G.S.

THE RED RIVER VALLEY
1811–1849

THE RELATIONS OF
CANADA AND THE UNITED STATES

A SERIES OF STUDIES
PREPARED UNDER THE DIRECTION OF THE
CARNEGIE ENDOWMENT FOR INTERNATIONAL PEACE
DIVISION OF ECONOMICS AND HISTORY

JAMES T. SHOTWELL, *Director*

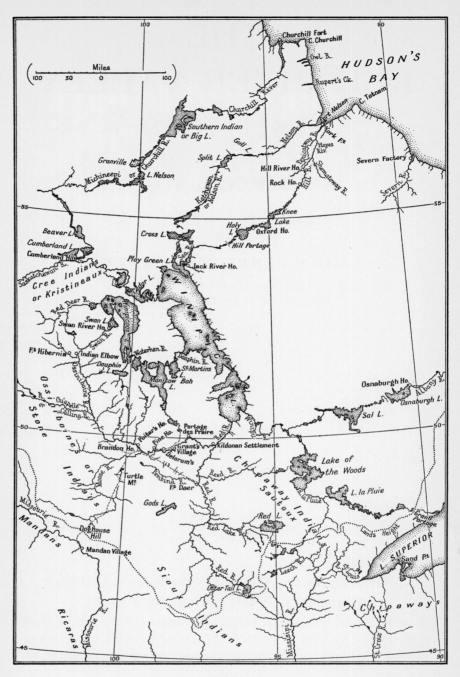

After a Manuscript Map in the Selkirk Papers, St. Mary's Isle, Kirkcudbright, Scotland.

THE
RED RIVER VALLEY
1811–1849

A REGIONAL STUDY

BY

JOHN PERRY PRITCHETT

QUEENS COLLEGE OF THE
COLLEGE OF THE CITY OF NEW YORK

NEW HAVEN : YALE UNIVERSITY PRESS
TORONTO : THE RYERSON PRESS
LONDON : HUMPHREY MILFORD : OXFORD UNIVERSITY PRESS
FOR THE CARNEGIE ENDOWMENT FOR INTERNATIONAL
PEACE : DIVISION OF ECONOMICS AND HISTORY
1942

TO
REGINALD GEORGE TROTTER
THIS VOLUME
IS GRATEFULLY DEDICATED

INTRODUCTION

FOR those who live in the east central section of the continent, and that means the largest part of the population of both Canada and the United States, nature itself seems to have provided an inevitable boundary between the two nations. For over a thousand miles, great lakes and swift-flowing rivers furnish a natural barrier to political encroachment, while offering at the same time a neighborly means for commercial intercourse and common travel. Again, in the Rocky Mountains at the west and the rugged wilderness at the northeast, the two nations are divided by more than an imaginary line, like that which stretches across the prairies of the Northwest. But there are three river systems which definitely cut across the border, running north and south, all of them opening gateways to movements of history, of which the record has now become a common heritage of both nations. In the East the basin of the Richelieu, running from Lake Champlain to the St. Lawrence, furnished a natural pathway for invasion both ways in the French and Indian War, as well as in the period of the American Revolution. The symbols of this danger are still to be seen in the fortifications on lake and river, although now that chapter of history has passed forever into the era of romance. The interplay of peaceful rivalry—none too peaceful at times—in the fur trade and the commerce of the early nineteenth century that centered in the St. Lawrence Valley on the one hand and the Hudson Valley on the other has been told with graphic power in one of the volumes of this series, *The Commercial Empire of the St. Lawrence* by D. G. Creighton. Also in the West a similar romance has now shaped itself out of the frontier history of the Oregon Territory, to which the vast stretches of the Columbia River gave access from the north, while rival adventurers rounded the Horn or worked their way up the Missouri to gather the rich fur trade at the mouth of the river on the Pacific. This story of exploration and settlement has now taken on almost the character of a Homeric saga of strength and courage battling both the elements of nature and the dangers of conflict. The volume which carries the story of the Northwest out of these beginnings which now seem so far away is the joint product of three authors, Judge F. W. Howay and Professors W. N. Sage and H. F. Angus, and is entitled *British Columbia and the United States: The North Pacific Slope from Fur Trade to Aviation.*

The present volume deals with the third of these trans-border river systems, the Red River Valley, which stretches from the low highlands of South Dakota and Minnesota and through the gently sloping plain to

Lake Winnipeg and the far-off reaches of Hudson Bay. Again the story begins with exploits utterly foreign to the America of today and especially of the Middle West, to the annals of which it forms an alluring prelude. Indeed the opening theme of Professor Pritchett's volume seems to have less of the hard reality of history than did the push of contending forces which met at the St. Lawrence and the Columbia. It is true that the background is much the same, that of the great fur-trading interests organized into vast empires by the two companies of the North, the Hudson's Bay Company and the North West Company of Montreal. Their southern and western rivals, which centered at St. Louis and at Astoria or New York, lie outside the central narrative of this volume. The areas of exploitation for the trapper and the trader were not bounded by any nice dividing line of political allegiance. The royal grant of Charles II to the Hudson's Bay Company gave substantial sovereign rights over an area so vast as to make it almost impossible to define. It is with the advent of settled life that hard and fast frontiers become necessary and the fur trader was the last person to promote settlements. It was only by chance that the obstructive monopoly of the Hudson's Bay Company was broken down to allow the rich soil of the Red River Valley to be plowed by pioneer colonists. The story which follows is at first mainly that of the life of Thomas Douglas, fifth Earl of Selkirk, who was shrewd enough to buy a nominal controlling interest in the Company when, between 1806 and 1808, Napoleon's Berlin decrees caused a vast decrease in the price of its shares. By this shrewd business deal he acquired the right to send a band of settlers into the Red River Valley and so became the founder of what was later to develop into the Province of Manitoba.

It is to be hoped that Professor Pritchett from his researches at St. Mary's Isle, the Selkirk family estate, will some day give us the rest of the story of this remarkable man whose figure dominates the first phase of the Red River Valley history. Even in these few pages we see a strange mingling of persistent purpose with youthful enthusiasm. Although he was uplifted and almost carried away by the great high winds and glorious promise of the first years of the French Revolution, he was, nevertheless, a lifelong friend of Walter Scott, who was no radical, and he had studied under Adam Smith. Instead of revolution, he planned escape from the hardships of the old world to the promise of the new, little aware of the extent to which hardship was the daily lot of the colonist.

If the founding of the colony was inspired by altruism, the first years of its history, as recorded here, were filled with strife and disappointment. Fortunately the settlers came of that sturdy stock which was kin with most of those who conquered the American wilderness. It was impossible to escape involvement in the warfare of the rival companies, and dissension, treachery, and even murder, darkened the early annals of the settlement. Although the country was rich in wild fowl and herds of buffalo, at times the settlers faced sheer starvation. But they were pioneers of the heroic mold, and they showed it in many ways that should give their records rank with the greatest in the early history of America. There is no section of the narrative that is more appealing than the incident of the trek of a score of these settlers who journeyed in 1819 in the depth of winter to Prairie du Chien, more than six hundred miles to the south, to buy new seed. And there is nothing more significant than the way in which the old trails through the wilderness became veritable caravan routes in a country still wild and rough and infested with hostile Indians. It is doubtful if even the Marco Polo route from old China could make a better showing than this where, before many years, "Red River carts," built entirely of wood and leather and drawn by oxen or shaggy little Indian ponies, rattled along, two hundred or so in a single caravan.

Meanwhile the colony was spreading out in the valley of the Assiniboine River as well as the Red; and Fort Garry, now Winnipeg, at the confluence of the two rivers, had become a post of some importance, matched as it was by Fort Snelling, guarding the Mississippi at the point where the twin cities of St. Paul and Minneapolis now stand. But little if any attention was paid by the early settlers to the political frontier that stretched its imaginary line along the highlands south of the Assiniboine. Their trade was purely local in any case, restricted to the simple needs of colonial life. In the mid-thirties, however, the political frontier began to take on importance, when the sixth Earl of Selkirk returned his grant to the Hudson's Bay Company, and, with the grant, all authority reverted to the Company. Export and import taxes were imposed and the traders on their way to Minnesota were stopped by armed police. But more than the traffic in furs was now involved, and Fort Garry became the center, not only of an effort to block commercial intercourse with the South, but of real oppression of personal as well as economic liberties. The story which follows is traced by Professor Pritchett in terms that have a universal appeal, although the scene of the drama was an isolated frontier colony, most of the inhabitants of which were French or English half-breeds, or *métis*. It was these unlettered frontiersmen who became the leaders of a protest which was carried to London and presented to the imperial authorities. Again, as in the case of the Stamp Act, legalism prevailed, and the charter rights were re-asserted. The result of this repressive action was a tiny revolution led by *métis* who had never heard of the great movements of history, of which their protest formed an obscure but real counterpart; for these unlettered *métis* added to the slogan "*Le commerce est libre!*" that of "*Vive la liberté!*"

The leader of the little revolution of 1849 was one Louis Riel, who voiced the opposition of the *métis* to the heavy-handed action of the chartered Company. But the predominantly French element in the *métis* had then to watch with uneasiness the increase of the English-speaking population; and when, in 1869, the territorial rights of the Hudson's Bay Company were transferred to the Dominion of Canada, it was Louis Riel's son who, by a strange paradox, followed his father's footsteps in protest against the new regime. This story of frontier unrest, which finally culminated in the second rebellion of 1885, is now beginning to take its proper place in the perspectives of history. The central theme of the history of the Northwest, like that of the rest of the continent, is that of ever-advancing frontier, as wilderness and prairie were made into farmlands and lonely posts became villages and towns. But this forward movement of civilization was by no means the harmonious process which it seemed to be in the careless retrospect of later days. The settlements which became the nurseries of democracy had to establish their rights against vested interests in a longer, if less dramatic, struggle than that against the Indian. It is with the origins of this complex movement of social and political forces that the present volume deals. The epic of those early pioneer days is not merely the prelude to the history of the Northwest but is an intrinsic part of it. This has been made clear in the scholarly analysis of the whole movement to be found in the works of the Canadian editor of this series, Professor Chester Martin, and in another series of studies carried on by the coöperation of American and Canadian scholars, "Canadian Frontiers of Settlement."

The Red River carts no longer creak along the highways of the frontier, for the wilderness to the east has now been pierced by more than one line of transcontinental railway, while to the south the great railway empires of the Northern Pacific and the Great Northern Railways, link the Assiniboian country with the valley of the Mississippi. The way in which the American creation of a great Canadian, James J. Hill, was countered in Canada by his American-born rival, Sir William Van Horne, in the effort to divert the trade of the growing Province of Manitoba to Canadian ports, has been told in two volumes of this series, *The Railway Interrelations of the United States and Canada*, by Colonel William J. Wilgus, and *A History of Transportation in Canada*, by G. P. de T. Glazebrook. The trading post at the junction of the two rivers has become the great city of Winnipeg, the metropolis of the Canadian Northwest. But it still preserves a section of the gray stone wall of old Fort Garry, as the symbol of an era almost as far away from that of the busy city as the feudal castle of Oxford is from the interests of the England of today. In place of the isolation of colonial life, world citizenship finds one of its most inspiring leaders in John W. Dafoe, the editor of the Winnipeg *Free Press*. The purpose of Selkirk's great design has now been realized, not in terms of escape, but of full acceptance of the responsibilities of membership in a world community.

Long years of preparation lie behind the writing of the present volume. After his student days at Stanford University, and his doctorate in history at Queen's University in Canada, where he also taught, Professor Pritchett held a professorship at the University of North Dakota, located in the Red River Valley, and from that point of advantage was able to study the history of the local colonial development in all its aspects. Meanwhile, with scholarly devotion, he pursued his researches wherever the source material was to be found, in the libraries and archives of Canada and the United States, and in St. Mary's Isle, Selkirk's home in Scotland. Fortunately, his later academic posts in the East have by no means lessened his interest in this field, to which he now brings so distinctive and notable a contribution.

JAMES T. SHOTWELL

PREFACE

THE subject of this volume is a phase of regional history. As such it derives its unity and purpose from the nature and the events of a certain geographical area. The country which is drained by the Red River of the North enjoys a natural integrity which no political or other force is likely to destroy; and its early recorded history found its contours shaped largely by geography. These considerations form the chief basis for the limits of this study. In the course of time political forces superimposed themselves on the regional elements in Red River; at first lightly, and more in theory than in practice; later, with a vigorous and permanent dividing authority; and the invisible forty-ninth parallel of latitude became a stronger power than the unifying features of nature. But with the development of the Northwest into one of the greatest agricultural areas of the world, much of the practical unity that the Red River Valley had lost through politics was regained in economics; and with the recent institution of regional historical studies, interest and theory have further repaired the division. The plan of the volumes which are being published under the general title of "The Relations of Canada and the United States" not only suggested the framework and provided the immediate impulse for the writing of this book, but also indicated suitable bounds for its extent. As the period after 1849 has already been treated in detail by Professor Lester Burrell Shippee in his volume on *Canadian-American Relations, 1849–1874,* in this series, and by Professor Chester Martin in his work on *"Dominion Lands" Policy* in the "Canadian Frontiers of Settlement" series, it seemed convenient as well as proper to continue the main part of this study no further than the middle of the nineteenth century.

Perhaps the most outstanding single aspect of the history of the Red River Valley, and one that appears to make it peculiarly appropriate in a series devoted to Canadian–American relations, is its international character. Especially in its earlier years the Valley aroused the interest and attracted the energies of Frenchmen, Englishmen, Canadians, and Americans. It was long doubtful who would exercise final sovereignty in the region; and the settlement of the question by an arbitrary division emphasized and perpetuated its international aspect. In the following pages this element of Red River history is duly stressed. Otherwise the plan of the volume involves emphasis on the colonization of the Red River Valley as the most important feature of its early history, and on the part played by Thomas Douglas, the fifth Earl of Selkirk, the chief and indispensable promoter of settlement and fur trading, as the liveliest and most dramatic thread running through the whole.

The fur trade and the people who lived in the Red River country before the arrival of Selkirk's first contingent of settlers in the year 1812 are described in an introductory chapter. The background of Selkirk's North American interests and work is treated at some length later, as are also the advance of the American frontier and settlements toward the Red River Valley from 1783 to 1850, and the appearance of a western-expansion movement in the Canadas in the decades before Confederation. The reason why the part played by Americans is given such comparatively little space is a simple one: Americans played little part in the story. It will be shown that, as in Oregon, the British were not only the first but were for a long time the only tillers of the soil in the Red River Valley. The fact is stressed by the circumstance that the earliest permanent settlers in what is now the State of Minnesota were emigrants from the Selkirk Settlement. That settlement began as an advance post of civilization far-flung in a wilderness. The American agricultural frontier did not really reach the Red River Valley until the decade following the year with which this study closes. American fur traders did appear earlier, and their activities are given their due place.

The main body of the volume is devoted to the Red River Colony in the years from 1811 to the middle of the century, particularly to events in the vital decade from 1811 to 1821, when the future control of the Red River country was largely decided. Most of the wider aspects of the subject are reviewed and discussed in the concluding chapter; but the geographical features which give topical unity to the whole are described at the outset.

The writer is conscious of obligations beyond the power of a Preface to express, much less repay. Indebtedness for sources of information is acknowledged in the proper places in the text; but the invaluable aid and the kindly interest and encouragement of friends cannot be so easily and explicitly recognized, and can be given only general though most grateful acknowledgment. In particular the writer is indebted to his good friend Mr. Don J. Pierce, Toronto, for counsel and material aid; to Mr. F. J. Wilson, Queen's University, for suggestions as to style and syntax; to Professor Chester Martin, Head of the Department of History, University of Toronto, for many constructive suggestions and criticisms of detail; to Professor J. Bartlet Brebner, Department of History, Columbia University, for advice and assistance of the highest value; to Professor James T. Shotwell, Director of the Division of Economics and History, Carnegie Endowment for International Peace, for the benefits of his wide knowledge and mastery of the historical art, and to the Endowment itself for its generous financial support of both researches and publication; to Sir Charles and Lady Hope-Dunbar for their kindness and their permission to use the Selkirk Papers at St. Mary's Isle, Kirkcudbright, Scotland; to Mr. Arthur E. McFarlane, editorial reader for the Carnegie Endowment, for his valued assistance in overcoming difficulties encountered both in the text itself and in its preparation for the printer; and especially to Professor Reginald George Trotter, Head of the Department of History, Queen's University, for the stimulus of his broad scholarship no less than for his keen and constructive criticism.

JOHN PERRY PRITCHETT

Queens College of the
College of the City of New York
January, 1942

CONTENTS

ABBREVIATIONS

CHR: Canadian Historical Review, Ottawa.

G: Public Archives of Canada, G Series (dispatches from the Colonial Office to the Governments of Upper and Lower Canada, originals).

Rufus King: The Life and Correspondence of Rufus King, C. R. King, ed. (New York, 1894–1900).

Miles Macdonell, Selkirk Settlement, PAC: Miles Macdonell, Selkirk Settlement, 1811–1812, And Various, 1763–1812, Public Archives of Canada, Ottawa.

MHC: Minnesota Historical Collections, St. Paul.

MHQM: Minnesota History, A Quarterly Magazine, St. Paul.

Narrative of Occurrences: A Narrative of Occurrences in the Indian Countries of North America since the connexion of the . . . Hon. the Earl of Selkirk with the Hudson's Bay Company and his Attempt to establish a Colony on the Red River (London, 1817).

N. Y. Col. Docs.: Documents Relative to the Colonial History of the State of New York, E. B. O'Callaghan, ed. (Albany, 1853–1887).

PACR: Dominion of Canada, *Public Archives of Canada Report.* Ottawa.

PAC SP: Selkirk Papers, Public Archives of Canada, transcripts from St. Mary's Isle, Kirkcudbright, Scotland.

Papers Relative to Settlement: Papers Relating to the Red River Settlement: 1815–1819 (Great Britain, Parliamentary Papers, House of Commons, No. 584). Ottawa.

PP GB, HC: Great Britain, Parliamentary Papers, House of Commons.

Q: Public Archives of Canada, Q Series (correspondence of the Colonial Office with the government of the old Province of Quebec and the governments of Upper and Lower Canada, transcripts from the Public Record Office).

Report on H.B.C.: Report from the Select Committee on the Hudson's Bay Company; together with the Proceedings of the Committee, Minutes of Evidence, Appendix and Index (Great Britain, Parliamentary Papers, Commons, 2 Session, XV, No. 240.260).

Robertson's Correspondence: Colin Robertson's Correspondence Book, September, 1817 to September, 1822, E. E. Rich and R. Harvey Fleming, eds. (London, 1939).

RSC: Royal Society of Canada, Ottawa.

SP SM: Selkirk Papers, St. Mary's Isle, Kirkcudbright, Scotland. Originals.

SbP MHS: Sibley Papers, Minnesota Historical Society, St. Paul. Originals.

Statement Respecting Settlement: Statement Respecting the Earl of Selkirk's Settlement upon the Red River, in North America; its Destruction in 1815 and 1816; and the Massacre of Governor Semple and His Party (London, 1817).

THE RED RIVER VALLEY

CHAPTER I

THE NEW-WORLD SCENE

THE valley of the Red River of the North is a geographical unit lying at the heart of the continent of North America. Situated at the south-ernmost limits of the drainage basin which holds the Nelson River and slopes down to the north and to Hudson Bay, it is separated only by short distances and a low divide from waters which flow south to the Mississippi, and is even more easily accessible from other streams and lakes which lead eastward to the margin of the St. Lawrence drainage basin. By nature and in historical times it was mostly a treeless plain, clothed in the richest of soils and supporting a dense growth of grassy vegetation on which vast herds of bison, or buffalo, fed. A description of this region by a recent writer perhaps cannot be excelled within equal limits as an accurate account of the main elements of its nature and ex-tent:

The Red River Valley, stretching from Lake Traverse in Minnesota to Lake Winnipeg, bounded on the east by the Precambrian Shield and on the west by the Manitoba Escarpment, is geographically a unit, not so much because it is a single drainage basin as because its plain was built by the deposits of the glacial Lake Agassiz. As the ice-sheet retreated, water was ponded in a vast shallow lake whose ancient beaches form the present boundaries of the Red River Valley. The waters of this lake retreated, leaving the Red River meandering northward through a level grassland plain, and leaving remnants of itself in Lakes Winnipeg, Manitoba, and Winnipegosis.

The whole of the Red River Valley has an annual rainfall of 18 to 21 inches, of which 11 to 12 inches normally falls between April 1 and Sep-tember 1. . . . The mean summer temperature (62°–64° . . .) is higher than that in any other part of the Canadian West, except that in the centre of the semi-arid belt. The growing season ranges from 160 to 170 days . . ., a period exceeded only by that of southern Alberta. "The climate favours the growth of all classes of farm crops, both cereals and grasses."[1] This rela-tively warmer, more humid climate, promoting abundant growth of grasses, has converted the clay deposits of Lake Agassiz into a rich black clay loam. The tenacious black surface soil ranges from 4 to 12 inches in depth. It con-tains greater quantities of nitrogen and phosphorus than any of the western soils except the best of the Park Belt soils.

The surface is characteristically flat, broken only by the shallow channels

1. R. W. Murchie and H. C. Grant, *Unused Lands of Manitoba* (Dept. of Agricul-ture and Immigration, Winnipeg, 1926), p. 24.

of the rivers. In contrast with the Park Belt, trees grow only along the rivers. The level topography has made it necessary to supplement natural drainage by extensive systems of open drains. In the heavy clay districts good wells are uncommon, and the chief source of water for farm use is the surface water stored in "dug-outs," or reservoirs dug in the clay.

Though drainage is still a problem, the Red River Valley contains a larger proportion of arable land than any other division of the Canadian West. It is estimated that out of a total of more than 2,000,000 acres of land, 70 per cent is suitable for cultivation, 15 per cent is marginal, and 15 per cent is not suitable for cultivation.[2]

Such was, essentially, the character of the region whose change from a fur-producing wilderness to a comparatively civilized agricultural community is here to be traced. From the above quotation, it is clear that in spite of the cold winters and the high latitude of Red River, the fertile soil was potentially one of the finest in the world for the purposes of northern agriculture. It was in this region that men pushing up the three great river systems of the Nelson, the St. Lawrence, and the Mississippi naturally met; and whether they came in search of furs or of food or of good land, it was here that they could find all three, and other men, too, to quarrel with over the spoils. It is true that from time immemorial the country had been occupied by tribes of native Indians. But these were so weak economically, and had such a loose hold on the soil, that the incoming whites found them easy to dispossess, and comparatively willing tools for commerce in food and furs.

It was not from the Indians that newcomers might have expected trouble, but rather from other newcomers like themselves. For those men who penetrated early to the valley of the Red River were for the most part adventurers seeking wealth, men who for one reason or another found it more desirable to travel far afield in the hope of gain than to pursue a more regular and traditional course at home; and such men are not likely to hesitate to adopt irregular courses in scenes far removed from the forces of law when any situation arises which seems to threaten their most cherished interests. Now the wealth of the Red River country conspired with the location to produce just such situations. The most apparent and available wealth at first was furs. But the quantity of furs was limited, and fur traders converging on the country from two or more directions were sure to have opposing aims and to pursue mutually hostile courses. This was what happened, and the conflict involved murder and other crimes. There was later a more

2. W. A. Mackintosh, *Prairie Settlement: The Geographical Setting* ("Canadian Frontiers of Settlement," W. A. Mackintosh and W. L. G. Joerg, eds., Toronto, 1934), I, 86 f.

fundamental cause for quarrel, however, between those who came for furs and those who came for land. Agriculture destroys the fur trade. The introduction of settlers into the region of the Red River precipitated a struggle more violent than anything known before, a struggle which was rendered still more deadly by being merged in the fur war. But when civilization is advancing across a country, the fur trade inevitably gives way to settlement. It is the series of events by which the fur trade gave way to settlement in the Red River Valley that forms the subject of this work.

The story of the Red River fur trade goes back to the seventeenth century and to the rival overseas ventures of England and France. It was not until late in the century that the Mississippi River was explored and its adjacent lands annexed by subjects of Louis XIV, but already for many decades Frenchmen had been trading, exploring, and colonizing in the valley of the St. Lawrence; and the English, through their explorers, had long possessed some knowledge of, and some claim to, the regions lying about Hudson Bay. While it was to be many years before the valley of the Red River was to enter directly into the fur contests between men from the St. Lawrence and men from the Bay, and then, indeed, only after France had abandoned the scene, peculiarly enough the Red River area played some part in the laying of the foundations of the future fur struggle. Shortly after the middle of the seventeenth century two Frenchmen, Radisson and Groseilliers, made several expeditions far up the St. Lawrence River system. Their chief purpose was to make money out of the fur trade; and this may help to account for the vagueness of that part of their written records which deals with their most western travels. It is known that they penetrated the country lying to the southwest of Lake Superior, and met some Sioux Indians. But whether they traveled farther west and north into the valley of the Red River is only a matter of conjecture.[3] What gives their voyages significance for this study, however, is the fact that they tapped the fur region of which the Red River Valley was a part, and they helped to bring about not only a flow of furs from Red River to the St. Lawrence, but also a rival flow from Red River to Hudson Bay. When the partners returned to Montreal in the year 1660 with a very rich cargo of furs, Groseilliers was imprisoned and a great part of the furs were seized by the Governor; as a result of this the angry traders, having appealed in vain to the government of France, went over to Eng-

3. See particularly Albert M. Goodrich and Grace Lee Nute, "The Radisson Problem," *Minnesota History, A Quarterly Magazine*, XIII, 245 ff. (hereafter, *MHQM*); Hjalmar R. Holand, "Radisson's Two Western Journeys," *MHQM*, XV, 157 ff.; Grace Lee Nute, ed., "Radisson and Groseilliers' Contribution to Geography," *MH QM*, XVI, 414 ff.

land with their knowledge and their desire for revenge; and partly owing to their activities in England in the ensuing years, the Hudson's
Bay Company was chartered in 1670 by Charles II, and was given the
ownership and the control of the lands whose waters flow into Hudson
Bay.[4] The purpose for which this company was formed was to acquire
the North American fur trade as far as it might be carried on through
Hudson Bay. Part of that trade was to consist of furs from Red River,
diverted from a stream of trade already beginning to flow toward the
St. Lawrence. Thus as early as the third quarter of the seventeenth century an embryonic fur rivalry between the Hudson Bay region and the
St. Lawrence region, and involving the Red River Valley, had come into
existence, partly through the changing loyalties of two fur-trade partners. It was to be over a century before the traders from the two regions were to come into direct conflict in the Red River country itself;
but in the meantime their hostility was to be manifested intermittently
at other points.

The "Company of Adventurers of England trading into Hudson's
Bay," as it was known officially, whose charter of incorporation included a monopoly of the trade in furs in the charter lands, was not
slow in taking advantage of its opportunities. Immediately upon incorporation it began operations on the shores of Hudson Bay, and by
the year 1685 had founded trading stations at a number of strategic
points—Albany River, Hayes Island (near Moose River), Port Nelson,
and New Severn, from each of which it carried on a lucrative trade in
furs with the Indian tribes of the interior.[5]

No sooner had the Hudson's Bay Company established itself in the
field than it came into direct conflict with the French in the St. Lawrence Valley. The early movements of the English in the Bay were noted
by their rivals with uneasiness. Five months subsequent to the charter-
ing of the English company the Intendant of New France, Jean Talon,
reported to the French Minister, Colbert, that "two European vessels
[English] have been seen very near Hudson's Bay, where they wig-
wam";[6] and again a year later the French Government was advised that
"two English vessels and three barks wintered [1670–71] in the neighborhood of that bay, and made a vast collection of beavers there."[7]

4. *Hudson's Bay Company. Copy of the Existing Charter or Grant by the Crown
to the Hudson's Bay Company; . . .*, pp. 3 ff. (Great Britain, Parliamentary Papers,
House of Commons, 1st Sess. 1842, XXVIII, No. 547). Hereafter, *PP GB, HC.*

5. John Oldmixon, *The British Empire in America* (London, 1741), I, 544, 559 ff.
Joseph Robson, *An Account of Six Years' Residence in Hudson's Bay, From 1733 to
1736, and 1744 to 1747* (London, 1752), p. 71, Appendix No. I, p. 11.

6. E. B. O'Callaghan, ed., *Documents Relative to the Colonial History of the State
of New York . . .* (Albany, 1853–87), IX, 67. Hereafter, *N.Y.Col.Docs.*

7. *Ibid.*, pp. 72 f.

Three months prior to the writing of this latter communication Talon had dispatched Father Albanel, a Jesuit missionary, and the Sieur de Saint Simon, a young Canadian, to Hudson Bay, with instructions to draw up a memoir of all they discovered, "drive a trade in furs with the Indians, and especially reconnoitre whether there be any means of wintering ships in that quarter, in order to establish a factory. . . .' They were also expected to examine thoroughly the English "Establishment."[8]

At this time the French did not admit the validity of the Hudson's Bay Company's charter, or the pretensions of King Charles of England to possess the power to grant lands and fur monopolies in the Hudson Bay region. All lands lying to the north and west of their settlements on the St. Lawrence they regarded as belonging to France by right of both charter and exploration. Cardinal Richelieu had granted all these regions to the Company of New France; and the Council of New France had caused it to be inscribed in its records under the date of August 26, 1656, that Jean Bourdon in 1656 "ran along the entire coast of Labrador with a vessel of 30 tons, entered and took possession of the North Bay"[9]—that is, Hudson Bay. But in the seventeenth century neither European governments nor their subjects overseas were accustomed in their attitude to newly found lands to value charter privileges above prescription, or to respect claims based on more or less authentic stories of discovery, when they coveted a piece of territory and had the strength to take it. The French were certain that their title to Hudson Bay was better than that of the English; and, having assured themselves on this point, they turned to the main business of driving out their rivals and seizing the lucrative fur trade for themselves. A violent but indecisive struggle ensued. Adventurous Canadian merchants and fur traders banded themselves together and attempted to take by force what they regarded as their own property by right. At times they were successful, killing or driving out the English and seizing the fur posts and the furs. At times they themselves were worsted and evicted. Conflict continued spasmodically until the year 1697 when, by the Treaty of Ryswick, England recognized France as the owner of Hudson Bay. From then until the Treaty of Utrecht in 1713 the French held all the Hudson's Bay Company's posts except Albany—and even Albany should have been theirs according to the eighth article of the Treaty of Ryswick.[10]

Though the Treaty of Utrecht gave French recognition to the Eng-

8. *Ibid.*   9. *Ibid.*, pp. 268, 304.
10. *Ibid.*, pp. 72 f., 268, 428, 797 ff., 918 f. Robson, *Six Years' Residence in Hudson's Bay*, Appendix No. I, pp. 7 ff.

lish claim to the Hudson Bay region (without fixing distinct boundaries) and led at once to the Hudson's Bay Company reëstablishing itself on the Bay, traders from Canada continued to invade the Company's charter lands. Following the route provided by the Great Lakes and dependent waters, they pushed farther and farther to the west into the interior of the continent. The La Vérendryes, father and sons—the most famous of the later French-Canadian fur traders—went up the Great Lakes and thence by river, lake, and portage to the Great West: across Lake of the Woods, down the Winnipeg River, and up the Red River to "the Forks," where the Assiniboine makes its junction from the west. This was during the years 1731 to 1738. The elder La Vérendrye, after a two days' sojourn at the Forks in the latter part of September, 1738, ascended the Assiniboine to the prairie portage where Portage la Prairie now stands. Here he built a large fort, Fort La Reine. Later in the same year he was in the Mandan country, *un peu éloigné* from the Missouri River. During the first part of the next decade the intrepid La Vérendryes continued the exploration of the West and the establishment of trading posts—"the establishment of posts being significantly to the fore."[11] Early in January, 1743, François and Louis-Joseph de la Vérendrye had pushed their way across the great central plain to the foot of what, probably, were the Rocky Mountains.

Following closely in the footsteps of these pioneer traders and pathfinders came a scramble of fur traders. They advanced rapidly and within a few years had made considerable progress in the occupation of the West. Here and there they built trading posts, usually at the forks of rivers and at the heads of lakes, or at other points of vantage. In a very short time a profitable trade was developed—for this was the very center of the beaver El Dorado—and a rich stream of furs began to move over the Winnipeg River–Lake Superior water route into the trading houses of Montreal and Quebec. Now most of these furs were secured on lands whose waters flowed into Hudson Bay and which were therefore charter lands of the Hudson's Bay Company and subject to the English fur monopoly.[12] Thus, several years before Canada became British there had grown up the successful practice of Canadians poaching on the fur preserves of the Hudson's Bay Company. The Red River

11. Arthur S. Morton, "La Vérendrye: Commandant, Fur-trader, and Explorer," *Canadian Historical Review,* IX, 297. Hereafter, *CHR.*

12. Some Account of the Trade Carried on by the North West Company, *Dominion of Canada Report of the Public Archives for the Year 1928* (Ottawa, 1929), Appendix E, pp. 58 f. Hereafter, Trade Carried on by N.W. Co., *PACR, 1928.* Alexander Mackenzie, *Voyages from Montreal, on the River St. Lawrence, through the Continent of North America to the Frozen and Pacific Oceans; in the Years 1789 and 1793. With a Preliminary Account of the Rise, Progress and Present State of the Fur Trade of that Country* (London, 1801), pp. iii ff. Hereafter, Mackenzie, *Voyages.*

Valley formed a part of these preserves and lay right on the line of march followed by the interlopers in their penetration of the Great West.

The Seven Years' War made a complete break in the northwestern fur trade from Canada. Many of the French traders withdrew to the eastern settlements, forts and canoes were left to decay, the portages were obliterated by wilderness growth, and the flow of furs to Montreal and Quebec ceased. These conditions, however, were only temporary. When Montreal capitulated to General Amherst in the year 1760, Britain had won in the long struggle for the control of the fur trade in North America, and many British merchants and traders lost no time in setting to work to rebuild the fur-trade business which had passed out of the hands of the French. Although the traditional English policy in prosecuting the trade was to have the Indians bring their furs and peltries to the frontier settlements, it was followed only partially in Canada after 1760. As soon as peace had been secured a number of traders left the settlements and took the fur route to the West.[13]

But scarcely had the old French trading posts on the Upper Great Lakes been reoccupied than the Pontiac War broke out. Then for nearly two years the whole inland fur traffic was suspended.[14] Sir William Johnson, Superintendent of Indian Affairs in the northern district of America, said in 1767, in one of his letters to Shelburne, Secretary of State: "Our most valuable frontiers were depopulated, our outposts with most of their garrisons destroyed and the Trade ruined; all the Traders at the posts, and the much greater part of those who were on their way with cargoes were plundered; and many of them were murdered."[15] It was not until after the cessation of hostilities in 1764 and 1765 that the trade was in any measure resumed. Then there began a second rush into the wilderness. In less than a decade Canadian traders, chiefly from Montreal, had gone far beyond the regular old French limits. Even before the end of the 'sixties a few of the more energetic and adventurous were trafficking as far as the Saskatchewan.[16] Thus almost

13. Alexander Henry, *Travels and Adventures in Canada and the Indian Territories between the Years 1760 and 1776* (New York, 1809), Pt. I. Hereafter, Henry, *Travels*. Mackenzie, *Voyages*, p. vii. Trade Carried on by N.W. Co., *PACR, 1928*, Appendix E, p. 59.

14. Adam Shortt and Arthur G. Doughty, eds., *Documents Relating to the Constitutional History of Canada, 1759–1791* (2d ed., Ottawa, 1918), Pt. I, p. 233 (Sess. Pap. No. 18, Canadian Archives).

15. *N.Y.Col.Docs.*, VII, 962.

16. Henry, *Travels*, Pt. II, pp. 192–330. Mackenzie, *Voyages*, pp. viii ff. Harold A. Innis, *The Fur Trade in Canada* (New Haven, 1930), pp. 192 f. Arthur S. Morton, *A History of the Canadian West to 1870–1871* (Toronto, n.d.), pp. 263 ff. Hereafter, Morton, *Canadian West*. Gordon Charles Davidson, *The North West Company* (Berkeley, 1918), VII, 33 ff.

immediately after the Conquest—of French Canada, that is, by England—the practice of open and wholesale violation of the Hudson's Bay Company fur monopoly was reëstablished, and this time under British auspices.

These Montreal traders were a heterogeneous collection. Some were natives, others were newcomers. After the Conquest many daring men had come to Canada from the English-American colonies—chiefly from New York, Massachusetts, and New Jersey. A large number were Scottish, or of Scottish extraction. In some cases their fathers had left Scotland after the Forty-five, the Jacobite uprising of that year, and had taken refuge in the New World. Then, too, there were English and Scots who had recently come over. There was also a sprinkling of the sons of officers who, in the Seven Years' War, had fought for Britain in America. Finally, in addition to these exotic elements there was a strong substratum of French-Canadian and métis-voyageurs, trappers, and traders. All of these widely diverse elements eventually found a certain unity in a common occupation—the fur trade.

Some of the Montreal traders acquired quick prominence. As early as the autumn of 1761 the enterprising Alexander Henry, well stocked with trading goods from Albany, advanced westward from Montreal over the Ottawa route to Michilimackinac. The next spring he went on to Sault Ste Marie, where he met for the first time the noted French fur trader, Jean-Baptiste Cadotte. Cadotte had married a squaw and had acquired great influence among the Indians. During the Pontiac War, and shortly after Fort Michilimackinac was taken by the "Chipewyans," Henry was captured by the savages, but finally escaped and reached Niagara in safety. With the restoration of amicable Indian relations in 1765, he was granted an exclusive license for the trade around Lake Superior. In July of the same year he and Cadotte formed a partnership and succeeded in sending home a succession of rich cargoes of furs. They not only exploited the Lake Superior regions, but also carried on trade as far west as the Saskatchewan River. They were soon followed into the interior by James Finlay, the first English fur trader from Montreal to reach the Saskatchewan; Thomas Currie, who was "determined to penetrate to the furthest limits of the French discoveries"; Peter Pond, the Connecticut Yankee; Thomas and Joseph Frobisher, and many others, some of whom became, like those just named, famous in the annals of the western Indian trade. Thus it came about that the northwest fur trade became almost the exclusive property of the Montreal merchants. They supplied the capital and the enterprise, and enjoyed most of the profits. The actual work, however, was entrusted to hired servants. Of these the most necessary as well as the most picturesque were the voyageurs—swift, strong, and daring on river, lake, and portage, and almost invariably good-natured and lighthearted. Between them and their leaders, the merchants, there sprang up a kind of magnetic attraction. Both spoke the same tongue, French, with ready facility, shared at times the dangers of the wilderness trail, and found their best interests served by concerted action and mutual devotion. Besides the voyageurs there were, among the hired servants, numbers of clerks, interpreters, laborers, guides, and others.[17]

Until about 1783 the fur traffic conducted from Montreal was largely in the hands of independent traders, although from time to time there was some concentration of interests. The French fur-trading policy was replaced almost from the first by a system of free and open trade. It is true that some remnants of the system in vogue before the Conquest were adhered to in particular districts until after 1765, "in virtue of grants from military commanders," e.g., the monopoly of the Lake Superior trade given to Alexander Henry by the commandant at Fort Michilimackinac. But, by the end of the 'sixties the provisions of the Proclamation of 1763 were quite generally in force. The consequence of throwing open trade to everyone, with licenses given gratis, was a cutthroat system of competition attended by great disorder and much crime. Fraud, chicanery, and concomitant evils were employed freely to secure the Indian barter. In spite of this state of affairs, however, and of the resultant Indian hostility, the unrestricted trade acquired considerable proportions and diminished the profits of the Hudson's Bay Company which, from the cessation of the French trade and probably until about 1770, had been enjoying the advantages of an almost exclusive business with the Indians west of Lake Superior, who "were obliged to go to them for such articles as their habitual use had rendered necessary."[18]

The Hudson's Bay Company had been from its very inception aristo-

17. Henry, *Travels*. Mackenzie, *Voyages*, pp. viii ff. Arthur S. Morton, ed., *The Journal of Duncan M'Gillivray of the North West Company at Fort George on the Saskatchewan, 1794–1795, With Introduction, Notes and Appendix* (Toronto, 1929), pp. xxvi ff. Edward Umfreville, *The Present State of the Hudson's Bay, Containing a full Description of that Settlement, and the Adjacent Country; and Likewise of the Fur Trade* (London, 1790), pp. 70, 214. For a detailed, interesting, and scholarly treatment of the voyageur see Grace Lee Nute, *The Voyageur* (New York, 1931).

18. Henry, *Travels*, Pt. II, pp. 192 f. Mackenzie, *Voyages*, p. vii. Umfreville, *Present State of the Hudson's Bay*, pp. 56, 70 f., 101 f., 205 f. Trade Carried on by N.W. Co., *PACR, 1928*, Appendix E, p. 60. The Memorial & Petition of McTavish, Fraser & Co. and Inglis, Ellice & Co. of London, Merchants on their own behalf & on behalf of the other Persons interested in the North West Company of Fur Traders of Canada, Colonial Office Records, Series Q, Vol. 130, Pt. II, p. 287, Public Archives of Canada. Hereafter, Memorial of McTavish, Fraser, *Q130*.

cratic in its membership and pompous and dignified, sometimes even aloof and inhospitable, in its dealings with the Indians. The latter were forced, if they wished to trade, to bring their furs right down to the Company's factories on Hudson Bay. Often they were refused admission to the barter establishments and were merely allowed to exchange goods through an open window. They were treated decidedly as inferiors. Very different were the methods employed by the traders from Canada both before and after the Conquest. These traveled far afield, met the Indians on or near their hunting grounds, and mixed with them as equals. Nothing but the lack of a vigorous competition and the making of a wide margin of profit enabled the English company to pursue its slothful methods with success as long as it did.

The Canadians, in fact, had by 1770 so advantageously established themselves in the upland country on the lakes and rivers leading to the fur posts of the Hudson's Bay Company that the chartered trade was in a great measure cut off from its usual channel. It was no longer necessary for the Indians to make the long, toilsome, and perilous journey down to the Company's factories, because they were now well supplied at their very doors with the goods they required.

To such an extent was the Hudson's Bay Company's fur traffic intercepted that in 1773 its officials planned, as a countermeasure against the Canadians, to extend operations into the interior. In the following year, 1774, Samuel Hearne built a fur post called Cumberland House on the southeastern shore of Cumberland, or Pine Island Lake, within five hundred yards of a Canadian trading post. The Company had begun to fight back by taking the offensive. From this time on until early in the next century the chartered traders continued to follow the "Canadians to their different establishments," building rival forts and laying plans to supplant their opponents, whom they regarded with open contempt and stigmatized as "pedlars, thieves, and interlopers."[19] The movement to expel the intruders, the vicious competition among the *bourgeois*, a smallpox epidemic which, during 1781 and 1782, killed off thousands of the Indians, and, finally, the need of much capital and an extensive credit system led to the organization of a most redoubtable Canadian combination against the English company. In the winter of 1783–84 most of the individual traders and a group of Montreal merchants, mainly Scottish who had come to Canada during the 'sixties and the 'seventies and who for years had been pursuing similar occupations, united under the leadership of Benjamin and Joseph Frobisher and Simon McTavish. The partnership was called "The North West Com-

19. Mackenzie, *Voyages*, pp. vi ff., ix. Umfreville, *op. cit.*, pp. 56 ff., 68 ff., 101 ff., 116, 203 ff.

pany."[20] Even before the time of its organization a number of different Canadian fur-trade partnerships had been formed, and several of them had also been known in their time as the "North West Company." Alexander Henry and Jean Cadotte, as was noted above, formed such an association, but not of the above name, in the year 1765. Ten years later the principal trade in the Saskatchewan River Valley was being carried on through joint-stock arrangements. Whether this was true for the next year is not known definitely because the license returns for 1776 are missing;[21] but for the following two years there is definite evidence of an amalgamation of interests. In 1779 the "different Traders for their Common safety in a country where they had no protection from their Government entered into Agreement and united the Trade" for one year.[22] This gentlemen's agreement was renewed in 1780 for a period of three years, but "at the end of Two years it was discontinued and feeble and unprofitable attempts were made to carry on the Trade on grounds of separate interest."[23] Northwestern trade conditions already noted then brought about the formation of the North West Company of 1783–84. In the following winter, as a result of the omission of small independent traders from the ranks of the newly created partnership, a second Montreal fur-trading company was formed, that of Gregory, McLeod and Company. This partnership maintained an independent business for two years. Then it was dissolved, and its members joined the older organization.[24]

The North West Company was not an incorporated body with exclusive privileges; it was a partnership among a group of individuals, voluntarily maintained and claiming rights in the fur trade by virtue of discovery and of priority in trade. From the time of its inception it grew very rapidly, and before many years had passed it succeeded in establishing fur-trade routes which extended across the continent from Montreal by way of the Ottawa River, Lakes Huron and Superior, and the western river systems, to the Pacific Coast, and also penetrated well into the regions farther north and south. From the start, and for

20. Memorial of McTavish, Fraser, *Q130*, Pt. II, p. 287. Trade Carried on by N.W. Co., *PACR, 1928,* Appendix E, p. 61. Mackenzie, *Voyages,* pp. xiv ff. *Bourgeois* was the familiar name of those North West Company merchants who took part in the fur trade, whether they carried it on in Canada or went into the interior. Shares in the North West Company were held by merchants in Montreal, known as agents, and by partners who wintered in the fur country and were known as "wintering partners," or "winterers." The agents did the buying and selling for the company while the winter partners engaged directly in the trade for furs.

21. H. A. Innis, "The North West Company," *CHR,* VIII, 311.

22. Memorial of McTavish, Fraser, *Q130*, Pt. II, p. 287.

23. Trade Carried on by N.W. Co., *PACR, 1928,* Appendix E, p. 61.

24. Mackenzie, *Voyages,* pp. xix, xx. R. Harvey Fleming, "McTavish, Frobisher and Company of Montreal," *CHR,* X, 136 ff.

long afterwards, the chief enemy to be feared by this Canadian organization was not the difficulties of the trade, or hostile traders from without, but rather defections from its own ranks. After the initial cleavage
mentioned above all went well for a time. Then, from 1793 to 1804, the
success of the Canadians was again jeopardized. Cupidity and disaffection among the principal traders caused the formation of another rival
combination under the auspices of the powerful firm of Forsyth, Richardson and Company of Montreal. This grouping of merchants was
known during the course of its existence by five different names: The
New North West Company; Sir Alexander Mackenzie and Company,
when, after 1801, Sir Alexander Mackenzie, the great explorer, was its
guiding light; the Little Company—a name given in derision by the
powerful Simon McTavish, who now perhaps was the chief partner of
the North West Company; and the New Company, or, more commonly,
the X Y Company. This last name had its origin in the marks used by
the company to brand its bales of merchandise and furs. The older company used the brand N W, the initial letters of its name; the new rival
took as its mark the next two letters in the alphabet, X and Y. For
nearly a decade a deadly rivalry marked the relations of the two companies. At times there was bloodshed and great loss of property. So
fierce was the struggle that at one time the contending parties bade fair
to ruin each other. Such an outcome was averted, however, after, and
partly as a result of, the death of Simon McTavish. This occurred in
July, 1804. Within a few months a reconciliation was arranged—"the
ancient establishment consenting to ingraft on their own original compact, the concessions made to the other party." Once again the North
West Company was predominant in the West.[25]

The consolidation of the Canadian fur interests in 1804 led to a
phenomenal development in trade, and it was only a short time until
the "North-westers" had regained their former vigor. Plans were elabo-
rated to meet the opposition of the Hudson Bay traders, who as early
as 1793 had advanced into the valleys of the Assiniboine and Red
rivers.[26] For the next few years the Red River Valley was the center of
the fighting ground of the two great rivals. As has been well said, although it is an understatement, "for keen, hard, shrewd efficiency, the
North-West Company was perhaps the most terribly effective organi-

25. Trade Carried on by N.W. Co., *PACR, 1928,* Appendix E, p. 61. Alexander
Mackenzie to John Sullivan, October 25, 1802, with enclosure John Richardson to
H. W. Ryland, October 21, 1802, *Q293,* pp. 225–238. R. Harvey Fleming, "The Origin
of 'Sir Alexander Mackenzie and Company,'" *CHR,* IX, 137 ff. Fleming, "McTavish,
Frobisher and Company of Montreal," *CHR,* X, 141 ff.

26. John Macdonell Journal, August 26, 1793, Masson Collection, McGill University
Library. Trade Carried on by N.W. Co., *PACR, 1928,* Appendix E, pp. 69–70.

zation that had ever arisen in the New World";[27] so it is not surprising that the first phase of the battle for the Western fur field was decidedly in favor of the Canadians.

The opposition from the Hudson's Bay Company, however, was gradually becoming more intelligent, vigorous, and effective. The stake was well worth fighting for. Profits on furs were enormously high and easily repaid the great expense of building and maintaining trading posts in the interior. Besides, the Bay traders had a far shorter distance to cover than the Canadians, from tidewater to the Western plains. By 1810 the Hudson's Bay Company had gone far toward abandoning its "jog-trot mode" of trade. It was operating posts at almost all the points in the transprairie region where its rival had erected establishments and rivalry grew ever keener until blood began to be spilled. Competition is said to be the life of trade, but when competition reaches a certain point it ceases to be competition and becomes war. Before long "financial ruin was staring all branches of the fur-trade in the face."[28] The activities of a number of private traders made the situation still more difficult. Most of these had made their first appearance in the fur market about 1805. The great majority were hunters, trappers, and voyageurs who had been discharged from the service of the X Y Company after the coalition of that organization with the North-westers. Instead of returning to Canada after their discharge they had remained in the Western country, engaging independently in the fur traffic, especially along the Pembina and Red rivers, and eventually becoming, in the eyes of the North West Company, "as great a nuisance . . . as their former employers."[29]

These free traders were not the only inhabitants of the Red River Valley at this time. Besides the constant stream of fur traders coming and going between Canada and Hudson Bay, there was a considerable native population made up of Indians and half-breeds. The Indians of the plains and prairies subsisted chiefly on the trophies of the buffalo hunt and as a result frequently moved from place to place; but bands of at least four great Indian nations, Chippewas, Crees, Assiniboines and Sioux, found a more or less permanent home in the regions about Red River and eastward to Lake Superior. The Chippewas were called Saulteurs or Saulteaux because of the fact that they had once lived in large numbers about Sault Ste Marie. The original inhabitants of the

27. Chester Martin, *Lord Selkirk's Work in Canada* ("Oxford Historical and Literary Studies," Oxford, 1916), VII, 31. Hereafter, Martin, *Selkirk*.

28. Memorial of McTavish, Fraser, *Q130,* Pt. II, p. 228. Selkirk to Macdonell, December 23, 1811, Selkirk Papers, p. 125, Public Archives of Canada. Hereafter, *PAC SP.*

29. Elliott Coues, ed., *New Light on the Early History of the Greater North-west* (New York, 1897), I, 268 f.

Valley were the Crees,[30] a nation kindred to the Chippewas. They were a sturdy race, and easily capable of adapting themselves to the demands of a changing environment. To the west of the Crees, and in the lands drained by the Assiniboine River, lived the Assiniboines, congeners in blood to the Sioux. These bands of Saulteaux, Crees, and Assiniboines formed the bulk of the population of the Red River country at the opening of the nineteenth century. Then, too, as in earlier years, it was not unusual for parties of Sioux, the "tigers of the plains," to wander or raid northward from their homelands farther south.

Before the Conquest of Canada, when the French trafficked in the Northwest, a new type of inhabitant began to appear, the métis or half-breed. Just when the first Red River métis were born cannot be definitely determined; but there is certain proof that there was a prairie métis population in existence before the year 1775;[31] and there are good grounds for believing that it originated as early as the 'forties and 'fifties of the eighteenth century. After the Conquest, when the fur trade from Montreal had grown into a regular and permanent industry in the interior, the métis element increased in numbers rapidly. Around the forts and trading posts established by the Canadian traders the voyageurs built their huts and the Indians set up their tepees. Morganatic-like marriages—"marriages of the country"—between the white traders and the Indian women became common. When the trader returned to the East to live, as he usually did sooner or later, he "pensioned off" his Indian wife, or gave her to some other trader or voyageur. Many of the voyageurs and laborers, too, secured wives directly from the tepee; and as their residence in the country was generally permanent, their marriages, as a rule, were bona fide. The issue of these unions soon formed a numerous progeny, particularly on the prairies, and thus grew up around the trading posts large numbers of French, Scottish, and English métis. Whenever the means were available these dusky children were sent down to Montreal or Quebec for a time and given educational and religious instruction.[32] Almost invariably, however, they returned to the land of their birth, and mixed with their friends and relatives who were similar in origin to themselves.

30. In colloquial use the Red River Valley was commonly abbreviated to "the Valley." Similarly, the Red River Settlement or Colony became simply "Red River." The shorter terms will frequently be used hereafter.

31. Henry, *Travels,* Pt. II, p. 249. L. A. Prud'homme, *L'Elément Français au Nord-Ouest,* p. 29, gives the year 1775 "as the possible, if not the probable, date of the unions of the French with the native women." It is recorded that Henry Kelsey, a Hudson's Bay Company explorer, returned to Fort York from the interior in 1692 with an Indian woman.

32. John Macdonell to Miles Macdonell, June 27, 1812, Miles Macdonell, Selkirk Settlement, 1811–1812, And Various, 1763–1812, p. 149, Public Archives of Canada. Hereafter, Miles Macdonell, Selkirk Settlement, *PAC.*

As a result of this fusion of races and the attraction of common interests and a common origin an extensive half-breed community appeared on the plains between the Saskatchewan and Red rivers some time during the last quarter of the eighteenth and the early part of the nineteenth century. Its members called themselves by various names. Being of a *gens libre* they were "free men," or "free Canadians." Because of their dark skins they were bois-brûlés, or "charcoal faces." By way of distinction and self-approval they were "the New Nation." Being of mixed blood, for the French fur traders, the bourgeois, and voyageurs, they were métis, or bois-brûlés, and these two latter names will generally be used here. The Caucasian strain, whether of French, English, or Scottish source, exhibited itself in marked degree, while at the same time characteristics peculiarly Indian were still present. These métis were stalwart, muscular, and active, excitable, imaginative and ambitious, passionate and restless, easily amused and commonly devout. With the horse, the gun, and the paddle they were equally skillful; they were masters of the art of trapping; and in the pursuit of the buffalo they acquired the daring, precision, and tactics of trained cavalrymen.[33]

Such was the population of the Red River Valley before permanent and civilized settlement was begun. Far removed from the outermost limits of the slowly advancing agriculturalists to the east and south, its members might have lived out their wild and colorful, but hard and unfruitful careers for decades to come without being disturbed greatly by the inroads of civilization, had it not been for certain conditions and events in the distant British Isles. There, circumstances conspired to bring an unexpected flow of settlers with agricultural ambitions to the Red River Valley. Owing to a number of causes, large sections of the rural population of the British Isles were suffering from extreme want and all the terrible uncertainties that afflict the newly poor; and just when the times seemed ripe for wholesale emigration to a new and kindlier world a man appeared fitted by instinct, education, and inheritance to lead the unfortunate people out of their wilderness and into their promised land. This man was Thomas Douglas, the fifth Earl of Selkirk, a wealthy, educated, and philanthropic Scottish nobleman.

33. Simpson to Colvile, May 31, 1824, Selkirk Papers, St. Mary's Isle. Hereafter, *SP SM*. The Earl of Southesk, *Saskatchewan and the Rocky Mountains, A Diary and Narrative of Travel, Sport and Adventure, during a Journey through the Hudson's Bay Company's Territories, in 1859 and 1860* (Edinburgh, 1875), pp. 360 f. Viscount Milton and W. B. Cheadle, *The North-West Passage by Land* (London, 1865), pp. 42 ff. The term "Free Canadians" was also used to designate men either white or of mixed blood, who had been born in Canada and who trafficked in furs independently of the fur-trade companies.

CHAPTER II

THE OLD-WORLD SCENE

On the southwestern coast of Scotland, in the stewartry of Kirkcudbright at the mouth of the River Dee, is the beautiful, sequestered St. Mary's Isle,[1] the ancient seat of the Douglas family. Here on June 20, 1771, was born Thomas Douglas, fifth Earl of Selkirk, Baron Daer and Shortcleugh, and the youngest of the seven sons of Dunbar (Hamilton) Douglas. The families from which Thomas was descended,[2] the Douglases, the Marrs, and the Anguses, had for centuries played a bold and prominent part in the history of Scotland; and when the seventh son was born it was scarcely suspected that he alone of that generation of Douglases would add luster to the great name he bore.

From early boyhood to maturity Thomas Douglas was subjected to influences which were likely to fire with enthusiasm the mind of an imaginative and sensitive[3] youth. The country round about his birthplace was replete with historical remains and traditions. Only a short distance below the town of Kirkcudbright, on a small island in the River Dee, was the gaunt medieval fortalice, Threave Castle, the handiwork and onetime aerie of such doughty warriors as Archibald the Grim and the Black Douglas. Eastward about five miles from St. Mary's Isle, on the banks of the Abbey Burn, stood the noble ruins of Dundrennan Abbey, founded in the twelfth century and rendered more historic by having afforded shelter to the ill-fated Mary Stuart previous to her flight into England. The very building in which Thomas lived had originally been, in part, a priory, the "Prioratus Sanctae Mariae de Trayll," founded during the reign of David I of Scotland.

It was not the past alone, however, which stirred and left its impress on the mind of the youthful Douglas. He was born in, and lived through troublous times. During the years of the American Revolutionary War, when Britain was struggling with a multiplicity of foes, the British coasts were raided frequently by enemy privateers. One of these found

1. St. Mary's Isle is today a peninsula of about a mile and a half in length and three eighths of a mile in mean breadth, formed by the main channel of the River Dee on the west and Kirkcudbright Bay on the east. The recession of the sea, so noticeable along the whole coast of Kirkcudbrightshire, is remarkably observable from the peninsula. At one time St. Mary's was an isle, most of its present surface being covered by the sea.

2. Sketch of Selkirk Family, *SP SM*.

3. Selkirk to Thomas Douglas, July 14, 1793; Thomas Douglas to Selkirk, August 16, 1793, February 8, 1794; Selkirk to Thomas Douglas, March 27, 1794, *SP SM*.

its way to St. Mary's Isle. On June 14, 1777, the Second Continental Congress had invested Captain John Paul Jones with the command of the *Ranger*, a new ship-rigged corvette. Jones was a native of Arbigland, Kirkcudbrightshire, and a sometime resident of St. Mary's Isle, who had gone to America at an early age, had eventually settled in Virginia, and at the beginning of the Revolution had thrown in his lot with the "patriots."[4]

On April 10, 1778, the captain, having "girded himself for his first great enterprise in foreign seas," sailed from Brest on a cruise in British waters. Shortly afterwards the *Ranger* was in the Irish Channel and John Paul was near the place of his birth. After an abortive attempt to burn the shipping at Whitehaven, the *Ranger* sailed into Kirkcudbright Bay. The captain and a marauding party put to shore at St. Mary's Isle and, being informed that Lord Selkirk was not at home, contented themselves with carrying off the family plate. It had been Jones's intention to capture Selkirk and hold him "until, through his means, a general and fair exchange of prisoners, as well in Europe as in America, had been effected." Later he repented of his venture even to the extent of buying the stolen plate from his men and returning it to Lady Selkirk.[5]

The Paul Jones raid made a deep and lasting impression on Thomas Douglas; he was only seven years old at the time and was driven to terror by the rough sailors as they came to take his father prisoner, and made off with their plunder. In later years, after he had become Earl of Selkirk, he wrote: "This was a momentous event in my life. I was terribly frightened. The firing of the cannon during the night terrified me . . . and when I was but a youth I developed an antipathy for the United States due almost solely to the buccaneering of John Paul."[6] Perhaps this may help to explain why the Earl, when considering possible sites in America for colonization projects, was decidedly in favor of districts lying in British territory rather than in the more temperate regions of the United States.

A more worthy tradition was implanted in Thomas Douglas' mind by the political atmosphere of the region in which he grew up. The county

4. Mrs. Reginald De Koven, *The Life and Letters of John Paul Jones* (New York, 1913), I, 257.

5. Lady Selkirk to Countess of Morton, April 23, 1778; Lady Selkirk to Selkirk, April 23, 1778; Jeffrey to Selkirk, April 23, 1778; Lady Selkirk to Selkirk, April 24, 1778; Lady Selkirk to Countess of Morton, May 15, 1778; Jones to Lady Selkirk, May 8, 1778; Lord Daer to Blane, May 27, 1778; Selkirk to Le Despencer, n.d.; Le Despencer to Selkirk, June 22, 1778; Selkirk to Jones, June 9, 1778; Lady Selkirk to Witham, April 25, 1778; Mary Elliott to Grieve, May 6, 1778; Blane to Selkirk, May 2, 1778, *SP SM*.

6. Selkirk to Halkett, June 21, 1813, *SP SM*.

of Wigtown and the stewartry of Kirkcudbright, which constitute the
ancient district of Galloway, used to be called the "Whig Country."
Here in the past had lain the chief strength of the Covenanters, who had
fought for the common rights of the individual and against tyranny in
government. The aristocracy of Galloway, the Gordons, Kennedys,
Douglases, McCullochs, and Maxwells, were comparatively free from,
and opposed to, the narrow-mindedness which commonly afflicts ruling
classes. As a result Thomas imbibed, as he grew up, not a few social and
political principles that were radical.[7] Nevertheless, these principles
were always, in his case, to be restrained and directed by a powerful and
cultivated mind. Naturally gifted with a strong intelligence,[8] from his
earliest years he was exposed to the influences of broad culture. Brilliant men were always welcome at the Douglas family seat, as the fourth
Earl of Selkirk loved and patronized letters. Among others, Robert
Burns and Dugald Stewart, the philosopher, were guests from time to
time. It was on his first visit there that Burns extemporized the well-
known "Selkirk Grace":[9]

> Some ha'e meat and canna eat,
>   An' some wad eat that want it;
> But we ha'e meat, an' we can eat,
>   An' sae the Lord be thankit.

Such contacts as these were among the influences that helped to mold
the boy's character and mind.

As a younger son, especially as the youngest of seven, Thomas fully
expected that he would have to make his own way in the world, and at
fifteen he was registered at, and attended classes in, the University of
Edinburgh where he remained for four years.[10] At that time the city of

7. Selkirk to Lord Daer (Basil William), February 12, 1785; Lord Daer to Alexander Douglas, August 10, 1790; Lord Daer to Brissot, n.d., c. July, 1792; Selkirk to
Alexander Douglas, December 9, 1792; Alexander Douglas to Selkirk, n.d., c. December, 1792, SP SM.

8. Selkirk to Lord Daer, January 17, 1785; Selkirk to Thomas Douglas, July 14,
1793; Thomas Douglas to Lord Daer (John Douglas), January 25, 1796; William
Barbauld to Lady Selkirk, May, 1821, SP SM.

9. Sketch of Selkirk Family, SP SM.

10. Selkirk to Lord Daer, January 17, 1785, SP SM. Although young Thomas was
sent to Edinburgh to study law, he apparently devoted his time to studies other than
law. In a letter to his brother John (January 25, 1796, SP SM), speaking of his
knowledge of law, he writes: "You know I never attended a class, and I don't know
how far that may be an obstacle in the way. . . ." See, however, Sir James Hall, his
brother-in-law, to Selkirk, May 3, 1817: "I gave him a piece of information which
came upon him like a flash and at once cleared up many Points in your history which

Edinburgh held a leading position among the centers of culture and learning in Great Britain. Robertson, the historian, was Principal of the University. Dugald Stewart was professor. The great economist, Adam Smith, was living out the years of his retirement in the city.[11] Within the student body itself there was keen activity and brilliant promise. Literary societies, involving debates and the reading of essays, played an important part in academic life. In the year 1788 "The Club," later to become famous in the history of the university, was formed by an unusual group of students, young Douglas and Walter Scott being two of its original members, and friends throughout their lives.

It was the custom for the members of the club to meet once a week. After the reading of papers and open discussion they "usually adjourned to sup at an oyster tavern" where they made merry until a late hour. There is no contemporary evidence, however, that Douglas ever took a leading part in the activities of the club. And although he was won by "the literary and humanitarian spirit" displayed,[12] he was reticent, reserved, and very timid, characteristics of which he was conscious but which he was never able to overcome completely.[13]

While he was attending the university, the French Revolution broke out. Like Wordsworth, Coleridge, and other young men of promise, he became deeply interested in the great and many-sided upheaval, and finally crossed the Channel to study it at first hand.[14] Then, when he returned to Scotland, he began to study Highland life and to learn the Gaelic tongue with a view to fitting himself to help improve the condition of the Highland poor.

There lay a field well worth the attention and generosity of a philanthropist. Since the Forty-five uprising the clansmen of the Highlands had found it ever harder to make a living. As soon as the rebellion was crushed, the British Government had taken effective steps to prevent a recurrence. The clan system was broken up and the social scale radically altered. From early times the land had belonged not to the chiefs

he had been at a loss to comprehend. I mean the circumstance of your having been bred a lawyer." *PAC SP,* p. 6156.

11. While in Edinburgh, young Thomas occasionally listened to public addresses of Adam Smith; he was an ardent admirer of the economist. See Notebook, *SP SM.*

12. Martin, *Selkirk,* p. 16.

13. Selkirk to Thomas Douglas, July 14, 1793; Thomas Douglas to Selkirk, August 16, 1793, February 18, 1794; Selkirk to Thomas Douglas, March 27, 1794, *SP SM.*

14. See especially letters: Thomas Douglas to Selkirk, November 16, 25, December 5, 13, 1792; Thomas Douglas to John Douglas, October 29, 1793; Thomas Douglas to Selkirk, December 27, 1793, and the two Thomas Douglas French diaries, November 8, 1792—December 30, 1792, *SP SM.*

alone, but to the clans as units. The chiefs themselves were elected by the clansmen and, although given implicit obedience, had no more ownership of the soil than had their meanest followers. The clansman's life was lonely, but independent. Around his rude hut he grew a little corn for his family and a little fodder for his cattle. His small flock of sheep provided wool which his womenfolk carded, spun, and wove. The life of the men was one of comparative indolence, broken by brief periods of work when they sowed or reaped their crops, or it was sharply broken by the clarion call to arms when, by means of the Fiery Cross, their chief assembled them to defend their homes or engage in a raid or a campaign.

All this was altered fundamentally after the Forty-five when, with baleful effects, the British Government confiscated the land and gave it to the chiefs. It is true that at first little change was felt; the old leaders treated their followers very much as before. But with the rise of a new generation the economic innovation began to affect social relations markedly. The young lords were usually sent to southern Scotland or England for their education. Here they not only lost the peculiar love of the Gael for his kinsmen but also developed expensive tastes and ambitions which the customary rents were too meager to support. The result was a great and sudden increase in rents; and the tenants felt the unaccustomed burden severely. This was not all. The last quarter of the eighteenth and the first part of the nineteenth century witnessed the spread of the agrarian revolution into Scotland; it had begun in England in the middle of the eighteenth century, and by the 'nineties, when Douglas was studying economic conditions in the "straths," the wide and open Highland valleys, it was sweeping rapidly over Scotland. Speculators from the south, traveling through the Highlands, had been quick to grasp the sheep-raising possibilities of this land of heather, grass, and winter snow; and they had offered the new owners much higher rents than the clansmen, now reduced to the permanent level of tenants, could pay. Within a few years, as a result, hundreds of families were evicted by the modernized chiefs; lands were enclosed on a large scale; and where there had once been men there were now sheep, cattle, and deer. Half-despairing, the homeless people drifted either to the seashore to win a dangerous and precarious livelihood by fishing or to the new industrial centers—already the Industrial Revolution had also extended from England into Scotland—to become wage slaves in the factories. As they grew ever more poverty-stricken in their new environments, these dispossessed people turned at length to the idea of emigration; and before the close of the eighteenth century thousands of them left Scotland forever to seek in the New World the living which was denied to them at home.[15]

Such was the condition of the Highlands in 1792 when Thomas Douglas, prompted by "a warm interest in the fate of my countrymen," made a tour of northern Scotland. In the course of this journey he ascertained clearly "that Emigration was an unavoidable result of the general state of the country"; that, in fact, it was "the only solution of a bad situation." He also learned that the great majority of the emigrant Highlanders "were dispersing to a variety of situations, in a foreign land, where they were lost not only to their native country" but to the Empire. He was opposed to this expatriation; he was a firm believer in the desirability of a colonial empire; and he had no sympathy with those who "insinuated that the colonies are altogether of little use . . . ; that all the continental colonies, and particularly the Canadas, must inevitably fall, at no distant period, into the hands of the Americans." The best way for Britain to maintain control over her colonies, Douglas believed, was, first, to adopt a liberal policy of colonial administration and, secondly, to secure the large number of outgoing Scots "to our own colonies, rather than abandon them to a foreign country."[16]

Such, however, was the pressure of the French war at the time that he was not encouraged to make definite proposals to the government. As yet, too, he was only a "younger son." But when, in 1797, the last of his six brothers died, he became Lord Daer and heir to his father's earldom; and his philanthropic plans must have taken on wider scope and further detail when he realized that some day he would have large resources and great influence. That day came on May 24, 1799, when, with the death of his father, he became Earl of Selkirk. The upbringing which he had received now proved to be of vast advantage to him. He was not only a great nobleman but "an educated man with the broad outlook on life and the humanitarian sympathy which study and experience bring to a generous spirit."[17] He now decided to use the new means at his disposal to carry out his earlier plans: he would better the economic and social status of the Highlanders by providing for them new homes across the Atlantic, and he would at the same time help to save Britain's colonial empire by peopling the open spaces of her continental colonies.[18]

15. Thomas Douglas, Correspondence and Diaries on Highland Tour, 1792, *SP SM*. Earl of Selkirk, *Observations on the Present State of the Highlands of Scotland, with a view of the Causes and Probable Consequences of Emigration* (London, 1805), *passim*. Hereafter, Selkirk, *Observations on Highlands*.

16. *Ibid., passim. PAC SP,* p. 13231.

17. George Bryce, *The Life of Lord Selkirk, Coloniser of Western Canada* (Toronto, n.d.), p. 14.

18. Selkirk to Hobart, November 30, 1802, *Q293,* pp. 256 f. *PAC SP,* p. 13231.

CHAPTER III

"WITH A VIEW TO THE PUBLIC SERVICE"

Selkirk's first definite step in carrying out his emigration theories was an appeal to the British Government for land on which to settle colonists. At the moment it was not Scotland but Ireland which goaded him to action. Few European countries of the old regime were more assiduously misgoverned than Ireland. Political oligarchy, Catholic disabilities, alien and absentee landlordism conspired with a variety of concomitant evils to make Ireland a most miserable and dejected land. The war of the American Revolution was in some wise Ireland's opportunity: the crisis enabled the Irish to wring certain concessions—nominal home rule and some commercial favors—from an obdurate British Parliament. Despite these gains, however, economic and social conditions in the country were little alleviated. The great majority of Irishmen still remained the economic helots of Britain. Hence, when the French Revolution broke out and England entered the war on the Continent, in 1798 Ireland again took advantage of England's difficulties and revolted. The British, however, fearful of great economic loss and of greater military danger, crushed the ill-starred rising with savage fury.

Selkirk had watched the course of the Irish rebellion with keen interest, and when he saw it "throttled down in sullen despair, his feelings were fully aroused."[1] For several months he studied carefully the economic, especially the agrarian, and the social problems in the unfortunate island,[2] and finally came to the conclusion that his solution for similar conditions in Scotland—assisted and systematic emigration—would also be the best remedy for Ireland's woes. In consequence, he prepared a memorial entitled "A Proposal tending to the Permanent Security of Ireland"; and, in the winter of 1801–2, he sent it to the Colonial Office.[3] For permanent Irish security, it was urged that a colony be founded in North America expressly for Irish Catholics, and that assistance be given for its establishment from the Public Purse.

Selkirk was confident that if such a colony were established a very large number of Irishmen might be induced in the course of a few years

1. See the Selkirk Irish manuscripts (three in number, not dated, all probably written in the winter of 1801–2), *SP SM*. Helen I. Cowan, "Selkirk's Work in Canada," *CHR*, IX, 301.

2. From early in January until late in August, 1802, Selkirk traveled extensively through Ireland, carefully observing economic, social, and political conditions. His findings were painstakingly recorded in five volumes. *SP SM*.

3. *PAC SP*, pp. 13893–13897.

to emigrate to it; and that the emigration might be so managed as to free Ireland in a relatively short time of all its most troublesome elements

of those whose disaffection is most noted & violent, of those turbulent & restless characters who would be most likely to be active leaders of future disturbances, of those who from extreme poverty would be most readily tempted into such scenes, of those whose habits of idleness and irregularity render them most difficult to be converted into useful & industrious subjects.

In the Proposal, the Earl was specific as to a site for the colony. The situation chosen must be possessed of a favorable climate, a fertile soil, and an extensive water system for navigation purposes. It was his opinion that the remaining unsettled territories of British North America were unsuitably located for colonization. Hence he eliminated it from his colonizing project and instead suggested Louisiana as being most desirable, "a situation in which every advantage would be united; in which there would be the fairest prospects both of the internal Prosperity of the Colony, & of its becoming a valuable acquisition to the Commerce of Britain."

Sufficient contemporary evidence is available to explain what Selkirk meant when he made the suggestion to the Addington Ministry that Louisiana might be secured by Britain in the "haste and secrecy" of "the negotiation then pending": he alluded to the recent Spanish retrocession of Louisiana to France, and the Anglo-French negotiations of 1801–2 that culminated in the Treaty of Amiens, March, 1802.

In a preliminary treaty of October 1, 1800, Spain had ceded New Orleans and Louisiana west of the Mississippi to France. Despite all endeavors of the signatory powers to keep the treaty a secret, the news of the retrocession soon leaked out in Europe. By the winter of 1801–2, the thing had become common knowledge. Thus it was that Selkirk suggested to Downing Street "that if the circumstances of the negotiation now pending open any possibility of procuring the Cession of Louisiana, it would be a situation in which every advantage would be united."

This was not the first occasion on which Selkirk had thought of territories in North America outside the British possessions as a fitting sphere for organized colonization. Several years earlier a tract of land in New York State, bordering on Lake Ontario and situated about the mouth of the Great Salmon River, had been purchased by an agent for the Selkirk estate. Although disagreement over the ownership of the border districts in the region of the Great Lakes had caused much hard feeling between the United States and Great Britain, by the late 'nineties the dictates of both common sense and common gain had gone far to remove it. In spite of the patriotic zeal of John Graves Simcoe, then Lieutenant Governor of Upper Canada, British emigrants and British capital were flowing in increasing volume into the northern states. Even before the Jay Treaty had in 1794 definitely settled the boundary question, shrewd Scotchmen in close connection with members of the British Cabinet had purchased large holdings in western New York State. Shortly after the signing of the treaty, and some four months subsequent to the British evacuation of Fort Ontario, the Selkirk purchase was made.[4] The real ownership, however, was not made public until the year 1800, when an Act was passed in the state legislature enabling aliens to hold land. The Act was pushed through for private reasons and by the efforts of British and American land speculators. Selkirk was now able to assume personal ownership of his holdings at the mouth of the Great Salmon.[5]

Although he thus possessed New York lands very suitable for colonization, he was anxious to obtain territory, adaptable to his purposes, within the Empire. Hence his suggestion that the government might acquire Louisiana. There was sufficient historical evidence to warrant Selkirk making such a proposal. Since 1763 English statesmen had been wary lest France try to reëstablish herself on the North American continent;[6] in 1783 Lord Lansdowne, the British Foreign Secretary, had urged the exchange of Gibraltar for Louisiana and the Floridas;[7] in 1790, when Great Britain and Spain were at variance, Pitt had "contemplated a seizure of both the Floridas and Louisiana";[8] and six years later had come the Chisholm–Blount–Liston conspiracy, which planned an invasion of Louisiana and the Floridas and had been for a time approved at Downing Street.[9] Furthermore, in 1801 British statesmen were moved by the news of the retrocession of Louisiana to express their

4. Franklin B. Hough, *A History of Jefferson County in the State of New York, From the Earliest Period to the Present Time* (Albany, 1854), p. 63. Grisfield Johnson, *History of Oswego County, New York, With Illustrations and Biographical Sketches of Some of its Prominent Men and Pioneers* (Philadelphia, 1877), p. 52. Book of Deeds, 36, Land Office, Albany, N.Y.

5. Oneida Records, I, 144, Oswego, N.Y.

6. *PACR, 1891*, pp. xxxvi ff. F. J. Turner, "The Diplomatic Contest for the Mississippi Valley," *The Atlantic Monthly*, XCIII, 678 ff.

7. Charles R. King, ed., *The Life and Correspondence of Rufus King* (New York, 1897), IV, 93. Hereafter, *Rufus King*.

8. William Spence Robertson, *The Life of Mirando* (Chapel Hill, 1929), I, 108. Ripley Hitchcock, *The Louisiana Purchase and the Early History and Building of the West* (Boston, 1903), p. 55.

9. Arthur Preston Whitaker, *The Mississippi Question, 1795–1803. A Study in Trade, Politics, and Diplomacy* (New York, 1934), pp. 107 ff. J. Fred Rippy, *Rivalry of the United States and Great Britain over Latin America, 1808–1830* (Baltimore, 1929), pp. 24 ff.

strong disapproval of the exchange, and even to indicate some intention of using force to secure the territory for Britain.[10]

To what extent Selkirk was aware of the official attitude toward Louisiana in 1801, and how far it may have determined his suggestion that Britain might acquire the territory, are not known. But the official mind soon changed. By the winter of 1801–2 the British Government, though still reluctant to see the country west of the Mississippi remain in the hands of France, was no longer considering the possibility of using force to achieve this purpose, nor even ready to bring the matter up for discussion in the negotiations for peace then being carried on at Amiens.[11] When Selkirk learned of the new official attitude, he wrote a new "Proposal Tending to the Permanent Security of Ireland," dated March 31, 1802, and formally submitted it to the Secretary of State, Lord Pelham. In this document he drew the attention of the government to "the dangerous situation of a Kingdom where a great Majority of the people are so obstinately disaffected that no concession softens their animosity"; and, again, supervised emigration was suggested as a radical cure such as military coercion could not effect. Downing Street was urged to establish a colony "expressly for Irish Catholics in some unoccupied part of North America," making every arrangement there in accord with their religious and racial prepossessions. In his own words, deeply impressed with the importance of

these views, the Memorialist would not hesitate to devote his personal exertions & the best years of his life to the Service of his Country, in carrying them into execution—& if his plan should be adopted by Government, he would undertake to settle the proposed Colony in America, provided he were assured of effectual support, & that a situation were chosen, possessed of those natural advantages which are requisite for success. Such he trusts may be procured in a climate, where the attention of the Colonists may be directed to the objects of cultivation, not only useful to the Commerce of Britain, but for which at present she depends chiefly on the territories of her habitual enemies.[12]

In this "Proposal" the author concentrated his attention on points only of essential consideration, and, until a later date, postponed making public the areas in America most favorable for colonization. It was on April 3 that Selkirk, in "Observations Supplementary to a Memorial relative to the Security of Ireland,"[13] addressed to the Colonial Office, discussed possible sites. On the day preceding the writing of this document Selkirk had been in conversation with Lord Pelham, and the latter

10. *Rufus King*, III, 469, IV, 241.
12. *SP SM. Q293*, pp. 172 ff.
11. *Ibid.*, IV, 56 ff., 241.
13. *Ibid.*, pp. 178 ff.

had attacked the whole Irish plan with many arguments, including "some secret view."[14] But it would seem that he had not declared himself to be completely hostile to the Earl's views on the matter, because only on the next day Selkirk, in his "Observations Supplementary," described with exuberance the Red River Valley as the ideal site for the location of a colony. Nowhere in the document is Louisiana mentioned specifically, although at one point the author observes that a "concurrence of circumstances" might some day "lead to the acquisition of territory on the Upper Mississippi." Just what were the exact implications of this statement is difficult to determine. The United States owned the region to the east of the Mississippi; France had recently acquired the land to the west. Did the writer hope that negotiations might in the future secure some United States territory? More likely he was insinuating that a good way to meet the French threat from Louisiana was to let him colonize Red River.

It was probably after a reading of Sir Alexander Mackenzie's account of his Northern and Western explorations, as published in 1801, that Selkirk conceived the idea of planting a colony in the distant interior of British North America.[15] The great explorer, who had penetrated the Northwest to the Arctic Ocean in 1789 and to the Pacific Ocean in 1793, had described, on the whole favorably, the climate and the soil of the territory between Lake Superior and the Saskatchewan River.

It becomes obvious from a reading of "Observations Supplementary" that Selkirk drafted that document with a copy of Mackenzie's *Voyages* before him, although he allowed himself to give a more vivid

14. Conversation with Lord Pelham, April 2, 1802, *PAC SP,* p. 13902.
15. The extent to which Selkirk was indebted to Mackenzie's *Voyages* is difficult to determine. To quote from George Bryce, "Mackenzie, Selkirk, Simpson," *Makers of Canada* (Toronto, 1905), VII, 94: "From the Earl of Selkirk's own lips we learn that it was this book which first called his attention to Rupert's Land, and led him to lay the foundation of his colony on the Red River." Martin, in *Selkirk,* p. 17, is of the opinion that "Count Andreani, the traveller . . . was probably the first to direct Douglas's attention to the promise of the New World." The present writer went through the Selkirk materials at St. Mary's Isle very carefully and he was unable to find any direct evidence to support the contention of either Bryce or Martin. In a letter to his father written from Lucerne on May 6, 1794, Selkirk says: "I am only sorry I could not remain longer with Count Andreani to whom Sir James Hall recommended me, and who received me very kindly. He was not at Milan when I passed there, but I saw him at a country house on the road to Switzerland." *SP SM.* This is the source of evidence cited by Martin. Selkirk in his *Sketch of the British Fur Trade in North America* (London, 1816), pp. 36 f. (hereafter, Selkirk, *British Fur Trade*) quotes from the Andreani "Journal" as extracted by La Rochefoucault-Liancourt, in *Voyages dans l'Amérique,* but nowhere in this volume does he state or even suggest that the Count was the first to direct "his attention to the promise of the New World."

and optimistic description of the Red River prairies than had the man who wrote from long and personal experience. Downing Street was advised that no large tract of land on the Atlantic seaboard remained unsettled "except barren & frozen deserts." If a sufficient extent of good soil in a temperate climate was to be found, it would be necessary to go far inland. This, however, was not to be regarded as an insurmountable obstacle to the prosperity of a colony; in fact, the advantages of a site in the interior considerably outweighed all the drawbacks:

At the Western extremity of Canada, upon the Waters which fall into Lake Winnipeck [Winnipeg], & uniting in the great River of Port Nelson, discharge themselves into Hudson's Bay, is a Country which the Indian Traders represent as fertile, & of a Climate far more temperate than the Shores of the Atlantic under the same parallel, & not more severe than that of Germany & Poland. Here, therefore, the Colonists may, with a moderate exertion of industry, be certain of a comfortable subsistence, & they may also raise some valuable objects of exportation. . . . To a Colony in these territories, the Channel of Trade must be the River of Port Nelson.

In the eyes of the author of "Observations Supplementary" the greatest impediment to the establishment of a colony in the Red River prairies appeared to be the monopoly rights of the Hudson's Bay Company, which the possessors could hardly be expected readily to relinquish. This, however, the greatest obstacle, might be surmounted with comparative ease. The Hudson's Bay Company's monopoly could be abolished with ample indemnification, certainly without any burden, and "perhaps even with advantage to the Revenue." There was little in the Earl's adjustment scheme which was new or original. It called merely for the revival and application of the old French fur-trade licensing system:

An annual duty should be paid for a license by every person trading with the Indians in the Countries connected with Hudson's Bay, each individual being limited to a particular district, in which no other should be allowed to interfere: that from the funds thus arising the Proprietors of Hudson's Bay Stock should receive an annual dividend equal to their net profits on an average of bye gone years.

It was not regarded as too sanguine to expect that in due course of time the duty from trading licenses would be large enough not only to defray the expense of the whole civil and military administration of a colony, but "even to become a productive source of Revenue to the Mother Country."

The Irish security plan, however, did not meet with the general ap-

proval of His Majesty's Government. Nearly two months elapsed before
Selkirk received even official acknowledgment of his addresses. Finally,
late in May, Lord Pelham pronounced emphatically against the "Proposal": he was definitely opposed to "colonizing at all en masse"; he
saw "great difficulties & objections to Government undertaking to
Transport & settle people from Ireland or elsewhere"; and, furthermore, any interference with Hudson Bay trade, "which takes such good
care of itself," could not be brooked.[16] Lord Hobart, the Secretary for
War and Colonies, considered a reply unnecessary, even when the Earl
wrote to ask for the return of his memorial, urging that it surely could
not be the wish of Government that he should remain pledged to services
which they did not intend to accept.[17] Dugald Stewart was most curt
and officious in his unpublished "Observations," warning Selkirk that if
he pushed his requests too vehemently, he would be accused of stimulat-
ing emigration, and that in any case he could more advantageously employ his services at home.[18]

Despite such discouraging opposition, Selkirk was not daunted in his
colonizing ambitions. In June he sought an audience with Lord Hobart.
It was granted for the eleventh. The "Proposal tending to the Permanent Security of Ireland" was reviewed and explained by the author in
every detail. Lord Hobart gave the Earl little encouragement, but did
promise to reconsider the whole proposition and to give the government's final decision "in a few weeks." It would seem that at this stage
of events the section of the "Proposal" which dealt with the prospect of
a colonization site in the interior of British North America met with
most objection. The Secretary hinted at this interview that the government would probably be more willing to grant lands for settlement in
Prince Edward Island than in the West.[19]

Several weeks now passed and Selkirk received no word from Downing Street. This silence on the part of the officials was irritating and
disturbing. By the time July had arrived without any answer forth-
coming, the Earl had lost hope that his Red River suggestion would be
taken up. He now decided to cease all agitation on the subject. Not that
he was willing to forego his project for Irish security. He was merely
giving up his hopes that the government would support him in the
realization of his desire to colonize Red River.[20]

To bring his plans as nearly as possible in line with the wishes of the

16. Pelham to Selkirk, May 27, 1802, *Q293*, pp. 167 f.
17. Selkirk to Hobart, June 9, 1802, *Q293*, p. 188.
18. Dugald Stewart, "Observations on American Plan," 1802, *PAC SP*, pp.
13903 ff.
19. Selkirk to Hobart, July 6, 1802, *Q293*, pp. 201 f.   20. *Ibid.*

government Selkirk now turned his attention from the Hudson's Bay Company's territories to Prince Edward Island and Upper Canada. On July 6 he wrote to Lord Hobart asking for grants of land on the Island, and at Sault Ste Marie.[21] In his letter the Earl stressed his desire for land around the Sault rather than on Prince Edward Island, not because he believed the soil richer or the climate more salubrious in this vicinity, but rather because he recognized the fact that Sault Ste Marie was the only communication on British soil between the Canadas and the Northwest, and if the latter were ever to be colonized by His Majesty's subjects, it was of the greatest importance "to secure this pass, & to be before hand with the Americans in establishing a respectable settlement there."[22]

Late in July the officials of the government had come round to a position more or less favorable to the idea of overseas colonization. At any rate, Selkirk was promised a tract of land about Sault Ste Marie on certain conditions—the main one being that "the Settlement should be begun with people more tractable than the Irish." After having duly considered the government's wishes, the Earl in August entirely acquiesced.[23]

Selkirk decided to take action at once while the political skies were still clear. Perhaps for this reason he acted too hastily. An emigration plan was prepared and advertised in western Scotland—where large numbers of recently evicted Scottish tenants were about to emigrate to the United States—"with the view of diverting the current towards His Majesty's Colonies," and especially to Sault Ste Marie. The Earl and his agents were not without success. About a hundred families, chiefly from the island of Skye but partly from Ross, Argyll, and Inverness, were persuaded to go out to Upper Canada instead of to the Carolinas. This was an encouraging beginning, but Selkirk was soon dismayed by his discovery that the expense of the venture would be such as to require a far larger financial backing than he could supply out of his own resources. "Prudence," he wrote to Lord Hobart on November 30, "requires me to pause, till I am informed what specific assistance I may expect from Government to alleviate the burthen, or what indemnification I have to look to in case I take it on myself."[24] Prudence might well have intervened a little sooner. The government had stated its conditions explicitly and Selkirk had accepted them unreservedly.

21. *Ibid.* Hobart to Selkirk, July 30, 1802, *PAC SP,* pp. 13851 f. *PAC SP,* p. 13234.

22. Selkirk to Hobart, August 21, 1802, *Q293,* pp. 219 f.

23. *Ibid.,* pp. 221 f. *PAC SP,* pp. 13234 f.

24. *Ibid.* Downing Street to Hunter, September 4, 1802, *Q293,* pp. 83 f. Selkirk to Hobart, November 30, 1802, *Q293,* pp. 256 ff. Selkirk to Hobart, January 25, 1803, *PAC SP,* pp. 13234 f., 13847 f.

Negotiations with the government were begun again, but at first brought no success. When interviewed by Selkirk, the Prime Minister, Addington, would promise nothing.[25] Finally in January, 1803, after discussing the matter with a number of close friends, the Earl decided to try to force the government's hand. On January 25 he wrote to Lord Hobart explaining how circumstances had compelled him to change his plans:

Your Lordship is informed that I entered into terms with a number of emigrant families, and to induce them to alter their destination, have been under the necessity of making stipulations which will incur a considerable expence, and by which I shall suffer great loss if I do not make immediate preparations.

Tho' this has been incurred with a view to the public service I do not mean to complain, as I can turn these expences to very good account by a purchase in the Western Territory of the United States.

But however profitable such a speculation would be, I can assure your Lordship that little short of absolute necessity would make me think of this resource, & that I shall feel most sincere regret in being compelled thus to counteract the very object with a view to which I entered upon the business. That object however is not for an individual to undertake without public aid or any prospect of indemnification; & if His Majesty's Ministers do not think it adviseable to make an effort for attracting the Emigrants to our Colonies, I trust that being thus engaged in this business, I shall not be blamed for proceeding in the only way, in which I can avoid a total sacrifice of my own interest. . . .[26]

This letter had the desired effect, and in February the Ministry came to terms. Selkirk was granted a magnificent strip of land, with liberal concessions, on the eastern peninsula of Prince Edward Island and promised a tract of 1,200 acres in any township in Upper Canada "not already appropriated which he may prefer," with "a further quantity at the rate of Two hundred acres for every Family he may induce to settle there."[27]

In July, 1803, 800 settlers crowded into three ships and set sail for Prince Edward Island. It had been the Earl's intention to go out to the Island "some time before any of the settlers" should arrive there, "in

25. *Ibid.*, p. 13847.   26. *Ibid.*, pp. 13847 f.

27. *Ibid.*, pp. 14149 f. Selkirk to Addington, February 1, 1803, *PAC SP*, pp. 13853 ff. Selkirk to Hobart, February 9, 1803, *PAC SP*, pp. 13856 f. Selkirk to Addington, February 10, 1803, *PAC SP*, p. 13858. Hobart to Selkirk, February 12, 1803, *PAC SP*, pp. 13849 f. Selkirk to Sullivan, February 13, 1803, *PAC SP*, pp. 13859 f. Proposition and Memorandum, *PAC SP*, pp. 13861 ff. Sullivan to Selkirk, March 30, 1803, *PAC SP*, p. 13863. Hobart to Hunter, February 28, 1803, Colonial Office Records, Series G, Vol. 54, Pt. I, pp. 90 ff., Public Archives of Canada. Hereafter *G*.

order that every requisite preparation might be made"; but private
duties caused him such delay that he did not arrive until early in August. One ship's passengers had already landed, and the others came
along within a few days. August and September were busy months.
There was much to be done. Trees and underbrush had to be cut away,
though this was not such an arduous task since the land had once been
cleared by the French. Surveys had to be made, lands distributed, and
winter houses built. Selkirk remained with his colonists until the most
pressing affairs of settlement had been completed. Then, leaving an
agent to carry on in his stead, he hurried away to the United States.[28]

It was partly with a view to investigating settlement conditions near
his own holdings in western New York that the Earl visited the United
States on this occasion. From October, 1803, until June of the following year he traveled in the States, principally in New York, noting
everywhere details of settlement schemes—road construction, quality of
soils, land prices, methods of sale—and stowing away the information
in a diary which, for the journey, runs to twelve valuable volumes. Particular attention was paid to the conditions obtaining on those lands
which were being developed by his fellow Scots. One of these ventures
exemplifies in such complete detail every settlement method and device
brought forward later by Selkirk that it must undoubtedly have made
a strong impression upon him. This was a million-acre tract in the
Genesee country, under the general management of Charles Williamson,
son of the secretary of the Earl of Hopetown. No expense had been
spared in its development. Roads, hotels, schools, churches, and pure-
bred stock had all been supplied by the promoters. Its attractions were
widely advertised; but up to the time of Selkirk's visit the expenses had
proved far greater than the returns, and the promoters of such a "hot-
bed settlement" had lost much from extensions that lacked caution. Selkirk examined the whole scheme closely, not only by making several
visits to the settlement itself but also by questioning the chief agents at
headquarters. An examination of other New York hot-bed settlements
showed similar if less expensive failures. The colonizing nobleman was
impressed, but not favorably. He sold his New York holdings and returned to Canada, more firmly than ever bent on securing government
coöperation in British North American settlement enterprises.[29]

During his sojourn in New York Selkirk carried on a correspondence
with the Government of Upper Canada with a view to securing suitable

28. Selkirk, American Diary, 1803–1804, I, 6 ff., *SP SM*. Hereafter, Selkirk Diary.
Selkirk, *Observations on Highlands,* pp. 190 ff.

29. Selkirk Diary, II, IV, *SP SM*. Cowan, "Selkirk's Work in Canada," *CHR,* IX,
303 ff.

lands for prospective settlers. Lord Hobart had already, in February, 1803, instructed the Lieutenant Governor of Upper Canada, Peter Hunter, to make land grants of the same nature and under the same terms as had been made in Prince Edward Island. Selkirk selected land, finally, in the townships of Chatham and Dover, in western Upper Canada between Lakes Erie and Huron. Before leaving Scotland for Prince Edward Island, he had also made arrangements for settlers to come to Upper Canada. During the year 1803, 111 families were recruited. After wintering at Kirkcaldy, they sailed for Canada, and after landing at Montreal, proceeded to Queenston, where they met the Earl. Baldoon Farm, the new settlement site, was reached after a laborious journey by lake, river, and portage.[30]

Selkirk himself did not go back to Baldoon Farm, but left to agents the work of establishing the settlers on the land and of distributing among them cattle and sheep which had been purchased and sent on ahead.[31] But in any case his presence could scarcely have made Baldoon Colony a success. The site was unhealthy, the land being too low and wet. Within a year of their arrival forty-two of the settlers died from fever or dysentery. Others left to seek more attractive localities. Those who still remained were fairly successful until the War of 1812, when successive invasions ruined most of their property. A few years later, in 1818, Selkirk himself, wearied of settlement enterprises for the time, sold his lands in the Lake St. Clair region.[32] In spite of early hardships and disasters, however, several Baldoon families clung grimly to their farms, and today many of their descendants are still to be found in the locality.

Except at Baldoon, Selkirk did not succeed in starting any settlements in Upper Canada. In August, 1803, he offered to build a highway through the province from York, now Toronto, to Baldoon. In return for such road work, which was to cost about £40,000, he asked the Upper Canadian government for a grant of certain unoccupied Crown lands along the proposed route.[33] Such roads were needed badly in Upper Canada at that time, and the government lacked the necessary funds for building them; but a political clique which ruled the country

30. Colonial Secretary to Grant and Gore, *G55*, Pt. I, pp. 89 f. Selkirk Diary, V, 13 ff., IX, 15 ff., *SP SM. PAC SP*, pp. 13234 f.

31. *Ibid.*, IV, 68, 75, 106, V, 13 ff. Selkirk spent most of June and a part of July, 1804, in the St. Clair country exploring, surveying, planting, and in general preparing for the arrival of the settlers. Selkirk Diary, V, 13 ff., VI, 1 ff., *SP SM*.

32. Land Book G, Upper Canada, February 28, 1806, to March 29, 1808, pp. 8, 16, 215, *PAC. PAC SP*, pp. 6918, 14528, 14592, 14601. Halkett to Colvile, November 22, 1821, *SP SM*.

33. Baldoon, *SP SM*.

and which had been notoriously generous in land grants to its own members, declined the Earl's offer. Later, however, in 1805, his proposal to colonize one of the "Mohawk townships" on the Grand River was accepted. Two years afterwards a purchase of a tract exceeding 30,500 acres in extent was made near the mouth of the river. The unsettled condition of Europe, however, and the distracting of Selkirk's attention to other and more important colonizing ventures prevented the materialization of the Grand River plans; and before many years had passed most of the Upper Canadian properties were sold at tremendous losses.[34]

In the late summer of 1804, after the Baldoon colonists had left Queenston for their settlement, Selkirk went back to Montreal.[35] Here he was entertained lavishly by the leading merchants, chief among whom were the North-westers. Many of the latter were men who had engaged personally in the Western fur trade; and Selkirk was interested in, and thrilled by the stirring tales they told of their adventures in the great Northwest.[36] They invited him to the meetings of the famous Beaver Club, whose membership was limited solely to those engaged in the fur trade, and whose motto, "Fortitude in Distress," was engraved on a gold medal worn by the members. On these occasions Selkirk was regaled with forest delicacies—venison, bear meat, and buffalo tongue— ate and drank from the beaver-crested silver plate and cut glass of the club, and joined in frequent toasts to the fur trade and its heroes, while all sang French-Canadian boat songs.[37] Such experiences could hardly have failed to arouse his dormant interest in the distant Northwest. But neither in his mind nor in those of his fellow revelers could there have been as yet any foreboding of the strife and bitter feeling which the future was to bring between them.

Late in September, 1804, before leaving America, Selkirk visited his colonists in Prince Edward Island, where he was pleased to find that his plans had been followed up with attention and judgment, and progress had been made with satisfaction to all concerned.[38] In this case the future did not bring disappointment. To this day the descendants of the

34. *PAC SP,* pp. 6917 ff., 6981, 14424, 14448.

35. This was his second visit to Montreal. Earlier in the year he had spent two weeks there. Selkirk Diary, III, 105 ff., *SP SM.*

36. In western New York, Upper Canada, and at Detroit Selkirk learned much about the Northwest—the nature of its soil and climate, its inhabitants, and its fur trade. Selkirk Diary, III, IV, V, VI, VII, VIII, *SP SM.*

37. *Ibid.,* X, 10 ff. *A Narrative of Occurrences in the Indian Countries of North America, since the connexion of the Right Hon. the Earl of Selkirk with the Hudson's Bay Company, and his Attempt to establish a Colony on the Red River . . .* (London, 1817), pp. 1 f. Hereafter, *Narrative of Occurrences.*

38. Selkirk Diary, X, 61 ff., *SP SM. Observations on Highlands,* p. 206.

Selkirk settlers on the Island are among the most successful and progressive of its inhabitants.

For several months after his return to St. Mary's Isle, in 1804–5, Selkirk busied himself with the writing of his first book: *Observations on the Present State of the Highlands of Scotland, with a View of the Causes and Probable Consequences of Emigration*—"a strikingly clear, well-written work,"[39] advocating Highland colonization within the Empire. "Now it is our duty to befriend this people," he wrote. "Let us direct their emigration; let them be led abroad to new possessions. Give them homes under the flag and they will strengthen the empire." The object in the publication of this volume was in part to meet the "calumnious reports" that had been spread abroad, with the sanction of some highly respected names, concerning his emigration schemes. Despite this openly acknowledged purpose, the author presented the political and economical effects of the changes Scotland was then undergoing, with great precision and accuracy. Ten years subsequent to the publication of *Observations on the Present State of the Highlands* a certain John Campbell, describing conditions in Scotland to Lord Bathurst, then Secretary for War and the Colonies, observed:

Lord Selkirk's book upon the subject of Emigration, and of the population in the Highlands contains many principles and remarks which are well founded, and which have been evinced since that publication. I am so much satisfied with the interesting remarks made by his Lordship that it entirely supersedes many observations that are obviously just in regard to the Highland as it respects both the state of proprietors, & of the tenants and cottagers. His book was received at the time with some prejudice & excited considerable opposition. But it has been found that it contains much truth.[40]

In 1806 Selkirk definitely entered the political arena of Great Britain as one of Scotland's sixteen representative peers. Chosen again in 1807, in August he addressed the House of Lords in a "Speech on the Defence of the Country." In this speech, published at once in pamphlet form, he argued that "every young man between the ages of eighteen and twenty-five, throughout Great Britain, should be enrolled and completely trained to military discipline." During the same year he and Wilberforce debated the best methods for the civilization and improvement of the Indians of British North America. Many of Selkirk's ideas concerning their proper treatment, especially his "reservation" theory,[41] were

39. *Dictionary of National Biography*, V, 1256.
40. October 14, 1815, *Q135*, Pt. I, pp. 216 f.
41. Selkirk, *Observations on a Proposal for forming a Society for the Civilization and Improvement of the North American Indians within the British Boundary* (London, 1807). Selkirk, *On the Civilization of the Indian in British America* (n.d., n.p.).

carried out later in the nineteenth century as essential features of the Indian administrative systems in Canada and the United States. Early in March of 1807 the Earl was appointed Lord Lieutenant of Kirkcudbright. The following November he married Jean Wedderburn-Colvile of Ochiltree and Crombie. This marriage was to prove of vital importance in his later colonization ventures, for members of the Wedderburn-Colvile family were principals in the Hudson's Bay Company.

In 1808 he was made a Fellow of the Royal Society in recognition of his distinguished contributions in the realm of knowledge. Soon afterwards he published a brochure, *On the Necessity of a More Effectual System of National Defence*, in which was largely anticipated the modern volunteer system. This, like the *Speech on the Defence of the Country*, drew forth considerable discussion. Both of these tracts, as well as *Observations on the Present State of the Highlands*, reveal clearly the ardent patriotism of their author. A *Letter on the Subject of Parliamentary Reform* was published early in 1809.

By this time, however, Selkirk's active participation in British politics had almost come to an end. During the interval since his visit to America his faith had not waned, but had continued to grow. Six years of experience in the art of colonization, however, had done much to moderate his expectations and to concentrate his interests. His indiscriminate altruism had given way to a more scientific grasp of his problems. In 1808 a rare chance to secure land for settlement in the trans-Red River country presented itself, and this opportunity the philanthropic nobleman was not slow in seizing.

CHAPTER IV

ASSINIBOIA

FROM the information about the Northwest which he had gleaned in Canada and elsewhere, Selkirk came to the conclusion, about 1807,[1] that the only feasible way of colonizing the Red River Valley was to ally himself with one of the great fur-trading companies—either with the North West Company operating from Montreal or with the chartered English company established on Hudson Bay. He feared that in the fur-trade war which was growing constantly more bitter between the two great rivals, neutral intruders, especially settlers entering the key region of the Red River, might expect to suffer from the hostility of both sides and to enjoy the friendship and support of neither. No longer did he believe that by any system of indemnification and license fees could the fur traders be reconciled to colonization within the heart of the fur country.

After having considered the question long and carefully, and from various angles, Selkirk decided to throw in his lot with the Hudson's Bay Company, and attempt to colonize the Red River region by using, as far as it might be possible to do so, the Company's charter, resources, and friendship. At first glance this might easily seem to have been an unwise choice. At this time, in 1808, the Company was on the verge of insolvency. For the few preceding years dividends had steadily shrunk, and in 1808 the directors neither declared a dividend nor submitted a financial statement to the stockholders.[2] As a matter of fact they had made no profits to declare. It seemed as if its Canadian rival had finally succeeded in beating the English company to its knees. Trade rivalry, however, was not the only, nor even the chief, cause of this state of affairs. Since 1806 Napoleon had been enforcing with great rigor his famous continental policy—the exclusion of British goods from the markets of Europe. Consequently, the foreign fur buyers, German, French, and Russian, who had been the Hudson's Bay Company's best customers, had failed to come to London for several years. In 1808 the Company's warehouses were piled high with the greater part of three seasons' peltries; and there was no prospect of their sale.

1. *PAC SP*, pp. 13283 f.
2. Memorial of McTavish, Fraser, *Q130*, Pt. II, p. 286. Simon McGillivray to McTavish, McGillivray & Co., June 1, 1811, *Q153*, Pt. III, pp. 615 ff. *PAC SP*, pp. 13247, 13284. Memorandum by the Earl of Selkirk, *SP SM*. Hereafter, Selkirk Memorandum, *SP SM*.

So critical did the corporation's financial condition become that late in December the directors were driven to petition the Chancellor of the Exchequer for temporary assistance. In the following month the petition was transmitted by the Lords of the Treasury to the Board of Trade. After considering the request the Board reported that it "contained no proposition on which the Lords of this Council could offer any opinion to the Lords of the Treasury."[3] A short time afterwards the Company asked the government for a loan of £60,000. This request likewise met with a refusal. The government did, however, grant the Company permission to store furs for twelve months free of duty.[4]

As a result of these contingencies, not only had the Hudson's Bay Company ceased to pay dividends but the market value of its stock had also fallen far below its normal level—from £250 to less than £60 a share.[5] Selkirk now realized that the Company's misfortune might be his advantage, since for a comparatively small sum he might buy up a controlling interest and thus insure for his Red River Settlement project the favor and assistance of the fur-trade organization which, nominally at least, owned and controlled the whole Red River Valley and the approaches from Hudson Bay.[6]

Before committing himself to the venture, however, he made careful inquiries into the content and the validity of the charter of 1670 under which the Company was operating. In the course of these investigations five of the leading jurists of Great Britain were consulted—Sir Samuel Romilly, William Cruise, and John Bell, as well as the two distinguished pleaders, James Scarlet and George Holroyd. In view of the fact that the place and the time were preëminently favorable to rendering sacrosanct the property rights of large proprietors, the answer was never much in doubt. The gentlemen of the law were unanimous in declaring that the charter, lengthy and sweeping though it was, nevertheless was quite valid: that it made the Hudson's Bay Company sole proprietor of all the territories granted, with full powers of government, including the appointment of sheriffs, the trial of lawbreakers, and the leasing or alienation in fee simple, of any part of its domain.[7]

Convinced that the charter was invulnerable, Selkirk began to buy

3. Board of Trade Papers, Series I, Vol. 42, No. 36, and Series V, Vol. 18, No. 438, Public Record Office, London.

4. John Perry Pritchett, "Some Red River Fur-Trade Activities," *Minnesota History Bulletin,* V, 404 n. Hereafter, *MHB.*

5. Memorial of McTavish, Fraser, *Q130,* Pt. II, p. 286.

6. Selkirk Memorandum, *SP SM. PAC SP,* pp. 13245, 13283 f.

7. *PAC SP,* pp. 13245 f., 13284. *Statement Respecting the Earl of Selkirk's Settlement upon the Red River, in North America; its Destruction in 1815 and 1816; and the Massacre of Governor Semple and His Party . . .* (London, 1817), p. 2, Appendix A, pp. i ff. Hereafter, *Statement Respecting Settlement.*

Hudson's Bay stock. This was in the summer of 1808. In the first few months of buying he was not alone. Singularly enough, associated with him in his purchases was none other than the famed explorer, and now chief London director of the North West Company, Sir Alexander Mackenzie.[8] But this strange buying partnership did not continue long. As soon as Selkirk's ulterior motive became apparent, that his investments in Hudson's Bay Company stock were more than mere financial speculations, Sir Alexander abruptly broke with him. Mackenzie, it would seem, had undertaken the speculation with a view to making the Hudson's Bay Company a North-westers' concern. William McGillivray, however, another North-wester, stated most emphatically some nine years afterwards that this was not so, that his partner had acted "without any definite object . . . beyond possibly a re-sale at an enhanced price, when a sufficient amount [of stock] should have been procured to enable them to exercise a beneficial influence in the management of the Company's concerns, and thereby to increase the value of their stock." But McGillivray's evidence on matters connected with this fur-trade struggle is not very reliable. He was an interested party and, like most of the successful Canadian fur traders, he would have disapproved of Henry Clay's preference for "being right." At any rate, Mackenzie never succeeded in gaining a controlling voice in the affairs of the older company because, after much wrangling and many threats of legal proceedings, Selkirk secured control of the majority of the shares acquired in joint account, and his opponent ceased purchasing.[9]

The quarrel with Mackenzie did not discourage Selkirk. On the contrary, it stimulated him; and he continued quietly and astutely to increase his holdings of Hudson's Bay Company stock. Owing to the poor prospects for the future value of the shares, owners in many cases were anxious to sell. Selkirk's marriage into the Wedderburn-Colvile family was likewise of much help to him, for not only were the members of that family induced to increase their holdings but influential friends of both families were also persuaded to buy stock. In time the group as a whole constituted about one third of the total shareholding interest.[10]

8. Mackenzie to Selkirk, June 27, 30, 1808; letter neither addressed nor signed, June 29, 1808; Alexander Mundell to Selkirk, June 30, 1808; Mackenzie to Selkirk, October 29, 1808, *PAC SP*. Mackenzie to Selkirk, July 9, 1808; Mackenzie to Colen, July 11, 1808; Colen to Mackenzie, July 14, 1808; Mackenzie to Selkirk, July 15, 1808; Selkirk to Mackenzie, July 16, 29, 1808; Mackenzie to Selkirk, August 8, 1808; Selkirk to Mackenzie, October 13, 1808; Mackenzie to Selkirk, March 18, 1809; Selkirk to Mackenzie, May 16, 1809; Mackenzie to Selkirk, August 19, September 11, 1809; Account of Purchases of Hudson's Bay Company Stock for Selkirk and Mackenzie, March 10, 1810, *SP SM. PAC SP*, pp. 13245, 13284.

9. Selkirk Memorandum, *SP SM*. Selkirk to Mackenzie, March 10, May 31, 1810, *SP SM. Narrative of Occurrences*, pp. 32 f.

10. The total joint stock bought up by Selkirk and his connections is estimated at

Having thus secured an influence in the Hudson's Bay Company's affairs far greater than that of any other individual or group, Selkirk proposed to the directors that settlement be undertaken on certain parts of the charter lands south of Lake Winnipeg, in which he himself would assume only the nominal position of director in the enterprise. But the suggestion, accepted by the Governor and Committee without enthusiasm, proved to be far from welcome to the officials of the Company at Hudson Bay. William Auld, Superintendent at York Factory, "wrote letters to his employers calculated to induce them to abandon" the venture, and "entirely neglected the instructions which had been given him respecting the formation of a colony at Red River." When Selkirk late in 1810 again urged upon the directors his desire to people the Red River Valley, and offered to take the responsibility for the enterprise more directly upon his own shoulders, he was asked for a statement of the terms upon which he would agree to take over from the Company, and hold in his own name, a tract of land for colonization. He was also asked to specify in particular what restrictions he would be willing to have imposed on the settlers and how he would guarantee to protect the Company from any infringements upon its trade and other rights and privileges. "In these circumstances Lord Selkirk was induced to make a proposal which met the views of the Directors, viz. to take upon himself the charge of forming the intended settlement on condition of the Company granting him a sufficient extent of land to afford an indemnification for the expense."[11]

It was on February 6, 1811, that Selkirk's statement was duly submitted to the Governing Committee of the Company. For several succeeding weeks the Governor and Committee discussed the proposals. Much bitter opposition was expressed. Certain members of the Committee felt that grave consequences might arise from a departure from "traditional policy," from a sacrifice of "loyalty to the noble, the ancient founders," and from a violation of the "spirit of reverence for the history of our Company"; but all to no avail. Selkirk's wishes in the end prevailed. Before, however, such an important and unprecedented transaction could be properly effected, it was necessary to secure the approval of a majority of the shareholding interests in General Court assembled. It was Sir Alexander Mackenzie who insisted most strongly upon this procedure being followed. At once Selkirk and the directors

---

between £35,000 and £40,000. The Company's total stock in 1810–11 was held to have been from £103,000 to £105,000. See Letter from the Agents of the North West Company to H. Goulburn, March 18, 1815, *Q133*, p. 241. Simon McGillivray to McTavish, McGillivray & Co., June 1, 1811, *Q153*, Pt. III, p. 616. Memorial of McTavish, Fraser, *Q130*, Pt. II, p. 286. *Narrative of Occurrences*, p. 4.

11. Selkirk Memorandum, *SP SM. PAC SP*, pp. 12641 ff., 13284 ff.

took steps to insure success for their project; and then the meeting of the General Court was announced for May, 1811. The Court assembled and the stockholders were informed that the Governor and Committee deemed it advantageous to grant the Earl of Selkirk 116,000 square miles of territory in Rupert's Land on condition that he establish an agricultural colony and comply with certain specific terms.[12]

At once opposition was aroused, not so much within the Company itself as among the representatives of the North West Company in England. The leading North-wester in Britain at the time was Sir Alexander Mackenzie, a strong figure and the man who, outside North America, was to be Selkirk's principal antagonist in Red River colonizing activities. Born about 1755 at Stornoway in the Hebrides, Mackenzie, after receiving some education, had gone to Canada at a very early age and worked as a clerk for a few years in a Montreal commercial organization connected with the fur trade. "Endowed by Nature with an inquisitive and enterprising spirit," the young Scotchman turned from office work to the fur trade itself, and went into the wilderness as an independent trader. Before long the real greatness of his character thrust him into prominence and power. As an explorer he won fame and a knighthood; and as a leading member of the Canadian fur-trade oligarchy he became the strongest rival, and finally one of the chief partners of the North West Company. At a comparatively early age he retired from active participation in the fur business and went to live in England. But he still continued there to be a powerful and zealous guardian of the interests of the North West Company.

When the Governor and Committee of the Hudson's Bay Company announced to the General Court assembled in May, 1811, that they concurred in the plan for colonizing the Red River Valley, the North-westers in London became alarmed. It cannot be said that they were surprised, because Mackenzie had known of the design several months earlier, and as soon as he had become estranged from Selkirk had told all he knew to his fur-trade partners. "He will put the North-West Company to a greater expense," he wrote to one of them, "than you seem to apprehend, and, had the Company sacrificed £20,000, which might have secured a preponderance in the stock of the Hudson's Bay Company, it would have been money well spent." Events were to show that Mackenzie's mind had lost none of its perspicacity at this time; but his warning was not heeded, and the North-westers desisted completely

12. Selkirk Memorandum, *SP SM. PAC SP,* pp. 1920 f., 12644 ff., 13285 ff. *Q133,* pp. 59 ff. Letter from the Agents of the North West Company to H. Goulburn, March 18, 1815, *Q133,* pp. 241 f. Extract of a letter from Simon McGillivray to William McGillivray, May 25, 1811, *Q153,* Pt. III, pp. 621 f. *Statement Respecting Settlement,* p. 7. *Narrative of Occurrences,* pp. 4 f.

from any further purchases of Hudson's Bay Company stock.[13] When in 1811 they realized the gravity of the situation, it was too late for them to repair the blunder.

The London agents of the North West Company were of the opinion that Selkirk's project was simply a part of the Hudson's Bay Company's campaign of opposition to the Canadian fur traders. It was well known that colonization, as far as it progressed, would injure the trade. But that was not the chief danger to be feared by the Canadians. Insofar as they regarded the move as a phase of the fur-trade war, they could scarcely have considered it likely that the Hudson's Bay Company would promote extensive settlement of the Northwest, because such a course would be as fatal to one group of fur traders as to the other. What they really feared most was something different from colonization as such. The Red River Valley was a vital link in their line of communications between the Great Lakes and the whole Northwest; it was also a vital source of the special food staple of the fur brigades. This was pemmican, or the preserved and concentrated meat of the buffalo. Settlement under the auspices of the Hudson's Bay Company might easily destroy both these values. Of course the North-westers feared settlers too. They realized that if settlement was once begun in the Northwest it might easily spread far beyond the Red River Valley. Up to that time the fur traders from Canada had carefully suppressed all favorable reports of the agricultural possibilities of the regions west of the Great Lakes; and hitherto they had been opposed in that territory only by other traders. Now at last the dreaded settlement seemed to be threatening them; and Mackenzie and the other leading North-westers in Britain, especially John Inglis and Edward Ellice, decided that the snake must be scotched at all costs. At first they were content to ridicule the scheme, hoping that it would fall of its own weight; but when the enemy secured a preponderating influence in the English company, and that company expressed approval of "the great design," their anxiety became deeper, and they resorted to contemptuous and abusive criticism.[14]

Immediately upon the announcement of the colonization project to the General Court that body was adjourned in order that the partners

13. Louis-François-Rodrigue Masson, *Les Bourgeois de la compagnie du Nord-Ouest; Reminiscences of Roderic McKenzie* (Quebec, 1889), I, 52 f. Letter from the Agents of the North West Company to H. Goulburn, March 18, 1815, *Q133*, pp. 241 f.

14. Simon McGillivray to McTavish, McGillivray & Co., June 1, 1811, *Q153*, Pt. III, pp. 611 ff. William McGillivray to Major Loring, November 28, 1815, *Q133*, pp. 227 ff. Letter from the Agents of the North West Company to H. Goulburn, March 18, 1815, *Q133*, pp. 241 ff. Selkirk to the Governor, Deputy Governor and Committee of the Hudson's Bay Company, February 14, 1815, *PAC SP*, p. 1918. Selkirk Memorandum, *SP SM*.

might have time to secure fuller information and study the proposed measure in detail. All stockholders were given the opportunity to inspect the terms of the proposed grant at the office of the Secretary of the Company.[15] This adjournment gave Sir Alexander Mackenzie and the other North-westers in London a much desired chance to organize a formidable opposition. They began by making a vigorous attempt to prejudice the British public. Newspapers were persuaded to describe the Red River country as a Cimmerian desert of primeval solitudes quite unsuited for the habitation of man and intended by nature to be permanently nothing but a breeding ground for wild animals. One of Selkirk's acquaintances exclaimed to him: "By God, sir, if you are bent on doing something futile, why do you not sow tares at home in order to reap wheat, or plough the desert of Sahara, which is so much nearer?"[16]

On May 30 the General Court reassembled. Just two days before the Court opened three North-westers, Edward Ellice, John Inglis, and Simon McGillivray, suddenly purchased some Hudson's Bay Company stock. This purchase was not made with a view to influencing the Court's decision; shareholders were not entitled to a vote until they had held stock for six months or more. But it gave them the right to attend Court meetings, enter into debates, and secure firsthand information in regard to all proceedings.[17]

Probably never in the previous history of the Hudson's Bay Company had there been a session of the Court as exciting as that which now began. The three North-westers present, Sir Alexander Mackenzie, Edward Ellice, and John Inglis, stormed and argued. A number of the older "subscribers" joined them when the Secretary again presented the Selkirk request. The demand was clear. Selkirk wanted a grant in fee simple of a fertile tract in Rupert's Land, preferably on the Red River, for purposes of colonization. Assurances were given that it would be settled in a limited time, that the whole expense of establishment, of government, and of the satisfying of Indian claims to the soil, would be met by the proprietor. In return for the grant of land the Hudson's Bay Company would be paid "ten shillings of lawful money of Great

15. *PAC SP*, pp. 12, 645 ff. Extract of a letter from Simon McGillivray to William McGillivray, May 25, 1811, *Q153*, Pt. III, p. 622.

16. Beckles Willson, *The Great Company (1667–1871)*, *Being a History of the Honourable Company of Merchants-Adventurers Trading into Hudson's Bay* (London, 1900), II, 143.

17. Minute by Miles Macdonell, Golden Square, May 24, 1811, Colonial Office Records, *Q133*, pp. 66 f. Hereafter, Minute by Miles Macdonell, *Q133*. Simon McGillivray to McTavish, McGillivray & Co., June 1, 1811, *Q153*, Pt. III, pp. 611 ff. Simon McGillivray to the Wintering Partners of the North West Company, April 9, 1812, *Q150*, Pt. I, p. 180. *Statement Respecting Settlement*, pp. 7 ff.

Britain," supplied with two hundred servants a year for a period of ten years (their wages to be paid by the Company), and given in addition a guarantee that the proposed colony would not encroach upon the fur-trade monopoly.[18]

This second announcement of the Selkirk undertaking drew from the opposition a "Protest" in the form of a lengthy document[19] attacking the whole settlement scheme from a variety of angles. Much of it was a very plausible defense of the interests of the Hudson's Bay Company as a fur-trading concern. It was, indeed, true that there was no "adequate consideration stipulated for between the said Company and the said Earl." Certainly ten shillings, and the promise of supplying servants *which the Company was to support*, was an insignificant price to pay for "a territory of about seventy thousand superficial miles, containing about forty-five millions of acres, of that part of the territory which is most valuable [and] fit for cultivation." Surely, too, it was only fair to the Company's subscribers "to expose" the land "to public sale, or at least give such notoriety to the transaction, as to admit of competition between individuals who may be inclined to purchase." There was reason and soundness, also, in some other particulars of the "Protest." Precedent went strongly to prove that

evils . . . had formerly arisen from the possession of a tract of land by one person, who could seldom, even in the vicinity of a populous country, procure a sufficient number of settlers to satisfy the Creditors of the original Grant. . . . How much more insurmountable must be the difficulty of peopling a region two thousand miles from any seaport, and out of the reach of all those aids and comforts which are derived from Civil Society.

Time was to prove the validity of another objection, namely, that "private traffic would be carried on between the settlers and the Indians, and clandestinely with traders from the United States and Canada"; and time was to vindicate completely the contention that colonization was at all times unfavorable to the fur trade. Finally, it was also to prove true that the Company had not "full power to exercise a final jurisdiction."

In the case of other points, however, the "Protest" was unfair. An unbiased judgment might well have ascribed for the grant some other

18. Grant of Assiniboia to Lord Selkirk by the Hudson's Bay Company, June 12, 1811, *SP SM*.

19. Protest of Stockholders and Proprietors of the Hudson's Bay Company against the Grant to Lord Selkirk, May 30, 1811, *Q134*, Pt. II, pp. 333 ff. The Protest is signed by William Thwaits, Robert Whitehead, and John Fish, stockholders of long standing in the Company; also by Edward Ellice, John Inglis, and Alexander Mackenzie, principals in the North West Company.

motive than to secure to Selkirk's posterity, at the expense of the stock-holders of the Company, an immensely valuable landed estate. One has only to consider Selkirk's earlier colonizing activities in Prince Edward Island and at Baldoon to realize that this charge was manifestly false. Nor was it reasonable to suppose at that time that for at least many years to come the settlers would be more tempted to look for commercial intercourse to the then-distant American settlements in the Mississippi West than to the ports on Hudson Bay. Prophetic, however, was the fear expressed that an insufficient "regard is had to the difficulties in the way of carrying it [the project] into effect, or to the sacrifices which the Company may be called upon to make." No truer prophets of the future of the contemplated colony could have been found, indeed, than the men who signed the Protest. Three out of the six were principals in the North West Company. Were they thinking, when they signed, of the "difficulties" and "sacrifices" with which they would try to burden the chief promoter of the emigration scheme if, as they feared, he should succeed in securing his grant? It is very probable, so prompt were they to prove in having recourse to questionable ways and means of impeding his project. At any rate, their Protest seems at least slightly ridiculous in view of their affiliations outside the Hudson's Bay Company.

At the very time when they and their colleagues in British North America were engaged in a deliberate and unscrupulous struggle to beat the English company from its ancient-charter fur preserves, they were righteously protesting against possible injury being done to that company by a grant of lands to the Earl of Selkirk. As subscribers, of course, they had the right to protest. But they seem to have forgotten the words of their proud motto, "Fortitude in Distress." For, having invested in the stock of a company in which a majority of the subscribers ruled, they failed to accept calmly the decision of such a majority; and they gave vent to bursts of rage and chagrin when they realized that they were being beaten in a game which they had entered with motives at least as selfish as those of their opponents and with an equal knowledge of the rules. But of course the truth is that the North-westers, for the most part, were men who owed their success not so much to the possession of what are usually known as virtues, as, rather, to the lack of them. They lived at a time and in places where for a variety of reasons the reign of law had largely given place to the rule of force and cunning. Their ethics were not very different from those of the jungle, and the jungle knows neither restraint in moments of victory nor courage and resignation in defeat. The North-westers respected no verdict but that of success; when they failed, they naturally acted like children and barbarians. This is not to imply, of course, that all the virtue was on one side. No doubt some of the associates of the chartered company foresaw the possibility of using a settlement on the Red River as a weapon against even the legitimate trade of the Canadian concern. But they were not prepared, as were their opponents, to resort to murder as an instrument of trade. The moral difference between the two groups was infinite.

As was inevitable, the Protest proved ineffectual. The total amount of stock represented at the meeting was £44,850. Of this amount, £29,-937 was in the hands of Selkirk and his friends. William Thwaits and Robert Whitehead, who were in opposition, owned about £13,000, while Alexander Mackenzie, John Inglis, and Edward Ellice—the two latter being unable to vote—together held only some £2,500. When a show of hands was called for, two thirds of those who could vote were in favor of the proposal.[20] The proceeding was momentous. Selkirk secured, for the nominal sum of ten shillings, 116,000 square miles—a district about five times the size of Scotland, or only 5,115 square miles less than the entire area of the United Kingdom of Great Britain and Ireland, and most of it was land as fine and fertile as any in the world. A deed was drawn up and completed on June 12, 1811, making Selkirk owner of the grant in fee simple. The boundaries of the "District of Assiniboia," as it was called, were defined in the deed as follows:

Beginning on the western shore of Lake Winnipic otherwise Winnipeg at a point in fifty two degrees and thirty Minutes north latitude and thence running due West to the Lake Winipigoos otherwise called Little Winnipeg then in a Southerly direction through the said Lake so as to strike its western shore in latitude fifty two Degrees then due west to the place where the parallel of fifty two degrees North Latitude intersects the western branch of Red River otherwise called Assiniboyne River then due South from that point of intersection to the height of land which separates the waters running into Hudson's Bay from those of the Missouri and Mississippi then in an Easterly direction along the said height of land to the source of the River Winipic or Winnipeg (meaning by such last mentioned River the principal branch of the waters which unite in Lake Saginagas) thence along the main stream of these waters and the middle of the several Lakes through which they flow to the mouth of the Winipic River and thence in a Northerly direction through the middle of Lake Winipic to the place of beginning.

More generally speaking, the District extended from Big Island in Lake Winnipeg south to the height of land separating the Red River Valley from the Mississippi drainage basin, and from almost the source of the Assiniboine River on the west to the Lake of the Woods on the

20. *PAC SP,* p. 12646. *Narrative of Occurrences,* p. 5.

east. An examination of a present-day map of the country will show that Assiniboia included parts of what are now the province of Manitoba and the states of Minnesota and North Dakota.

In securing all this land in fee simple and practically gratis, Selkirk had made a long stride toward the fulfillment of his Red River project. Just what his motives were at the time was a question which evoked many and conflicting comments from his contemporaries. Some, among whom were certain North-westers, even declared that his mind was unbalanced. Others inferred that he was seeking wealth through a speculation in real estate. William McGillivray attributed to him "an unquenchable thirst for land, and the speculations to which it gives rise." The majority of the North-westers were of the firm opinion that his one and only object was to introduce into the Red River country "a sufficient number of persons to carry into effect . . . plans of aggression and competition against the North West Company"; in other words, "the Noble Lord's plot . . . marked with more than the precaution of the American land-jobber," was to strike a blow at "the root of the North West Company, which it was intended to ruin."[21]

On the other hand, the actual evidence available as well as Selkirk's expressed purposes go to show almost beyond question that his motives were largely philanthropic: that he hoped to gain for himself only remuneration for his outlay and his due share of honor and fame as a national benefactor and empire builder. The principles "upon which I have acted," he wrote in 1816, "were based upon the importance of the Settlement on Red River in a national point of view,"[22] and were concerned with "the important question whether extensive and fertile regions in British North America are ever to be inhabited by civilized society."[23] So determined was he "upon proving that it [the Red River Settlement] was neither a wild and visionary scheme, nor a trick and a cloak to cover sordid plans of aggression,"[24] that he consistently rejected the idea of a coalition of the Hudson's Bay and North West

21. Simon McGillivray to McTavish, McGillivray & Co., June 1, 1811, *Q153*, Pt. III, pp. 617 f. Extract of a letter from Simon McGillivray to William McGillivray, May 25, 1811, *Q153*, Pt. III, p. 623. William McGillivray to Major Loring, November 28, 1815, *Q133*, pp. 227 f. McTavish, Fraser & Co., Inglis, Ellice & Co. to H. Goulburn, March 18, 1815, *Q133*, pp. 236, 238. Minute by Miles Macdonell, *Q133*, pp. 66 f. Selkirk to the Governor, Deputy Governor and Committee of the Hudson's Bay Company, February 14, 1815, *PAC SP,* p. 1918. Macdonell to Auld, December 25, 1811, Miles Macdonell, Selkirk Settlement, p. 283, *PAC*. John Strachan, *A Letter to the Right Honourable the Earl of Selkirk, on His Settlement at the Red River, Near Hudson's Bay* (London, 1816), p. 10. Hereafter, Strachan, *Letter. Narrative of Occurrences,* pp. 9 f.

22. Selkirk to McDouall, March 30, 1816, *PAC SP,* p. 2126.
23. *Statement Respecting Settlement,* p. vii.
24. Selkirk to Colvile, December 11, 1819, *SP SM.*

companies. There is no good reason for disbelieving either that Selkirk was convinced that the great colonization movement in the United States could be duplicated in British North America or that he was anxious to add luster to the Douglas name by associating with it great plans of imperial settlement.

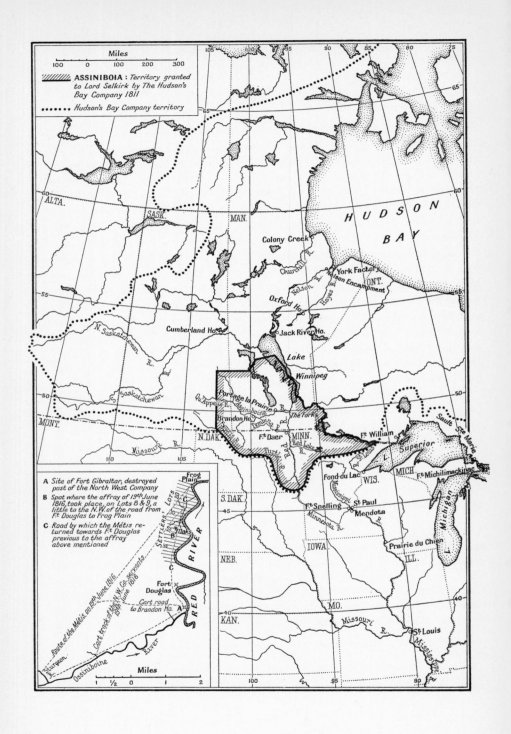

CHAPTER V

"A HERCULEAN LABOUR"

THOUGH it was on June 12, 1811, that Assiniboia was officially deeded
to Lord Selkirk, tentative plans for its settlement had been worked out
carefully several months earlier, and in many respects they were already well on the way to realization. The colonists were to be sent to
the Red River by the northern route. They would travel to the shores
of Hudson Bay in the Company's ships; land at York Factory on the
narrow strip of territory lying between the mouths of the Nelson and
Hayes rivers; and thence make their difficult way by river, lake, and
portage to the Forks of the Assiniboine and the Red. Selkirk had foreseen that the season would be well advanced before he secured Assiniboia, and that if settlers were to go out with the fur fleet in 1811, they
would have to be recruited with dispatch. Unless all were in readiness by
midsummer, when the Company's ships left for America, the expedition
would have to be postponed until the following year. This Selkirk was
anxious to avoid; and hence for several months prior to his actual purchase of Assiniboia he was engrossed in the work of securing the first
band of emigrants.

As a preliminary step he had prepared an "Advertisement and Prospectus"[1] in which he outlined the inducements offered by Assiniboia to
prospective investors and settlers, a document "well calculated to
quicken the spirits of emigration which so universally prevailed in Ireland and in the Highlands of Scotland."[2] The importance of this document, which has been misrepresented and misused by both propagan-
dists and historians, may be estimated by a consideration of it in detail. It reads as follows:

A Tract of Land, consisting of some millions of acres, and in point of soil
and climate inferior to none of equal extent in British America, is now to be
disposed of, and will be sold extremely cheap, on account of its situation,
which is remote from the present establishments. If a tract of the same extent and fertility were offered for sale in Lower Canada or Nova Scotia, pur-
chasers would be eager to obtain it at one hundred, or perhaps two hundred
thousand guineas, and at that price would make an ample fortune in the

1. Lord Selkirk's Advertisement and Prospectus of the New Colony, Q134, Pt. II,
pp. 338 ff.
2. Donald Gunn and Charles R. Tuttle, *History of Manitoba from the Earliest Settlement to 1835 and from 1835 to the Admission of the Province into the Dominion*
(Ottawa, 1880), p. 68. Hereafter, Gunn and Tuttle, *Manitoba*.

course of some years, by retailing it in small lots at an advanced price to actual settlers. The lands in question, no ways different in advantages, may be purchased for about £10,000 Stg. The title has been submitted to Lawyers of the first eminence in London, and is declared to be unexceptionable; but the situation is such that the population of the older Settlements cannot be expected, in the natural course of things, to be spread into it for a long period of time, and till that takes place, the disadvantage of its remote situation must be an insuperable objection in the eyes of any unconnected individual who is looking out for Lands to establish his family. Hence the prospect of finding Settlers to purchase the Land in small Lots is remote, and on this account the Proprietors are willing to part with it for so inconsiderable a price. But the obstacles which, to an unconnected Adventurer, may be justly deemed insurmountable, may be overcome with ease by the combined efforts of many; and an adequate sum of money judiciously expended in removing the first difficulties of an infant settlement, may place this Tract of Land in circumstances as advantageous to the Proprietors as if it were in the immediate vicinity of populous Colonies. The expences, however, would be too great for an Individual: it is therefore proposed to form a Joint Stock Company, in 200 shares of £100 each, so as to raise a sum of £20,000 of which a moiety to be employed in the purchase of the Land in question; the remainder, in those expences which are necessary for bringing Settlers, and thereby rendering the Land valuable. To those Settlers, Lands will be disposed of, either in the way of Sale, or Lease in perpetuity, at the option of the Settler, on terms very encouraging to him, and abundantly advantageous to the Proprietors.

As there are serious objections against receiving into the proposed Settlements any Americans of the description of those who are likely to offer themselves, the Settlers must be emigrants from Europe; and the most feasible plan seems to be, that they should be selected from those parts of the United Kingdom which are most overburdened with Inhabitants, vizt.: the Highlands of Scotland, and some parts of Ireland; a small proportion of the Emigrants who now go from these Districts to the United States of America, would be more than sufficient for the object in view. Such a change of their destination would injure no part of the Kingdom, and would save to the Empire, subjects who would otherwise be entirely lost to their country. To facilitate an object thus equally advantageous to the Public, and to the Parties concerned, it is proposed that a preference should be allowed to Subscribers who are personally connected with these Districts of the Kingdom, and whose local influence may be of service in promoting the desired change in the destination of those who are determined to emigrate. The Settlement is to be formed in a Territory where religion is not the ground of any disqualification, an unreserved participation in every privilege will therefore be enjoyed by Protestant and Catholic without distinction; and it is proposed that in every parochial division an allotment of Land shall be made for the perpetual support of a clergyman of that persuasion which the majority of the Inhabitants adhere to.

As the Lands in question possess important natural advantages over any which now remain unoccupied in Nova Scotia, and the adjacent Colonies, it cannot be deemed unreasonable if the Settlers in general are charged for their Lands at the lowest rate which they would pay in these Provinces. On the other hand, they will naturally expect to be conveyed to their land without incurring more expence than if they were to settle in these Maritime Colonies. The Managers of the Concern must therefore undertake to provide conveyance at moderate rates, for the Emigrants who go out under their Patronage. The rate of passage money paid on board of other ships bound to America may be taken as the criterion. These rates being always proportioned to the prices of freight and shipping at the time, no material loss can be apprehended upon the Sea Voyage. But as the place of Settlement is at a considerable distance from the sea, an extra expence must be incurred for the inland conveyance, which the Emigrants cannot be expected to pay, if they are to be charged for Land at the rate of the Maritime Colonies; the expence which may thus fall upon the Proprietors, may be estimated at about £10 for every family of Settlers at an average. This, however, will be amply reimbursed in the price of land. The lowest price of land in the Maritime Colonies, when sold to actual Settlers, and possessing any tolerable advantages of Situation, is at the rate of 10s. per acre, if sold; or if leased for a perpetuity, 1s. per annum. Every Family of Settlers may be expected to take up at least 100 acres. They are allowed some accommodation of time for the payment, and 100 acres at the above rate, will amount to £50, leaving a nett advantage of £40, after reimbursing the charge of bringing in the Settler. If he should prefer leasing, his rent will in two years repay the charges, and will remain afterwards as a clear income to the Proprietor. As the inland situation of the Settlement will preclude the Settler from some of the sources of profit which are enjoyed in maritime situations, it becomes necessary to provide substitutes. The cultivation of Hemp is peculiarly calculated for Inland Situations, as that Article is so valuable in proportion to its weight, that it can bear the expence of a considerable inland Navigation. This cultivation is also a favourite national object, and the Settlement will derive benefit from the public encouragement which is held out for promoting it. A still more beneficial object of attention is the growth of fine wool, an article so valuable, that it would bear any expence of Inland conveyance, and one for which the country is peculiarly adapted. In the vicinity of the proposed Settlement, there are immense open plains without wood, fine dry grass Land, much of it capable of immediate cultivation, and all well fitted for pasturage, particularly sheep. This is an advantage that no other part of British America possesses by nature, and to which the Colonists of the Maritime Provinces cannot attain without the laborious and expensive operation of clearing. If to this advantage the Proprietors add that of a good breed of Spanish Merino Sheep, the Settlers can never meet with any difficulty in paying the price or rent of their land. The fleeces of ten or twelve sheep will pay the Rent of 100 Acres, and with the produce of a very small flock the price of a Lot of Land may be paid off in three or four years. With such advantages, the Settlers must thrive rapidly; and it will soon become apparent to them, that the Land is worth a much higher price. At first, however, it cannot be supposed that the common Emigrants will understand, or become capable of appreciating these advantages. On the contrary, it is to be expected that they will be diffident and afraid of venturing to a new and (to them) an unknown country; it will therefore be necessary to give some extraordinary encouragement to a few of the first who enter into the plan. From this, and other causes, the commencement of the undertaking must be subject to expences, which will not continue permanently when the Settlement is well established; but, it is only by means of this first outlay, that we can expect to attain the ultimate advantages which are to accrue to the Proprietors. There is no room to believe, that these expences will exceed the sum which is proposed to be raised; but it must be sometime before the Settlers can be numerous enough to pay much either of rent or purchase money. Ten or twelve years must therefore elapse before the profits of the undertaking can be sufficient to afford a dividend to the Proprietors. After that period, the returns may be expected to increase rapidly, and will soon form an ample indemnification to the Subscribers, for the loss of interest on the money in the meantime. The amount to which the profits may ultimately arise, seems almost to baffle imagination upon any principle of calculation which can reasonably be adopted; the result comes out so extraordinarily great, that it might appear like exaggeration to state it.

But the difference between buying land at 1d. or 2d. per acre, and selling at 8s. or 10s. is very palpable, and does not seem to require much comment. The speculation may not suit those who require an immediate income; but for any one who is desirous to provide before hand for a young Family, such an opportunity seldom occurs.

This "Advertisement and Prospectus," valuable though it is as a storehouse of Selkirk's first definite plans for the colonization of the Red River Valley, and enticing though its terms to investors and settlers may have been, nevertheless not only failed in its main object of attracting capital but offered the colonizer's enemies an opportunity for attack. Due to the troubled political skies over Europe at the time, investors were loath to embark in far-off and uncertain ventures. Consequently the attempt to build up a joint stock company all but failed. Only relatives and a few personal friends of Selkirk subscribed to the stock.[3] Thus the enterprise, lacking the large financial support the promoter had hoped for, had to be narrowed to a scope proportionate to its backing. The Prospectus itself "was neither advertised, nor published, nor, in any shape, publicly circulated"; only a few copies were printed and privately distributed "among a very limited number of . . . friends."[4] But the opponents of Red River colonization secured copies,

3. *PAC SP,* pp. 65, 119.   4. *Statement Respecting Settlement,* p. 118.

analyzed to the last element the plans formulated in the document, and found artful deceit and prospects of future calamity lurking in almost every detail. These baleful criticisms were disseminated most ingeniously in those parts of the British Isles where it was hoped that they would do the most injury to the scheme of colonization. Nor, though they came in some instances from gentlemen of very upright and religious pretensions, men who had a high reputation for honor and integrity, were they lacking in guesswork, exaggeration, deception, and meanness. The Advertisement and Prospectus was described as "a paper neatly drawn up, but, alas! destitute of truth."[5] Dr. John Strachan (later, Bishop Strachan), Rector of York in Upper Canada, a Scotchman who had done well in the New World, took it upon himself to address a letter to Selkirk on the error of his ways.[6] "It is, indeed," he declared, "impossible to behold with complacency a British Peer turning a land speculator, at a moment when his country was in imminent danger, and, instead of flying to her assistance, and disdaining to survive her fall, anticipating that melancholy event, by anxiously preparing an asylum in a distant corner of the earth."[7]

Such was the construction commonly placed upon Selkirk's intentions when he was endeavoring to relieve and at the same time preserve for the Empire the miserable rabbles which had been created in the north of Ireland and in the Highlands of Scotland largely by the political, social, and economic mistakes and the injustice of the leaders in the very country he was accused of betraying. His earlier colonizing ventures, which have briefly been described above, were declared to have been "singularly unsuccessful . . . though marked with more than the precaution of an American land-jobber."[8] As for those former ventures, Dr. Strachan went on,

you might have been deceived and really supposed that the conditions offered on both occasions were extremely liberal; but, after the experience which they must have given you, and your visit to America, it will not be so easy to excuse you for offering worse conditions to emigrants, going to an infinitely worse situation, where they can only meet with disappointment and misery. Your projected settlement at the Red River, or third attempt at colonization, appears to me, not only more extravagant than either of the former, but one of the most gross impositions that ever was attempted on the British public, and must be attended with the most baneful consequences to all those unfortunate men, who, deluded by the false promises held out to them, shall leave their homes for such a dreary wilderness.[9]

5. Strachan, *Letter,* p. 3.   6. *Ibid.*
7. *Ibid.,* p. 9.   8. *Ibid.,* p. 10.
9. *Ibid.,* pp. 10 f.

The North-westers in Great Britain and the Canadas, having gone through the Prospectus critically, summed up their findings.[10] "We have shewn," they declared,

That . . . Selkirk's title to Assiniboia is insecure;

That the settlement can receive neither protection nor assistance from the British colonies;

That the communications by Canada and Hudson's Bay are impracticable for the purposes of commerce;

That there is no market for grain or provisions of any sort;

That only one article, viz. wool, can be pointed out capable of paying transport;

That this article may not succeed, on account of the wolves, the soil, and climate;

That the difficulty of communication will prevent the colonists from receiving any supplies, unless at an enormous expence;

That the price of the land to settlers is a shameful imposition, and supported by statements that are false;

That the foundation for serious contention is laid, in not having satisfied the claims of the natives before the settlement was attempted;

That there is the strongest probability that the first colonists will be massacred by the Indians;

That all the promises urged in the Prospectus to leave Great Britain are false or delusive;

That the colony, if it succeed, must, of necessity, from its frontier, become dependent on the United States, and, at length, an American colony;

That to encourage emigration to Red River, is to sacrifice the superfluous population of Great Britain and to injure her American colonies.

It can be seen that the authors of this criticism were anything but restrained in stating their case against Selkirk. Every point they made was set down absolutely, disregarding the qualifications which in many instances would promptly occur to an informed reader. Time has amply refuted them on several points. But this manifesto was designed for a British public which was almost completely ignorant of central North America and which had no great reason to suspect that the fur traders had a vital interest in keeping secret the character of the Red River Valley. The North-westers felt that they were facing war and possible destruction if settlement succeeded at the nodal point of their far-flung,

10. Selkirk to the Governor, Deputy Governor and Committee of the Hudson's Bay Company, February 14, 1815, *PAC SP,* pp. 1914 f. William McGillivray to Sir F. P. Robinson, August 15, 1815, *PAC SP,* pp. 1620 f. Letter from the Agents of the North West Company to H. Goulburn, March 18, 1815, *Q133,* pp. 242 f. William McGillivray to Major Loring, November 28, 1815, *Q133,* pp. 227 ff. "Highlander" in the Inverness *Journal,* June 21, September 12, 1811, *PAC SP,* pp. 133–148. Simon McGillivray to Bathurst, June 19, 1815, *Q134,* Pt. II, pp. 377 f. Strachan, *Letter,* pp. 50 f.

precarious, fur empire, and they were prepared to wage war in reply, beginning with an appeal to an ignorant public opinion and proceeding to violence if preservation of their concern should seem to demand it. The debatable land at the crossroads of the continent was so remote from governmental authority that it had always made its own law and order in terms of the survival of the fittest. The Montrealers had inherited from the French a stringent, exacting, economic contest with the Hudson's Bay Company in which their investment of capital, men, and skills was very large and their margin of success very narrow. They believed that they must assuredly fail if control of the Manitoba Basin passed to their rivals from the Bay, and they did not mean to fail. In spite of the presence among the North-westers of men of probity like Mackenzie and McGill, the majority at headquarters and in the field were prepared, if they judged it necessary, to go to almost any lengths to defend their intricate creation and their livelihood.

To the philanthropist or the benevolent sympathizer, however, who aims at helping suffering humanity, it is often not the machinations of enemies, or the trouble, the self-sacrifice, and the expenditure of money that is the chief obstacle, but rather it is the bitterness, the distrust, the narrow-mindedness, and the general unworkableness of the poverty-stricken themselves. "Poverty in its worst form is a gaunt and ravenous beast, that bites the hand of friend or foe that is stretched out toward it." So Selkirk found it, when he undertook to help the unfortunate people of northern and western Ireland and the Scottish Highlands. "He had the sympathising heart; he had the true vision; and he had as few others of his time had, the power to plan, the invention to suggest, and the skill and pluck to overcome difficulties, but the carrying out of his intent brought him infinite trouble and sorrow."[11] His prospectus was an entirely worthy document, offering to the poor what the author believed to be a home of ultimate plenty on the fertile banks of the Red River. But the cotters were timid, and they loved even their miserable hovels. Assiniboia looked terribly far away. If they were to be persuaded to go, much encouragement would be needed. The sympathetic Earl understood all this very well; he knew, too, that his enemies in Britain would use every artifice to defeat his project at its beginning. To meet both difficulties, he selected three recruiting agents who, he believed, were well fitted by both character and training for the task of securing emigrants for Red River in spite of opposition.

The man he picked for recruiting in Ireland, a man who was to play a leading part in the first years of the Red River venture, was Captain

11. George Bryce, *The Romantic Settlement of Lord Selkirk's Colonists* (Toronto, 1909), pp. 45 f. Hereafter, Bryce, *Romantic Settlement*.

Miles Macdonell, a Glengarry Highlander from Upper Canada. Miles Macdonell was born in Inverness, Scotland, but a few years later, in 1773, his family had emigrated to New York and settled in the Mohawk Valley under the protection of Sir William Johnson. When the Revolutionary War broke out the Macdonells stood with the British Government. Miles's father—known as "Spanish John"—raised a company of one hundred men among the Loyalists in the vicinity of Johnstown, led them across the rebel lines and down to Montreal. Soon afterwards he settled in Quebec not very far from the frontier. John and Miles, the two eldest sons, although not much more than boys at the time, served in the King's Royal Regiment of New York, more familiarly known as the Royal Greens, as captain and ensign, respectively. With the close of the war both went to Canada as Loyalists and settled, like most of the King's Royal Regiment, in Glengarry County in the Ottawa Valley. When Selkirk visited the Canadas in 1804, he met Miles, then a captain in the Canadian militia, living on a small and backward farm near Osnabruck. Apparently, too, Miles found mere farming hardly sufficient to support his family as he wished. Perhaps this was because he was by instinct and training far more suited to the adventurous life of a soldier than to the regularity of farming.[12]

Selkirk must have been strongly attracted by Captain Macdonell, because soon after first meeting him he spent several days as a guest on the farm at Osnabruck; and in the years that followed he continued to correspond with him. Probably another reason for this rather unusual intimacy was the fact that Miles's brother John had, since 1797, been a wintering partner in the North West Company, and Selkirk was beginning to be strongly interested in the Northwest.[13] Many of John's letters to Miles are full of details about the prairie country. In one instance the *bourgeois* writes:

From the Forks of the Assiniboine and Red Rivers the plains are quite near the banks, and so extensive that a man may travel to the Rocky Mountains without passing a wood, a mile long. The soil on the Red River and the Assiniboine is generally a good soil, susceptible of culture, and capable of bearing rich crops. . . . The buffalo comes to the forks of Assiniboine, besides in these rivers are plenty of sturgeon, catfish, goldeyes, pike and whitefish—the latter so common that men have been seen to catch thirty or forty apiece while they smoked their pipes.[14]

12. Selkirk Diary, III, 89 f., IX, 50, 53, 55, *SP SM*. A. G. Morice, "A Canadian Pioneer: Spanish John," *CHR*, X, 222 ff.
13. Selkirk Journal (a manuscript volume of 59 pages of heterogeneous materials), p. 38, *SP SM*. Hereafter, Selkirk Journal, *SP SM*.
14. John Macdonell Journal, Masson Collection, McGill University Library.

Perhaps it was descriptions such as these that connected Selkirk's interest in Miles Macdonell with his interest in the Red River country. However that may be, when Selkirk came to seek a leader for his western venture, he offered the position to his former host. Doubtless John Macdonell's letters had aroused in his soldierly brother a desire to see for himself the half-unknown wilderness beyond the Great Lakes. Doubtless, too, he was heartily sick of the humdrum life of a backwoods farm. Probably the superintendency of the Red River Colony and the governorship of Assiniboia promised to fulfill his fondest hopes. When he was offered them—the one by Selkirk, the other by the Hudson's Bay Company—he accepted both with alacrity. In the winter of 1810–11 he went to England, and shortly after his arrival was sent to the western parts of Ireland to advertise the settlement scheme, secure subscriptions of stock, and recruit laborers and settlers. At this time emigration from Ireland was in rapid progress, and Selkirk hoped that Miles, being a Roman Catholic, might the more easily persuade some of the Catholic Irish to go to Assiniboia instead of to the United States.[15]

Next to Miles Macdonell, the most promising of the men picked by Selkirk as emigration agents was Colin Robertson, a native of the island of Lewis in the Hebrides. Robertson had spent six years in the Indian country in the employ of the North West Company. He had served his employers with fidelity and zeal, and had been put in charge of a fur post on the Saskatchewan. But he was not happy in the service of the North-westers. Since the various Canadian fur factions had united to enforce monopoly, the prospects of promotion for the lower ranks had shrunken considerably. It seemed that the only way to find favor with superiors now was to be conspicuous in mistreating Indians and Hudson's Bay traders. Such conduct was very distasteful to the high-minded Robertson. His predicament made his thoughts turn to service with the Hudson's Bay Company; and his great powers of observation had convinced him that the "Achilles' heel" of the North West Company lay in the potential secession of the wintering partners.

That judgment, made by such a man, was as portentous as the course he now adopted. Having approached an official of the Hudson's Bay Company on the subject of a change of allegiance and having received an encouraging reply, Robertson soon found himself a free man. Probably a violent quarrel with another North-wester had something to do

15. Selkirk to Miles Macdonell, December 6, 1809, February 10, 1810; Miles Macdonell to Douglas, May 31, 1811; Selkirk to Miles Macdonell, June 13, 1811; Miles Macdonell to Selkirk, July 4, 1811, Miles Macdonell, Selkirk Settlement, pp. 84, 88, 131, 135, 253 f., *PAC*. Miles Macdonell to Auld, December 25, 1811, *PAC SP*, pp. 101 f. Morice, "Sidelights on the Careers of Miles Macdonell and his Brothers," *CHR*, X, 313. Miles Macdonell to Colvile, February 1, 1820, *SP SM*.

with the change; and there is some evidence to show that he was actually dismissed. The fact that he went away with very bitter feelings toward his former associates might indicate that he was discharged. More likely the move was in accordance with his desires. What is certain is that he had contemplated leaving for some time and that he received a glowing testimonial and an expression of good wishes from his late employers. But he was a man quick of temper and uncompromising; and when he reached Britain late in 1809 his mind was busy elaborating plans by which the Hudson's Bay Company might defeat and destroy their formidable Canadian rivals. Robertson succeeded, early in 1810, in bringing his views to the attention of the Company's Committee; but though the Committee was in an innovating mood, owing to its recent reverses, the ex-North-wester's plan, which called for a heavy outlay, was not accepted for immediate use. It was kept on file, however, because it was admirably suited to the Company's purposes; and events were to show that it was, ultimately, of decisive value. But at the moment its chief significance for Robertson was that, directly or indirectly, it brought him into contact with Selkirk. It has been said that the two men had met in Montreal in the year 1804, and that the fur trader had told the nobleman glowing tales of the wonders of the distant West. But no real evidence has been found to prove this. Probably Selkirk had never heard of him before he, Robertson, seemingly unemployed, returned home in 1809.[16]

Being possessed, however, of a very fine plan of campaign and even of the ability requisite to implement it successfully, is not sufficient for a man who has no independent income; and the truth is that when he came back in 1809 to his native land the trader was out of work. And Selkirk met him then. Many long talks followed, and Selkirk was so impressed with the capacity and ideas of the ex-North-wester that he offered him the position of agent in his Red River project. Robertson accepted eagerly. Within two weeks he was busy promoting Selkirk's plans in the Hebrides, especially in his native island of Lewis. And partly because of his native ability and his intimate knowledge of the far West, and also because of his hostility to the North West Company, he was to prove of great value to the cause.

Selkirk's third emigration agent was Captain Roderick McDonald, and the third place of muster for Assiniboia was Glasgow, the center of Scottish industrialism. For many years indigent Highlanders in large

16. McTavish, McGillivray & Company to Robertson, September 15, 1809; Selkirk to Semple, April 26, 1816, *PAC SP*, pp. 990, 2213. Lady Selkirk to Halkett, November 2, 1817, *SP SM*. E. E. Rich and R. Harvey Fleming, eds., *Colin Robertson's Correspondence Book, September 1817 to September 1822* (London, 1839), pp. xxiv-xxxi. Hereafter, *Robertson's Correspondence*.

numbers had been leaving their native valleys and pouring into Glasgow in search of a living. Economic conditions in the city being so bad during the first decade of the nineteenth century—thousands were barely keeping themselves alive—Selkirk thought it should be comparatively easy to engage large numbers of Glasgow men as laborers for the Red River Settlement and the Hudson's Bay Company. Having discussed the matter with the Directors of the Company, he sent Captain Roderick McDonald, a Highlander and a fairly capable man, to Glasgow to hire men for both settlement and company. The task proved difficult and eventually almost fruitless. Though McDonald was a Highlander and depicted the glories of Assiniboia in attractive terms, he found most of his listeners unwilling to undertake a voyage to such a far-off and unknown country. It was only by means of persistent urging and haggling, with final promises of exorbitant wages, that he persuaded a few to contract for the trip. Of these fewer than forty reached the appointed rendezvous; and those who did so were discovered later to be shiftless in character and a constant source of trouble. The promises of higher wages made to these men likewise were to prove a bone of contention all the way out to Red River.[17]

Besides these contingents from Lewis and Glasgow, and that from Ireland, a number of settlers were secured in scattered groups from various parts of the Highlands, from other islands in the Hebrides, and from Stromness in the Orkneys. All were to assemble in Stornoway, the chief port of the Hebrides, in time to sail on the Hudson's Bay Company's ships on their annual voyage to America.[18]

While the work of the emigration agents was being pushed with energy and rapidity, opposition forces were being put in motion to delay and, if possible, to nip the project in the bud. The British representatives of the North West Company, Mackenzie, Inglis, and Ellice, thwarted in their efforts to prevent Selkirk from securing Assiniboia, resorted to various devices to foil his further efforts.[19] Inverness was made one of their centers and the Inverness *Journal*, the most widely circulated newspaper in northern Scotland, was bought up for the cause. Within a week after the official deeding of Assiniboia to Selkirk

17. Miles Macdonell to Selkirk, July 4, 25, October 1, 1811; Miles Macdonell to Auld, December 25, 1811, Miles Macdonell, Selkirk Settlement, pp. 254, 255 f., 259, 260, 264 f., 270, 281, *PAC*.

18. Miles Macdonell to Selkirk, July 25, 1811, Miles Macdonell, Selkirk Settlement, pp. 255 ff., 261, *PAC*. Journal of John McLeod, Sr., Chief Trader, Hudson's Bay Company, 1811–42, 1, *PAC*. Hereafter, McLeod, Journal, *PAC*.

19. Simon McGillivray to McTavish, McGillivray & Co., June 1, 1811, *Q153*, Pt. III, pp. 612 ff. Selkirk to the Governor, Deputy Governor and Committee of the Hudson's Bay Company, February 14, 1815, *PAC SP*, pp. 1914, 1918 f. Miles Macdonell to Auld, December 25, 1811, Miles Macdonell, Selkirk Settlement, pp. 282 f., *PAC*.

there was published in the *Journal* an effusive article on Selkirk's venture, signed "Highlander."[20] It was written by Simon McGillivray,[21] a brother of William McGillivray, and pretended to offer a friendly warning to anyone so imprudent as to think of settling in Assiniboia. The rigors and dangers of the British Northwest were described in vivid colors and full detail. Nothing was left to the imagination. Miles Macdonell, Colin Robertson, and Roderick McDonald were characterized as liars and dissemblers, and it was the same with Selkirk. His patriotism and philanthropy were only assumed; in reality he was a "designing and dangerous character," bent solely on enhancing "the value of his own transatlantic territories." This tirade, when scattered industriously far and wide through the Highlands and the Isles, did the Red River Settlement cause much damage. The sources of this and other underhand attacks, however, were not unknown to their objects.[22] Late in May, 1811, Miles Macdonell had called upon Sir Alexander Mackenzie at his John Street house in London, and there the North-wester had unequivocally denounced the plans of Lord Selkirk as nothing but a "mad scheme" intended to ruin the North West Company; and at the same time he pledged himself uncompromisingly to offer all the opposition in his power, whatever the consequences.[23] In early July Miles wrote to his chief: "Sir A. [Alexander Mackenzie] has pledged himself as so decidedly opposed to this project that he will try every means in his power to thwart it."[24] The Inverness *Journal* attacks showed that these were not empty threats.

In spite of the insidious work of the North-westers, however, a heterogeneous group of would-be colonists straggled slowly into Stornoway during the summer of 1811. Some were men in the prime of life anxious to found in the New World the homes and the prosperity which had been denied to them in the Old; others were youths who had eager visions of the deer hunt, wild Indians, and social freedom; a goodly sprinkling were "failures," seeking to shake off the stigmas of the past and begin life anew; and not a few were malcontents who were not at all certain that they really wished to make the venture. By far the greater number were of Scottish blood. Some had been hired as "servants" of

20. *PAC SP*, pp. 133 ff.

21. Simon McGillivray to the Wintering Partners of the North West Company, April 9, 1812, *Q150*, Pt. I, p. 181. Simon McGillivray to Bathurst, June 19, 1815, *Q134*, Pt. II, p. 377. Selkirk Memorandum, *SP SM*.

22. Miles Macdonell to Selkirk, July 25, 1811, Miles Macdonell, Selkirk Settlement, p. 257, *PAC*. Inverness *Journal*, September 12, 1811, *PAC SP*, pp. 140–148.

23. Minute by Miles Macdonell, *Q133*, pp. 66 f.

24. July 4, 1811, Miles Macdonell, Selkirk Settlement, p. 254, *PAC*.

the Hudson's Bay Company; the rest, known as "His Lordship's servants," were engaged to work for a fixed time, at the end of which each would be given, free of charge, one hundred acres of land. Not until the following year would ordinary settlers and their families be brought out. In the meantime accommodations for families would be begun by the indentured servants. The number of those who assembled at Stornoway, however, was far smaller than Selkirk had expected. The paucity of investors, noted above, the work of the North-westers, and the difficulty of handling the sort of men his agents had been instructed to approach, together well-nigh ruined his plans for 1811. Of seventy men expected from Ireland, fifteen reached Stornoway; and the other contingents were only less disappointing. Then, too, the difficulties of recruiting and assembling delayed and disorganized the whole expedition. It was not until well on in July that final preparations for sailing were under way.[25]

The place from which the Hudson's Bay Company's ships usually set out for America was Gravesend on the Thames. Every year at least one ship made the round trip to and from the Bay. At times, when the fur posts needed an unusually large consignment of goods or when the fur returns were particularly heavy, two or even three would be sent out. It happened that in 1811 three ships were being sent to the Bay. Two of these, the *Prince of Wales* and the *Eddystone*, were for the service of the Company. They were well equipped and well manned. The third, the *Edward and Ann*, was a wretched old hulk of a vessel, poorly appointed and understaffed. She was for the use of the Selkirk expedition. Her character and equipment seemed to indicate that there were strong influences at work within the Company against the colonization project.[26]

Owing to delays in starting and to contrary winds, it was not until July 17 that the *Eddystone* and the *Edward and Ann* reached Stornoway. The *Prince of Wales* came in six days later, having stopped at Stromness to pick up 59 Company servants and emigrants. For the next ten days Miles Macdonell was busily engaged among his 125 motley followers in settling a host of perplexing problems. Some of the men were naturally disagreeable and faultfinding. Others were jealous of the higher wages promised to the men from Glasgow. A number began to waver in their intention to go on. The Galway men failed to turn up. A few laborers received advances of pay, and threatened to desert. Some

25. Miles Macdonell to Selkirk, June 27, July 4, 25, 1811, Miles Macdonell, Selkirk Settlement, pp. 253, 255 ff., *PAC*. Selkirk Memorandum, *SP SM*.

26. Miles Macdonell to Selkirk, June 27, July 4, 25, October 1, 1811, Miles Macdonell, Selkirk Settlement, *PAC*.

did desert. There were protests about quarters on shipboard. And, meanwhile, the expenses of the expedition were mounting alarmingly.[27]

The character of the emigrants and the character of the expedition would by themselves have made Macdonell's work at Stornoway extremely difficult; but the continued intrigues of the North-westers made it almost unbearable. The minds of the men were constantly being poisoned against both the project and its promoter. Present discomforts, the low rates of pay, the dangers of ocean travel, the prospects of a severe winter, the labor and drudgery of the life in the New World—all these and other real or imagined grounds for dissatisfaction were exploited to the full. Chief among the intriguers was Collector Reid—"an old, weak & dissipated man"—who was customs officer at Stornoway. As an official, his duty was to lend every assistance to Macdonell. But his wife was Sir Alexander Mackenzie's aunt; and family ties prevailed over the claims of office. He went about among the assembled people, deliberately urging them to desert before it was too late. He assured them that neither Selkirk nor the Hudson's Bay Company could force them to embark, and could only seek redress by law for violation of contracts and to recover advances in pay already made.

Reid's efforts were ably seconded by those of his son-in-law, Captain John McKenzie, described by Miles Macdonell as "a mean fellow." The captain came to Stornoway ostensibly in quest of recruits for the army; in reality he was a secret agent of the North-westers. His method of attack was to induce a discontented settler or laborer to "take the King's shilling," and then arrest him as a deserter from His Majesty's service. He even went aboard the *Edward and Ann* with a recruiting party, "and with his own hand gave Money as Inlisting money to some of our men"; but "the men he was not allowed to take away and himself and party were sent from the ship." A little later in the day, however, he returned with half-a-dozen soldiers. This time he was not permitted to go on board; but customs officials forthwith appeared, went on board the *Edward and Ann*, and offensively performed their duties. "The muster was gone through, the Clause of the Emigration Act regulating the provisions for passengers was read, & then most officiously, a public declaration was made to know if every man was fully satisfied, & if he was going entirely with his own free will & consent, as otherwise . . . they might go on shore & several said they were not willing." A few of the emigrants then returned to shore, Captain McKenzie very obligingly conveying some of them. The captain made still another trip to the emigrant ship to help deserters get to shore, but

27. Miles Macdonell to Selkirk, July 4, 25, 1811, Miles Macdonell, Selkirk Settlement, pp. 253 ff., *PAC*. Selkirk Memorandum, *SP SM*.

some hostile hand on board scuttled his boat with a nine-pound shot, and he was forced to row back to avoid sinking. Before he could retaliate, a wind had sprung up, and the *Edward and Ann* had put to sea.[28]

Those deserters whom Captain McKenzie was unable to ferry to shore had been taken ashore by the revenue cutter and the collector's boat. Many departed so hastily that they left their baggage behind. One incident of this kind had serious consequences later. A Moncrieff Blair, one of the most conspicuous of the deserters, had gone ashore "on pretence of some business," and there had decided not to return. His baggage was forgotten by the collector until after the vessel had sailed. This gave Blair a grievance against Selkirk and the Hudson's Bay Company; and shortly afterwards the North-westers were using him effectively as an agent of propaganda against the Red River enterprise.[29]

Finally, after all these provoking delays, the expedition was ready to start. Miles Macdonell was weary and disconsolate. "This, My Lord," he wrote to Selkirk a few hours before departure, "has been a most unfortunate business. . . . I condole with Your Lordship for all these cross accidents. . . . It has been a Herculean labour."[30]

28. Miles Macdonell to Selkirk, July 25, October 1, 1811, Miles Macdonell, Selkirk Settlement, pp. 257, 259 f., 261 ff., *PAC*. McLeod, Journal, 1, *PAC*. Selkirk Memorandum, *SP SM*.

29. Miles Macdonell to Selkirk, July 25, October 1, 1811, Miles Macdonell, Selkirk Settlement, pp. 261 ff., 269, *PAC*. Miles Macdonell to Selkirk, June 20, 1811, *PAC SP*, p. 712. Alexander MacDonald to Archibald McDonald, April 3, 1812, *PAC SP*, 288. John Macdonell to Miles Macdonell, August 6, 1812, Miles Macdonell, Selkirk Settlement, p. 157, *PAC*.

30. Miles Macdonell to Selkirk, July 25, 1811, Miles Macdonell, Selkirk Settlement, pp. 259, 262, *PAC*.

CHAPTER VI

STORNOWAY TO RED RIVER

WHEN the three Hudson's Bay Company ships at last set sail from Stornoway on July 26, 1811, only 105 of the men collected by Selkirk's agents were on board. Thirty-five of these were indentured servants of the Company; the others were settlers for the prairies of Assiniboia. Of the whole number 76 had quarters on board the *Edward and Ann*. Owing to the prevalence of French privateers in British waters a man-of-war accompanied the ships on the first stages of the journey. About 400 miles out the convoy turned back and left the three transports to make their difficult way to Hudson Bay.[1]

The weather was bad throughout most of the voyage. On the rare days when the passengers could come up on deck, Macdonell, as governor-to-be, set to work to carry out certain instructions that had been given to him by Selkirk who had put them in these words:[2]

It is of great importance to introduce and keep up from the first habits of exact subordination; but in doing this it is necessary to avoid exciting the jealousy of the people, who might think they were kidnapped if the forms of military service were prematurely introduced. On the passage the practice of keeping watch and the various observances which the regulations of a ship require, afford sufficient opportunities for enforcing the essential principles of obedience and discipline. After you leave the Factory [York Factory] on the inland route, the propriety of guarding against surprise from Indians, etc., afford an evident reason for introducing some military observances, as to watches, sentinels, etc. After your arrival at the Settlement this reason will become so evident, that the forms of a regular garrison may be introduced, and when the people see distinctly the nature of the undertaking, from the occupations in which they are employed, they will probably consent without difficulty to practice military evolutions.

The Governor found the instructions easier to interpret than to execute. He understood as well as did Selkirk the need for military drill among the colonists for Red River; but the material with which he had to work was most difficult. "There was never a more awkward squad—not a man or even officer of the party knew how to put a gun to his eye or had even fired a shot"; and these were mostly men from the country which had bred Montrose and Claverhouse. Nor was ignorance their

1. Miles Macdonell to Selkirk, July 25, October 1, 1811, Miles Macdonell, Selkirk Settlement, pp. 259, 261, 263 ff., *PAC.*
2. *PAC SP,* p. 168.

only drawback. The rough weather made seasickness more prevalent than usual. Close confinement, narrow quarters, and the poor quality of the food augmented their discomforts and dangers. Dr. A. Edwards, the ship's surgeon, toiled constantly among the wretched people. No serious epidemic, however, developed during the voyage, although some of the men who had contracted social diseases in Stornoway just prior to embarkation were in a miserable plight before the journey's end.[3]

A prominent personage on the *Edward and Ann* was "a careless-hearted cleric, whose wit and banter" provided welcome diversion throughout the voyage. This was the Reverend Charles Bourke, an Irish priest who had stolen away from Killala without his bishop's permission. Unfortunately the good father's overfondness for "a sup of the *creature*," his too-frequent indulgence in nonsensical jests, and certain "eccentricities" made him undesirable as a chaplain to the Catholics on board. Nevertheless, he was kindhearted and willing; and both before and during the voyage his services to the expedition were numerous.[4]

It was not until the middle of September that the ships reached Hudson Bay. The voyage had been long, stormy, and dreary, and the *Edward and Ann* was much the worse for it. It took almost ten more days to cross the Bay to York Factory—an unnecessarily long time. The *Prince of Wales* arrived on September 24; the *Edward and Ann* a few hours later on the same day. The *Eddystone* was to have gone to Fort Churchill, but because of the lateness of the season she, too, went to York Factory. All three ships anchored in the shallow waters off the western shore, near the mouths of the Hayes and Nelson, and at last the weary and disheartened emigrants disembarked. Great was their relief to find themselves once again on solid ground. They had been on board ship for sixty-one days, the longest passage "and latest ever known to Hudson's Bay."[5] After the trials of departure from the Old World and the perils of a storm-tossed ocean, they were at last face to face with a primeval wilderness. In spite of their joy at having landed, their first impressions of the New World were discouraging enough: all around them lay the barren rocks and the stunted forest growth of the storm-swept coasts of the Bay.

On October 5 the Company's ships sailed for home, taking with them about twenty Orkneymen, who had served out their time in the fur

3. Miles Macdonell to Selkirk, October 1, 1811, Miles Macdonell, Selkirk Settlement, pp. 265 f., 268 f., *PAC.*

4. Miles Macdonell to Selkirk, July 25, October 1, 1811, Miles Macdonell, Selkirk Settlement, pp. 256, 269, *PAC.*

5. Miles Macdonell to Selkirk, October 1, 1811, Miles Macdonell, Selkirk Settlement, pp. 265 ff., 270, *PAC.* McLeod, Journal, 1, *PAC.* John McLeod to D. McKenzie, *PAC SP,* p. 149.

trade, and two members of the Assiniboia contingent who had become incapacitated through injury or disease.[6] Prior to the fleet's departure Miles Macdonell spent several hours trying to persuade some of the Orkneymen who were going home to remain and contract for service in the colony for a year or two. His labor, however, was practically fruitless. The men "formed a combination . . . against remaining longer in the country." Only one, William Finlay, could be prevailed upon to stay, and his services were secured only by a promise of exorbitant wages.[7]

Immediately upon his arrival at York Factory, Miles Macdonell commenced the arduous task of preparing for the approaching winter. He and Selkirk had planned, originally, that the expedition should proceed to Red River a very short time after disembarking. But the lateness of the season made it necessary to give up the plan and, instead, to winter on Hudson Bay.[8] The disembarked settlers were first marched a short distance over a rough road along the north bank of the Hayes River to York Factory, where they received "a very cold & haughty reception."[9] The Hudson's Bay Company officers at York, William H. Cook, Governor of York Factory, and William Auld, Superintendent of the Northern Department, were not disposed to be particularly friendly to the newcomers, although at first Macdonell was inclined to feel that both men were in sympathy with Selkirk's views.[10] Not many days had elapsed, however, before he discovered that neither of the men, and especially Auld, despite their expressions to the contrary, favored the Earl's policies of Hudson's Bay Company rejuvenation and Red River colonization. The reorganization of the Company on a distinctly efficiency basis met with the disapproval of most of the Bay traders, who were so accustomed to the jog-trot mode of administration that they found any change, no matter how much benefit it might promise to the Company, quite repugnant. The planting of a colony in the center of the fur domain they regarded as a foolhardy venture and definitely undesirable from their point of view.[11]

6. Miles Macdonell to Selkirk, October 1, 5, 1811, Miles Macdonell, Selkirk Settlement, pp. 268, 270, 276 f., *PAC*.

7. Miles Macdonell to Selkirk, October 5, 1811, May 31, 1812, Miles Macdonell, Selkirk Settlement, pp. 276, 323, *PAC*.

8. Selkirk to Miles Macdonell, June 29, 1811; Miles Macdonell to Selkirk, June 27, July 4, 25, October 1, 1811, Miles Macdonell, Selkirk Settlement, pp. 141, 254, 257 f., 273, *PAC*.

9. McLeod, Journal, 1, *PAC*.

10. Miles Macdonell to Selkirk, October 1, 1811; Miles Macdonell to Auld, December 25, 1811, Miles Macdonell, Selkirk Settlement, pp. 269, 288, *PAC*.

11. Miles Macdonell to Selkirk, May 29, 1812, Miles Macdonell, Selkirk Settlement, pp. 319 f., *PAC*. Auld to Selkirk, September 12, 1812, *PAC SP*, p. 479. Selkirk to Miles Macdonell, December 23, 1811, *PAC SP*, p. 125.

Late in June, 1811, Selkirk had suggested to Macdonell that if the Company's ships reached Hudson Bay too late in the season to permit the colonists to go on to Assiniboia that year, York Factory might be utilized as a shelter for the winter; and that the men might be employed to advantage in building a new factory on the Seal Islands near by, a project which the Company had much to heart, but had never yet had sufficient man power to accomplish.[12] A brief inspection of York Factory, however, revealed to the Governor that it was almost as uninviting to the emigrants as were the local traders. At that time the Factory stood a little more than half a mile up the Hayes River and "at the distance of 100 yards from the North Bank . . ., in low miry ground without a ditch." All about were stagnant swamps. A single row of pickets about eighteen feet high and "so slender & so open that they could give no security against an enemy," enclosed the principal buildings. The biggest of these structures was "two storeys high & covered with lead—the whole badly planned & as badly constructed, . . . inconvenient in every respect, & not at all calculated for a cold country." It is difficult to understand how such conditions could have existed when one considers that for years York Factory had been a post of considerable importance, being the distributing and receiving station for the whole of the Company's prairie fur trade. Apart from the Factory buildings there was practically no sign of human life for vast distances around, save a few Indian tepees near by and some log shanties which housed the Company's voyageurs.[13]

After the inspection of the Factory as a possible winter camp for the colonists, Macdonell, Auld, and Cook held a conference at which they discussed the whole question. At this meeting Macdonell suggested that since the accommodations at the Factory were so evidently inadequate for his men, being already crowded, and the neighborhood far from reassuring in respect to sanitary conditions, a new camp should perhaps be constructed on a better site not far away. Auld and Cook, who had already thought of such a solution before the arrival of the ships, gladly agreed. To Macdonell's chagrin, Auld went further and peremptorily chose the site. But the man knew the country, as the Governor did not, and the location was well chosen.

The place was a narrow clearing on the north bank of the Nelson River facing the upper and largest Seal Island, with a high bluff at the rear. Close by stood clusters of the stunted timber typical of the coun-

12. Selkirk to Miles Macdonell, June 29, 1811, Miles Macdonell, Selkirk Settlement, p. 141, *PAC*.

13. Miles Macdonell to Selkirk, October 1, 1811, May 29, 1812, Miles Macdonell, Selkirk Settlement, pp. 275, 316 ff., *PAC*.

try—larch, poplar, alder, willow, and white spruce. But the spruce was large enough to be used in the building of log cabins.[14] As the air was already getting frosty and the winter with all its northern ferocity was only a few weeks distant at best, Macdonell, on October 4, dispatched his men to the new site to begin building operations. Three days later he himself arrived, having been delayed by work and snowstorms. Since the men under his command were not skilled in the use of the axe, Macdonell was forced to instruct them while the work went forward. This was not the only difficulty with which he had to cope. The tools were of a very poor quality;[15] the Orkneymen were naturally slow and clumsy; the Glasgow recruits were lazy and faultfinding; the Irish were addicted to quarreling and fighting. The Governor, by nature somewhat temperamental, berated his followers frequently and developed an overly brusque manner toward them.

About the middle of October Macdonell and William Hillier, a Company magistrate, agreed that the men destined for Red River should be separated from the Company's servants and housed by themselves. By this arrangement Macdonell retained control over about thirty-six men —ten or eleven Glasgow clerks, a few Highlanders, some Irish, and some Orkneymen; the remaining men were placed directly under Hillier's management. The division produced good results. The work went forward more rapidly than before, and by October 26 was finished. The buildings which had been erected proved so satisfactory that in the ensuing winter, in spite of Arctic weather without and much quarreling within, no complaints were raised against them.[16]

As soon as the main task of building houses had been completed, Macdonell divided his followers into two groups: one was set to work building fences with snares in them for catching deer; the other was instructed to cut firewood and bring it within easy reach of the cabins. Nelson Encampment, as it was called, was no sooner ready than the Northern winter was upon it. The snows fell, the winds became fiercely cold, the rivers froze over, and the shores of Hudson Bay were piled high with shining, jagged mounds of ice.[17]

It proved to be a difficult winter for Macdonell. From the first the

14. Miles Macdonell to Selkirk, May 29, 31, 1812, Miles Macdonell, Selkirk Settlement, pp. 318, 321, *PAC*.

15. Miles Macdonell to Selkirk, October 1, 5, 1811, May 15, 1812, Miles Macdonell, Selkirk Settlement, pp. 271, 276 f., 321, *PAC*.

16. Miles Macdonell to Selkirk, October 1, 5, 1811, May 31, 1812; Miles Macdonell to Auld, December 25, 1811, Miles Macdonell, Selkirk Settlement, pp. 270 f., 277, 281 f., 321 ff., *PAC*.

17. Miles Macdonell to Selkirk, October 5, 1811, May 31, 1812, Miles Macdonell, Selkirk Settlement, pp. 276, 322 f., *PAC*. John McLeod to —, June 29, 1812, *PAC SP*, p. 154.

Hudson's Bay men at York Factory, particularly the "old hands" and some of the leading officers, did their utmost to prejudice the newcomers against the Company's service and the country itself.[18] The officious Auld lost no opportunity to gibe at the Irish, to find fault with Macdonell, to malign the Red River project surreptitiously, and to chafe generally under his new obligations.[19] A week after the expedition arrived he wrote to Andrew Wedderburn, one of the principals of the Hudson's Bay Company, that the Irish were constantly quarreling and fighting and that many of the laborers were "indifferently qualified for our sort of management." Many of the men hired in 1811, Auld complained, were "ancient servants," old men who were "wholly unfit to earn their Salt."[20] From their first meeting he had disliked Macdonell. The Governor, he wrote, was all ardor and contempt for obstacles.[21] Selkirk was advised confidentially that he had been imposed upon.[22] On the other hand, Macdonell's estimate of the Company's men, "old hands" and officials, was in no wise flattering. He tried in his dealings with them to be tactful and conciliatory;[23] but in this he was not always successful. Throughout the winter, relations between Nelson Encampment and York Factory remained anything but amiable. Macdonell allowed his men to go down to the Factory only when necessity required it, but each visit brought forth a fresh crop of ill feeling. In this matter the Factory people were not the sole offenders. Many of the settlers were born troublemakers.[24]

One typical source of friction was the question of antiscorbutics. Fresh food proving very scarce, as the winter progressed the newcomers were attacked by scurvy. In vain Macdonell pleaded with the Company officials for adequate medicines. Finally, in despair, he resorted to Jacques Cartier's remedy when in similar straits, a drink prepared from the leaves of the white spruce. Only one of his men died from the dis-

18. Miles Macdonell to Selkirk, May 29, 1812, Miles Macdonell, Selkirk Settlement, p. 319, *PAC*.

19. Auld to Selkirk, October, 1811, September 12, 1812; Selkirk to Auld, June 15, 1813, *PAC SP*, pp. 59, 499 f., 689 f.

20. October 3, 1811, *PAC SP*, pp. 70, 74 ff. Auld to Miles McDonell [Macdonell], October 16, 1811, *PAC SP*, p. 91.

21. Auld to Wedderburn, October 3, 1811, *PAC SP*, p. 81.

22. Auld to Selkirk, October, 1811, *PAC SP*, p. 59.

23. "Numerous letters passed between me and Messrs. Auld and Cook. . . . Mine are chiefly in reply and in justification of ourselves and measures, and as moderate as I could possibly word them, to avoid giving the least shadow of umbrage that might occasion the withholding any support required. . . ." Miles Macdonell to Selkirk, May 29, 31, 1812, Miles Macdonell, Selkirk Settlement, pp. 318 ff., 330 f., *PAC*.

24. Miles Macdonell to Cook, January 9, 1812; Miles Macdonell to Auld, May 4, 1812; Miles Macdonell to Selkirk, May 31, 1812, Miles Macdonell, Selkirk Settlement, pp. 291 ff., 308 f., 326 ff., *PAC;* Cook to Miles Macdonell, December 29, 1811, January 10, 1812, *PAC SP*, 129, 278.

ease. But the incident served to widen the gulf between the settlers and the traders.[25]

The restoration of the men's health was only a prelude to new troubles, most of which were due to bad management and to the natural propensities and idle condition of the subordinates. Two groups of men, living in the same encampment and under different regulations and officers, are prone to form opposing interests. Even on board ship there had been a tendency toward this.[26] After all were settled for the winter, cliques became well established. The Connaught Irish formed one group, the Orkney laborers another; and the Glasgow men refused to associate with either the Irish or the Orkneymen. Grievances, real and imaginary, developed in each of the several groups.[27] Under the circumstances Hillier and Macdonell were almost powerless; but they exerted themselves to do the best they could to calm the troubled waters.

By the middle of winter Macdonell was suffering from strain. He became moody and pessimistic. Three months earlier he had been confident that he could surmount all difficulties that might arise.[28] Now he began to have doubts, though he did not really lose hope of ultimate success. He unburdened himself frequently in his letters to Auld and Cook. The Orkneymen, he wrote, were lazy, spiritless, and ill-disposed, with gluttonous appetites, and so ungrateful that they would exult in the ruin of those who furnished them the means of subsistence. The Glasgow men were insubordinate, and "a more . . . cross-grained lot were never put under any person's care." As for the Irish, they were worthless blackguards, in need of the lash.[29] Little consolation did he receive, however, from the Hudson's Bay nabobs; they were secretly happy over the turn Macdonell's affairs seemed to be taking.

Bickerings within Nelson Encampment finally flared into open violence. The time was New Year's Day; the immediate incitement, a liberal supply of liquor; the aggressors, the Irish. Before the mêlée was over seven Irishmen had suffered and five Orkneymen were so "severely

25. Miles Macdonell to Cook, November 30, 1811, January 9, 21, 26, February 9, 1812; Miles Macdonell to Auld, December 25, 1811, February 27, May 12, 1812; Miles Macdonell to Selkirk, May 29, 31, 1812, Miles Macdonell, Selkirk Settlement, pp. 287 f., 290 f., 296 ff., 302 ff., 310, 318 f., 322 ff., PAC. John McLeod to —, June 29, 1812, PAC SP, pp. 154 f.

26. Miles Macdonell to Selkirk, October 1, 1811, Miles Macdonell, Selkirk Settlement, p. 265, PAC. Selkirk to Auld, July 15, 1813, PAC SP, pp. 689 ff.

27. Miles Macdonell to Auld, February 27, 1812, Miles Macdonell, Selkirk Settlement, p. 302, PAC.

28. Miles Macdonell to Selkirk, October 1, 1811; Miles Macdonell to Auld, December 25, 1811, Miles Macdonell, Selkirk Settlement, pp. 274, 282 f., 288, PAC.

29. Miles Macdonell to Auld, December 25, 1811, February 27, 1812, May 15, 1812; Miles Macdonell to Selkirk, May 29, 31, 1812, Miles Macdonell, Selkirk Settlement, pp. 287, 301 f., 312 f., 319, 324, PAC.

cut, bruised and maimed" that their lives hung in the balance for several weeks.[30] Macdonell and Hillier arrived on the scene after most of the fighting was over. They had recently been appointed civil magistrates and justices of the peace for the Indian Territories not within the limits of either Upper or Lower Canada.[31] On the days following the brawl they received charges and took evidence. There is good reason for thinking that Macdonell did not probe very deeply into the real causes of the trouble; but, on the whole, justice seems to have been done. All the assailants were forced to make a money payment to the injured and to give security for their future good behavior. James Hart and Michael Higgins, held to be "worthless blackguards" and the real instigators of the fracas, were to be sent home with the next fur shipment. Anthony Macdonnell, who had led the attack, was forgiven, partly because he could not speak English, and no doubt, too, because he had numerous relatives and friends in Ireland who were regarded as possible emigrants for the Red River Colony.[32]

The New Year's disorder had no sooner been liquidated than an insurrection of dangerous proportions broke out in the Encampment. The prime mover and cause of it was William Finlay, the Orkneyman hired by Macdonell in October at York Factory. For quarreling and insubordination he had been confined to a specially constructed jail, a brush hut. His fellow countrymen, whose loyalty to authority he had been busy undermining, thereupon released the prisoner and set fire to the hut. As the building burned, they danced and shouted triumphantly "in the most audacious manner." When they were brought before the court, they listened to the evidence and then walked out contemptuously. For the next four months they kept the Encampment in constant confusion and, after they had secured arms, in alarm; and both at the Factory and in the Encampment they were openly aided and abetted. Finally Macdonell and Hillier called upon Auld for help.[33] After several unsuc-

30. Evidence delivered on oath at Nelson Encampment, January 2, 3, 1812, *PAC SP*, pp. 260–277. Miles Macdonell to Auld, February 27, 1812; Miles Macdonell to Selkirk, May 31, 1812, Miles Macdonell, Selkirk Settlement, pp. 302, 323 f., *PAC.* Auld to Selkirk, September 12, 1812, *PAC SP*, pp. 497 f.

31. State Book, Lower Canada, *G139, PAC.*

32. Evidence delivered on oath at Nelson Encampment, January 2, 3, 1812, *PAC SP*, pp. 260–277; Miles Macdonell to Auld, February 27, May 4, 1812; Miles Macdonell to Selkirk, May 31, July 4, 1812, Miles Macdonell, Selkirk Settlement, pp. 302, 308, 323 f., 338, *PAC.*

33. Miles Macdonell to Cook, February 14, 15, 1812; Miles Macdonell to Auld, February 27, April 18, May 4, 12, 15, 24, 1812; Miles Macdonell and Hillier to Auld, May 15, 1812; Miles Macdonell to Selkirk, May 31, June 19, 1812, Miles Macdonell, Selkirk Settlement, pp. 299 f., 302 f., 304 f., 306, 307 f., 309 f., 311 ff., 315 f., 323 ff., 332 f., *PAC.* Auld to Miles Macdonell, April 30, May 13, 16, 1812; Auld to Miles Macdonell and Hillier, May 13, 1812, *PAC SP*, pp. 309 ff., 337 ff., 340 f., 367.

cessful attempts to bring the mutineers to terms by informal advances, Auld began formal action against them on May 13 by issuing a notification which he requested Macdonell and Hillier to read to the entire Encampment. It ran as follows:[34]

The Servants of the Hudson Bay Compy who were put off duty by Captn Miles Macdonell a chief Factor in this service on the 12th Feby in consequence of their riotous & mutinous conduct on that night are hereby warned of the evil consequences which must follow from their obstinate refusal to return to their duty after so much pains have been taken not only by Captn Macdonell but also by myself to lead them to a proper line of conduct. I have now finally to inform them that if they shall instantly return to their duty they will be taken on the books again & that all punishment will be referred to the Honble Committee's decision. But on no consideration shall they be allowed pay or wages for the time during which they have continued in defiance of their Factor's authority.

If they refuse the above terms they are to be now told that they shall be sent home close prisoners on board the Company's ship or ships to be delivered up at the first port in Britain to the Civil Power or in case of necessity put on board any of his Majesty's ships for security until they shall be demanded for trial.

Macdonell and Hillier called a general assembly of the Encampment at twelve o'clock on May 15. The insurgents were present at the meeting, where Macdonell read Auld's notification; but one left before the reading, and the others, having absolutely rejected the proffered terms, again marched off home. Meanwhile three officers had gone to the insurgents' camp to seize their arms; but they were too late, and were met by refusal and insults. They then departed, but soon returned with Macdonell and some armed men. The Governor found that the mutineers had taken advantage of the interval to secrete their arms. He again read the notification, but it had no effect except to call forth defiance and threats of open violence. Macdonell then informed Auld of his failure, but for the time being no further action was taken. In June, however, the rebels were forced to come to terms. A number of them had gone to York Factory for food supplies and were unable to return owing to the breakup of the ice on the river. Refused admittance to the Factory, they were helpless. At last they acknowledged their guilt and threw themselves entirely on the mercy of the Company's officials. Thereupon they were admitted into the service of the Hudson's Bay Company. They were no longer regarded as fit material for colonization purposes.

Thus ended the most serious crisis of the winter. Just who was most to blame for it, aside from the insurgents themselves, is difficult to de-

34. *PAC SP*, pp. 342 ff.

termine from the evidence. Auld's letters to Selkirk throw most of the blame on Macdonell. But probably the latter's account, though biased in his own favor, is much closer to the truth. No doubt the Governor was indiscreet and lacking in tact in dealing with his men; but neither is there much doubt that Auld and Cook and some of their "old hands" were definitely to blame. "Every time a party was sent to the Factory the men were tampered with"; and after the insurrection had broken out, Cook and his men openly encouraged the ringleaders. The fact that the mutineers were taken into the service of the Company after their surrender, and long after they had refused all terms, is a clear commentary on the situation. The natural hostility of the fur traders to settlement was merely giving another instance of its ineradicable character.[35]

But despite all the turbulence and hardships, the months spent by the emigrants on the Bay were not without their amenities. Throughout the winter Macdonell kept up a regular mess in his house on the south bank of the Nelson. Here he had a variety of company, more or less congenial—Hillier, Father Bourke, and Dr. Edwards, as well as a number of petty officers and clerks, chief among whom were Michael McDonnell, John McLeod, Kenneth McRae, and a Mr. Whitford. Although fresh meats were scarce during the months of January, February, and March, in April fresh venison and partridges were secured in abundance. No one in the Encampment would eat any more salt meat. "From the 27th April to 15th May . . . no less than 3,000 Deer crossed the river below the Seal Islands." "People may complain of bad living in Hudson Bay," Macdonell wrote to Selkirk, "but it is certain we have all got fatter than when we came to it."[36] With the approach of spring the days grew longer and warmer, waterfowl appeared in myriads, and life, if not feeling, improved daily among the restless emigrants.

Throughout the months of spring Macdonell and his men were busy preparing for the journey inland. The season was the latest ever known at the Bay. The ice usually left the rivers in May or early in June. This year it was still coming down long after the middle of June. At the suggestion of Auld, Macdonell sent two officers with the most effective of the men to the Factory on May 22 "to be ready there to take early advantage of the opening of the Hayes River for transporting a cargo to

35. Miles Macdonell and Hillier to Auld, May 15, 1812; Miles Macdonell to Auld, May 15, 1812; Miles Macdonell to Selkirk, May 29, 31, June 19, 1812, Miles Macdonell, Selkirk Settlement, pp. 311 f., 312 f., 319, 323 ff., 332 f., *PAC*. Auld to Miles Macdonell, April 30, May 13, 1812; Auld to Miles Macdonell and Hillier, May 16, 1812; Auld to Selkirk, September 12, 1812, *PAC SP,* pp. 311 ff., 337 ff., 367, 496 ff.

36. Miles Macdonell to Cook, January 26, 1812; Miles Macdonell to Selkirk, May 31, 1812, Miles Macdonell, Selkirk Settlement, pp. 296, 328, *PAC*.

the Rock." This party was not able to set out until June 10. Twelve days later Macdonell and the remainder of the party left the Encampment for the Factory in four unwieldy boats. They lost one boat in the ice, but saved its cargo. Part of the group was forced back once to the Encampment, but on June 25 all were at York. Final preparations were now rushed. During the winter Macdonell had had four flat-bottomed boats, similar to those he had seen used on the rivers in New York State, constructed at the Factory. These were now loaded with baggage and supplies. They were poorly built and were to prove very unsatisfactory for inland transport.[37]

By July 4 all was ready for the start. Macdonell wrote a last letter to Selkirk,[38] explaining why he was sending four of the men home. This letter, with others he had written during the winter, would go to Britain in the fall on the Company's ships. They were to provide Selkirk with his first news of the expedition since his reception of letters in the fall of 1811. They described in detail the course of events at the Bay up to July 4, 1812. Two days later the Governor set out with his men for the distant Red River Valley.[39]

Contrary to what might be expected, the Nelson River is not the most navigable waterway from Hudson Bay to the Red River. It is a swift stream full of dangerous rapids and waterfalls. It was seldom used by the Hudson's Bay Company voyageurs. Their usual route was by way of the Hayes and Hill rivers and a chain of connected lakes and streams. This was the course chosen for the Red River settlers.

At best the journey was a long and tedious one. The first hundred miles were comparatively easy. In the lower reaches of the Hayes the banks are low and about a quarter of a mile apart, and the river flows at the rate of about two miles an hour; farther up, however, the banks are higher and closer together, and the waters are more rapid. The real difficulties of the expedition began when the "Rock" portage was reached. Here the Hayes falls perpendicularly for ten feet. It took five hours of hard labor to unload the boats, carry them and their cargoes to a point above the falls, and reload. This was the colonists' first experience of a portage. It was a painful enough experience and it was to be repeated often in the course of the ensuing weeks.[40]

Progress up the Hill River was slow and tiresome, owing to the swift-

37. Miles Macdonell to Selkirk, May 31, June 29, July 4, 1812, Miles Macdonell, Selkirk Settlement, pp. 329, 331, 333 f., PAC. The Rock was on the Hayes River route about 130 miles above York Factory.

38. Miles Macdonell, Selkirk Settlement, pp. 334 ff., PAC.

39. Miles Macdonell to Selkirk, August 11, 1812, PAC SP, p. 445.

40. McLeod, Journal, 2, PAC. John McLeod to —, June 29, 1812, PAC SP, p. 153. Auld to Miles Macdonell, October 16, 1811, PAC SP, p. 97.

ness of the stream and the numerous rapids. Many times both the boats
and their loads had to be lifted up the steep banks, as at the Rock, and
"packed" past roaring cataracts or surging rapids. Sometimes it was
only necessary to remove the cargo or a part of it and carry it over
the portage trail, while the boats were left in the water and "tracked."
Portage trails were often almost as difficult as racing rapids, being usually circuitous, steep, rough, and long. Such traveling was all in the
day's work where only experienced voyageurs were concerned. But the
poor emigrants, awkward and inexperienced, found it the most crushing
sort of toil. Their work would have been hard enough with fragile birch-
bark canoes; but the heavy and clumsy *bateaux* presented tremendous
difficulties. It took several men to carry each of these boats over the
steep and rugged trails, and, when the distances were great, much time
was consumed. Of Macdonell's men the Orkneymen and the western
Scots proved to be the most willing and useful. The Irish and the Glasgow men found the work very irksome and disagreeable. Most of them
wished they had stayed at home; and Macdonell heartily concurred.
Their complaints were equaled in frequency and vigor only by the curs-
ings and beratings from the officers.

Slowly the brigade advanced. Often, after a long day of the most toilsome and wearying exertions, during which the men had constantly
pushed the boats up long rapids with poles at a very slow pace and
portaged and tracked repeatedly, they found themselves only two or
three miles from the encampment of the previous night. As the weather
grew warmer, vast clouds of mosquitoes appeared and the nights became
almost as trying as the days. Fortunately there were a few things to be
grateful for. A number of the experienced servants of the Hudson's
Bay Company who were returning to the inland fur posts accompanied
the expedition and gave much-needed assistance and information. Then,
too, there were stretches of comparatively easy going when the trail
followed a quiet stream or led across the calm waters of a lake.

After what seemed endless toil and discomfort the colonists reached
Oxford House, a Company post on the southeastern shore of Holy
Lake. Here the weary, blistered, and now sunburned emigrants came in
contact with the first real traces of civilization they had encountered
since leaving York Factory. Then, after two days of welcome hospitality and rest, they parted with the Hudson's Bay men who had accompanied them. On July 30 the brigade, augmented by three experienced men and two large boats procured at the Post, put off in the best
of spirits. There were still many miles of very difficult traveling before
them, however; and it was not until the middle of August that they
came to Norway House, a Company fur post on Playgreen Lake close

to the source of the Jack River. They were ragged, footsore, mosquito-bitten, and weather-beaten, but they had put behind them 430 strenuous miles since leaving York Factory.[41]

After resting briefly at Norway House the expedition undertook the last stage of the long journey. Upon rowing about a mile they entered the waters of Lake Winnipeg and, skirting its eastern shores to avoid the dangers of sudden storms, came in about two weeks' time to the mouth of the Red River. On August 30, 55 days after leaving Hudson Bay, having covered in all about 700 miles, the first brigade of Red River settlers arrived at the forks of the Red and the Assiniboine.[42]

41. John McLeod to —, August 7, 1812, *PAC SP*, p. 160; Miles Macdonell to Selkirk, August 11, 1812, *PAC SP*, pp. 443 ff.
42. Miles Macdonell to Selkirk, July 17, 1813, *PAC SP*, pp. 764.

CHAPTER VII

"THE LAND OF PROMISE"

THE force of men with which Miles Macdonell had set out from Stornoway in the summer of 1811 had dwindled sadly by the time he reached Assiniboia at the end of August, 1812. What with the necessity of sending some back home, and allowing others to take service with the Hudson's Bay Company, he found on preparing to set out from York Factory to Red River that he had only nineteen effectives. It is true that on July 1, when the force at the Factory was divided up, twenty-two were assigned to him for the Settlement. Three days later, however, he was still uncertain about how many he would have. "The people are so fluctuating," he wrote to Selkirk, "that I cannot yet send a list of my party. A man of one nation is prejudiced against going with one of another. I shall go on with any number, take possession of the tract & hoist the standard."[1] On the morning of July 6, just before the brigade was to leave, three Orkneymen arrogantly informed him that they were not going to Red River. They took service with the Company. In their place the expedition secured three experienced men at Oxford House. These were engaged for a year, at advanced wages. Somewhere on the Sea River a young Indian, Tipotem, volunteered his services as a guide. At Playgreen Lake, on August 11, Macdonell was able to send a "return" to Selkirk of "twenty-three effective men." All of them reached the Forks.[2]

This number was considerably smaller than Selkirk had counted on when issuing his general instructions to Macdonell before the fleet left Stornoway. At that time the Earl was of the opinion that of the men gathered at Stornoway, 40 ought to be taken for the Settlement—certainly not less than 30; and of these he desired that 12 or 15 should be Irish, the rest Highlanders picked from among the Glasgow recruits.[3] As yet, of course, Selkirk was quite unaware of the poor quality of the men recruited by Roderick McDonald. As it turned out, only 19 of the men engaged in 1811 reached Assiniboia. Of these 8 were Irish, and the others mostly from the Orkneys and western Scotland. The nationality of the 3 men engaged at Oxford House is not definitely known, but probably all were Orkneymen.[4]

1. Miles Macdonell to Selkirk, July 4, 1812, Miles Macdonell, Selkirk Settlement, pp. 334 f., *PAC*.
2. Miles Macdonell to Selkirk, August 11, 1811, *PAC SP*, p. 443.
3. Instructions to Miles Macdonell, 1811, *PAC SP*, p. 168.
4. Miles Macdonell to Selkirk, August 11, 1812, *PAC SP*, p. 443. "List of Men be-

Upon their arrival at the Forks the settlers pitched camp on the east side of the river opposite Fort Gibraltar, the North West Company's trading post for the vicinity, along with a group of Hudson's Bay Company traders from the East Winnipeg district and Brandon House. The traders had been encamped there for several days before the colonists arrived; they were "waiting the arrival of carts to transport part of their goods by land" to their respective posts.[5] As soon as the tents were up Macdonell set his men to hunting and fishing. Food stores were low. Despite all the promises of Auld, the Company's posts in the interior had made no preparation for the coming of the settlers. "Not one bag of Pemican or any other article of provision" except a few potatoes had been reserved. This was very bad for in the fall months the buffalo were at a great distance from the Forks, and "nothing was to be procured from the natives," who lived only from hand to mouth. The Company's men were almost as badly off as the colonists; they had only a few bags of pemmican. During the few days now spent at the Forks, the Red and Assiniboine rivers were the main resource of all. Owing, however, to a scarcity of hooks, the quantity of fish caught was small, and quite inadequate to meet the needs of so many people. Macdonell was forced to buy supplies, especially meat, from the Northwesters at Fort Gibraltar.[6]

Hardly had the Governor and his men got their tents up than they were "chilled to the marrow with a sudden terror." From over the plain there suddenly rushed toward them a wild-looking band of horsemen, accoutred in war paint and feathers, and brandishing tomahawks. The first fear of the settlers was that they were being attacked by Indians; but when the riders came within close range, yelling and gesticulating, it was evident that they were not Indians but bois-brûlés decked out in

longing to R.R.S. arrivg in H. Bay in 1811 & Brought from York Factory July 1812," Miles Macdonell, Selkirk Settlement, p. 151, *PAC*.

5. Miles Macdonell to Selkirk, July 17, 1813, *PAC SP,* p. 764.

6. Miles Macdonell to Selkirk, July 17, 1813, *PAC SP,* p. 764. Extract of a Letter from a Proprietor of the North West Company, August, 1813, *Q134,* Pt. II, pp. 347 f. According to the North-wester the Hudson's Bay Company traders who arrived at the Forks in August, shortly before the colonists, "endeavoured to obtain from the Natives a Supply of provisions for the Settlement"; but "all the provisions which the Natives could procure . . . had previously been secured by the N.W. Co. for the support of their Establishment in that quarter & when . . . Miles McDonell [*sic*] arrived with the Settlers, he had no means of finding subsistence for them but by making immediate application to the N.W. Co. for provisions, whereof in consideration of the case, and from motives of humanity a temporary supply was given to them." It is very probable that the North-westers had deliberately secured all the natives' supplies so that Macdonell could not buy them. Later on in the winter this was done. Narrative of John Pritchard of the Red River Settlement, May 4, 1819, Colonial Office Records, Series Q, Vol. 153, Pt. III, p. 739, Public Archives of Canada. Hereafter, Pritchard, Narrative.

Indian costumes for the sake of effect. They had come to inform Macdonell, which they did in no uncertain terms, that the Red River Valley was a fur-trade domain, that farmers were not wanted, and that the settlers must go elsewhere. In equally plain language the Governor retorted that the Red River Valley belonged to Lord Selkirk, and that if anyone were forced to go elsewhere, it would be the fur trader and not the settler. Thereupon the dusky riders withdrew. They had come from Fort Gibraltar, and their hostile gesture had been prompted by the men in charge there—John Willis, Alexander Macdonell—cousin and brother-in-law of Miles—and Benjamin Frobisher. The whole incident seemed trifling in immediate retrospect, but it was prophetic of future calamities for the colony.[7]

Despite this display of hostility from the North West Company traders, the ceremony of delivery and seizin of Assiniboia took place with dignified formality on September 4. At his camp on the eastern bank of the Red River Macdonell, with a guard of officers under arms and with colors flying, took formal possession of Assiniboia in the name of the Earl of Selkirk. Besides the colonists there were present at the ceremony the Hudson's Bay Company traders from Brandon House and the East Winnipeg district, a number of free Canadians and Indians, and three North West Company gentlemen from Fort Gibraltar. The North-westers "did not allow their people to cross" over, although they had been invited. William Hillier, acting on behalf of the Hudson's Bay Company, made the delivery. The patent and Macdonell's commission were read in French and English—Hugh Heney, a Hudson's Bay Company officer, having prepared translations. At the conclusion of the conveyance "7 swivels were discharged and 3 cheers given." All the gentlemen, including the three North-westers, then assembled at Macdonell's tent, where they "partook of a cold snacke . . . and drank toasts appropriate to the occasion." "A Keg of Spirits was turned out to the people."[8]

Thus, at last, the colony of Red River, long planned by Selkirk, was an established if not an imposing fact. But the same enemies who had tried sedulously to nip the venture in the bud in the old land were even now taking steps to destroy the first shoots before they had grown too vigorous in the new. The North West Company gentlemen had accepted Macdonell's hospitality with a fair show of friendliness; and they had

7. Pritchard, Narrative, *Q153,* Pt. III, pp. 735 ff. Alexander Ross, *The Red River Settlement: Its Rise, Progress, and Present State* (London, 1856), p. 21. Hereafter, Ross, *Red River Settlement.*

8. *PAC SP,* p. 16743. Miles Macdonell to Selkirk, July 17, 1813, *PAC SP,* pp. 764 f. McLeod, Journal, 2, *PAC.* Miles Macdonell and Dr. Edwards spent the evening of September 4 at Fort Gibraltar as guests of the North-westers.

seemed strongly impressed by his expression of authority. But secretly they were all opposition. In addition to sending the métis to frighten and intimidate the settlers, they had forbidden their men to cross the river to witness the transfer of the grant; and as soon as the ceremony of delivery and seizin was over, they made detailed reports of the proceedings for the information of the partners who would meet at Fort William.[9]

The Governor's next duty was to carry out Selkirk's advice as to the location of the colony.[10]

On your arrival in Red River the first and most important point will be the choice of a situation for the settlement. For the sake of health, a dry and airy situation is essential and may be sought with most probability where the River approaches the high or outer bank. To unite every advantage this should be in a plain of tolerable extent, yet near the edge of the woods, and the plain should both be of fertile soil and of sufficient extent to allow a number of settlers to be spread out on separate lots, each enjoying the advantage of wood, water and open lands fit for immediate cultivation. The country from the mouth of the River to the Forks and for some distance farther is described as generally wooded, with only a few small and insulated plains which would not probably answer the purpose. If it is necessary to go up the River to the edge of the great plains, some time must be occupied in examining both branches so as to choose a good situation; and it would be a great loss, if the people were to remain all this time idle. It may therefore be advisable to make a halt at the first tolerable situation that you find, and set the men to work there with spades to turn up some ground for winter wheat, while you go with a small party to explore. Perhaps the best spot for this halt will be that marked in P. Fidler's survey by the name of Pelican Ripple, which he describes as the first plain in going up, and also as nearly dead water from the Lake, so that a sailing vessel might probably be able to reach it. If so this must become in time a place of consequence though the country appears to be too low to be chosen as the permanent situation of the first establishment. It is probable however that a house may be built and a few people left without danger through the winter, to guard the crop and extend the improvements there, while the main body proceed farther up the River. It will be extremely important that you should be able to remove to the ultimate situation before the setting in of winter; so that during the winter some progress may be made in clearing and on the opening of the Spring every exertion for bringing into cultivation as much land as possible. If your arrival in Red River be very late it may be a matter of necessity to remain for the winter at Pelican Ripple or in the first spot that you stop at. In that case it will be necessary to remain there till after the Spring seed time is over not to interrupt the exertions for so important an object as the *first*

9. *Ibid.*
10. Instructions to Miles Macdonell, 1811, *PAC SP*, pp. 173 ff.

crop. It will be easy to move up in course of the summer before the . . . season comes on, which ought not by any means to be passed in the low and moist country. There will, however, be considerable inconvenience in removing from a place where a considerable quantity of work has been employed, and where much crop has been sown; but if your arrival is very late in the season, it is perhaps impossible to avoid this inconvenience.

All this, however, must depend on local circumstances. . . .

Macdonell followed these instructions closely. According to the best information at his disposal, the country below the Forks was the most suitable for a permanent settlement.[11] A few days after formally taking over the country the Governor led a boat's crew down the Red River to explore. In three days he examined both banks of the stream thoroughly for a distance of several miles. He finally located what he thought to be the most eligible spot about two miles below Fort Gibraltar on the west bank of the Red at "an extensive point of land [later named Point Douglas] through which a fire had recently run and destroyed the wood, there being only burnt wood & weeds left." To this place they now brought a bull, a cow, winter wheat, and some other stores which had been brought with the party from York Factory. The men were set to work at once building a storehouse and clearing a tract of land in which to sow winter wheat. Leaving his men at work, Macdonell then returned to the Forks to complete the arrangements he had already begun to make for the maintenance of the settlers through the approaching winter.[12]

In taking over the District of Assiniboia and selecting a site for the establishment of the colony, Miles Macdonell had formally and actually completed his duties as an emigration officer; he was now officially the first Governor of the Red River Colony. As an emigration officer he had accomplished much, and that in the face of great and constant obstacles. Throughout the vicissitudes he had experienced since first coming into the employ of Selkirk, he had acted with painstaking perseverance and energy and, for the most part, with admirable self-control. A lesser man might well have been daunted by any single phase of the trials through which he had passed since going to Britain—the annoyances and hindrances propagated by the agents of the North West

11. Miles Macdonell to Selkirk, July 17, 1813, *PAC SP,* p. 765. John Macdonell (brother of Miles) had written to Miles from Bas de la Rivière House, June 27, 1812 (Miles Macdonell, Selkirk Settlement, p. 149, *PAC*): "The safest places from the incursions of these barbarians [the Sioux Indians] and the best lands lay between our post of the Forks or junction of the Red & Assinibouan Rivers and Lake Winipick. . . ." John Macdonell was an employee of the North West Company; he had been in the western fur trade eighteen years, twelve of which were spent on the Assiniboine.

12. Miles Macdonell to Selkirk, July 17, 1813, *PAC SP,* pp. 765 f.

Company, the apathy and even hostility of many of the Hudson's Bay Company officials, the perils and discomforts of the Atlantic, the deadly monotony and the insubordinations of Nelson Encampment, the seven hundred grueling miles between the sea and Red River, and at all times the heartbreaking deficiencies of so many of his followers. Throughout all this he had been sustained by the courage and stamina which had won him respect as a soldier, and by that devotion to a leader and a cause which had held him to the losing side in the Revolutionary War and had brought him afterwards as a Loyalist to Canada. The remuneration which he might have hoped ultimately to receive as leader of the expedition and Governor of Assiniboia, though fairly large, was too uncertain to have prompted him as a sole motive. That Selkirk was assured of this fact, and that he entertained a high regard for his subordinate, is evident from many of his letters, especially from the one which gives the details of Macdonell's material prospects in the Red River colonization enterprise. On June 13, 1811, Selkirk wrote to Macdonell:[13]

In the event of any accident to myself it is proper that you should be enabled to refer those who may succeed to the management of my affairs to some permanent evidence of the terms under which you have engaged your services for the management of the Colony which you are now proceeding to form in the Territories of the Hudson's Bay Company. In this view I have to state that you are to receive a grant of fifty thousand acres, to yourself and your heirs. This grant must be subject to the general conditions imposed by the Company in their grant to me, and also to any general regulations which may be adopted for the purpose of preventing one proprietor from alluring away settlers brought to the country by another; but it shall not be burdened by any particular stipulations of settlement. In the particular location of this grant, I shall have every disposition to qualify your own wishes, consistently with those general principles which must be adhered to in the distribution of land. Besides this particular grant you are to have an interest in a joint Stock Company to which I purpose to assign a large proportion of the Territory granted to me, on condition of establishing a fund for its settlement; and on the formation of this Company shares shall be reserved for you, equivalent to a subscription of five hundred pounds sterling.

You are also to receive a pecuniary salary at the rate of three hundred pounds a year, so long as you continue in the management of the Colony; which salary is at present current from the 29th, ulto. On the formation of the Company to which I have already alluded, the payment of your salary will probably devolve upon them, but I have no doubt that your management of the business entrusted to you will be such that they will be anxious

13. Miles Macdonell, Selkirk Settlement, p. 137, *PAC*.

to retain you in their service, so long as you find it convenient to remain in that remote country.

I trust that you will not quit the Colony till it is fairly established, and past the dangers of an infant settlement; but if your inclination should then lead you to resume your residence in a less remote part of the world, you may depend on my most strenuous endeavours to promote your interest and to obtain for you an advantageous establishment.

A short time later Selkirk gave Macdonell further proof of the confidence which he placed in him by providing him with written authorizations to name and to appoint his second in command, and his successor if such should prove necessary.[14]

Having accomplished as instructed all tasks preliminary to the actual foundation of the colony, the Governor proceeded with unabated diligence to care for the welfare of the settlers in the Land of Promise. On September 6, before setting out to search for a colony site, he sent most of his men to Pembina, at the junction of the Red and Pembina rivers, some sixty or seventy miles up the Red from the Forks, and the site of both a North-wester and a Hudson's Bay Company post. He took this step because of the scarcity of food. Macdonell blamed this scarcity on the agents of the Hudson's Bay Company, especially Auld, who had been instructed to arrange for food supplies.[15] But his prejudice against Auld and his desire to justify himself in the eyes of his superior to the disadvantage of the Superintendent seem to have led him to misrepresent the situation. He pretended to Selkirk that he believed Auld had never sent on the instructions regarding foodstuffs, when he actually knew that this was not true. As early as October 16, 1811, he had been told in a letter from the Superintendent that William Sinclair of Brandon House was to secure a supply of provisions for him at Red River—even to the extent of planting potatoes "near the bottom of the Red River out of the way of all Indians." The potatoes were planted in June, 1812, and "two men were left all the summer to attend them."[16] When the brigade of colonists arrived on the Red River shortly below the Forks, they came in sight of the potato "plantation." In his letter of July 17, 1813, to Selkirk, complaining about the failure of the Company's agents to provide supplies at the Forks, Macdonell stated that not a single item of food had been reserved for the colony

14. Blank Signed by Selkirk Enabling Miles Macdonell to Appoint Successor . . . June 29th, 1811, enclosed with letter from Selkirk to Miles Macdonell, June 29, 1811, Miles Macdonell, Selkirk Settlement, pp. 141, 143, PAC.

15. Miles Macdonell to Selkirk, July 17, 1813, PAC SP, pp. 764 f.

16. PAC SP, pp. 94 f. Auld to Selkirk, October, 1811, September 12, 1812; Auld to Wedderburn, October 3, 1811, PAC SP, pp. 61 f., 86, 490 f.

despite all the orders that had been given.[17] He forgot to mention the potato plantation, probably because it would not have fitted into the unfavorable picture of Auld that he was building up in Selkirk's mind.

Nevertheless there was actually an alarming shortage of food at the Forks in the fall of 1812, although Auld and his men were in no way to blame for the situation. The Company's traders were almost as badly off as were the colonists. The winter of 1811–12 was the most severe that the Northwest had experienced in more than twenty years. Both the traders and the Indians had been reduced to dire necessity, and in some parts the natives had been driven to "the most horrible & revolting means of eking out a wretched existence"—cannibalism and even "the disinterment of the Dead."[18] Although conditions had improved considerably by the close of the summer of 1812, there still existed an unprecedented scarcity. What little pemmican and wild rice the Indians and the métis had secured during the season had all been bought up by the shrewd North-westers before the first brigade from the Bay reached the Forks. It is true that the men in charge of Fort Gibraltar offered to sell to the colonists such commodities as barley, oats, and poultry. But the prices they asked were high and the amounts available were limited.

Conditions being such at the Forks, Macdonell soon realized that it would be highly inexpedient to attempt to winter his whole force there. Besides, he had information that food could be secured in almost unlimited quantities a short distance up the Red. In those years millions of bison roamed the Western plains. "Herds of these animals often darkened the horizon like a slowly moving cloud." In summer they penetrated far to the north, feeding upon the prairie grass. In winter they sought the higher levels where the snow was scanty and the dried grass could be got at easily. As a rule, however, they went no farther north in the winter than the region of the Pembina. It was to reach this locality that the majority of the settlers had set out on September 6.[19]

It was on September 9 that Macdonell, leaving at work the men who had been exploring with him below the Forks, "set off on horseback for Pembina with an escort of three men." It took him three days to make the journey. The settlers who had preceded him, under the command of John McLeod and Dr. Edwards, had reached the Pembina with the stores only a day earlier. They had traveled by boat with Heney and his party and had made the trip without mishap. On September 13 the Governor spent two or three hours on horseback reconnoitering the

17. *PAC SP*, p. 764.
18. G. McBride to Hugh McBride, September 1, 1812, *PAC SP*, pp. 454 f.
19. Miles Macdonell to Selkirk, July 17, 1813, *PAC SP*, pp. 765 f. McLeod, Journal, 2, *PAC*.

surrounding country, and finally chose a point of land on the south bank of the Pembina, where it met the Red, as a site for a fort. There on the evening of the same day his men set up their leather tents. Early on the following morning all hands began the construction of a storehouse. A Canadian was engaged to catch fish. "He made his hooks out of nails, and was tolerable successful."[20]

Across from this encampment, on the north side of the Pembina, stood the North West Company trading post. It had been abandoned for about two years; but, just a few days before the settlers arrived at Pembina, the company had reëstablished it "for the purpose of opposing the colony in the purchase of provisions."[21] Not far away the Hudson's Bay Company, too, had a trading house. The colony encampment and the two trading posts were all within a radius of half a mile. Finally, in the immediate vicinity were considerable numbers of Indians, métis, and free Canadians.[22] These people, faithful to the tradition of mutual aid which had grown up with European ventures into the wilderness, were disposed at first to be friendly toward the settlers, for their lives and ways had not yet been seriously shaken by the moves and countermoves of the contest between Selkirk and the North-westers.

By the time the colonists had reached the Pembina, the supplies brought from Hudson Bay and those they had purchased from the North-westers at Fort Gibraltar were almost exhausted. It was indeed fortunate that the native population was inclined to be friendly, else the emigrants would now have found their condition terribly precarious. During the fall months, however, Macdonell's men did not want for food, as the natives and "freemen" generously brought in large quantities of buffalo meat, wild berries, and "prairie turnips." In fact, so abundant were these supplies that a boatload of buffalo meat and prairie turnips was sent down late in September to the party working below the Forks.[23]

Shortly before the end of September the Pembina storehouse was completed, a substantial structure well calculated to meet the needs of a settlement of more than a hundred people, and the men were busily engaged in the building of living quarters. "The work fairly agoing," on October 1 Macdonell went off to the Forks, taking along with him two horses and a harrow. The horses had been purchased from the

20. *Ibid.*

21. *Papers Relating to the Red River Settlement: 1815–1819,* p. 153 (Great Britain, Parliamentary Papers, House of Commons, No. 584). Hereafter, *Papers Relating to Settlement.*

22. Miles Macdonell to Selkirk, July 17, 1813, *PAC SP,* p. 774; *Narrative of Occurrences,* pp. 19 f.

23. Miles Macdonell to Selkirk, July 17, 1813, *PAC SP,* p. 766.

métis at a rather high price, while the harrow had been borrowed from the local post of the Hudson's Bay Company.[24]

The men at the Forks had not worked particularly well during the absence of the Governor. A storehouse had been built, but it was poorly constructed and quite inadequate for practical purposes; a quantity of hay had been cut, but had not been stacked; a tract of land had been cleared for the winter wheat, but it was insufficient. After Macdonell's return, however, the men began to work harder and with better results. By October 7 five acres of land back from the western bank of the river had been cleared and sown with wheat. Unfortunately the wheat had to be covered by the hoe, as the harrow which the Governor had carried down from Pembina had no teeth, and there was no blacksmith at the Forks who could supply the deficiency.[25]

After the wheat was in, all the men were set to work building houses. A Canadian who had a general acquaintance with the Indians in the vicinity was hired "to trade meat from them & also Skins when they should offer them"; he was also expected to fish and to assist in the building operations. An Indian was engaged to hunt, to provide fresh meat. A supply of pemmican was bought from the Indians and put in the storehouse for the support of a second contingent of colonists which was daily expected to arrive from the Bay. Finally, after the completion of all the necessary arrangements for the welfare of the men he was leaving at the Forks, and for the reception of the incoming settlers, Macdonell returned to Pembina on October 18. Only five men were left to winter at the Forks; the rest went up to Pembina.[26]

On arriving at the upper encampment after his two weeks' absence at the Forks, the Governor found that his people "had wrought well." The living quarters for the winter, however, were not yet ready for occupation. This slowness in building construction was due largely to the lack of expert axe men. At this time there were at Pembina only two good axe men. When, shortly afterwards, the second contingent of emigrants arrived, the number was increased to five; and then the work of erecting dwellings was pushed with such speed that the buildings which were to house the settlers and the laborers were ready by November 21. Quarters for the Governor and the officers were not finished until December 27. "As soon as the place took some form & a decent Flag Staff was erected in it, it was called Fort Daer."[27]

Before the fort was completed, winter was well upon the country. In October the nights had become cold and even frosty; in November severe northern winds and flurries of snow interfered with the labors of

24. *Ibid.*   25. *Ibid.*
26. *Ibid.*, pp. 767 f.   27. *Ibid.*, pp. 768 f.

the workmen; by the middle of December the Red River plains were covered with deep snow.[28] But considering the lateness of the arrival of Macdonell and his party in the country, the meager preparations which had been made to receive them, the character of the emigrants themselves, and the necessity of dividing the brigade and preparing two winter camps, one is bound to concede that the Governor had made the best of a bad job.

28. Extract of a Letter from a Proprietor of the North West Company, August, 1813, *Q134*, Pt. II, pp. 348 ff.

CHAPTER VIII

MORE SETTLERS

SINCE the departure of the first group of Red River colonists from Stornoway, Selkirk had been busily engaged in raising and sending out the second contingent, and in maturing plans for schools, extensive agriculture, and the reign of law and order under the jurisdiction granted in the Company's charter.[1] The task of recruiting emigrants had been rendered exceedingly difficult by the continued activities of the North-westers in Britain. Pledged to "unequivocal and decisive" opposition to the Red River Settlement, by all the means in their power,[2] the British agents of the Canadian company were leaving no stone unturned in their endeavors to ruin the project. During the summer and fall of 1811 and the winter and spring of 1812 a number of meetings of the most prominent agents took place in London and at various centers in western Scotland, and plans were carefully laid with a view to prejudicing everyone who might be of importance to Selkirk's venture, especially those high in government circles, and such people in Ireland and Scotland as were likely to be influenced by emigration agents and advertisements.

In this business the efforts of Sir Alexander Mackenzie, Simon McGillivray, and Edward Ellice were the most effective. Ellice, being a member of Parliament, accomplished much in the political sphere; Mackenzie, widely known for his explorations and for his extensive knowledge of the Northwest, dissuaded many prominent men of means from becoming stockholders in the Red River Company; and McGillivray, by his deceptive letters, published and copied in several of the leading Scottish newspapers, according to his own words "saved many cottars and evicted tenants in western Scotland from becoming the dupes of 'the Chief of Land-jobbing Speculators.' "[3] If the work of each of the three

1. See especially Selkirk to Miles Macdonell, December 23, 1811, June 20, 1812; Selkirk to Auld, June 18, 1812; B. H. Everard to —, April 20, 1812, *PAC SP,* pp. 126 ff., 304 f., 384 ff., 712 ff.

2. Miles Macdonell to Auld, December 25, 1811, Miles Macdonell, Selkirk Settlement, p. 283, *PAC.*

3. Selkirk to Miles Macdonell, March 24, June 20, 1812; Selkirk to the Governor, Deputy Governor and Committee of the Hudson's Bay Company, February 14, 1815, *PAC SP,* pp. 292, 712, 1918 f. Selkirk to Alexander McDonald, March 10, 1812, *PAC SP,* Vol. 79, pp. 53 ff. Alexander MacDonald to Archibald McDonald, April 3, May 14, 1812, *PAC SP,* pp. 288, 291. Simon McGillivray to the Wintering Partners of the North West Company, April 9, 1812, *Q150,* Pt. I, pp. 180 ff. Selkirk wrote the name Alexander "McDonald."

could be accurately appraised, it would probably be found that Ellice's was in the long run the most fruitful because, among people connected with the government, he succeeded in gradually building up a prejudice against Selkirk which was to have in future years the most deadly results. But in the early stages of the struggle the work of McGillivray and Mackenzie was more evidently effective.

When the North-westers first pledged themselves to resist the colonization of Assiniboia, Selkirk considered their carpings mere idle menaces; he did not think that they would take any definite action or resort to devious ways. Even after the first contingent had sailed, he felt sure that his opponents would realize that they could not hope to defeat him and would gradually come to acquiesce in his plans.[4] When, however, he began to recruit for the second contingent, he came to a full understanding of the deadly seriousness of the North-westers' intentions, and the almost irreparable harm which had been done his cause in some parts of Scotland. "In the Highlands," he wrote to Miles Macdonell in March, 1812, "we have met with so much obstruction, that I doubt whether it will be effectually overcome."[5] Again in June of the same year he wrote to the Governor:

Our adversaries have been very busy in the Highlands & have succeeded for the present in narrowing our supply of men from that quarter. The 'Hr' ["Highlander"] continued his lucubrations in the Inverness Journal with more & more personality: & in the course of the Winter Sir Alexr & his colleagues got hold of Mff Blair whom they induced to put his name to an affidavit grossly misrepresenting the transactions of Stornoway. . . . These calumnies . . . made a great impression, & deterred many from engaging in the Service.[6]

While the North-westers were thus carrying out in Britain their policy of opposition to the colonization of Assiniboia, other members of the company in Canada and the Northwest were also formulating plans for the same purpose. As early as May 25, 1811, when Selkirk's settlement schemes were before the Hudson's Bay Company, Simon McGillivray wrote to his brother William,[7] in Montreal, gave him every detail of the Earl's designs, and described in a rather optimistic vein the intrigues and counteractivities of the London agents. Selkirk was characterized as a designing and dangerous man of whose real nature Mackenzie had not been sufficiently aware. This, however, was not really

4. Selkirk to the Governor, Deputy Governor and Committee of the Hudson's Bay Company, February 14, 1815, *PAC SP*, pp. 1918 f.

5. *PAC SP*, p. 292.

6. Selkirk to Miles Macdonell, June 20, 1812, *PAC SP*, p. 712. "Mff." was Moncrieff Blair.

7. *Q153*, Pt. III, pp. 621 ff.

true. For at least a year and a half Mackenzie had been warning his fur-trade partners of the "dangerous" intentions of the Scottish nobleman. It was not Sir Alexander Mackenzie, but his friends in the North West Company, who had underestimated the capacity of Lord Selkirk.

On June 1, 1811, McGillivray addressed a long communication to McTavish, McGillivray and Company of Montreal,[8] describing the success of Lord Selkirk's transactions with the Hudson's Bay Company and the particulars of the Red River project, and urging that the Montreal traders and winterers prepare strenuously to oppose both the English traders and the establishment of settlers. McGillivray wrote:

I have had this morning a meeting with Sir Alexander McKenzie [sic] and Mr. Ellice, and I am authorized to state to you and to their connexions, as our unanimous opinion, that you should immediately on receipt of this, dispatch an Express to the Interior with notice to prepare your people for a year of Trial. If possible your posts should be strengthened with men and extra supplies of goods, and measures should be taken for a vigorous opposition. . . . We forbear to suggest the particular details of this opposition, as you will be better able to judge of them than we are, but the opposition ought to be general and followed up at almost any expence. . . . The object in view is well worth making sacrifice for. . . . The Hudson's Bay Company . . . by their grant to Lord Selkirk . . . are striking at the very root of . . . [your] Fur Trade. In short, no means should be left untried to thwart Selkirk's schemes.

Simon McGillivray was not content to let the Montreal associates alone instruct the wintering partners of their company. On April 9, 1812, as an old friend with "a *family claim* to the feelings and opinions of a North-wester," he addressed communications[9] to them that were not merely formal. With much subtlety he expressed his sentiments, as he chose to call them, on several matters of interest to them, which had been much in discussion in prominent circles during the past season. The details of the purchase of Assiniboia were referred to in a general way; but the activities of the North-westers in Britain were set forth in vivid detail; and the winterers were urged to do their share in helping to defeat the Earl. In McGillivray's words:

The Committee of the Hudson's Bay Company is at present a mere machine in the hands of Lord Selkirk, who appears to be so much wedded to his Schemes of Colonization in the Interior of North America, that it will require some time, & I fear cause much expence to us, as well as to himself, before he is driven to abandon the project, & yet *he must be driven to abandon it,* for his success would strike at the very existence of our trade.

8. *Ibid.*, pp. 611 ff. 9. *Q150*, Pt. I, pp. 180 ff.

Thus it came about that by the summer of 1812 every wintering partner of the North West Company—even in the distant Athabasca region—had been fully informed of what had been going on in Britain. Before the first settlers had left Hudson Bay, "a North-wester who had wintered at Lesser Slave Lake, 2,500 miles by canoe in the interior," talked familiarly with Macdonell of the details of the troubles at Stornoway in 1811, "Selkirk's reputation among the North-westers—'his Lordship with all his visionary projects passes among us for a parsimonious *scrub*'—the scanty success of Selkirk's previous colonizing enterprises in Upper Canada, and the probabilities of failure at Red River."[10] All this displays not only the remarkable efficiency of the North West Company's organization, but also the fact that the leaders of that concern were at last aware of the seriousness of the danger that threatened them. They saw the cogency of Sir Alexander Mackenzie's prediction of a few years earlier. The Hudson's Bay Company was now beginning to feel the stimulus of Selkirk's enthusiasm. Signs of this renascence were quite evident in London. Easy-going traders in America could not be transformed so quickly; but exact and detailed instructions were being sent to the men at the Bay, and there was every reason to expect that they would produce, in part at least, their intended effect.[11]

The first direct move instigated by Selkirk against the North West Company fur trade was an expedition to the upper Churchill.[12] Unfortunately Selkirk was as yet unaware of the extent to which the Northwesters had grown in strength since his visit to Canada in 1804; and also, that they were not as gentle in their methods in the fur country as they were at the meetings of the Beaver Club in Montreal. The course upon which he was now embarking was to bring quick enlightenment. His purpose was merely to enforce the claim made by the Hudson's Bay Company, in virtue of its charter, that all the land drained by the waters flowing into Hudson Bay was under its jurisdiction. The Red River Colony project, though not necessarily a part of this plan, was certainly not in conflict with it. The upper Churchill expedition, however, was purely a Company move. It was put under the control of

10. John Macdonell to Miles Macdonell, June 27, August 6, 1812, Miles Macdonell, Selkirk Settlement, pp. 149, 157, *PAC*. Martin, *Selkirk*, p. 45.

11. Hudson's Bay Company Instructions to Auld, June 18, 1812, Selkirk Papers, pp. 382 ff. Hereafter, Auld, Instructions, *PAC SP*. Selkirk to Hillier, June 18, 1812, *Q134*, Pt. II, pp. 366 ff. Inglis, Fraser & Co. to Goulburn, May 29, 1815, *Q134*, Pt. II, pp. 358 f.

12. Originally it was intended that Hillier should "form a new Settlement at East Winipick to keep the Canadians from Trading on the H.B. Co. Territories." See John McLeod to —, June 29, 1812, *PAC SP*, pp. 153 f. Selkirk to Hillier, June 18, 1812, *Q134*, Pt. II, p. 366.

William Hillier, who was to act principally in the capacity of magistrate. According to the Hudson's Bay Company instructions sent to the officials at the Bay, the Hillier expedition was to be considered as of peculiar importance, and its success was to be estimated

> by a very different standard, than a bare comparison of the expence incurred with the value of the returns received. If in this one instance the violence of the Cans. [Canadians] . . . [was] effectually repressed, they . . . [would then] learn to respect the H.B. Co. & alter their tone throughout the whole of their establishments. On the other hand, if they should succeed in frustrating the object of the expedition . . . [the Bay traders] could expect a double portion of violence whenever . . . [they met with them]. The object of primary importance . . . [was] therefore to gain a solid footing & shew . . . their adversaries what . . . [they could] do, much more than to carry on the trade of the season in an economical & profitable manner.[13]

Hillier was definitely instructed to treat the Canadians as trespassers and poachers on private property. In repelling the violent aggressions of the North-westers, he was never to "exceed the bounds of moderation," or allow any provocation to lead him into "an imitation of their lawless proceedings." At all times, however, he was to assert the unimpeachable rights of private property, and to enforce them whenever he had the physical means. If the Canadians should make a forcible resistance, they would be acting illegally and could be held responsible for the consequence of their actions. "*You are safe,*" Hillier was advised, "*so long as you take only the reasonable and necessary means* of enforcing that which is your right."[14]

This change of policy, when it became known, produced considerable surprise and even astonishment among the more dominant partners of the North West Company.[15] Hillier's upper Churchill instructions were regarded as audacious. Even the old servants of the Hudson's Bay Company under the leadership of Auld and Cook were amazed at the idea of taking aggressive steps against their rivals without the "aid of the Legislature to support the Company's property." The possibility of securing such aid, however, was precluded by the prejudice then obtaining in Great Britain against the Company's monopoly; and Selkirk explained this rather bluntly to the Bay traders. "It is altogether visionary," he wrote to Auld, "to look for the aid of the Legislature to support the Company's property & I am surprised that after all the

13. Auld, Instructions, *PAC SP,* pp. 384 f. Selkirk to Hillier, June 18, 1812, *Q134,* Pt. II, pp. 366 ff.
    14. *Ibid.*
    15. Inglis, Ellice, McTavish, Fraser & Co. to Goulburn, May 29, 1815, *Q134,* Pt. II, pp. 356 ff.

explanation which was given you can still harp on that idea."[16] As a matter of fact, neither company was desirous of an appeal to the courts to decide upon the legality of its position in the Northwest. Each feared to lose what it already held in fact or by implication, and preferred to settle the question *in loco*. "I have serious thoughts," wrote Selkirk to the officials at the Bay, "of paying you a visit next year, at the head of such a body of men, as will overawe any attempt to resist the lawful authority of the Company. For that purpose I must bring out not less than 4 or 500 men, with whom it will be my object to proceed . . . directly to the Settlement."[17] But the Earl was careful, meanwhile, to avoid an overdisplay of force. Macdonell was cautioned repeatedly not to give the Settlement too military a character. What Selkirk was aiming at was the exercise of a jurisdiction dependent directly upon the British courts and entirely independent of Canadian interference.[18]

While he was planning thus to curb the future activities of the North West Company, Selkirk, through the work of his agents in the spring and early summer of 1812, had succeeded in persuading a second company of emigrants to agree to set out for Red River. The party that had gone out in 1811 was expected to prepare as thoroughly as possible for the coming of the second group. Thus in the following year recruiting efforts were directed especially toward securing a number of families who would settle permanently as units on farms. Selkirk saw clearly that if the colony was to be a success a large number of families with permanent interests in the land must be established in it at the earliest possible date. The brigade recruited in 1811 had contained only indentured servants, permanent settlers and their families not being allowed to enlist, because Selkirk realized that the hardships suffered by the first group going out might easily be too great for women and children, and for men with family cares. Now that the trail had been broken, however, and the initial difficulties overcome in part, it seemed feasible to send out permanent settlers. Of course, the indentured servant, too, could take up land if, when his contract had expired, he should wish to remain in the country as a settler. But such people could not be depended upon to found a permanent colony.[19]

Most of the emigrants selected for the second contingent were secured in western Scotland and western Ireland. The principal recruiting

16. Auld, Instructions, *PAC SP*, p. 401.   17. *Ibid.*
18. Instructions to Miles Macdonell, 1811; Selkirk to Miles Macdonell, June 13, 14, 1813, April 12, 1814; Selkirk to Colvile, June 5, 1813, *PAC SP*, pp. 169, 646, 670 ff., 682, 1044.
19. Selkirk to Alexander McDonald, January 9, 1812, *PAC SP*, Vol. 79, pp. 48 f. Selkirk to Miles Macdonell, June 20, 1812; Alexander MacDonald to Archibald McDonald, January 26, 1812; B. H. Everard to —, April 20, 1812, *PAC SP*, pp. 285, 304 f., 712 f.

agents this year were Alexander MacDonald, Charles McLean, a Mr. Geddes, Archibald McDonald, and Owen Keveny. Geddes, Alexander MacDonald, and Archibald McDonald worked in the northern and northwestern counties of Scotland, Geddes confining his activities to Sutherland and Caithness, the others to Ross and Inverness; Charles McLean recruited mostly in Argyll and on the Isles of Tiree and Mull; Owen Keveny, a hotheaded Irishman, spent all his time in western Ireland, mainly in the county of Sligo.[20]

In the early summer of 1812 Selkirk himself entered the recruiting field. For several weeks he was in the Highlands, attempting to counteract the opposition of the North-westers. In June he was in the city of Sligo, "exercising a personal supervision over the men chosen for the settlement and drawing up instructions for those who had already gone out." Sligo had been chosen early in the season as the place of final rendezvous for the contingent.[21]

Toward the middle of June the agents and their recruits began to reach Sligo; and by June 22 all those who were expected had arrived. The men who had been secured in Sutherland and Caithness crossed over to Stromness and were picked up there by the Hudson's Bay Company ships. All the people recruited in western Scotland—the majority were from Argyll—gathered at Tobermory, and were transported from there to Sligo in a specially chartered sloop.[22]

Some time in June Keveny was appointed commander of the expedition. His experience as a leader of men had not been considerable. For the four preceding years he had worked in a countinghouse. But he had come to Selkirk with the best of recommendations; there were "ample proofs of his steadiness, activity & integrity." So pleased with him was the Earl that on June 20, 1812, he recommended him to Miles Macdonell as a suitable second-in-command in Assiniboia.[23] Selkirk was not a good judge of men.

20. A List of Servants, Settlers, engaged in the Island of Tyre for the Honble H.B. Co. & the Right Honble the Earl of Selkirk, 1812; A List of Settlers & Servants engaged in Ross, Brolas, Greenburn &c in the Island of Mull for the service of the Honble H.B. Coy & the Right Honble the Earl of Selkirk; 1812, O. Kevenys Return of men classed; Alexander MacDonald to Archibald McDonald, January 26, 1812; Selkirk to Miles Macdonell, June 20, 1812, *PAC SP*, pp. 285, 295 f., 558 f., 560 ff., 712 ff. Selkirk to Alexander McDonald, January 9, May 5, 9, July 9, August 4, 1812, *PAC SP*, Vol. 79, pp. 14 f., 48 f., 60 f., 64 f.

21. Alexander MacDonald to Archibald McDonald, May 14, 1812, *PAC SP*, p. 289. Selkirk to Alexander McDonald, May 5, July 9, 1812, *PAC SP*, Vol. 79, pp. 60 f., 64. Martin, *Selkirk*, pp. 50 f.

22. Selkirk to Alexander McDonald, May 5, July 9, 1812, *PAC SP*, Vol. 79, pp. 60 f., 64. Alexander MacDonald to Archibald McDonald, May 14, 1812; Selkirk to Miles Macdonell, June 20, 1812, *PAC SP*, pp. 289 f., 712 ff.

23. Selkirk to Miles Macdonell, June 20, 1812, *PAC SP*, pp. 713 f.

The exact number of people who rendezvoused at Sligo is not known. According to Keveny's "return" to Lord Selkirk, made out after the expedition had reached York Factory, there were seventy-one: some six families, four or five girls of marriageable age, a large number of young and unmarried men, eleven children less than eight years old, and four between eight and fifteen.[24]

The Hudson's Bay Company ships put into Sligo on June 16, and for the next six days the town was all a-bustle with the final preparations for sailing. The ship which was to carry the Red River settlers and servants was the *Robert Taylor*. Compared with the *Edward and Ann*, and even the *Eddystone*, she was rather prepossessing. At least she was seaworthy and properly manned.[25] The *Robert Taylor* and another ship, the *King George*, carried large consignments of goods for the Settlement. At a considerable expense Selkirk had purchased for the colony substantial quantities of wheat and oats, twenty-one Spanish merino sheep, and a few agricultural implements. Unfortunately even yet far too little effort was being made to equip the settlers properly with farm implements. Most of the grain and supplies were loaded on the *Robert Taylor*. The *King George* carried half the sheep, some supplies, and some seed grain. The sheep on board the *Robert Taylor* were put under the care of Alexander McLean, formerly a tacksman, i.e., lessee, from Kingerar, recruited for Red River by Charles McLean. Some one had recommended him to Selkirk as a good farmer of a "fair & honourable character." On the other hand, Selkirk knew that in the conduct of his own affairs he had "not shewn much steadiness," and that he had a reputation for being somewhat "wild." Nevertheless, in June, 1812, Selkirk not only gave him the eleven sheep put on the *Robert Taylor*, but also promised him a township of 10,000 acres in Assiniboia, and the maintenance of his family and two servants for the first year after his arrival at Red River.[26] Here again the Earl showed poor judgment. The McLeans proved to be a source of much trouble and worry in the New World.

By June 24 all was in readiness for the departure of the second Red River contingent. At noon of that day Selkirk dined with the officers on board the *Robert Taylor*, remained on the ship until Sligo Bay was cleared, and then watched the ships put to sea.[27]

24. 1812, O. Kevenys Return of men classed, *PAC SP,* pp. 560 f. Selkirk to Alexander McDonald, May 5, July 9, 1812, *PAC SP,* Vol. 79, pp. 60 f., 64.

25. Selkirk to Miles Macdonell, June 20, 1812, *PAC SP,* pp. 712 f.

26. *Ibid.,* pp. 715 ff. Selkirk to Auld, June 18, 1812, *PAC SP,* pp. 394 f.

27. Selkirk to Alexander McDonald, July 9, 1812, *PAC SP,* Vol. 79, p. 64. Thomas M'Keevor, *A Voyage to Hudson's Bay, During the Summer of 1812* (London, 1819), p. 1.

Although the departure was earlier than that of the preceding year, the voyage was of equal length. Nor was it a happy one. At first all seemed to go well enough, but before long "a fierce spirit of discontent seemed to spread from one bosom to another."[28] The ringleader in the trouble was Andrew Langston, an Irishman picked up by Selkirk in the city of Sligo. The Earl had been much impressed by him and had recommended him very favorably to Keveny. The latter afterwards was of the opinion that had Langston not been aboard the *Robert Taylor*, there would have been no trouble. As it turned out, several men had to be returned for misconduct. The principal charge cited against the Irishman was that he made the people on board the *Robert Taylor* discontented by telling them that they were not well treated; that they were not used according to Selkirk's instructions; "that they all should have grog; that they were treated unlike men and with Tyranny, and, last and worst of all in fomenting Jealousy between the Scotchmen & Irishmen by representing to the latter that the former were used more kindly and better in every respect."[29]

Langston's charge that the settlers and servants on the *Robert Taylor* "were treated unlike men and with Tyranny" probably contained some truth. Keveny was a hard taskmaster and his measures of discipline were severe. It was reported

and not contradicted, that for the most trivial offence he would order the offending party to be put in irons; in other cases the unfortunate culprit was made to run between two lines of men drawn up fronting each other, and each man prepared with a cudgel to commence the strange, and to one party concerned, unpleasant operation of belabouring the object of their chief's resentment as soon as he entered between their ranks.

Langston ran the gantlet in this fashion several times during the voyage to Hudson Bay.[30]

About two weeks out from Sligo a number of passengers conspired with several members of the crew to mutiny. Chief among the conspirators were Langston, Randle McDonell, and Humphrey George, all three

28. Gunn and Tuttle, *Manitoba*, p. 75.
29. Keveny to Selkirk, September 8, 1812; Auld to Selkirk, September 12, 1812; Selkirk to Keveny, June 15, 1813, *PAC SP*, pp. 462 f., 484, 698 ff.
30. Selkirk to Alexander McDonald, January 6, 1813, *PAC SP,* Vol. 79, p. 66. "My Irish Supercargo, who had charge of the ship from Sligo, appears to have been rather rough in proceedings & no observer of the *suaviter in modo;* but he maintained very strict discipline, & kept his Paddies to their tackle very effectually, tho' at the expense of much grumbling, which was most improperly countenanced by the second in command." See also Selkirk to Keveny, June 5, 1813; Miles Macdonell to Selkirk, July 17, August 31, 1813; Auld to —, September 26, 1813, *PAC SP,* pp. 698 ff., 772, 818, 840. Gunn and Tuttle, *Manitoba,* p. 74.

originally hailing from the same town in Ireland. Their plan was to overpower their officers, "seize the ship and take her to some country at War with Great Britain and sell ship and cargo to the best advantage and divide the proceeds among the captors." Fortunately the mutineers were betrayed before they were ready to act, and the plot was nipped in the bud. When the captain and Keveny learned what was afoot, armed men were placed as guards at the hatches, and "the quarter guns were loaded with grape shot and pointed forward." When the conspirators attempted to come on deck they were forced back into the hold and quickly subdued. Thus ended the most serious disturbance of the journey. The guilty were punished chiefly by being put in irons and by being made to run the gantlet. The leaders suffered most.[31]

After the attempt at mutiny the voyage was quiet enough. In July the Hudson Straits were reached. The speed of the *Robert Taylor* was hampered greatly by ice floes and the other ships caught up with her. The Bay was entered on August 21. Then came "three days of almost incessant squalls, sleet, rain, and a most boisterous sea." On August 24 a terrible storm arose. For almost twenty-four hours there seemed every likelihood that the ship would go down with all on board. In the midst of the terror and confusion one of the women, Mrs. McLean, was seized with labor pains, and while the storm was still raging, gave birth to a daughter. A day later, the storm having abated, a schooner from York Factory came out to meet the ships and brought badly needed fresh provisions. The *Robert Taylor* dropped anchor about five leagues from the Factory.[32] The second Red River contingent had reached the New World.

Within the next two days the passengers were ferried ashore, and by September 1 all the cargo had been unloaded. Accommodations at York Factory being quite inadequate for so many people, tents were pitched, on Auld's advice, near the shore on the original site of York Factory. Every precaution was taken to prevent intercourse between the newcomers and the old hands. The experiences of the preceding year provided more than sufficient argument in favor of such a course. Only the McLean family, and Dr. M'Keevor, who had accompanied the expedition, were given quarters in the Governor's house.[33]

The brigade was detained at the Bay longer than had been intended. There were several reasons for this: "the difficulty of procuring a suffi-

31. Keveny to Selkirk, September 8, 1812; Auld to Selkirk, September 12, 1812, *PAC SP*, pp. 462 ff., 484. Gunn and Tuttle, *Manitoba*, p. 75.

32. Keveny to Selkirk, September 8, 1812, *PAC SP*, p. 460. M'Keevor, *Voyage to Hudson's Bay*, pp. 2 ff., 46 f.

33. Keveny to Selkirk, September 8, 1812, *PAC SP*, pp. 464 ff. M'Keevor, *Voyage to Hudson's Bay*, pp. 47 f.

cient number of old hands to take the boats inland"—many of the old hands "being found difficult to engage anew, their contracts being expired"; an insufficiency of boats, as only six were ready; and a lack of coöperation on the part of the Company's officials. Cook and Auld were "all indifference." Auld kept referring to the way he was sacrificing the fur-trade interests to those of the colonial enterprise. But his vaunted sacrifices were mostly imaginary; he was actually doing little for the expedition. By September 6, however, enough men had been engaged and the required number of boats and canoes secured; and during the next three days final preparations for departure were completed.[34]

Before leaving the Bay, Keveny made arrangements with Auld to have four of his men sent home. These were Andrew Langston, Randle McDonell, Humphrey George, and John Douglas. Three of them had taken leading parts in the abortive mutiny on board ship. Douglas had created trouble after reaching the Bay shore. His offense was not very serious, but Keveny represented him to Selkirk as most culpable.[35] In this incident, as in several others, the commandant showed little tact or good sense. A small measure of conciliation would have worked wonders with most of the emigrants. Quite likely there would have been no serious disturbances either during the voyage or at the Bay had Keveny been less harsh and overbearing. Selkirk had made a serious mistake in putting such a man in command of the expedition.[36]

On September 7, 8, and 9 the party set out for Assiniboia in eleven boats and three canoes. The division into three groups was made to facilitate progress. The first section was under the command of George Holmes, "an ingenious young gentleman." Kenneth McRae, whom Macdonell had sent down from Red River to meet Keveny, was in charge of the second division. The third was under the guidance of Keveny himself. The McLean family, with their little flock of sheep, traveled with Keveny. McLean and Auld had engaged in considerable argument over the animals. The settler insisted on taking them with him to Red River. Auld was opposed to this because of the large number of men needed to handle them. Finally the Superintendent gave in and assigned six men to the task. Eight more were needed for the McLeans and their baggage. No wonder that Auld became short-tempered.[37]

34. Keveny to Selkirk, September 8, 1812; Auld to Selkirk, September 12, 1812, *PAC SP,* pp. 461, 468, 484 ff.

35. *Ibid.,* pp. 462 ff., 484 f. Douglas to Keveny, January 30, 1813, *PAC SP,* p. 565.

36. Selkirk to Keveny, June 15, 1813; Miles Macdonell to Selkirk, August 31, 1813; Auld to —, September 26, 1813; Keveny to Selkirk, September 8, 1812, *PAC SP,* pp. 464 ff., 698 ff., 818, 840. Selkirk to Alexander McDonald, January 6, 1813, *PAC SP,* Vol. 79, p. 66.

37. Keveny to Selkirk, September 8, 1812; Auld to Selkirk, September 12, 1812; Miles Macdonell to Selkirk, July 17, 1813, *PAC SP,* pp. 468, 485, 490, 767 f.

The trip inland, though long and strenuous, was made without serious mishap, and in good time. At Norway House Keveny met Hillier; and here the Company's servants left the expedition. The settlers reached the Forks late in October.[38]

Macdonell had left orders with the men at the Forks that the second contingent on its arrival was to proceed immediately to Pembina.[39] The journey was made under the guidance of a band of Salteaux Indians and bois-brûlés, who on this as on other occasions showed themselves most friendly, albeit somewhat given to practical jokes. Alexander Ross, the pioneer historian of Red River, gives a picturesque description of the making of the contract between Keveny and the Indians, and the subsequent trip from the Forks to Pembina. He wrote:

The settlement of this contract between parties ignorant of each other's language furnished a scene as curious as it was interesting; the language employed on the one side being Gaelic and broken English, on the other, an Indian jargon and mongrel French, with a mixture of signs and gestures, wry faces, and grim countenances. The bargain proved to be a hard one for the emigrants. The Indians agreed to carry their children and others not able to walk, but all the rest, both men and women, had to trudge on foot; while all their little superfluities were parted with by way of recompense to their guides. One man, for example, had to give [up] his gun, an old family piece, that had been carried by his father at the battle of Culloden, which, under any other circumstances, no money would have purchased. One of the women also parted with her marriage ring, the sight of which on her finger was a temptation to the Indians. . . . The journey to Pembina exhibited a strange perversion of things: the savage, in aristocratic independence, was completely equipped and mounted on a fine horse, while the child of civilization, degraded and humbled, was compelled to walk after him on foot. No sooner had the gipsy train got under way, than the lords of freedom scampered on ahead, and were soon out of sight with the children, leaving the bewildered mothers in a state of anxious foreboding, running and crying after them for their babes. This facetious trick, as their guides doubtless thought it, was often played them.[40]

Despite all pranks, the Indians and bois-brûlés carried out their promises faithfully and, indeed, with a large measure of thoughtfulness. Throughout the trip they showed themselves to be really mild, generous, and trustworthy. Many of them had been among the armed and terrifying band which had greeted Macdonell's men so threateningly on their arrival at the Forks from the Bay. In making that hostile gesture they had acted under the influence of the North-westers. But in guiding

38. *Ibid.*   39. *Ibid.*
40. Ross, *Red River Settlement*, pp. 21 f.

Keveny and his followers they were free and acting for themselves, all of which plainly indicates "that when not influenced or roused by bad counsel, or urged on to mischief by designing men, they were naturally humble, benevolent, kind, and sociable."[41]

It was on October 27, six weeks after the arrival of the first Red River settlers, that the second group of emigrants, tired, sunburned, and with blistered feet, trudged into Macdonell's camp on the Pembina. Here Keveny surrendered his authority to the Governor of Assiniboia.[42] The newcomers mingled with the first arrivals, with whom they were to spend their first winter in the New World, enjoyed for a short time a long-awaited rest, and then set about helping to prepare the still un-finished encampment for the approaching winter. Selkirk's enterprise had now advanced another difficult step toward success.

41. *Ibid.,* pp. 22 f.
42. Miles Macdonell to Selkirk, July 17, 1813, *PAC SP,* pp. 767 f.

CHAPTER IX

WINTER AT PEMBINA

THE winter of 1812–13 was anything but pleasant for the Red River settlers. Although their lot had been hard enough in the Old World, it was far worse now. Those who had wintered at Nelson Encampment had expected to find, when they reached Red River, that their troubles and hardships were over. All had looked forward to discovering in Assiniboia a Land of Promise. All, however, were destined to disappointment.

As the plains about Fort Daer had been swept by fires early in the autumn, the buffalo during the late fall and winter failed to come down the Pembina as far as usual. Provisions therefore became scarce as the year drew to a close. The emigrants were too inexperienced to hunt buffalo with success, so the bois-brûlés and the Indians did the hunting, and sold the meat to the newcomers at a price. The price they charged, however, was high; and they could not be depended upon for a steady supply. Often, instead of selling their supplies to the settlers as promised, they disposed of them entirely to the North-westers. Nor was the total quantity of food available on the whole sufficiently large. The natives in the vicinity of Fort Daer "never made pounds to catch buffaloe," and hence secured few during the winter. The Crees, Assiniboines, and other tribes to the west, who hunted in that way with some success, were too far away to provide the colonists with regular supplies.[1]

At first the settlers used dogs and horses to drag their buffalo meat from the hunting grounds to the fort. But they had only a few of these animals, and early in the winter it became necessary for the men to harness themselves to the sleds in teams of two or three and drag part of their provisions themselves. This work was both difficult and dangerous. The Old World men were not skilled in the use of snowshoes and sleds. At times they suffered severely from frostbite. More than once parties of them were lost in blinding prairie blizzards, and were forced to burrow in the snow to keep from freezing, and to eat their dogs or beg from the North-westers to avoid starvation. Frequently by the time they had returned to the fort they had consumed most of the supplies for which they had set out.[2]

1. Miles Macdonell to Selkirk, July 17, 1813, *PAC SP*, pp. 769 f.
2. *Ibid.*, pp. 770 f. Extract of a Letter from a Proprietor of the North West Company, dated Red River, August, 1813, *Q134*, Pt. II, pp. 347 ff. Edwards to Selkirk, n.d.; Selkirk to —, n.d., *PAC SP*, pp. 513, 518.

Many and conflicting stories have been told of the events of this first winter. Miles Macdonell's letters to Selkirk form what may be called the official version of what happened. But though they touch in a general way upon the miseries and hardships suffered, they by no means tell the whole truth. The Governor always tended to minimize events which he feared might cast doubts upon his own competence. The stories told by Dr. Edwards, Kenneth McRae, William Auld, and the North-westers, on the other hand, can be accepted only with reservations. The doctor was no admirer of Macdonell; they had quarreled on several occasions. His letters to Selkirk are often little more than ridiculous tirades against the Governor. Some of his charges were based on facts but were so exaggerated as to be quite misleading; others appear to have had no basis in reality. His whole course in the matter seems to have been allied to Auld's campaign to discredit Macdonell in Selkirk's eyes, for Edwards and Auld were very friendly.[3] McRae, too, had quarreled with the Governor, and hence his statements are not very reliable, though they seem to be more truthful than the doctor's.[4] Little need be said of Auld's veracity. He rarely let slip a chance to strike a blow at Macdonell, especially after McRae had shown him copies of certain letters in which Macdonell had told Selkirk what he thought about him, Auld, and Cook.[5] The fact that the Governor had spoken truthfully in these letters did not help matters much. Of course Auld could describe the events of the winter at Pembina only from hearsay. But he made the most of what he heard.

The stories told by the North-westers likewise contain much that is false or misleading. In fact, they are for the most part skillfully constructed misrepresentations. It was the purpose of the North West Company to disseminate as widely as possible everything which might work to the detriment of Selkirk's colonial enterprise. The struggles and sufferings of the settlers made useful materials for propaganda, especially after they had been distorted, as they always were, by the hostile traders.[6]

All things considered, the winter at Pembina was not unbearably difficult. There were sufferings aplenty, of course, but they were not as acute as some of the evidence might lead one to suppose. In spite of

3. Edwards to Selkirk, n.d., and July 10, 1813; Edwards to Auld, July 10, 1813; Miles Macdonell to Selkirk, July 17, 1813; Selkirk to Miles Macdonell, April 12, 1814, *PAC SP,* pp. 518, 748 ff., 755 ff., 771 ff.

4. McRae to Auld, August, 1813, *PAC SP,* pp. 800 ff.

5. Miles Macdonell to Selkirk, September 9, 1814; Auld to Selkirk, n.d., *PAC SP,* pp. 511 f., 1216 f.

6. Extract of a Letter from a Proprietor of the North West Company, dated Red River, August, 1813, *Q134,* Pt. II, pp. 347 ff. William McGillivray to Robinson, August 15, 1815, *PAC SP,* pp. 1622 f.

their hostility to Selkirk's plans, the North-westers provided the colonists with a considerable quantity of food, though they charged high enough prices for it. This was in the earlier part of the season. As spring drew near food became scarcer. In January some families in which there were no very small children were sent, in company with the least effective among the unmarried men, to seek their living on the plains a hundred miles away in order to relieve the scarcity at the fort. The place to which they were ordered to go was the site of an abandoned trading post on the upper reaches of the Pembina River. The journey proved most trying. It was begun on a stormy day, and scarcely had the party "proceeded to the distance of eight or nine miles from Fort Daer, when many children and their mothers were severely frozen & obliged to put up [sic]. In four days did these hardy creatures, tramp through snow up to the knee, with their helpless children on their backs, at every step cursing bitterly *him* who had *thus* plunged them in misery." But this pictures things at their worst. Having arrived at their destination, they remained there until the last day of March, living rather well.[7]

When spring came the food supply at Fort Daer became so low that Macdonell "was obliged to send from the Fort every one that could travel. This was thought a great hardship, particularly by the families of the Settlers although the meat was ready killed & secured on Stages & they had only to go & eat it at the place."[8] Thus was solved the most pressing problem of the Selkirk Settlement during the first winter at Red River.

It was not the only difficulty with which Macdonell had to contend. The North-westers across the river also caused him trouble. The chief trader of the North West Company at Fort Pembina was his cousin and brother-in-law, Alexander Macdonell. During the early part of the winter the two, being, as far as Miles knew, on very good terms, were quite intimate and often together.[9] Their intimacy, in fact, was such that certain Hudson's Bay Company traders maliciously insinuated that Miles was being bribed by the North West Company. Auld told Hillier that he felt Miles was too intimate with the Canadians to be trusted with anything.[10] Of course there was no truth in the charge.

7. Extract of a Letter from a Proprietor of the North West Company, dated Red River, August, 1813, *Q134*, Pt. II, pp. 349 ff. Miles Macdonell to Selkirk, July 17, 1813, *PAC SP*, pp. 769 ff., 775.

8. *Ibid.*, pp. 770 f.

9. Auld to Wedderburn, September 16, 1813; Miles Macdonell to Selkirk, July 17, 1813, *PAC SP*, pp. 771, 777 f., 851.

10. January 29, 1813, and Auld to Hillier, January 27, 28, 1813; Auld to —, September 26, 1813, *PAC SP*, pp. 568, 573, 576, 838.

Miles Macdonell was not a disloyal man, his fault on this occasion lay, rather, in his being too trusting and somewhat obtuse. His cousin, on the other hand, was shrewd and unscrupulous. All the while that he was on friendly terms with Miles he was secretly trying to undermine his authority by tampering with his followers in order to make them discontented and to induce them to desert to the North West Company. In February, 1813, Dugal Cameron, a North-wester stationed on the Winnipeg River, paid a visit to Fort Pembina. He, too, engaged in "the same dishonourable proceeding." That is, he tampered with the Governor's following.

It was only in March, after both Alexander Macdonell and Dugal Cameron had departed, that Miles discovered how he had been tricked.[11] His gullibility in this affair is the more surprising when one considers that he was all the time fully aware of the sentiments which the heads of the North West Company entertained on the subject of the colony.[12] When he found that his kinsman had deceived him, he became indignant and expressed his feelings in a letter to Alexander: "Your insidious & treacherous conduct during the winter in endeavouring to swerve my people from their duty is fully known to me, as well as that of your colleague Mr. Dugal Cameron. I therefore trust that you will not attempt to intrude your visits here where you can no longer be received."[13] From the standpoint of morals it is perhaps all to the Governor's credit that he was trusting enough to be deceived, and frank enough to express his anger at the deception. But neither the one virtue nor the other was likely to be of any use in dealing as an opponent with the North West Company.

The bitterness of feeling engendered in Macdonell by such experiences during his first winter at Red River was betrayed in his letters to Selkirk in the following summer. "I have been interfered with & opposed on all sides—the N.W. Co. tampered with my people—the Indians threatened to destroy us [they had been incited by the North-westers][14] —Even some in the employ of the H.B. Co. acted with more hostility than friendship. My situation last Winter was uncomfortable in the extreme."[15]

11. Miles Macdonell to Selkirk, July 17, 1813; Miles Macdonell to Alexander Macdonell, April 18, 29, 1813; Alexander Macdonell to Miles Macdonell, April 18, 27, 1813; Miles Macdonell to Agents of the N.W. Co., June 1, 1813, March 8, 1814, *PAC SP*, pp. 593 ff., 596 ff., 626 f., 777 f., 967 f.

12. Selkirk to Miles Macdonell, April 12, 1814, *PAC SP*, p. 1049.

13. Miles Macdonell to Alexander Macdonell, April 18, 1813, *PAC SP*, p. 593.

14. McLeod, Journal, 3, *PAC*. McLeod to Hillier, February 17, 1813, *PAC SP*, pp. 581 f.

15. Miles Macdonell to Selkirk, July 17, 1813, *PAC SP*, p. 777.

Alexander Macdonell and Dugal Cameron, however, had not had much success in their efforts to persuade the settlers to desert. "The people, finding the fallacy of the overtures made them, repented & informed."[16] Only one man, John Walsh, actually deserted. He was taken by the North-westers to Lake Superior in the spring, but was sent back again in the fall of 1813, because the partners meeting at Fort William decided that such proceedings were as yet inexpedient.[17]

The cause of Macdonell's and Cameron's conduct is not far to seek. Simon McGillivray's letter to the Montreal partners notifying them of the North West Company meeting in London and of the unanimous opinion of those present that they "should immediately, on receipt of this, dispatch an Express to the Interior to prepare . . . [the winterers] for a year of Trial," and his letter directly to the wintering partners declaring that Lord Selkirk must be driven to abandon his colonial project, as his success would strike at the very existence of the company's trade, were beginning to produce their intended effect.[18]

On the other hand, it is interesting to watch the Hudson's Bay Company traders take an attitude to the colony similar to, if not as violent as that of the North-westers. Part of this hostility, of course, was personal. "You will find," Auld wrote to Selkirk, "I am little inclined to admire Cn. McD. [Captain Macdonell] management. To me he seems not possessed of those acts of conciliation which his situation so peculiarly requires. . . . He knows not how to attach hired, tho' he may command military servants."[19] The Superintendent's dislike turned to rage when he read the letter to Selkirk, referred to above, in which Macdonell blamed Auld and Cook for bad conditions at the Bay in the winter of 1811–12. For this "infamous & scandalous intelligence" Auld never forgave Macdonell, though the latter apologized and "expressed his sorrow & contrition." To Selkirk the trader accused Macdonell of shameless misrepresentation, confusion, and foolish and unprincipled management. To Wedderburn he asserted

without fear of contradiction from a human creature in this country, that if Ld Selkirk had advertized for a fool of the first magnitude he never could have better succeeded than he has done with the present man. He has disgusted every one of the Settlers & Servants of his own. He has disgusted the free Canadians. . . . He has encouraged the Canadian Traders to treat him with contempt by his childish partiality & unwise confidence reposed in them.

16. *Ibid.*, p. 778.
17. Miles Macdonell to Agents of the N.W. Co., March 8, 1814, *PAC SP*, pp. 967 f.
18. See above, chap. viii, 8 n., 9 n.
19. Auld to Selkirk, September 12, 1812, *PAC SP*, p. 499.

. . . He is not since his first arrival to the present moment accused of having done even by mistake one single thing right.[20]

A more serious charge preferred by the Bay official against Macdonell, namely, that he was too intimate with the Canadians to be trusted, has already been alluded to. In the summer of 1813 it was made the excuse for a most amazing performance at the Bay. The official letters to Macdonell which Selkirk had sent out on the Company's ships were opened by Auld and some of his subordinates; and a private letter, which was to be returned only in case of Macdonell's death, was sent back with an explanation.[21] Joseph Howse, a Company trader, wrote to Selkirk to say that many reports,

unfavourable to the character of Captn McDonnell are in circulation—and these reports are certainly of such a complexion as must induce a belief that if true he will be considered by your Lordship as ill calculated for conducting the undertaking confided to him—and consequently a very improper person to receive communications, of the nature which, from the injunction accompanying them, we presume these to be. In short the safer plan appears to me to be the suspending of the delivery of this packet till further orders rather than commit it to the discretion of a person labouring under so many imputations. . . .[22]

"The sea begets uncertain ways"; and so, apparently, did the North American fur trade. Here we have the Hudson's Bay traders, very much like the North-westers, taking the law into their own hands and confessedly stopping their very employer's letters in order to check an enterprise which was really none of their concern, aside from the orders they received, but which seemed to them to threaten their precious fur trade. There was more than personal animosity in this; and the future was to make the fact clear.

Despite all the charges made against Macdonell, nevertheless, Selkirk was too generous spirited and too well aware of the difficulties confronting the Governor to be easily influenced by the Company officials. "One of the letters which I sent to you last Autumn," he wrote to Macdonell on receiving the intercepted package, "was kept back and returned to me by Mr. Auld for reasons too impertinent and absurd for the most petulant school boy."[23] Selkirk then went on to encourage his lieutenant and promised him all the aid he could possibly give. At the

20. Miles Macdonell to Selkirk, September 9, 1814; Auld to Selkirk, n.d.; Auld to Wedderburn, September 16, 1813, *PAC SP,* pp. 511 f., 847, 849 ff., 852, 856 f., 1216 f.
21. Auld to Selkirk, September 26, 1813; Selkirk to Auld, June 15, 1813, *PAC SP,* pp. 692 f., 837 ff.
22. September 24, 1813, *PAC SP,* pp. 871 f.
23. April 12, 1814, *PAC SP,* p. 1051.

same time he urged him in the most friendly manner to proceed in all things with as little friction as possible. This, it must be admitted, was timely counsel. Macdonell was not a conciliatory man. He did not understand men; certainly he could not win them. Perhaps he was too distant and reserved to establish close relations with other men easily. During the winter at Pembina he quarreled with Dr. Edwards, Kenneth McRae, Owen Keveny, and Heney.[24] Yet these men may have been difficult to get along with; probably they were. Still, the Governor was undoubtedly guilty of arbitrariness and pettishness. Selkirk seems to have become aware of this, and said so himself.

I cannot help entertaining an apprehension[25] that there is too little of the *suaviter in modo* in your behaviour, to those who are placed under you. Before you left London while we were going about among the Tradesmen, one or two circumstances came under my view which, tho' trifling in themselves, if I had only considered at the time, ought to have led me to caution you on the Subject. I can perceive the same in the complaints of Edwards & McRae. Tho' both of these young men have proved themselves to be foolish and petulant & one of them a good deal worse, yet I remain of opinion that by suitable management, they might have been made to do their duty. I send you a long rigmarole of a complaint which Edwards has made. . . . I should not even take up your time in reading such a production, if it were not to remark that however persuaded I am that Edwards must have given you considerable provocation upon different occasions, which he refers to, yet the expressions he ascribed to you are such as ought never to be used by a person in a Situation of Command.

Tho' no complaint has been made by Mr. Keveny, & his language in speaking of you is perfectly respectful, it appears evident to me, that he has met some treatment which has given him disgust. . . . Your measures concerning him have not been well considered.

But when all the evidence has been sifted, and the nature of the situation examined, it becomes painfully clear that the Governor was in an exceedingly difficult position. In the first place the enterprise which he had undertaken—to plant an agricultural colony in the interior of the wilds of North America—was in itself an all but hopeless task in view of the difficulty of communication then obtaining between Red River and the sea. Then, again, the instruments at his command were woefully inadequate to accomplish the purposes for which they had been chosen: the doubtful character of most of the emigrants, already failures in the world where they had grown up; the meager and ill-chosen transport

24. *Ibid.,* pp. 1044 ff. Auld to Wedderburn, September 16, 1813; Miles Macdonell to Selkirk, July 17, 1813; Edwards to Selkirk, July 10, 1813, *PAC SP,* pp. 748 ff., 771 ff., 849 ff.

25. April 12, 1814, *PAC SP,* pp. 1043 ff.

and maintenance accommodations provided by the Hudson's Bay Company; the equipment, totally inadequate for an incipient agricultural community, sent out with the first, and even with the second expedition. Furthermore, there were the extremely trying natural conditions to be faced and overcome at Red River—the coldness of the winter, the lack of housing facilities, the uncertainty of the supply of the staple food, buffalo meat. Finally, there was the more or less active opposition to the whole project—not only that of the North-westers, which was to have been expected and might have been forestalled, but also that of the Hudson's Bay Company traders, which, though it might have been anticipated, was all the more trying because it came from those who were supposed to be friends, and who, from their position within the gates of the citadel, were able to accomplish by fraud what declared enemies could only attempt by force. All this, of course, does not excuse Macdonell's faults and mistakes. But it should prevent the historian, as it has not always succeeded in doing, from ascribing to the course and the character of the leader events which might easily have taken their way very much as they did from the nature of things which were quite beyond the control of any one man, however wise and virtuous he might have been.

CHAPTER X

RED RIVER FARMING

THE coming of spring terminated almost all the ills from which Macdonell and his followers had suffered during the winter of 1812–13. The departure of several of the more discontented among the settlers removed to a great extent the discord and pessimism which had been disturbing everyone.[1] As the days grew longer and warmer and the snow and ice disappeared, fish and wild fowl became abundant and the rapid growth of vegetation testified to the fertility of the soil and the salubrity of the climate. The people began to have hopes of an abundant harvest in the autumn. The camp at Pembina was now abandoned and the settlers returned to the Forks and set about creating a permanent agricultural establishment.[2] The name already chosen by Macdonell for the site he had selected and begun to develop was "Colony Gardens."

The manner in which actual settlement was to be started had been indicated by Lord Selkirk in his instructions to Macdonell. He had written:

All that needs to be observed is that the work of the first season ought to be concentrated as much as possible in the near vicinity of the fort, both for security and that the work may be carried on with more regularity and less loss of time. The men being all upon wages and therefore under complete command, may be employed in the most systematic manner, in distinct lands allotted for different branches of the work, each under their separate overseer. It is of evident consequence that the first crop should be as large as possible; and to animate the exertions of the people it may be held out that if the abundance of the harvest answers your expectations, they will receive their allotments of land without waiting the expiration of their contracts of service. In fact if the first harvest proves tolerably abundant, and the produce in any degree encouraging, the people should then receive separate allotments of land, to cultivate each for himself, with the promise that as soon as they have raised a sufficient crop to feed a family and build a house to lodge them, their friends from home shall be brought out to them. From the time that any man is thus set free to work for himself, his wages ought to cease. He must be assisted with a supply of provisions for the first year, as well as tools; for which if he has not the means of paying he should be charged as a debtor to the establishment; and a moderate charge should in like manner be added on account of the land allotted to him. A description of the land allotted to each should be sent home, so that a grant in due form

1. Miles Macdonell to Selkirk, July 17, 1813, *PAC SP*, p. 786.
2. *Ibid.*, pp. 779, 780, 783 ff.

may be sent out to be delivered to the settler, on payment of his debts. The price to be put on the first lots, is of little consequence except for the sake of the principle.[3] They may be laid out from 50 to 100 acres to each man, and should as far as possible combine wood and plain in every lot. If, however, the Indians should appear disposed to be troublesome so as to excite any apprehensions for scattered settlers, small lots of 5 or 10 acres may be laid out more closely adjoining to the fort and assigned to the men on a temporary tenure to cultivate till they can safely take possession of their full lots. The reinforcement sent out next year will probably do away all apprehension on this score.[4]

Selkirk never really feared that the settlers would be mistreated by the Indians. He even advised Macdonell that perhaps a supply of Indian corn might be obtained from the Ottawa and Bungee Indians at Dead River near the mouth of the Red.[5] Realizing the importance of securing the friendship of the natives and the danger of alienating them by an unceremonious invasion of their territorial rights, he tried to impress upon his agent the best course to pursue in dealing with them.

With respect to these and all other tribes of Indians with whom you have any intercourse, no precaution must be omitted to obtain their friendship as the party will not much exceed the numbers of an ordinary trading post, it may be hoped that in the first instance they will pass for such; and to countenance that idea it will be very useful if the Superintendent at York will send a trader with an assortment of goods for the Indians, to accompany the settlers. Though this idea cannot be of very long duration, it will be well to keep it up as long as possible, at least till the post is well established and fortified. When it can no longer be concealed that the establishment is to be permanent, if the jealousy of the Indians appears to be aroused, the proposal of purchasing the land must be brought forward. The purchase ought to be, in part at least and as much as possible by way of annuity, rather than a price to be paid at once. An annuity to be annually distributed among the tribes and families, who have a claim to the lands, will form a permanent hold over their peaceable behaviour, as they must be made to understand that if any individual of the tribe violates the treaty, the payment will be withheld. It is to be hoped that from your first arrival in the country an intercourse may be established with the neighbouring tribes and by personal attentions, presents, etc., the leading individuals may be conciliated which will greatly facilitate any general treaty. A boon of immense consequence may be held out in the communication of the vaccine. On this point it may be necessary to proceed cautiously to avoid misapprehension, but time and pa-

3. Selkirk was of the opinion that "few people set much value on what they get for nothing." See Selkirk to Alexander McDonald, November 8, 1811, *PAC SP,* Vol. 79, p. 41. Selkirk to Miles Macdonell, December 23, 1811, *PAC SP,* pp. 126 f.

4. Instructions to Miles Macdonell, 1811, *PAC SP,* pp. 179 ff.

5. *Ibid.,* pp. 175 ff.

tience will convince them, both of the value and the beneficence of the gift. Perhaps by judicious management on the part of the interpreters, they may be made to entertain very high ideas of the power of those who have such a command over nature. Much in all this must depend on the interpreters, and from the adjacent establishments of the Company, we may expect essential assistance. But after all the attentions which can be used for obtaining the friendship of the Indians, it would certainly be wrong to trust very much to it, especially after the threats which have been held out. A better security will be in the awe which they will entertain for so strong a post, if they see it guarded with unremitted vigilance, and especially if they find that any proceeding in the least degree savouring of insult or encroachment is repressed with a determined vigour.[6]

In most of their relations with the settlers, and in spite of the attempts of the North-westers to incite them to mischief, the Indians proved so consistently friendly and helpful, and rarely worse than tolerant, that Macdonell was able to devote practically all his attention to other problems. It is true that during the winter months at Fort Daer a few of the local Indians, aroused by North West Company traders, threatened to destroy the young colony; but they never attempted to carry out their threats.[7] At first both Selkirk and Macdonell were inclined to disregard these hostile utterances as merely the result of attempts on the part of the Canadian traders to check the growth of the colony by fear. Later, as "the virulence of the enemies" increased, they became somewhat alarmed. Even then they were concerned not so much over the hostility of the Indians as over that of the métis, who were more plastic material in the hands of the North-westers. The bois-brûlés, it would seem, had been given to understand that if they permitted a colony to be established at Red River, they would ultimately become slaves. A retired Montreal trader, in 1814, expressed grave concern for the safety of Miles Macdonell and the Settlement. "My greatest fear," he wrote, "is from the treachery and machinations to prejudice the natives [métis] against the colonists. . . . The strongest argument I have heard used, to raise jealousy in the Natives, is by inculcating on their minds a belief, that they are robbed of their lands without any indemnification. This I have heard a year ago from the mouth of a principal, & one of the Chief instigators of this enmity to the Colony."[8]

6. *Ibid.*, pp. 176 ff.
7. See above, chap. ix, n. 14, n. 15. Selkirk to the Governor, Deputy Governor and Committee of the Hudson's Bay Company, February 14, 1815, *PAC SP,* pp. 1914 ff. *Statement Respecting Settlement,* p. 5.
8. Selkirk to the Governor, Deputy Governor and Committee of the Hudson's Bay Company, February 14, 1815, *PAC SP,* pp. 1914 ff.

Meanwhile in the spring of 1813 Miles Macdonell took up the question of purchasing land at the Forks from the Indians for the use of the colony. On discussing the matter with the local Indians he discovered to his surprise that they did not call themselves the owners of the soil, although they had been long in possession. The country about the Red River had belonged in former times to the Crees, whom the Assiniboines had driven off. Such being the situation, the Governor was "at a loss in what manner to make a purchase from the natives"; but he informed Selkirk that a small annual present would satisfy the Indians at Red River and that if any others should make a claim later, a present would probably satisfy them too.[9]

The question of the Indian title to Red River being thus disposed of, and all the settlers brought back from Pembina to the Forks, the land at Colony Gardens was surveyed, divided into farms, and distributed among the immigrants. Each farm consisted regularly of one hundred acres, with an 880-foot frontage on the river. This was in accordance with Selkirk's instructions. Farms in Lower Canada had 660-foot fronts, and a great many of the first in Upper Canada had the same, but these had been found by experience to be too narrow. Macdonell was aware of this from his familiarity with farming in the Canadas, and decided to add for the sake of convenience the length of one square acre to the width of the Red River farms.[10]

In June and July the settlers began the construction of more or less substantial dwellings; at least they were more comfortably built than any that had been available for the expedition since its arrival in America. Their attempts at farming, however, were extremely discouraging. When they had been located on their lands as much seed (grain) as could be spared was given them.[11] Unfortunately, through oversight or mismanagement, very few agricultural implements, as observed above, had been sent out to Red River. A few had been brought out on the *Robert Taylor* in 1812, but most of these had been left behind at York Factory. The only implements available for breaking up the tough prairie sod were hoes. Furthermore, the quantity of seed distributed was small. Selkirk had sent out what he considered would be ample, but during the winter more than half of it had been consumed as food. Macdonell bought a small amount of wheat from the North-westers, but the settlers themselves had no money with which to buy any. Somehow they

9. *Ibid.*, pp. 1915 f.

10. Miles Macdonell to Selkirk, July 17, 1813; Selkirk to Miles Macdonell, June 20, 1812, *PAC SP,* pp. 724 f., 787.

11. Miles Macdonell to Selkirk, July 17, 1813, *PAC SP,* p. 787.

managed to secure a few potatoes, a small quantity of peas, some Indian corn and some fowl.

In the preceding year the workmen who had remained at the site of Colony Gardens had sown two or three acres of winter wheat. This, unfortunately, had been a failure, principally because it was sown "among the ashes of caustic vegetables without disturbing in the Slightest degree the soil below." The little wheat that did come up was choked by the weeds. The summer wheat, peas, English barley, and Indian corn planted in the late spring were equally unsuccessful. The season was too advanced, the seed old, and the ground insufficiently worked; everything, too, suffered from drought. The only crops which were at all satisfactory were the potatoes and the turnips; and these did very well. Some of the settlers had returns of forty-five or fifty kegs for each keg of potatoes planted, and the turnips grew to an extraordinary size. During the winter McLean's sheep had not fared well. They had been left at the Point along with a cow and a bull; and one ewe, two rams, and all the lambs but one had died. The summer did not seem to change their fortune, five more being killed by dogs. In the spring of 1813 Peter Fidler, a Hudson's Bay Company trader and surveyor at the Forks, bought from the North-westers three head of cattle—a bull, a cow, and a heifer—at the enormous price of £100. "He meant well of course in doing so," wrote Macdonell, "but had he not interfered, I think I could have had them for a great deal less." Shortly afterwards the bull became so vicious that he had to be killed.[12]

It is not surprising that these first attempts at farming in Red River were disappointing. Even the most fertile soils must be worked, if they are to yield; and while many of the colonists were willing enough workers, they had only the most rudimentary knowledge of agriculture and practically no suitable implements. The majority of them had been fishermen, not farmers, in the Old Country; and the new school was not a good one. To make matters worse, food was very scarce while the crops were ripening. Even the supply of fish, usually good, was very scanty this year. The fruits of the prairie were not much more encouraging. Berries were scarce. In their dire need the hungry settlers took to eating certain prairie weeds. The best of these was the "prairie-

12. Auld to Wedderburn, September 16, 1813; Miles Macdonell to Selkirk, July 17, 1813, July 25, 1814; Miles Macdonell to Auld, February 4, 1814, *PAC SP*, pp. 768, 784, 788, 853 f., 955, 1183. Selkirk to Alexander McDonald, February 26, 1814, *PAC SP*, Vol. 79, p. 128. The North-westers in *Narrative of Occurrences*, p. 20, maintain that they sold to Macdonell in the spring of 1813 "articles of various descriptions; potatoes, barley, oats, and garden-seeds, four cows, a bull, pigs, fowls, &c." Macdonell in his correspondence to Selkirk mentions having bought only one bull and two cows.

turnip," which had a large tap root and grew in abundance on the dry plains. Another favorite was a succulent weed known as "fat-hen."[13]

Conditions were made worse in June and July by a dangerous fever epidemic, a sort of bilious ague. Almost every person in the Settlement was afflicted by it; but only two died, Hector McLean, and a boy about twelve years of age. The disease was new to the country, the first ever known in Hudson Bay. Auld attributed it to "the deficient subsistence during the preceding winter, and the abominably filthy habits . . . of these civilized caffres afterwards." Macdonell, on the other hand, was unable to account for its source; he doubted that it had come from a deficiency of food during the winter, bad as times were.[14]

As the days at Colony Gardens passed, the settlers became more discouraged and full of regrets for having come to Red River. Their memories of the hopeless misery in which they had lived in the Old World had been dimmed or wiped out by the toil and the hardships of the New; and they now longed for a knowledge and the company of the friends they had left behind, and for a sight once more of the familiar scenes they had forever quitted. Coming as they had from a variety of places, and being unaccustomed to forming new friendships readily, they failed to find in contacts with their fellow immigrants the amenities upon which the pleasures of their simple lives so largely depended. Nor was there anything at Colony Gardens calculated to relieve their homesickness. The métis were at times hostile, and were always feared and distrusted. The Indians, though usually kind and generous, were strange and difficult to understand. The settlers' log houses were small and not very comfortable. Even the climate and the landscape were repellent. Instead of the changeable weather of the Highlands and of western Ireland there was a monotonous succession of warm dry days with a bright sun and an endless wearying breeze, broken, as a rule, only by alarming storms of thunder and hail. The nights were strangely cold. Not least among the settlers' regrets was the fact that their beloved Gaelic was at a distinct disadvantage in a country where English, French, and a variety of Indian dialects were the chief media of conversation.

Very different from this, however, was the attitude of Miles Macdonell to Red River. "The country," he wrote with enthusiasm, "exceeds any idea I had formed of its goodness. I am only astonished it has lain so long unsettled. With good management the Buffaloe in winter & fish in Summer are sufficient to subsist any number of people untill

13. Miles Macdonell to Selkirk, July 17, 1813, *PAC SP,* p. 788. Ross, *Red River Settlement,* p. 23.
14. Miles Macdonell to Selkirk, July 17, 1813; Miles Macdonell to Auld, February 4, April 12, 1814; Auld to Miles Macdonell, March 13, 1814; Auld to Wedderburn, September 16, 1813, *PAC SP,* pp. 790, 852 f., 955, 975 f., 1001 f.

more certain supplies are got out of the ground. . . . The land is most fertile & the climate most extraordinarily healthy."[15]

The harvest at Colony Gardens in 1813, however, was quite insufficient to feed the settlers through the succeeding winter. It was necessary, therefore, to return to Pembina in the fall. Macdonell took with him to Fort Daer all the servants and settlers except the McLean family and six men who were left at the Point to guard the establishment. The McLeans chose to remain on their land, having had "a tolerable house" built there.[16]

When the Governor and his followers reached Pembina they received a cold, if not surly reception from both the bois-brûlés and the Canadian traders. The North West Company had succeeded in prejudicing the bois-brûlés against the colony. The traders themselves were more openly hostile than the natives. At the annual summer meeting of the partners at Fort William much attention had been given to "Lord Selkirk's delirium" —as one North-wester was wont to speak of the Red River Settlement. The policy which was adopted at this meeting was to build up animosity against the settlers among the natives, especially among the bois-brûlés. This policy had now begun to bear fruit.[17]

Nevertheless, the winter now spent by the colonists at Pembina was comparatively agreeable. Provisions were plentiful, the weather was mild, and there was very little snow. Fortunately there were no Hudson's Bay Company traders in the locality, and very few Canadians. Within the little community of immigrants cordiality prevailed.[18] Dr. Edwards had gone off to Fort Churchill after he and Macdonell had settled their differences amicably. McRae was still present, but he had no one to intrigue with. Mrs. McLean was a troublemaker, but she was now at the Forks. During the preceding winter, spring, and summer, gossip had accused Macdonell and Mrs. McLean of serious improprieties.[19] There was probably no truth in the rumors. Dr. Edwards and Kenneth McRae were quite capable of inventing such stories. Auld, of course, gave them full credit, as they suited his purposes exactly.[20]

Although provisions were plentiful throughout the winter, they had to be brought from a great distance; the buffalo had never been known to keep so far away. Consequently Macdonell had to hire a number of

15. Miles Macdonell to Selkirk, July 17, 1813, *PAC SP,* p. 789.
16. Miles Macdonell to Selkirk, July 25, 1814, *PAC SP,* p. 1184.
17. *Statement Respecting Settlement,* pp. 10 f. Pritchard, Narrative, *Q153,* Pt. III, pp. 738 ff.
18. Miles Macdonell to Selkirk, February 14, July 25, 1814, *PAC SP,* pp. 956, 1184, 1186.
19. Miles Macdonell to Selkirk, July 17, August 31, 1813, July 24, 1814; Auld to Wedderburn, September 16, 1813, *PAC SP,* pp. 782, 817, 854, 856, 1177 f.
20. *Ibid.*

free Canadians to do the hunting for the community. Owing to the mildness of the weather and the light snowfall the hunting could be done on horseback. But while this insured a large kill, the meat had to be brought many miles, sometimes a hundred. It often took the men at the fort from six to ten days to make the round trip. On some of these expeditions they suffered considerably from cold and frostbite. Yet their sufferings were slight compared with those of the preceding year.[21]

In March the food supply was seriously endangered for a short time. Earlier in the season five free Canadians had been killed by the Sioux Indians; and when the latter went on the warpath in the spring, both Canadians and bois-brûlés quit the buffalo ranges. For a few days the Settlement was without meat. Then the Governor, to avoid a recurrence of semistarvation, armed twenty of his best men with muskets and bayonets and took them out on the plains beyond the Turtle River where the hunters, Indians, and freemen had retired with their families. With some difficulty Macdonell persuaded most of the natives "to return once more to the charge." All then journeyed to the upper reaches of the Goose River, where they remained three days, procuring as much buffalo meat as they could carry home. They now had enough meat to last them till spring. They met no Sioux on this expedition, "but some of the enemies' out scouts were seen by . . . [the hunters'] rear guard."[22]

During the winter, in the absence of a clergyman, Macdonell married two couples and baptized four babies. But there was no pleasure for him in these duties; he urged Selkirk to send out "some clergyman soon" to relieve him of these "awful" tasks.[23]

Fort Daer was not without its amenities in the winter of 1813–14. To dispel the gloomy impression left by the occurrences of the past year they were given liquor, and a dance at Christmas and New Year's. The weddings of the season, too, were occasions of much merrymaking and hilarity. Many of the French Canadians were good fiddlers; and the Red River jig seems to have become a popular favorite. Both the Scots and the Irish were beginning to adapt themselves to the customs of their adopted country.[24]

Spring came late, in 1814. The river did not break up until April 22. On May 1 Macdonell and the first division of settlers returned to Colony Gardens. The rest followed some time after. Michael McDonnell and six men were left at Fort Daer to build a stockade round the fort

21. Miles Macdonell to Auld, February 4, 1814; Miles Macdonell to Selkirk, July 25, 1814, *PAC SP,* pp. 956 f., 1184 f.

22. *Ibid.,* pp. 1185 f.　　　　　　　　　23. *Ibid.,* p. 1186.

24. *Ibid.*

—the pickets had been cut and shaped during the winter—and "to keep the place in order & cultivate some ground."[25]

Most of the settlers were glad to get back to their farms, and at once began work on them. There were some, however, who had no taste for farming; or, for that matter, for any other sort of labor. These were mostly "the refuse of the different Countries they came from."[26] In spite of the presence of such drones the future would then have begun to look fairly bright for the colony had it not been for the hostility of the North-westers. Early in January, 1814, Miles Macdonell had issued a proclamation[27] forbidding the export of provisions from the District of Assiniboia. The Canadian traders were not only irritated by Macdonell's audacity; they were alarmed for the prosperity of their trade. The embargo would at any time have been obnoxious in the extreme to the North West Company, depending as it did on the Red River country for most of the provisions required by its traders to the west and north. But late in the autumn of 1813 news of the American border successes in the War of 1812 reached Assiniboia; and the danger of a failure of supplies from Montreal gave to the local provisions a new and vital importance.[28] By late summer relations between the Settlement and the Canadians had become correspondingly tense; and the arrival in August of a third contingent of settlers from the Old Country only added fuel to the fire.

25. *Ibid.*, p. 1187.
27. *Q133*, pp. 55 ff.

26. *Ibid.*
28. *Narrative of Occurrences*, p. 23.

CHAPTER XI

THE SUTHERLANDERS

THE hardships and the discouragements which had attended the first two Red River colonizing expeditions, and which would have been sufficient to daunt many a man of more than ordinary caliber, neither deprived the Earl of Selkirk of his hopes for the future welfare of the Settlement nor constrained him to abandon the further prosecution of his plans. On the contrary, the keen opposition of Sir Alexander Mackenzie and his associates, combined with the fact that two bands of settlers had already reached Assiniboia and were in need of support, fired the Earl's mind anew and prompted him to make still greater efforts to collect and send out another body of colonists. The hour provided circumstances exactly suited to his needs.

Several years previously the Marchioness of Stafford and Duchess of Sutherland, the only child of the last Duke of Sutherland, following to an extreme degree the brutal practice of other Highland landholders, had begun to evict her tenants in large numbers in order to secure lands for sheep raising. She had done this on such a scale that in one year, in the parishes of Clyne and Kildonan, a hundred tenants had made way for a single sheep farm. The consequent distress, though great enough, would have been much worse had it not been for the scarcity of labor occasioned by the Napoleonic wars. In particular, large numbers of the best tenant farmers had been drawn off by British recruiting sergeants. Evictions became so wholesale, however, in 1812 and in the early part of 1813 that the people were driven to lose hope. Serious riots broke out and threatened to grow into a general rising. To put down the rioters and to cow the Highlanders who might be thinking of revolt, a British regiment was sent into the country.[1] When the crisis was at its peak, the dispossessed tenantry sent a delegate to London to ask the government for state relief to keep them from starving. The government, however, having paid for sending a regiment to keep the poor quiet, apparently had no funds to spare for keeping them alive; and the disappointed deputy was on the point of turning northward in despair, when Selkirk became interested in the situation.[2]

Here he thought he saw a chance to secure "a fine race of men" for Red River. "I feel," he wrote to Miles Macdonell, "quite as much interest in their success as if they were in my own immediate employment."

1. Selkirk to Miles Macdonell, June 12, 1813, *PAC SP*, p. 651.
2. Selkirk to Alexander McDonald, April 30, 1813, *PAC SP*, Vol. 79, pp. 109 f.

When he offered them lands in Assiniboia according to the terms of his colonization scheme, they accepted his proposals with joy and determined to emigrate all in one body. Altogether seven hundred applications were received. It so happened that an old Hudson's Bay Company trader, Donald McKay—the founder of Brandon House—had resided many years in Kildonan, and had often told the people about the fertility of the soil, the healthfulness of the climate, and the beauties of the country of Red River. For this reason the Sutherlanders were not as disinclined as were most Highlanders to emigrate to such a distant scene. Unfortunately, Selkirk found it impossible to accept all the applications received. Such a contingent would have been large enough to make it worth while to go in person to Red River and to establish his colony on such an extensive scale that its permanence would be assured. One of the chief obstacles to such a procedure was the inability or the unwillingness of the officials at Hudson Bay to prepare means of transportation for such a large number. Word was sent from York Factory that it would be impossible to have the required number of boats ready in time to receive the settlers for the journey inland. On this account Selkirk was forced to limit the number of applications accepted to about one hundred. He promised many others, however, that if they would "remain in their old habitations till next Spring," he would send them out then.[3]

The terms upon which the Sutherlanders were secured for Red River were similar to those offered in the preceding year. Credit for provisions was promised them for a period of twelve months; liberal terms would be provided for the purchase of tools and other necessary articles. The choicest lands were to be sold to them at 5s. cash or 10s. credit, per acre; or the Sutherlanders might lease in perpetuity at half a bushel of grain per acre annually. "The amount of money to be received from these people . . . [was, however,] a matter of very secondary importance in comparison with their being well satisfied."[4] Selkirk agreed to provide passage from Scotland to Assiniboia at the price of £10 per person. To secure the necessary funds the emigrants were forced, in most cases, to sell their little herds of black cattle and their scanty flocks of sheep. A few, however, were able, after paying their passages, to deposit with the Earl sums of money to be drawn upon when necessity should arise.[5]

Most of those who made up this third contingent were from the parish of Kildonan. Whole families moved away together. There were, however, a number of unmarried young men and women who were going to

3. *Ibid.* Selkirk to Miles Macdonell, June 12, 1813, *PAC SP,* pp. 650 ff.
4. *Ibid.,* pp. 652 ff.   5. Gunn and Tuttle, *Manitoba,* pp. 89 f., 106.

Assiniboia to secure land in preparation for the later emigration of
their relatives. "Two or three of the elderly people might have done
better to . . . [have stayed] behind but they could not be persuaded."
Besides those from Sutherland there were a few families and some single
men recruited by the Earl's agents from Lochaber and Isla, on the borders of Ross-shire and Sutherland, and from Ireland. There were, however, only eight Irishmen, and they were to be used in the Company's
service. After hearing of the activities of the Irish in the earlier contingents, Selkirk had come to the conclusion that he did not want "any
great proportion of that untractable race, till the police of the country
should be established on a footing of tolerable security."[6]

Of the Kildonan people there were scarcely any who could be called
outstanding men. On the other hand, they were not of inferior stock.
John Sutherland, Donald Bannerman, Donald Gunn, Alexander Gunn,
and George McDonald had all been involved in the insurrection against
the sheep farmers;

but none of them were previously under a bad name: & the Circumstances of
the case were such that . . . [Selkirk could not] consider their Conduct on
that occasion as any great imputation on their general Character. According
to the ideas handed down to them from their Ancestors, and long prevalent
among high & low throughout the Highlands, they were only defending their
rights & resisting a ruinous unjust & tyrannical encroachment on their property.

Sutherland was regarded as one of the "most respectable people
in the parish," and it was said that during the recent disturbances he
had exercised a healthy influence over the young people, restraining
many of them from acts of violence which they were on the point of
committing. Donald Bannerman was well liked; many of his neighbors
spoke of him as "a frank open hearted character." Donald Gunn was
one of the Kildonan recruits that Selkirk liked least; still, the minister
of the parish testified to his good character. George McDonald had a
troublesome temper, but he was "a keen little fellow." The McBeaths
were an energetic and respectable family who promised to make first-
rate settlers.[7]

Early in June Selkirk himself went to Sutherlandshire to superintend
the preparations for departure and to encourage the emigrants in their
great undertaking. After having made satisfactory arrangements with

6. Selkirk to Miles Macdonell, June 12, 1813, *PAC SP*, pp. 652, 654 ff. Selkirk to
Alexander McDonald, June 29, 1813, *PAC SP*, Vol. 79, p. 121.

7. Selkirk to Miles Macdonell, June 12, 1813, *PAC SP*, pp. 654 ff. See list of passengers on board the *Prince of Wales* for Red River Settlement, Miles Macdonell, Selkirk Settlement, pp. 165 ff., *PAC*.

them, and given his instructions to his agents, he went on to Thurso to make preparations for the reception of the colonists. This done, he crossed the Pentland Firth to Stromness, whence the expedition was to sail. After the emigrants had all gathered at Thurso, they were transported to Stromness on board the *Water-witch* and then lodged in private houses at the Hudson's Bay Company's expense.[8]

Those who sailed from Thurso had been preceded a few hours at Stromness by their "very old and very young friends and relatives" who had gone by sea from Helmsdale. Here they met other groups, too, bound for America—Orkneymen for the Company's service, Irish laborers, and Moravian missionaries bound for Labrador. Once again, as in 1811, there was trouble with the government officials. McLean, the secretary of the Transport Board, was still an enemy of Selkirk, and caused most of the trouble. He was well seconded in this, however, by others on the board, particularly by Douglas, a "waspish captious" character "who delights in doing an ill-natured thing."[9] On the other hand, the people of Stromness were very kind, though they took advantage of the increased demand for food to raise prices. A few of the people were given poor lodgings, but the majority were well housed,[10] and the delay at Stromness was brief. The last of the emigrants arrived on June 10 and the Hudson's Bay Company ships put into harbor the next day. After some further irritating interferences by officials, and several days of ill winds, the fleet put to sea on June 28. It consisted of the *Prince of Wales*, carrying the settlers and the colony laborers; the *Eddystone*, with the Company's servants; a Labrador brig, bearing the missionaries; and a government convoy, the *Brazen*.[11]

As usual, the first stage of the voyage was unpleasant in the extreme, owing to the prevalence of homesickness and seasickness. But the passage as a whole was good, and was declared to be the quickest in the history of the Company. Just before the Bay was reached, however, the *Eddystone* was overtaken by the *Prince of Wales*, which reported that typhus fever had broken out on board. This was a new thing in the experience of the Hudson's Bay Company, and had been induced, it was believed then, by inactivity and close confinement in narrow quarters. Seven were already dead. Thirty others were lying in the hold dangerously ill. The outbreak had begun a short time out from Stromness and

8. Selkirk to Alexander McDonald, April 30, 1813, *PAC SP*, Vol. 79, p. 110. Gunn and Tuttle, *Manitoba*, p. 92.

9. Selkirk to Alexander McDonald, June 29, 1813, *PAC SP*, Vol. 79, p. 121. Selkirk to Colvile, June 5, 1813, *PAC SP*, p. 546.

10. Gunn and Tuttle, *Manitoba*, pp. 91 f.

11. Selkirk to Alexander McDonald, June 29, 1813; Archibald McDonald to Alexander McDonald, June 23, 1813, *PAC SP*, Vol. 79, pp. 119, 121.

had spread in spite of every precaution. Early in its progress the disease had carried off the surgeon, Laserre, a Guernsey man and a relative of General Brock, whom Selkirk had entrusted with the chief command of the expedition until it should reach Red River. His death was a serious loss; he was a capable young man, full of vigor, and possessed of a good medical education. He was to have succeeded Dr. Edwards as colony surgeon on his arrival in Assiniboia. After his death the command of the expedition devolved upon Archibald McDonald, Laserre's coadjutor, a young Highlander who had been actively in Selkirk's service for a little more than a year, and who, at the Earl's expense, had been instructed in medicine in London during the winter of 1812–13. As commandant of the expedition he seems to have got through it wonderfully well, contrary to the derogatory opinion of the hypercritical Auld.[12]

To the unavoidable calamity of typhus the commander of the fleet, Captain Turner, seemingly through a combination of ignorance and obstinacy, now added another. As soon as the open waters of the Bay were reached, the *Prince of Wales* was steered not toward York Factory, as Turner had been directed, but toward Fort Churchill far to the north. Why this action was taken has never been discovered. Besides having his orders from Selkirk, Turner knew that the settlers could secure adequate supplies for the following winter nowhere but at Red River. As the season was not yet far advanced, there would have been sufficient time for the trip inland before the cold weather if the colonists had been landed at once at York Factory. Perhaps the captain was thinking of the orders he had received to return to England as soon as possible, and Fort Churchill was the nearest port. The excuse has also been put forward that he may have hoped to relieve the sick more quickly by landing them sooner. But it is hard to explain or excuse his conduct. He must have been aware that, had he put in at York Factory instead of going to Fort Churchill, the sick would have found immediate relief in an abundance of fresh provisions and in good time all would have reached their destination. Macdonell had come down to York Factory to meet the expedition; and he was furious when he heard the news. "I hope," he wrote to Selkirk, "he will be made to smart severely for his brutal stubbornness."[13]

12. J.S. (Lady Selkirk) to Kate, November 12, 1813, *SP SM*. Selkirk to Alexander McDonald, January 9, May 5, July 9, August 4, 1812, January, April 30, November 6, 1813; Selkirk to —, March 24, 1813; — to Selkirk, April 12, 1813, *PAC SP*, Vol. 79, pp. 14 f., 21 f., 24, 48, 60 f., 64 f., 74 f., 111, 123 f. Selkirk to Miles Macdonell, June 12, 1813; Miles Macdonell to Selkirk, August 31, 1813, *PAC SP*, pp. 657 f., 822 f. Auld to Wedderburn, September 16, 1813, *PAC SP*, pp. 837, 845.

13. *Ibid.*, pp. 843 f. Miles Macdonell to Selkirk, August 31, 1813; Miles Macdonell

The passage across the Bay had been smooth and rapid. But soon the scene changed decidedly for the worse. A few days after making land, with the typhus still raging, the settlers were disembarked at Sloop's Cove. Here nothing was in readiness to accommodate even the sick and the dying. Fresh food was very scarce. The Company officials at the Factory offered them no assistance. Most of the provisions available were those brought from the ship. The shelters were only such as the settlers could improvise from their belongings and from the scanty forest growth near at hand. In spite of the benefits of wind and sun the fever continued to carry off its victims. Those who escaped the disease were worn out with nursing and watching their friends and relatives. There can be little doubt that many of the deaths which took place after the arrival could have been averted had proper food and lodging been available, as they would have been at York Factory.[14]

In spite of all the attempts that were now made to have the settlers taken on to their proper destination before winter set in, nothing was done. Auld, as soon as he heard of Captain Turner's "treachery" in going to Fort Churchill, hurried north to Fort Churchill and ordered him to sail for York Factory at once. After much stupid and obstinate bickering, the settlers were taken aboard again. But, whether by accident or design, the ship was then run aground near the mouth of the harbor; and although she was set free soon afterwards, rough weather detained her until it was too late to make the voyage.[15] Even then Selkirk's agents continued to urge the move. On September 19 Owen Keveny, after a difficult and dangerous voyage, reached Churchill, and pleaded that while there was yet time the settlers should be taken up the Hayes River as far as the Rock, about a third of the distance from the Bay to Lake Winnipeg, and left there for the winter. But the stubborn Turner refused to budge, and the weakened condition of the colonists gave point to his refusal.[16] There was nothing to do but prepare for a winter at Churchill; and this the wretched people were forced to attempt at once, as the cold was increasing so rapidly that unless they were soon housed they would freeze in their miserable encampment. Even

to Archibald McDonald, September 7, 1813, copied in McDonald's letter to Selkirk, May 22, 1814, *PAC SP*, pp. 822 f., 1091 f. Selkirk to Alexander McDonald, November 6, 1813, February 26, 1814, *PAC SP*, Vol. 79, pp. 123 f., 125. J.S. to Kate, November 12, 1813, *SP SM*.

14. Auld to Wedderburn, September 16, 1813; Miles Macdonell to Selkirk, August 31, 1813; Miles Macdonell to Archibald McDonald, September 7, 1813, copied in McDonald's letter to Selkirk, May 22, 1814, *PAC SP*, pp. 822 f., 843 ff., 1091 f. Gunn and Tuttle, *Manitoba*, pp. 97 ff.

15. Auld to Wedderburn, September 16, 1813, *PAC SP*, pp. 843 ff.

16. Keveny to Miles Macdonell, September 26, 1813, *PAC SP*, pp. 886 f. Selkirk had sent out instructions that a post be established at the Rock.

the smug Auld was moved to pity: "What will become of these miserable people and ourselves, the God in heaven alone can know."[17]

Throughout the winter, however, Auld continued systematically to try to discourage Selkirk in his colonizing enterprise and to paralyze the movement itself at the Bay. Through his fellow intriguer, McRae, he annoyed Macdonell as much as possible. Keveny was persuaded to join the anti-Macdonell clique. Every effort was made to have Selkirk recall or replace his lieutenant. Even the colonists and their capable young leader Archibald McDonald were vilified by Auld in his letters to the Hudson's Bay Company headquarters and to agents of the Company: the colonists were "the largest dirtiest devils you ever saw," "damned savages from Scotland," and "miserably ineffective"; Archibald McDonald was a "stupid fellow" of "pride and folly," and utterly unfit to manage men. Auld was not in favor of Selkirk's rejuvenation of the effete Company, especially since that process had involved a checkup on the activities of self-seeking officials.[18]

In spite of these unpromising beginnings, the winter at Churchill did not prove as bad for the colonists as they had expected. Scarcity of building materials and official opposition made it necessary to pick a camp site some distance from the fort. A good place was found about fifteen miles up the Churchill River. Despite their bodily weakness and their ignorance of the use of tools, the men were able to put up a number of rough log huts. The settlers themselves, McDonald wrote, were by no means bad hands, but on the contrary uncommonly good as green hands and were all willing workers.[19] So well did the work progress that their quarters were ready for occupation on October 16. They were far from being luxurious. Logs had to serve as chairs, and mud flooring take the place of beds, tables, and the like. Nor for another month were disease and hunger banished. After the departure of the Company's ships there were two more deaths from fever, and one from tuberculosis.[20]

As the winter advanced the intense cold and severe storms of the

17. Auld to Wedderburn, September 16, 1813, *PAC SP,* p. 848.

18. Miles Macdonell to Selkirk, July 24, September 9, 1814; Auld to Wedderburn, September 16, 1813; Auld to Hillier, September 26, 1813; Auld to —, September 26, 1813; Auld to Miles Macdonell, March 13, 1814, copied in Macdonell's letter to Selkirk, July 24, 1814; Archibald McDonald to Selkirk, May 22, 1814, *PAC SP,* pp. 836 f., 845, 875 f., 1091 ff., 1176 ff., 1179 ff., 1216 ff.

19. Archibald McDonald to Selkirk, May 22, 1814, *PAC SP,* pp. 1091, 1095 f.

20. *Ibid.* Keveny to Miles Macdonell, September 26, 1813; Miles Macdonell to Selkirk, August 31, 1813; Auld to —, September 26, 1813; Auld to Wedderburn, September 16, 1813; Auld to Miles Macdonell, March 13, 1814, *PAC SP,* pp. 818, 840, 846 ff., 889 ff., 974. Selkirk to Alexander McDonald, November 27, 1814, *PAC SP,* Vol. 79, p. 132. List of passengers on board the *Prince of Wales* for Red River Settlement, Miles Macdonell, Selkirk Settlement, pp. 165 ff., *PAC.*

North descended upon "Colony Creek" as the Churchill encampment was called. From time to time the settlers were forced to travel the thirty miles to Fort Churchill and back to secure provisions. Some fresh meat, however, was usually available near the camp. In the first weeks of November "the willow grouse or white partridge became very plentiful." At Selkirk's suggestion several of the colonists had brought guns and ammunition with them. They were now able to put them to good use.[21] The conscientious Auld, nevertheless, was not able to watch with equanimity the plundering of his Company's game preserves. Early in December he demanded that all gunlocks be surrendered to him. It is not known how far the order was obeyed. But in the spring Auld wrote to Macdonell and stated that Selkirk should be asked to pay for the partridges eaten by the colonists during the winter. He urged that the partridges at Churchill were equal in value to English beef.[22]

During the winter there occurred two incidents which, though unfortunate in themselves, were not very serious and served to break the monotony for the snowbound emigrants. One of these was an absurd quarrel between McDonald, their leader, and Dr. Edwards. The latter had been persuaded, for a consideration, to remain at the Bay and attend the sick. Unknown to McDonald, he was also appointed by Auld and Keveny to take control of Colony Creek. Auld said nothing of the arrangement until McDonald and Edwards quarreled. But the former commandant quietly accommodated himself to his new status.[23]

The other disturbance was more serious and arose out of the colonists' habit of going down to the fort for supplies.

As they could not return to their families the same day they were permitted to lodge in a room in the lower story of the dwelling-house. Unfortunately, when a few of them were passing the night in a room assigned to them, the ceiling above them caught fire. . . . The entire house was reduced to ashes, and the settlers got the credit of what was no doubt accidental.

The loss was heavy, but probably not as great as Auld made out. He told Macdonell that his loss was "no phantom." "It is," he said, "turned beyond £200 exclusive of all my papers many of which are the collections of 20 years experience and sojourn in this country that no

21. Selkirk to Alexander McDonald, November 17, 1814, *PAC SP,* Vol. 79, p. 132. Auld to Miles Macdonell, March 13, 1814; Archibald McDonald to Selkirk, May 22, 1814, *PAC SP,* p. 974.

22. Auld to Miles Macdonell, March 13, May 11, 1814, *PAC SP,* pp. 979, 1080. Gunn and Tuttle, *Manitoba,* pp. 101 ff.

23. Archibald McDonald to Selkirk, May 22, 1814; Edwards to Auld and Keveny, September 19, 1813; Keveny to Miles Macdonell, September 26, 1813; Miles Macdonell to Auld, February 4, 1814; Auld to Miles Macdonell, March 13, 1814; Auld to —, September 26, 1813, *PAC SP,* pp. 836, 869, 888, 951 f., 973 f., 1097 ff.

money can replace hence no wonder I so bitterly mourn over our misfortunes."[24]

With the approach of spring the settlers began to prepare for the long journey overland to York Factory. An early start was desirable in order that the trip inland could begin when the ice left the rivers. The end of March found them ready with the necessary snowshoes, moccasins, sledges, and provisions. After some delay due to bad weather, they set out on April 6, leaving several old people and noneffectives behind them. The party consisted of thirty-one men and twenty women, some guides from the Factory, and several hunters. All went on snowshoes, the young men pulling the stores and provisions on rough, flat sleds. They traveled early and late in the long northern days. But the difficulties of the journey and the too-constant exertion at length began to show their effects. Stops to relieve "snow-shoe cramp" became frequent and the progress of the expedition became very slow. At last it was found necessary to divide the party, leaving the stragglers to follow with a hunter and an Indian guide. In this way all finally reached the Hayes River and pitched their camp some two miles from York Factory.[25]

About a month was spent in camp before the rivers were clear of ice. During this interval the immigrants fared well, there being plenty of game, and the Company officials being comparatively kind. On May 23 the whole party set out for Red River. They made good time on the long journey, reaching Colony Gardens after twenty-nine days, on June 21. Those who had been left behind at Colony Creek in April, some thirty men, women, and children, were brought to York Factory in the summer by boat. They reached Red River in August, in "good health & spirits."[26]

A few days after the first contingent of Sutherlanders arrived, the heads of families and some young men who represented families that were expected to come next year, were each put in possession of one hundred acres of land on the west side of the river below the Forks.

A few were supplied with two Indian ponies each, while their less fortunate brethren had to be content with one each. . . . In the course of a few days

24. Archibald McDonald to Selkirk, May 22, 1814; Auld to Miles Macdonell, March 13, 1814; Miles Macdonell to Selkirk, July 24, September 10, 1814, *PAC SP,* pp. 975, 1104 f., 1180, 1227 f. Gunn and Tuttle, *Manitoba,* pp. 102 f.

25. Archibald McDonald to Selkirk, May 22, 1814; Auld to Miles Macdonell, March 13, 1814; Miles Macdonell to Selkirk, July 25, 1814, *PAC SP,* pp. 974, 1106 ff., 1194, 2024. Selkirk to Alexander McDonald, November 17, 1814, *PAC SP,* Vol. 79, p. 132.

26. Archibald McDonald to Selkirk, May 22, July 24, 1814; Miles Macdonell to Selkirk, July 25, September 9, 1814, *PAC SP,* pp. 1113 ff., 1194, 1215, 1270. Selkirk to Alexander McDonald, November 17, 1814, *PAC SP,* Vol. 79, pp. 132 ff.

His Excellency mustered his men, servants and settlers. All were treated to a glass of spirits and furnished with muskets and bayonets and ammunition. Two of the settlers refused weapons. . . . The Governor, at the same time telling them, that according to the law of the land the strong dictated to the weak. The colonists were put in the possession of lands and ponies, but where were the implements of agriculture or even the iron to make them of. How strange there were none of these articles taken into the country. . . . Yet His Lordship did not forget to send a battery of field artillery with ammunition and tumbrels, with many chests of muskets and bayonets. . . . The newcomers expected to find a supply of clothing and furniture . . ., but these were not to be had either for love or money, and the only provisions obtainable were a scanty supply of pemmican and cat-fish, and that without the luxury of salt.[27]

Soon after their land had been assigned to them, the Sutherlanders began to plant potatoes and build homes. They formed a valuable and much-needed addition to the Settlement; they were by far the best contingent of colonists that had thus far reached Assiniboia.

27. Miles Macdonell to Selkirk, July 25, 1814; Archibald McDonald to Selkirk, July 24, 1814, *PAC SP,* pp. 1170 ff., 1194 f. Gunn and Tuttle, *Manitoba,* pp. 106 f.

CHAPTER XII

THE EMBARGO ON PROVISIONS

THE North West Company, having failed to prevent Lord Selkirk from securing a title deed to the lands of Assiniboia and having been unsuccessful in keeping him from sending settlers to Red River, was at the end of 1813 quietly awaiting a good opportunity to ruin the colony before it should become too strong to be attacked. This opportunity was provided by the Governor's proclamation forbidding the export of food stuffs from Assiniboia. Since it was Macdonell's embargo which finally led to open war between the Selkirk interests and the Canadian traders, it is important to examine the reasons for the move and to attempt to determine how far those responsible are to be blamed.

Before deciding to issue his proclamation Macdonell had given long and careful thought to the matter; and his reasoning had revolved around two main arguments: first, that the Earl of Selkirk held Assiniboia in fee simple; and secondly, that the food resources of the young Settlement should be safeguarded until the farms could provide sustenance for their owners.

As to the truth of the first of these contentions, Selkirk himself was in no doubt. He had secured the weightiest legal opinion available, and it was in the affirmative. He was able to assure Miles Macdonell that "with respect to our rights of landed property, these are universally considered as clear and indisputable."[1] His own deep conviction in the matter is proved, if further proof were necessary, by the startling risks he ran in promoting such an imposing venture. Even on the assumption that no one could successfully challenge his claim to Assiniboia, Selkirk was daring to the point of rashness in involving his own and his friends' fortunes, prospects, and reputations in Red River.[2] But later legal decisions were to confirm the Earl's contention. When the land was resold to the Hudson's Bay Company in 1836 and to the Dominion of Canada in 1870, it was in each case transferred in fee simple and on the assumption that the Company's right to sell was valid. The case was well summed up before the Select Committee on the Hudson's Bay Company in 1857 by Edward Ellice, onetime North-wester and bitter

1. Selkirk to Miles Macdonell, June 20, 1812, June 5, 1813; Selkirk to Auld, June 18, 1812; Selkirk to Hillier, June 18, 1812, *PAC SP*, pp. 401, 407, 629, 727.

2. Protest of Proprietors of the Hudson's Bay Company against the Grant to Lord Selkirk, May 30, 1811, *Q134*, Pt. II, pp. 333–337.

opponent of Selkirk, later a member and a champion of the chartered Company. Ellice declared:

I have taken the opinion of every lawyer against the company when I was opposed to them, and for the company since I have been connected with them. We have the opinions of Lord Mansfield, Sir Dudley Ryder, Sir Richard Lloyd, Lord Erskine, Gibbs, Romilly, Cruise, Bell, Scarlett, Holroyd; . . . and, I think the universal opinion, without an exception, of the eminent lawyers is, that the proprietary rights of the company cannot be disputed. . . . None of these eminent lawyers, and no lawyer whose opinion I have ever heard quoted . . . have expressed the least doubt as to the proprietary rights granted under the charter.[3]

Thus Selkirk no doubt had the law of England on his side in his claims to Assiniboia. But in the years of struggle and on the actual field of battle his opponents were quick to stigmatize the basis of his title as an absurdity and founded on mere unproved theory, and to resort to the weapons of war to dispute his claim.

As to the question of the scarcity of food for the settlers, Macdonell's experiences in his first year and a half at Red River had convinced him that it was the most pressing problem with which he had to deal, and that the North-westers were prepared to use starvation as a weapon against the colony.[4] The attitude of the traders had constantly grown more hostile since the arrival of the first settlers. In vain Macdonell assured them that his purpose in coming to Red River was "solely to form a Settlement for the purposes of agriculture & civilization of the natives"; and that he "had no orders nor was inclined to give any molestation to the N.W. Co. in the prosecution of their ordinary trade in Furs." By the middle of 1813, however, he was firmly convinced that it was impossible to dwell in amity with them. "From the insidious line of conduct towards us by the N.W. Co., I have," he wrote to Selkirk, "no further delicacy or hesitation in taking a decisive part against them."[5]

The North-westers were not only intriguing in Assiniboia for the purpose of breaking up the Settlement; they were actually taking large

3. *Report from the Select Committee on the Hudson's Bay Company; together with the Proceedings of the Committee, Minutes of Evidence, Appendix and Index,* pp. 327 f., *PP GB, HC,* 2d Sess., XV, Nos. 240. 260. Hereafter, *Report on H.B.C.*
4. Pritchard, Narrative, *Q153,* Pt. III, pp. 738 ff.
5. Miles Macdonell to Alexander Macdonell, April 18, 29, 1813; Miles Macdonell to Agents of N.W. Co., June 1, 1813; W. McGillivray, A. N. McLeod, and Alexander McKenzie to Miles Macdonell, July 22, 1813; Miles Macdonell to Selkirk, July 17, 1813; Miles Macdonell to Auld, April 24, 1814, *PAC SP,* pp. 593, 597 f., 626 ff., 777 ff., 792, 796 ff., 986.

food supplies out of the country while its legal owners or their agents went hungry. During the winter of 1812–13, and again in the following winter, they secured in the Red River area all the pemmican supplied to their Northern and Western fur brigades.[6] Meanwhile the settlers had suffered intermittently from hunger; and the prospects for the future looked worse at the beginning of 1814. The third contingent of emigrants, one hundred strong, was waiting at Fort Churchill to make the trip to Red River in the summer; and Selkirk had given notice that he expected to come out from Scotland in the same season with still another force which he hoped would far exceed in numbers any he had yet sent out. To the Governor of Assiniboia it might well seem that he and his employer were being egregiously imposed upon when he could write that "the N.W. Co. supply their distant trading posts with the provisions procured in this district, whilst we to whom the soil belongs are obliged to go to the expence & trouble of importing from Britain a considerable part of the subsistence of our people."[7]

Besides thinking carefully before acting on the matter, Macdonell had also consulted the opinions of others. He knew what Selkirk had advised the Hudson's Bay Company traders to do in their relations with the North-westers. The Earl had written thus:

You must give them solemn warning that the land belongs to the Hudson's Bay Company, and that they must remove from it; after this warning they must not be allowed *to cut any timber either for building or fuel. What they have cut should be openly and forcibly seized, and their buildings destroyed. In like manner they should be warned not to fish in your waters, and if they put down nets seize them as you would in England those of a poacher. We are so fully advised of the unimpeachable validity of these rights of property, that there can be no scruple in enforcing them whenever you have the physical means.* If they make a forcible resistance, they are acting illegally, and are responsible for the consequences of what they do, *while you are safe, so long as you take only the reasonable and necessary means* of enforcing that which is your right.[8]

But Macdonell went further than these instructions. In the summer of 1813 he advised Selkirk that in consideration of the number of people for whom he had to provide subsistence, it would be well to place an embargo on all food supplies in Assiniboia.[9] The letter reached Selkirk

6. Miles Macdonell to Auld, April 12, 1814; Miles Macdonell to Selkirk, July 17, 1813, *PAC SP,* pp. 793, 998 f.
7. Selkirk to Miles Macdonell, June 12, 1813; Miles Macdonell to Auld, April 12, 1814, *PAC SP,* pp. 650, 661, 998 f.
8. Selkirk to Hillier, June 18, 1812, *Q134,* Pt. II, pp. 368 f.
9. Miles Macdonell to Selkirk, July 17, 1813, *PAC SP,* p. 792.

in the winter of 1813, but before his reply could reach Macdonell the latter had already acted. Doubtless the Governor felt confident that his employer would approve of his course, or he would never have taken it. He had already consulted the Hudson's Bay Company officials at York Factory on the subject. At first Auld had been opposed to an embargo, but after the arrival of the third contingent he declared himself strongly in favor of the plan. He wrote to Macdonell:

It is useless to repeat my entire acquiescence in the whole Proclamation not only in substance but the language. . . . I do most entirely join with you in the absolute propriety & necessity of enforcing the measure of the embargo to the fullest extent especially against the Canadians and it must be truly familiar to you that I have never in practice for a moment separated *our* interests from *yours*.

The other Bay officials concurred. It was, wrote Macdonell, the decided opinion of every person last fall at York Factory that such a measure would be highly proper.[10]

The discussions which had preceded this agreement had taken place in the summer of 1813 while Macdonell was at the Bay awaiting the arrival of the third contingent. The development of subsequent events was such as to confirm the Governor in his course. When he returned from York Factory to Red River early in the fall and found his people still short of food, and when he was forced for the second time to remove them to Pembina to winter,[11] while the hostile fur brigades were well supplied with provisions, the irony of the situation must have struck him forcibly. Later, referring to the summer of 1813, he wrote: "I was not then prepared to restrain the practice, knowing that an order to that effect would not be quietly submitted to; and I had not then the means of enforcing it."[12] The quietness which reigned at Pembina during the winter seemed to offer a good opportunity for inaugurating the new policy. The trading posts had all been abandoned. "Everything," wrote Macdonell, "goes on smoothly with us this year."[13] It was under these circumstances that he proclaimed the food embargo on January 8, 1814.[14] After asserting Selkirk's right to the country of

10. Miles Macdonell to Auld, February 4, April 12, 24, 1814; Auld to Miles Macdonell, March 13, April 15, May 11, 13, 1814, *PAC SP*, pp. 957 ff., 977 ff., 985 ff., 997 ff., 1054 f., 1058, 1079, 1083 ff., 1300 ff.

11. Miles Macdonell to Auld, February 4, April 12, 1814; Miles Macdonell to Selkirk, July 25, 1814, *PAC SP*, pp. 955 f., 998 f., 1184 ff.

12. Miles Macdonell to Auld, April 12, 1814, *PAC SP*, p. 998.

13. Miles Macdonell to Auld, February 4, 1814; Miles Macdonell to Selkirk, July 25, 1814, *PAC SP*, pp. 955 f., 1186.

14. See above, chap. x, n. 27.

Assiniboia, and outlining the boundaries of the grant, the proclamation continues:

And whereas the welfare of the families at present forming settlements on the Red River, within the said territory, with those on their way to it, passing the winter at York or Churchill Forts in Hudson's Bay, as also those who are expected to arrive next autumn, renders it a necessary and indispensable part of my duty to provide for their support, in the yet uncultivated state of this country, the ordinary resources derived from the Buffaloe, and other wild animals, hunted within the territory, are not deemed more than adequate for the requisite supply; wherefore it is hereby ordered, that no person trading in furs or provisions within the territory for the Honourable the Hudson's Bay company, the North-West company, or any individual, or unconnected trader or persons whatever, shall take out any provisions, either of flesh, grain or vegetables, procured or raised within the said territory, by water or land carriage, for one twelvemonth from the date hereof; save and except what may be judged necessary for the trading parties at this present time within the territory, to carry them to their respective destinations, and [such individuals] also may on due application to me, obtain licence for the same. The provisions procured and raised as above, shall be taken for the use of the colony; and that no loss may accrue to the parties, they will be paid for by British bills at the customary rates.

And be it hereby further made known that whosoever shall be detected in attempting to convey out, or shall aid or assist in conveying out or attempting to carry out any provisions prohibited as above, either by water or land, shall be taken into custody and prosecuted as the Laws in such cases shall direct; and the provisions so taken as well as any goods and chattels of what nature soever which may be taken along with them, and also the craft, carriages and cattle instrumental in conveying away the same to any part but to the Settlement on Red River shall be forfeited.

It is indicated above that the policy embodied in this instrument was not inconsistent with the expressed desires of Lord Selkirk and with the actual situation of Macdonell and his followers. Neither was it out of harmony with wider and more political considerations. At this time Britain and Canada were at war with the United States. Even in 1812, when war was only threatening, Selkirk was concerned over the possibility of an American attack on Red River, should hostilities commence. Two days after the United States Congress declared war (June 20), he wrote a letter to Macdonell on the course to be pursued in the event of war. While a reading of this letter makes it clear that Selkirk overestimated both the possibility and the probability of the Americans attacking Red River, it also reveals the fact that he correspondingly underestimated the North-westers in the same respects:

The aspect of affairs between this Country and the American States[15] is very gloomy. . . . I doubt that Canada will make but a feeble resistance, & our situation in the N.W. will then become very critical. Yet I do not despair of holding our ground, even tho' Canada should be conquered. There are much greater natural obstacles against an invader in the N.W. than in Canada & to that we have to add that the Indian population is strongly attached to the English traders & averse to the Americans, so that if the two Companies [the Hudson's Bay and the North West companies] will coalesce cordially for mutual defence & employ their means with skill, I think the Americans could not accomplish their reduction, without a greater force than they can easily spare for the object.

The great difficulty will be to bring the N.W. Co. to coöperate cordially with their Rivals. Neither party will be willing to act under the other: & my only hope is that your personal influence with both, may be the means of bringing them together, & that the obvious interest of mutual defence may induce them to unite under your military command. To promote this junction, I have expressed my Sentiments strongly to Mr. Auld, who with his colleague, Mr. Thomas, would be well entitled in such an emergency to form some temporary agreement with the chief wintering Partners of the N.W. Co. for such an arrangement of their posts that neither party should sustain a permanent or disproportionate injury by detaching towards the American frontier as large a proportion of their men as can possibly be spared.

If from the dissentions of the Traders, or the magnitude of the force sent against you, you are unable to repel the enemy on the frontier, it will become necessary to abandon the Settlement for a time. . . . In quitting the Settlement you must leave the families in possession of the Stockades, with instructions to submit to the Americans, who will probably allow them to continue the cultivation of their farms.

The young men you must take along with you in your retreat; & there are then two different plans between which you have to chuse, 1. It may be proposed to retire towards the Coast & to hold out as long as possible in the Strong country east of Lake Winipic in hopes of being reinforced from England. But there is little prospect of success in this plan. From the nature of our navigation your reinforcements must be precarious & it is scarcely to be supposed that in such a country, you could hold out long enough; particularly as in the woody country you could have very little assistance from the native Indians. I think therefore there is a much better prospect in the other plan: viz:—to collect horses from the establishments of both companies & take to the plains with all your young men, joining with the Indians & exerting your policy to unite the different tribes in a protracted resistance. Their dislike to the Americans is strong, & if you can prevent their being discouraged, you may render yourself very formidable. By following the tactics of the ancient Scythians retiring before the enemy when you cannot otherwise avoid

15. *PAC SP,* pp. 729 ff.

an engagement you may in the boundless plains, keep the long knives at bay for any length of time. They will tyre of following you, & seeing no plunder to be got will content themselves with fortifying a few posts on the rivers, leaving you master of the open country, with your strength entire, & ready to resume the attack whenever circumstances are favourable. If on this plan you are cut off from the coast of the H.B. you can open communication with the Spanish Settlements of New Mexico, where the Commandants will seek no better recommendation for their aid than that you are enemies of the Americans. . . . If by these methods you can hold out for a while, & let me know where you are to be found reinforcements shall come to you thro' one route or another, & it will go hard with me, but I will have a share in your adventures.

So concludes the spirited Earl.

The contrast between the instructions sent by Selkirk to Hillier on June 18, 1812, which were quoted above, and this letter written two days later, is startling, to say the least. In the one, Selkirk advises the Company's agent to treat the North-westers as poachers. In the other, an alliance with them, *under the Governor of Assiniboia*, is suggested as desirable in case of war. But there was no opposition from among his own agents to either course. Auld promised the Earl that in the event of an American invasion the rival companies would unite in resistance under the leadership of Macdonell—at least the Hudson's Bay Company traders would have no hesitation in choosing Macdonell as their leader, though the North West Company's "more fastidious devotion might desire a more Conciliatory Commander."[16] Macdonell demanded from the North-westers "the co-operation of every good subject of His Majesty," and later, in 1814, proceeded to employ the suggested danger as an argument in vindication of his embargo. He declared:

There is no saying to what extent ambition might urge them [the Americans] to push their conquests: & these parts are not too remote for them to attempt to carry their arms to: I consider it therefore to be my indispensable duty to endeavour to secure to the British Empire this part of the Country. . . . In this view the propriety of the Embargo on provisions is sufficiently obvious as a precautionary measure for the public safety & would justify the enforcement of it more extensively than was at first contemplated, for the support of the Settlers.[17]

In view of the actual course of the War of 1812 as far as Macdonell could have foreseen it, this reasoning seems fallacious if not purely sophistical. To the North-westers it was merely a thin veil designed to

16. Auld, Instructions; Auld to Selkirk, September 12, 1812, *PAC SP,* pp. 402 f., 495 f.

17. Miles Macdonell to Wills, May 22, 1814, *PAC SP,* pp. 929 f.

cover a hostile act. They were well aware that as far as the effects of the war were concerned, they themselves were in far greater danger of scarcity than were the settlers in Red River. The Americans had decisively defeated the British on Lake Erie in 1813 and had thus closed the southern route from Montreal to the Northwest. Further enemy successes might easily lead to the complete disruption of the fur traffic between Montreal and the interior; and this was the time chosen by the Governor of Assiniboia to shut off the Montreal traders from the only sources of provisions that would be open to them if the Americans secured control of the Upper Lakes. In that event, and if the embargo were enforced in Assiniboia at the same time, the Athabasca brigades would be forced to discontinue operations and shift for themselves as best they could.[18] Nor were the North-westers alone in taking this view. Their rivals at the Bay, in concurring with Macdonell on the advisability of putting on the embargo, had fully anticipated that the Canadian traders would be beaten out of the field by the enforcement of the measure. Macdonell, too, expected their ruin, and was nothing loath to accomplish it. Such an achievement would not only pay off all scores for the irritations, indignities, and difficulties which he had suffered in his dealings with the North-westers but would prevent any recurrence of such troubles in the future. Best of all, it would completely vindicate the Selkirk title to Red River.[19]

The Governor had delayed proclaiming his embargo because he had lacked the means of enforcing it. But had his position improved by January, 1814, as much as he seemed to think? His language was confident enough, not to use a stronger term. "I look upon the present," he wrote, "to be the last struggle of an expiring party; and when once foiled in it they can never trouble us more."[20] Strangely enough, Auld seemed to agree with him, remarking that "the *Bourgeois* will bluster and strut a bit, and that will be all."[21] It is exceedingly difficult to believe that Macdonell, who had lived most of his life in America, and who had now had considerable experience of the North West Company's

18. William McGillivray for Self and the other Agents of the North West Company to Coltman, March 14, 1818; William McGillivray to Loring, November 28, 1815; William McGillivray to Harvey, June 24, 1815; Simon McGillivray to Bathurst, June 19, 1815, *Q148*, Pt. II, pp. 327 ff., *Q133*, pp. 31 ff., 229 ff., *Q134*, Pt. II, pp. 374 ff. Duncan Cameron, John McDonald, John Wills, J. D. Cameron to Miles Macdonell, June 16, 18, 1814; John Wills to Miles Macdonell, January 25, 1814, *PAC SP*, pp. 923 f., 942, 945 f. *Narrative of Occurrences,* pp. 23 ff.

19. Miles Macdonell to Auld, February 4, April 24, 1814; Auld to Hillier, April 8, 1814; Auld to Miles Macdonell, April 15, 1814, *PAC SP*, pp. 958, 985 ff., 993 f., 1054 f., 1058.

20. Miles Macdonell to Auld, February 4, April 12, 24, 1814, *PAC SP*, pp. 958, 985 ff., 998.

21. Auld to Miles Macdonell, April 15, 1814, *PAC SP*, pp. 1054 ff.

power and methods, should really have concluded that the Canadian organization was about to admit defeat. But Auld's concurrence is even more difficult to explain. Throughout his long career in the fur trade he had witnessed only too frequently the strength and the resourcefulness of the Montreal group; but now he seemed to have forgotten all this, or else he was shamming. Did he perchance hope to see Macdonell and his colony engulfed in the maw of the enraged enemy? This is not known. The Hudson's Bay Company traders in the Red River Valley did not share his optimism. They were distinctly hostile to the embargo.[22]

Yet they could do little about it because their movements were controlled from London, where Selkirk was supreme. Nevertheless, the North-westers did not openly blame Selkirk. "I know," wrote one, "indeed am certain from good authority, that they are plans (the proclamation of Jan. 8, &c.) entirely formed in this Country. His Lordship Selkirk never gave such orders—I am apt to think that that fellow Miles is a mere Desperado at the head of Banditti."[23] Certainly the North-westers were not without some excuse for suspecting that the Governor of Assiniboia had decided on his own responsibility to attempt to ruin their trade west of the Great Lakes.

The extent to which Selkirk may be held responsible for the proclamation of the embargo is not easy to determine. His instructions to the Hudson's Bay Company magistrates, as has been seen, called for a policy, in dealing with the North-westers, which was almost as drastic as the one adopted for Assiniboia. Macdonell was familiar with these instructions. But in the meantime the Earl had changed his mind. In the private letter of June 13, 1813, which was returned to him by Auld, he had cautioned Macdonell to be careful to avoid a collision with the Canadian traders. His insistence and repetition here are full of the theme:

Means will be found of bringing our legal rights to a fair trial before the supreme Tribunal in England; and in the meantime any exercise of jurisdiction on the part of the Company must be confined to what is strictly necessary for preserving the peace and good order of the settlement, avoiding carefully any step that could give a handle for misrepresenting these proceedings as directed to sinister objects and particularly to the invidious purposes of monopoly; keep clear of any unnecessary collision with N.W. Co. (remaining as to them decidedly on the defensive); you must take care to deal with perfect impartiality between the servants of the two Companies; in all occasions of collision with the N.W. people, it will be advisable to be

22. Miles Macdonell to Auld, February 14, April 12, 24, 1814; Auld to Miles Macdonell, March 13, 1814, *PAC SP,* pp. 978 f., 982 ff., 987.
23. James Hughes to J. D. Cameron, April 5, 1815, *PAC SP,* p. 8833.

very sure of your ground and to have a case very well made out before you take any strong measures.

In advising this course Selkirk had no thought of abandoning any part of his claim to the country. He only hoped to venture nothing and perhaps gain much by proceeding as carefully as possible. "With respect to our rights of landed property," he goes on to say, "that is universally considered as clear and unquestionable. But it is a point of prudence not to use these rights in an invidious manner, and for the reason which I have already stated, it would not yet be advisable to attempt forcibly to dispossess the N.W. Company of the posts which they occupy." Nevertheless he still hoped ultimately to oust the company from his territory:

The only point at present to be attended to is that they be not allowed to acquire any prescriptive right which they have not already gained. Twenty years uninterrupted possession though it does not give an absolute right, yet creates a title which cannot be overturned except by a process of peculiar solemnity:—but in any case where the Canadians have not occupied the same spot continually for that length of time, they may be summoned to remove, according to the common form of ejectment. . . . Even though this summons should not be followed by effective removal yet it will be sufficient to interrupt prescription, and this ceremony ought therefore to be used in every case where the N.W. Co. have possessed a post within our limits for nearly 20 years but have not beyond that period. The summons must be made before a number of witnesses so as to secure that the memory of the proceeding shall not be lost.[24]

But this letter, though it probably shows that Selkirk would not have sanctioned the proclamation when it was made, failed to reach Macdonell, and this failure really throws much of the responsibility back on the Earl. When the master changes his mind, the onus of making the change known to his servant is upon him. Of course, Auld was the real villain of the piece. But Macdonell's case is further strengthened by other facts. He had failed to receive notice of the new policy even after having advised Selkirk that

no Government is so fit for such an establishment [judicature], in the beginning as a military one. . . . Martial law might be established by a proclamation. . . . Should Military Law be established within the tract, all traders must take out a Licence, which may answer a good purpose with the N.W. Co. The present state of the country requires strong power to bring it

24. Selkirk to Miles Macdonell, June 5, 1813, *PAC SP,* pp. 629 ff. (June 13, 1813, *PAC SP,* pp. 678 ff. practically the same).

to order. . . . Seeing people well prepared often prevents mischievous consequences.[25]

Further, Selkirk had expressed his fixed intention of going to Red River at the head of such a body of men as would overawe any attempt to resist the lawful authority of the Company.[26] This was to be in 1813. He had not come, but he had sent out a shipment of small cannon, muskets, and ammunition, and Macdonell fully expected that the Earl would come out with a strong force in the following year.[27] As it was, a large reinforcement of men lay at Churchill and would reach Assiniboia in a few months. Then, too, he had the approval of the officials at the Bay. Finally, he lacked agricultural implements, and would have to depend for some time on the natural produce of the country. But when all this has been granted in defense of Macdonell's decision to proclaim the embargo, it must be admitted that he made a mistake. He committed the fatal blunder which no good commander ever commits—he unnecessarily brought on the battle at a moment when the forces of the enemy were stronger than his own. He knew that the greatest power in the country which might be involved in the struggle was the mounted bois-brûlés community; and he also knew that at the moment they were definitely on the side of the North-westers. This one fact is sufficient to throw upon Macdonell most of the blame for any bad results that necessarily flowed from the new policy.

Selkirk's reaction to the news of the proclamation was typical. He deplored the rashness of his subordinate but admitted that the course taken was legally and technically justifiable.[28] Had the Earl been prepared in 1814 to lead a large force to Red River, he would probably have congratulated Macdonell for his sagacity and daring. Certainly his own later conduct at Fort William makes such a conjecture seem reasonable. But as it was, he realized that his chances of success in Assiniboia had been unnecessarily jeopardized, and he feared what the future might bring as a result.

25. Miles Macdonell to Selkirk, May 31, 1812; Selkirk to Miles Macdonell, June 5, 1813, *PAC SP,* pp. 330, 629.

26. Auld, Instructions, *PAC SP,* p. 401.

27. Selkirk to Miles Macdonell, June 20, 1812, June 12, September 10, 1813; Selkirk to Auld, June 15, 1813, *PAC SP,* pp. 667, 669, 694, 719, 865.

28. Selkirk to Miles Macdonell, December 21, 1814, March 23, 1815, *PAC SP,* pp. 1288 f., 1493 f. Selkirk to Alexander McDonald, November 17, 1814, *PAC SP,* Vol. 79, p. 134.

CHAPTER XIII

THE ENFORCEMENT OF THE EMBARGO

From the very first attempt to enforce the food embargo, the Governor of Assiniboia found his course difficult. When his agent attempted to nail a copy of the proclamation on the door of a North West Company post John Wills, the trader in charge, refused permission. This was near Brandon House, a Hudson's Bay Company station a hundred miles west of the Forks, at the junction of the Souris and Assiniboine rivers. Wills, it is true, soon realized that he had taken too strong a line. News had just arrived that the headquarters and communications of his company were being threatened by the Americans. Moreover, Wills was not well and the forces immediately opposed to him were strong. He pleaded with Macdonell that the plan to deprive the Athabasca brigades of their only source of provisions was "a piece of inhumanity unheard of."[1] Auld was moved to rejoice at such a humble remonstrance. As he wrote to Hillier,

We are but poor matches for the Canadians either in cunning or unjustifiable aggressions. The present humiliated condition of these Traders can in no degree lessen my abhorrence or make me forget their abominable tyranny & oppression over us when our numbers were few & their power & State so great. All bullies & cowards are cruel & tyrannical in prosperity while in adversity they can cringe & fawn like Spaniel dogs.[2]

But he rejoiced too soon. Many of the Canadians in Assiniboia and elsewhere were so astonished when they heard of the embargo that they found it difficult to believe Macdonell could have taken such a step;[3] and they continued to buy pemmican from the métis and remove it to their posts. It became clear to the Governor that there would be a general resistance to the enforcement of his new policy.[4]

1. Holdsworth to Miles Macdonell, February 2, 1814; Certificate of Fidler and Stett, January 24, 1814; Wills to Miles Macdonell, January 25, 1814; Miles Macdonell to Selkirk, July 25, 1814; Miles Macdonell to Wills, May 20, 1814; A. N. McLeod to Cameron, July, 1814, *PAC SP,* pp. 919, 920 f., 923 f., 926 f., 1188 f., 8604.
2. April 8, 1814, *PAC SP,* p. 993.
3. Memorandum of a conference between Miles Macdonell and Wills, May 23, 1814, *PAC SP,* p. 931.
4. *Ibid.* Miles Macdonell to Wills, May 20, 1814; Miles Macdonell to Selkirk, July 25, 1814; Auld to Hillier, April 8, 1814; Holdsworth to Miles Macdonell, February 2, 1814; Wills to Miles Macdonell, May 21, 1814; Spencer to Miles Macdonell, May 30, 1814; Spencer to Selkirk, December 8, 1814, *PAC SP,* pp. 921 f., 926 f., 928, 932, 993 f., 1134, 1188. Pritchard, Narrative, *Q153,* Pt. III, pp. 740 f.

The way the allegiance of the natives would go in the impending struggle likewise soon became clear. From the first there was little likelihood the Indians would take part in it. They had nothing at stake and few, if any, strong sympathies. Their attitude was one of friendliness or indifference to both sides. But the métis were different. Many of them were connected with the Canadian traders, directly or indirectly, by ties of race, or culture, or industry; and all of them were more or less economically dependent on the organization which bought their particular product, pemmican. Macdonell, it is true, had made some attempts to win them, defending them against the Sioux and promising them land and seed grain; and after several of them had settled at Fort Daer, he had written to Selkirk that he expected "that in a few years a fine settlement will be made there."[5] But the métis might well have feared that their way of life was threatened by a colonizing project at Red River; and they soon realized that their very living would be in danger if the embargo should be enforced. When Macdonell sent John Spencer, his sheriff, to prevent the North-westers from removing their pemmican from the métis camp near the Turtle River, the hunters saw which side their bread was buttered on, and began definitely to throw in their lot with the Canadian traders.[6]

The latter, although they knew that they were as yet too weak and unorganized to resist the Governor by force, were determined to continue trading for provisions as a matter of policy. If they succeeded in getting food supplies out of the country, that was all to the good. If they failed, they would be forcing Macdonell to make them the injured party.[7] This policy had its first definite results in May. A cargo of pemmican was being taken down the Assiniboine by a crew of North West Company voyageurs. When they were warned that they would be stopped, they hid it. It took Macdonell's sheriff several days of humiliating search to find the cache.[8] In June the main supplies of pemmican began to come down the Souris and the Assiniboine to be stored at the North West Company fort, La Souris, where the rivers come together. When large stores had thus been collected, Macdonell began to fear that they might be smuggled out of the country by a new route, instead of coming past the Forks; so he sent his sheriff with Joseph

5. Miles Macdonell to Selkirk, July 25, 1814, *PAC SP,* pp. 1185 ff., 1199 f.
6. *Papers Relating to Settlement,* p. 155.
7. Miles Macdonell to Auld, April 24, 1814, *PAC SP,* p. 985.
8. Miles Macdonell to Selkirk, July 25, 1814; Miles Macdonell to Wills, May 20, 1814; Wills to Miles Macdonell, May 21, 1814; Spencer to Miles Macdonell, May 30, 1814; Depositions of Pierre Saucisse and André Portras, May 25, 1814; Depositions of Houle and François Jason, May 28, 1814, *PAC SP,* pp. 926 f., 928, 932, 933 ff., 935 f., 1189.

Howse, a Hudson's Bay Company trader, and three men from Colony Gardens, to seize them at La Souris.

When the agents appeared at the fort and asked to be admitted, the clerk in charge, John Pritchard, refused, and bolted the gate. But Sheriff Spencer, having anticipated resistance, had brought a warrant; and he now proceeded to execute it by force. Two pickets were removed from the stockade, the staples pulled from the storehouse door, and the provisions within were seized. Spencer thus secured 479 bags of pemmican, 865 pounds of dried meat, and 93 kegs of fat; in all, about thirty tons of food supplies. Most of it he sent across the river to Brandon House; the rest was taken down to the Point. Macdonell had sent a guard of armed settlers a short distance up the Assiniboine to prevent the Northwesters at Fort Gibraltar from stopping the return party; but the Canadian traders did not attempt to interfere. The Governor seemed to be having his way; the North West Company "had not met with such a bitter Pill to swallow for . . . many years past."[9]

Thus far the enforcement of the embargo had met with passive resistance only; but now the Canadians began to fight back. The decision to begin active opposition was made by the Athabasca traders; and the first of these to act was Duncan Cameron. Although the sheriff, following Macdonell's orders, had seized only Assiniboia stores and had left untouched what had come from outside Selkirk's territory, Cameron decided to treat the seizure as common theft.[10] Gathering a party of armed men, he captured the trader, Howse, as he was returning from La Souris to the Point, and carried him down to Fort Gibraltar with a view to sending him to Montreal to be tried for larceny.[11] Macdonell, when he heard of what had happened, replied by training guns on the river at the Point. The first fruits of this counterstroke were two North West Company light canoes from Lake Winnipeg, with twenty-one men and a chest of arms. The men were soon afterwards set free on a prom-

9. Miles Macdonell to Selkirk, July 25, 1814; William McGillivray to Pritchard, July 23, 1814; Pritchard to McGillivray, July 23, 1814; Spencer to Selkirk, August 10, December 8, 1814; Warrant of Commitment of Miles Macdonell, September 15, 1815, *PAC SP*, pp. 1134 ff., 1162 ff., 1165 ff., 1189 ff., 1304, 1617, 1696 f. Pritchard, Narrative, *Q153*, Pt. III, pp. 740 f. Simon McGillivray to Bathurst, June 19, 1815; William McGillivray to Major Loring, November 28, 1815; Journal of Transactions in Red River Department having reference to the Seizure and Plunder of the North West Company's Property by Mr. Miles McDonell (hereafter, Journal of Transactions, *Q133*), *Q134*, Pt. II, pp. 374 f., *Q133*, pp. 40 ff., 229 f. *Narrative of Occurrences*, pp. 28 ff.

10. Miles Macdonell to Selkirk, July 25, 1814; Proprietors of the N.W. Co. to Miles Macdonell, June 16, 1814; Miles Macdonell to Proprietors of the N.W. Co., June 17, 1814, *PAC SP*, pp. 942, 943, 1189 ff.

11. *Ibid.* Miles Macdonell to Proprietors of N.W. Co., June 15, 1814, *PAC SP*, p. 940.

ise of good behavior, but the arms were held until the disturbance should be at an end.[12]

Macdonell was determined that the North-westers should obey his decree. If they wished to remove provisions they would have to secure licenses from him.[13] But aside from this, he was prepared to be conciliatory. He had advised the traders that the embargo would not be enforced with unreasonable severity, and had offered to return some of the goods which had been seized. He had also offered the services of his surgeon to the ailing Wills. This kindness had been accepted;[14] but the North-westers were not to be conciliated. Their hopes rose as their strength increased. Between 200 and 300 voyageurs were already on their way to join the dozen traders and another 120 voyageurs already at the Forks; and a request for further help had been sent to Fort William.[15] The leaders warned Macdonell that they could count on the aid of all of the métis. "The Sentiments of the Natives, who are not ignorant of the state of things," they wrote, "will show you if rightly represented how far it is necessary for the existence of your infant Colony that a perfect understanding and an intercourse of mutual good offices should exist between us and you."[16] As a matter of fact, a number of armed métis were already at hand, and the North-westers had almost completed their plans for destroying the Settlement. Macdonell had only 88 effective men as against the 120 gathered at Fort Gibraltar.[17] Howse, shut up in the Fort, had learned something of the enemies' plans, and he begged Macdonell to "afford every facility for the adjustment of the present differences by such concessions . . . necessary for the attainment of so desirable an object."[18]

Just at this juncture the North-wester known as Crooked Armed McDonald, having come all the way from the Rocky Mountains, arrived at Fort Gibraltar.[19] He opposed further hostilities, urged conciliation, and finally won over to his point of view most of the winterers at the Fort. Then followed overtures for compromise. Macdonell was as anxious as anyone to promote a peaceful settlement; so, having discussed possible terms with his subordinates, he drew up a compromise

12. *Ibid.* N.W. Co. Proprietors to Miles Macdonell, June 15, 1814, *PAC SP*, p. 939.

13. Miles Macdonell to Proprietors of N.W. Co., June 17, 1814, *PAC SP*, p. 943.

14. Miles Macdonell to Wills, May 20, 1814, *PAC SP*, p. 927.

15. Miles Macdonell to Selkirk, July 25, 1814, *PAC SP*, p. 1193.

16. John McDonald, Duncan Cameron, John Wills, J. D. Cameron to Miles Macdonell, June 18, 1814, *PAC SP*, p. 946.

17. Pritchard, Narrative, *Q153*, Pt. III, pp. 740 ff. Miles Macdonell to Selkirk, July 25, 1814; Selkirk Memorandum, *PAC SP*, pp. 1191 ff., 1306.

18. Howse to Miles Macdonell, June 17, 1814, *PAC SP*, p. 944.

19. Miles Macdonell to Selkirk, July 25, 1814, *PAC SP*, pp. 1191 ff. Pritchard, Narrative, *Q153*, Pt. III, pp. 741 f.

agreement and sent it to Fort Gibraltar. The North-westers, on receiving the document, replied: "We acknowledge the receipt of your Letter and agree to the contents, . . . *tho' very hard upon us,* . . . rather than come to extremities."[20]

On the basis of the agreement thus reached the summer was passed in peace. Twenty kegs and 800 pounds of fat, and 200 bags of pemmican, were to be returned to the North-westers for their "outgoing" brigades, and 175 bags of pemmican for the "incoming." In return, the bourgeois promised to provide the colony with food next winter, and agreed to send canoes to Hudson Bay to bring up oatmeal or other provisions or stores for the Settlement; and for every bag of oatmeal or "piece of 90 lb. weight" the North-westers brought up from the Bay to the mouth of the Winnipeg River, Macdonell was to give a bag of pemmican in exchange. Finally, the Governor engaged to procure transport to England for any furs the North-westers might send to the Bay in the provision canoes;[21] but there was little concession in this, as the British Government had already granted the right, owing to the war.[22] Indeed, the whole agreement was little more than a formality. The winterers who made it for the North West Company might have known that the Montreal partners would never consent to such loss and humiliation. Nor did they; and most of the terms of the agreement were never fulfilled.[23] But in the meantime peace reigned in Red River, the traders from Athabasca went on to Fort William, and the provisions remained in Macdonell's hands.

But the Governor's position continued to grow more difficult as the effects of the embargo accumulated. After the wintering partners had started out for Fort William, he forbade the métis to run the buffalo.

20. *Ibid.* Howse to Miles Macdonell, June 17, 1814; John McDonald, Duncan Cameron, John Wills, J. D. Cameron to Miles Macdonell, June 18, 1814; Miles Macdonell to Proprietors of N.W. Co., June 18, 1814; John McDonald, Duncan Cameron, John Wills to Miles Macdonell, June 18, 1814, *PAC SP,* pp. 944, 945 f., 947, 948. Journal of Transactions, *Q133,* p. 44.

21. Miles Macdonell to Proprietors of the N.W. Co., June 18, 1814; Miles Macdonell to Selkirk, July 25, 1814, *PAC SP,* pp. 947, 1192.

22. John McDonald, Duncan Cameron, J. D. Cameron to Miles Macdonell, June 18, 1814; Draft letter H.B. Co. to Thomas, 1814, *PAC SP,* pp. 945, 1395. Prevost to Bathurst (with enclosure), November 24, 1813; Simon McGillivray to H. Goulburn, March 15, 1814; Joseph Berens (then Deputy Governor of the Hudson's Bay Company) to Bathurst, March 23, 1814; Inglis, Ellice & Co. and McTavish, Fraser & Co. to H. Goulburn, April 25, 1814, *Q123,* pp. 27 ff., *Q130,* Pt. II, pp. 274 f., *Q130,* Pt. I, pp. 66 ff., *Q130,* Pt. II, pp. 276 ff.

23. Miles Macdonell to Selkirk, June 20, 1815; Miles Macdonell, A Sketch of the Conduct of the North West Company toward the Red River Settlement from September 1814 to June 1815 inclusive, *PAC SP,* pp. 1561, 1764. Hereafter, Miles Macdonell, Conduct of North West Company, *PAC SP.* Pritchard, Narrative, *Q153,* Pt. III, pp. 744 ff.

The North-westers who had remained in Assiniboia quietly concurred;[24] but the resentment of the natives increased.

Strangely enough, Macdonell did not seem to realize that he was forging a weapon for the use of the North West Company. "It was . . . with the utmost surprize, that he found the measure [the embargo] subsequently to the arrival of Mr. Duncan Cameron, the ensuing fall, made a subject of accusation against himself, and represented to the free Canadians and half-breeds, as an infringement of their liberty."[25] The insidious opposition from his own side, however, disturbed him considerably. The Hudson's Bay Company traders were disgruntled over the seizure of their pemmican; and they were at the same time disgusted with the Governor's leniency toward their rivals.[26] Even Archibald McDonald protested to Selkirk that Macdonell should never have given up any stores, but should have taken the opportunity "to drive the North-westers entirely out of the river." He also revealed the fact that the Governor was not even master in his own house. "Since coming here," he wrote, "I won't hesitate to say that though Capt. McD. has officers under him they don't consider him their superior officer at all; Mr. Auld is the man they look upon, and are sure to communicate to him from time to time every movement Capt. McD. makes."[27]

Under the strain of so many difficulties Macdonell became pessimistic and discouraged. Late in July he begged Selkirk to relieve him of his post as soon as possible, urging that he was unequal to the task of reconciling so many different interests.[28] When he went down to the Bay in the early autumn he was further plagued by the petty and malicious accusations of the tortuous Auld.[29] Under the burden of all these worries his health threatened to fail.[30] But Selkirk, as before, stood by him, and though gently reproving him for his rashness in the matter of the embargo, spoke very generously on the whole. Macdonell was deeply moved. "I feel exceedingly oppressed," he wrote. "I . . . now think your presence here indispensably required." He realized fully that he had made a mistake in issuing his proclamation, when he read the letter Auld had returned to Selkirk, the letter "which had I received at the

24. Miles Macdonell, Conduct of North West Company, *PAC SP*, pp. 1767 ff. *Papers Relating to Settlement*, p. 158.

25. *Ibid.*, p. 158.

26. Miles Macdonell to Selkirk, June 25, 1815, *PAC SP*, pp. 1300 ff., 1580.

27. Archibald McDonald to Selkirk, July 24, 1814, *PAC SP*, pp. 1173 f.

28. July 24, 1814, *PAC SP*, p. 1179.

29. *Ibid.*, pp. 1176 f., 1180. Miles Macdonell to Selkirk, September 9, 1814; A. Edwards Diary, August 27–September 1, 1814, *PAC SP*, pp. 1207 f., 1216 ff. Hereafter, Edwards, Diary, *PAC SP*.

30. Miles Macdonell to Auld, September 3, 1814; Edwards, Diary; Thomas to Selkirk, September 20, 1814, *PAC SP*, pp. 1207 ff., 1213 f., 1240 f.

time would have been a caution to me in my proceedings since; and perhaps would have prevented me from falling so much into errors."[31] Nor could Auld refrain from heaping on one sort of coals of fire. "You may be assured," he wrote, on hearing of Macdonell's intention to resign, "that I will use my utmost endeavours to satisfy the Noble Earl of the Propriety and necessity of his accepting cheerfully your resignation by which you thus give a most feeling mark of your devotion to his interests while you follow the only road to your true happiness."[32]

But Auld's "sympathy" was wasted. Macdonell soon recovered his health and at the same time his old courage and optimism seemed to return. He decided not to resign, and his enemies at the Bay were much chagrined.[33]

On September 2 the *Prince of Wales* anchored at York Factory with fourteen men for the Settlement. She brought no families. Selkirk had held back a large number of Sutherlanders, whom he had promised to send out that year, because of the fate of the expedition of 1813, and until word should reach him that they were ready to receive them.[34] Those who did come were troublesome and not worth anything. "I am much afraid," wrote Macdonell to Selkirk, "that instead of tilling the ground they will be apt to run away in the Spring with the N.W. Canoes."[35]

Nevertheless, early in September the Governor set out with his men for Colony Gardens, the newcomers clamoring "for good fare & liquor." The trip was made without mishap and in good time. All reached the Settlement by October 19.[36]

Macdonell was well pleased with the progress that had been made at the Gardens in his absence. In less than four months the Sutherlanders had become quite well established. They had built comfortable houses and raised some crops. Large quantities of potatoes had been grown, Indian corn had done fairly well, the turnips again had grown to an extraordinary size, and the wheat and barley had yielded "tolerably." Best of all, the colonists were becoming attached to the country. "Young men & maids were not altogether idle in the matrimonial affairs. Many were waiting for the return of the Captain to join them in that humble embrace." There had also been additions to the rising col-

31. Miles Macdonell to Selkirk, September 9, 1814, *PAC SP,* pp. 1218, 1225 f.
32. Auld to Miles Macdonell, September 1, 1814, *PAC SP,* p. 1213.
33. Edwards, Diary, *PAC SP,* pp. 1207 ff.
34. White to Selkirk, June 15, September 10, 1814; Miles Macdonell to Selkirk, September 9, 1814; Miles Macdonell, Conduct of North West Company; Selkirk to Miles Macdonell, April 12, 1814, March 23, 1815, *PAC SP,* pp. 1006 f., 1148, 1221 f., 1225, 1230, 1495, 1763.
35. Miles Macdonell to Selkirk, September 9, 1814, *PAC SP,* pp. 1221 f.
36. *Ibid.* Miles Macdonell, Conduct of North West Company, *PAC SP,* p. 1763.

ony in the shape of several children born during the summer. The situation seemed so favorable that Macdonell decided to stand his ground and winter for the first time at the Gardens.[37] The wintering partners of the North West Company had returned from Fort William in August[38] and had caused some excitement in the Settlement; but the Governor felt that he was now in a position to defy their hostility. He would not have felt so confident had he known what was being prepared against him.

37. *Ibid.,* p. 1765. Miles Macdonell to Selkirk, July 25, 1814; Spencer to Selkirk, December 8, 1814, *PAC SP,* p. 1198.
38. *Statement Respecting Settlement,* p. 11.

CHAPTER XIV

"THE COLONY ALL KNOCKED IN THE HEAD"

WHEN the Montreal partners, gathered at Fort William to meet the fur brigades from the West, learned of the enforcement of the embargo and the humiliating agreement made with Macdonell in June, they were exceedingly wrathful. The news first reached them through Alexander Macdonell, who had traveled rapidly by light canoe. He had been the only bourgeois at Fort Gibraltar to persist in opposing the compromise; and he now declared that had not Crooked Armed McDonald arrived, an end would have been put to the colony, "as their plan of attack was so well arranged, that Captain Miles McDonell's party could not have escaped, and he himself would have first fallen, and by his, Alexander McDonell's ball."[1] The partners were of a like mind. "Keen, uncompromising, and resourceful," they put their heads together to evolve plans for revenge. Chief among them was Lieutenant Colonel William McGillivray, a justice of the peace and a member of the Council of Lower Canada. "It is the first time," he declared, "the North West Company has ever been insulted"; and he was determined to exploit to the full the peculiar strength of his organization in order to avenge the insult.[2]

For the winter partners and their servants promotion depended on success. Bitter reproof was now their meed. Pritchard, who had permitted the chief seizure of pemmican, was accused of cowardice. Crooked Armed McDonald, a brother-in-law of McGillivray, was anathematized as a peacemaker.[3] "Tearing people to pieces," wrote Alexander Macdonell, "seems to be the order of the day; judge then the situation of the absent when those on the ground can't escape what is here called censure."[4] *He* called it dourness and bullying. Duncan Cameron, who had remained at Red River, received a letter from Archibald Norman McLeod, McGillivray's second at Fort William, severely criticizing him and his fellow winterers. "The strange and disagreeable events that took place at Red River last spring," went the letter, "were much spoken of, severely animadverted on, and totally disapproved. . . . Mr. Wills escaped a decided and Public censure by his reported state of health.

1. Pritchard, Narrative, *Q153,* Pt. III, p. 742.
2. *Ibid.,* p. 744. *Papers Relating to Settlement,* p. 159. Martin, *Selkirk,* p. 77.
3. *Ibid.,* pp. 159 f. John McDonald to Dougal Cameron, July 19, 1814, *PAC SP,* p. 9008.
4. Alexander Macdonell to J. D. Cameron, July 23, 1814, *PAC SP,* p. 9006.

. . . I assure you my friend it will take years of Active and persevering industry to do away the impression made by the unfortunate compromise of our honour at Red River."[5]

Having thus keyed up the wintering partners to the desired pitch of zeal, the Montreal nabobs proceeded to bare to them their plans for revenge. Red River had been the scene of the humiliation; there, accordingly, vengeance would be exacted. The two chief agents selected for the purpose were Duncan Cameron and Alexander Macdonell; and they were anxious to regain favor by a signal success. "All the black sheep," wrote Alexander, "were to be turned out. . . . Matters to be carried with a high hand, and the concern to retrieve their honour."[6] Cameron was to offer the settlers free passage to Upper Canada, and to stop at little in persuading them to accept. Miles Macdonell was to be arrested and brought to Montreal a prisoner. McLeod, who was a magistrate, provided the necessary warrants. The American war had necessitated a policy of rigid economy; but now the bourgeois were lavish. The canoes going west were loaded with luxuries for bribes; the leading settlers were to receive generous presents, and instructions for the campaign were given by word of mouth, to insure secrecy and security.[7]

News of what was afoot, however, leaked out. One of Alexander Macdonell's letters fell into the hands of the enemy. It read:

You see myself and our mutual friend Cameron, so far on our way to commence open hostilities against the Enemy in Red River; much is expected from us, if we believe some; perhaps too much: one thing certain, that we will do our best to defend what we consider our rights in the interior. Something serious will undoubtedly take place. Nothing but the complete downfall of the colony will satisfy some by fair or foul means. A most desirable object, if it can be accomplished; so here is at them with all my heart and energy.[8]

This was grave news for Miles Macdonell and the friends of the colony. Montreal was much farther away than Hudson Bay; and the law, theoretically, was on Selkirk's side. But these very handicaps had forced the Canadian company on the one hand to develop a mobility and a striking power unknown among their rivals, and on the other to assume the resourcefulness and the unscrupulousness of the outlaw. Furthermore, the policy of penetration necessarily followed by the North-

5. July, 1814, *PAC SP,* p. 8604. Martin, *Selkirk,* p. 77.

6. Alexander Macdonell to J. Cameron, July 23, 1814, *PAC SP,* p. 9007.

7. Pritchard, Narrative, *Q153,* Pt. III, pp. 744 ff. Deposition of John Pritchard, February 18, 1817, *Q143,* pp. 332 ff. Hereafter, Pritchard, Deposition. Pritchard to Selkirk, June 20, 1815, *PAC SP,* p. 1547. *Papers Relating to Settlement,* p. 159.

8. Alexander Macdonell to John McDonald, August 5, 1814, *PAC SP,* p. 1204.

westers had led to the growth of the métis community on the plains and, as had been shown, to the attachment of its sympathies to its source. Clearly the colony would have to look well to its defenses in the face of such opposition. In faraway Montreal Colin Robertson, now in the employ of the Hudson's Bay Company, was organizing a strong force of voyageurs to invade the North West Company's fur fields in Athabasca. But in the meanwhile the Canadians' star was in the ascendant.[9]

Already, too, before Miles Macdonell had come back from the Bay to Red River, the enemy had commenced active operations. Spencer, the sheriff, had been arrested by Cameron on one of the warrants provided by McLeod, and removed first to Fort Gibraltar, then to Lac La Pluie, and later to Fort William.[10] On hearing the news Macdonell was furious.[11] But this was only the first of a series of defeats. The enemy was winning over the métis. Cameron had appeared decked out in sword and scarlet uniform and was posing as "Commanding Officer R.R.," and "Captain in the Voyageur Corps." The Corps had been disbanded a year before, but this was not known at Red River. McLeod had provided the uniform. Meanwhile Alexander Macdonell had gone up the Assiniboine to the center of the bois-brûlé "nation" at Qu'Appelle. Apparently on his advice the métis again defied the Governor by running the buffalo near Turtle River. Their attitude toward the settlers and the English company's servants grew more hostile; and they refused to let the newcomers hunt buffalo. When Macdonell protested, his messenger was detained. When he arrested Peter Pangman, a North-wester formerly employed by the Hudson's Bay Company, four of his men were seized by Cuthbert Grant, an outstanding young métis. Macdonell, fearing open war, held a conference with Grant at Pembina. Both men were conciliatory and agreed to exchange prisoners. But this was only a lull.[12]

The North-westers were making progress not only with the natives but with the settlers. Cameron's official appearance and ingratiating manners, supported by his warrants, made a few of the latter waver in their allegiance; and though the majority were willing and even anxious to defend their leader, the sheriff, by force of arms, the subordinate offi-

9. *Papers Relating to Settlement,* p. 160. Berens to Bathurst, December 20, 1815, *Q134,* Pt. II, p. 324.

10. Spencer to Selkirk, December 8, 1814; Miles Macdonell, Conduct of North West Company; Miles Macdonell to Selkirk, June 20, 1815, *PAC SP,* pp. 1138 f., 1561, 1763.

11. J. D. Cameron to N.W. Partners, January 3, 1815, *PAC SP,* p. 8745.

12. Miles Macdonell to Selkirk, June 20, September 19, 1815; Miles Macdonell, Conduct of North West Company; Statements by Settlers, York, February, 1816, *PAC SP,* pp. 1561 ff., 1700 ff., 1764 ff., 2004. Colville to the Governor, Deputy Governor and Committee of the Hudson's Bay Company, December 5, 1815, *Q134,* Pt. II, pp. 275 ff. *Papers Relating to Settlement,* pp. 161 ff.

cers lacked the courage to act; and those among the colonists who urged action were quieted by the traitorous. This made it possible for the North-westers to carry Spencer off to Fort William, and directly past the colony fort, while no one dared to interfere.[13]

During the fall and winter Cameron carried his subtle policy of corrupting the settlers' allegiance much further. By a judicious mixture of aggressiveness, gaiety, and Gaelic he so wrought upon them that by the New Year many were ready to listen to suggestions that they desert. When, early in January, the Governor was absent from Colony Gardens, Cameron wrote to two of the most dissatisfied settlers, offering them free transportation to Upper Canada and free lands on their arrival there. "I have no interest whatever," he declared, "in making you this promise—but what humanity points out to me." Selkirk, Auld, and Macdonell he stigmatized as the greatest enemies ever they had.[14] At the same time he reported progress to his chiefs. "I hope," he wrote, "in spite of every difficulty that is thrown in my way to prevent it, to take all Lord Selkirk's Colony, amounting to about 120 Souls, men, women, and children, for if they are allowed to remain here as free-booters, we may leave the Country to themselves."[15]

While Cameron was thus contriving, Macdonell was at Fort Daer, seemingly unaware of the dangerous progress being made by the trader, although he received repeated tidings from Archibald McDonald that the settlers were in a very turbulent state. It was only when two colonists arrived from the Forks in April to tell him "that all the settlers had gone to the North-West fort with their families and luggage" that he decided to return. On reaching Colony Gardens he heard the details of the disaster. Not all the settlers had deserted, but those who had gone over had taken the fieldpieces to Fort Gibraltar. This had occurred on April 3. The North-westers had supplied the plan, and it was carried out in broad daylight. The officers who might have interfered were locked up in their mess-room; and Cameron had congratulated the traitors and cheered them all with a glass of spirits.[16]

13. Statements by Settlers, York, February, 1816; Miles Macdonell, Conduct of North West Company; Spencer to Selkirk, December 8, 1814, *PAC SP*, pp. 1138 ff., 1763, 2004, 2006 f., 2013, 2030, 2040.

14. Cameron to Livingston and McEachern, January 10, 1815, *Q139*, pp. 208 ff. Miles Macdonell to Selkirk, June 20, 1815; Miles Macdonell, Conduct of North West Company; J. D. Cameron to Wintering Partners, January 3, 1815; Siveright to Taitte, March 16, 1815; Spencer to Selkirk, October 17, 1815 (with enclosures: affidavit of Hector McEachern, October 9, 1815 and letters), *PAC SP*, pp. 1561 ff., 1726 ff., 1764 ff., 1867, 8748.

15. Cameron to James Grant, March 22, 1815, *PAC SP*, p. 1865.

16. Miles Macdonell, Conduct of the North West Company; Miles Macdonell to Selkirk, June 20, September 19, 1815, *PAC SP*, pp. 1562 ff., 1700 ff., 1773 ff. Colvile to the Governor, Deputy Governor and Committee of the Hudson's Bay Company, De-

Of course, the North-wester's way was not all easy sailing. Many of the Highlanders refused every offer, even when threatened with the loss of their property and massacre by the Indians. But he held to the main parts of his plan. Miles Macdonell was to be seized and removed from Red River. "He must be taken," wrote Cameron's fellow plotter, "otherwise we never shall have peace—now or never, Cameron."[17] And the "red-coat" acted in the middle of April by sending John Siveright, with one of McLeod's warrants, to arrest the Governor.

When the warrant was served on him, Macdonell was at first ready to refuse service. Then he hesitated; and not without reason. His position was desperate enough. The métis formed the strongest force in the country and they were actively against him now. Prompted by the North-westers, they claimed ownership of the Red River country, and demanded compensation for the colony lands. Recently they had taken to singing war songs as they rode by the Settlement; and under cover of darkness they fired from the bushes toward the settlers' houses. The North-westers had established a camp at Frog Plain, about three miles north of the Gardens, with Alexander Macdonell in charge. From there they directed the campaign against the Settlement. The Indians refused to join in this attack, but the métis drove off some of the settlers' stock and broke open and plundered many of their houses. Alexander Macdonell set up a battery with the guns leveled at the colony fort; and scarcely was it completed when orders came from Fort William to push the attack.[18]

After nightfall on June 10 there was a preliminary exchange of shots. Early next morning the North-westers again opened fire. Two settlers were wounded by their bullets and two more by the explosion of a wallpiece inside the fort. Several more desertions followed. The settlers still remaining urged Macdonell to give himself up to stop the bloodshed. The Governor realized that it was not merely his own person that the North-westers sought, but the destruction of the colony itself. To give his people an opportunity of judging more clearly for themselves he resolved to conceal himself some days and accordingly, taking the chance of being misunderstood, he disappeared in the night, with one attendant.[19]

cember 5, 1815; Duncan Cameron to Archibald McDonald, April 3, 1815; Pelly to Bathurst, March 25, 1818 (with petition from Red River settlers, September 10, 1816 enclosed), *Q134*, Pt. II, pp. 278 ff., 287, *Q150*, pp. 362 ff.

17. Alexander Macdonell to Duncan Cameron, March 1, 1815; Duncan Cameron to James Grant, March 22, 1815, *PAC SP*, pp. 1865 f., 9028.

18. Miles Macdonell, Conduct of North West Company; Miles Macdonell to Selkirk, June 20, September 19, 1815, *PAC SP*, pp. 1563 f., 1702 ff., 1775 f. Pritchard, Deposition, *Q143*, pp. 334 ff. Pritchard, Narrative, *Q153*, Pt. III, pp. 749 f.

19. Miles Macdonell, Conduct of North West Company, *PAC SP*, pp. 1780 f.

Upon learning of Macdonell's departure Cameron, by letter, ordered all the colony and the Company's people to depart immediately from the river, and he signed himself "Captain, commanding officer in Red River." This order united in some degree the few men remaining, and they resolved to defend themselves to the last. Macdonell heard of this determination in his concealment, and came back on June 14, after an absence of three days.[20]

On the night of June 15,

the enemy came in force, surprised a number of people at the farm huts, and made many prisoners. . . . Archibald McDonald happened to be there, broke his way through them, was fired upon, but escaped unhurt. They established themselves there, having next morning taken down the fence that secured the grain, with which [sic] they made a rampart round the position, and mounted on it some pieces of . . . brass artillery; their horses they set to graze on the wheat fields and other crops. . . . The enemy seemed determined to destroy everything.[21]

On June 16, Charles McKenzie, another North West Company partner, reached Fort Gibraltar with further reinforcements. A deputation of settlers and servants was sent to him "to endeavour to procure a peace on some fair terms; but . . . McKenzie was not inclined to interfere." The deputation, which consisted of the members of Macdonell's appointed council, was informed that if the Governor would surrender himself, hostilities should cease instantly. Thereupon the deputation returned to the Settlement and urged Macdonell to give himself up for the safety of the colony. Verbal conditions of peace were then arranged between the North-westers and the council; and after they had been confirmed and listed in a memorandum, the Governor went to meet McKenzie, and walked with him to the fort. "The damned robber," as they called him, was caught at last, and the "Rascally Republic," as someone had named the Settlement, seemed to have been practically ruined. On June 22 Macdonell was embarked for Fort William.[22]

The main objectives of the North-westers were now almost attained. Alexander Macdonell was left at the Forks to complete the ruin of the Settlement. The settlers who were going to Upper Canada were paid for their agricultural implements and taken away in canoes. On June 25 those who remained behind were served with this notice: "All settlers to

20. *Ibid.*
21. *Ibid.*
22. *Ibid.*, pp. 1781 f. Duncan Cameron to James Grant, March 22, 1815; Miles Macdonell to Selkirk, July 2, 1815; Warrant of Commitment of Miles Macdonell, September 15, 1815, *PAC SP,* pp. 1582, 1696 f., 1865. Duncan Cameron to Servants of the Hudson's Bay Company and those of the Settlement of Red River, *Q134,* Pt. II, p. 285.

retire immediately from Red River, and no trace of a settlement to remain." It was useless to resist; and two days later thirteen families amounting to upwards of sixty persons, "houseless, wounded and in extreme distress, . . . took to boats, and saving what they could, started for Norway House (Jack River), declaring they would never return." The next day, North West Company clerks led forty or fifty bois-brûlés to the Gardens and set fire to all the houses, trampled down the crops— which, ironically, looked very promising that year—drove off or killed all the cattle and sheep, and stole all the colony's horses as well as those belonging to the Hudson's Bay Company.[23]

The news of these occurrences, coming to Fort William, caused great rejoicing. This time there were praises instead of curses and browbeatings for the winter partners. Cameron and Macdonell had retrieved their lost prestige; the insult of 1814 had been avenged. Cameron was the man of the hour; and he surely deserved the title of a most clever and successful villain. "I am happy to inform you," wrote Simon McGillivray to Archibald McGillivray, "that the Colony has been all knocked in the head by the N.W. Co."[24] Charles McKenzie wrote to his colleague, Siveright: "I hope that things will go on better now since the Colony is gone to the Devil."[25] Some of the partners, however, expressed their fear that the means employed had been too violent.[26] But they let no inkling of this get out to the lesser servants and the settlers. The former were regaled with feasts, fine wines, and presents, and were publicly thanked. The deserting colonists were treated considerately and promised comfortable transport to Upper Canada. The ringleaders were given sums of money proportionate to their services.[27]

But such generosity and rejoicing partly defeated its own purpose. It became quite clear to the settlers that humanity and philanthropy had not motivated their "benefactors." They began to feel dissatisfied. Many demanded better terms. Those who had come under pressure said openly that they had been duped. When they went on to Upper Canada the hardships of the journey increased their disillusionment. J. D. Cameron was at Sault Ste Marie when the expedition reached that point on August 21. "They arrived here," he wrote to his relative, Duncan, "quite a different people to whatever you saw of them, entirely dis-

23. John McLeod to Selkirk, August 5, 1815; Pritchard to Selkirk, June 20, 1815; Red River and Colonial Register; Miles Macdonell, Conduct of the North West Company, *PAC SP*, pp. 1547 ff., 1594, 1782, 9732 ff. Miles Macdonell to Selkirk, July 25, 1815; John McLeod to Thomas, August 5, 1815, *Q133*, p. 77, *Q134*, Pt. II, p. 295. McLeod to Simpson, n.d., McLeod, Journal, p. 371, *PAC*.

24. July 2, 1815, *PAC SP*, p. 1868.   25. July 15, 1815, *PAC SP*, p. 8534.

26. James Hughes to John McLaughlin, January 24, 1816, *PAC SP*, p. 1466.

27. Red River Colonial Register, *PAC SP*, pp. 9732 ff. *Papers Relating to Settlement*, pp. 173 f.

pleased with the payment they got for their things, mad with rage at seeing people who had been more against us than for us cross the lake in a vessel like Gentlemen and Ladies, while they who had always been ready to sacrifice their lives for us came all round the lake pulling at the oars like Slaves."[28]

The North West Company partners, too, had cause for restraining their exultation. There was always the possibility, as some realized, that there might come a day of reckoning, with consequences unpleasant for themselves. Nor had the obnoxious colony been completely smothered out. A spark of life still remained in one log cabin where John McLeod, a Hudson's Bay Company clerk, and three men, Archibald Currie, Hugh McLean, and James McIntosh, kept watch over both the Company's and the colony's property.[29]

28. *PAC SP*, p. 1464.
29. John McLeod to Simpson, n.d., McLeod, Journal, pp. 371 f., *PAC*. John McLeod to Selkirk, August 5, 1815, *PAC SP*, pp. 1594 f.

CHAPTER XV

THE RED RIVER COLONY RESTORED

WHILE the fortunes of his colony had waxed and waned in America, Lord Selkirk had remained in Britain, putting off his intended visit to Red River, making persistent attempts to send out more settlers and also trying to obtain government recognition in favor of the Hudson's Bay Company's charter rights, as against those of the North West Company. He found the latter task by far the more difficult of the two. The Hudson's Bay Company Directors and the North West Company agents were still afraid to risk an adverse decision for their respective organizations. The Canadian company had established for itself "a practical monopoly, based on a popular theory of open competition";[1] but they preferred to seek redress by their own hands rather than by the law,[2] and for more than thirty years they had successfully taken care of their interests.[3]

The English company, on the other hand, "had an unpopular theoretical monopoly," and a corresponding responsibility before the law, with which to face the keenest kind of competition. Such being the case, Selkirk was forced "reluctantly to depend as best he could, upon the rights conferred by the Charter."[4] Early in 1815 he prepared elaborate judicial instructions for the government of the charter territories. In June these instructions were formally completed and presented by the Company's Governing Committee to the Colonial Office, with an urgent request that "they should be submitted to the consideration of His Majesty's Attorney and Solicitor-General, for their opinion." But there was no response. The document was pigeonholed and the opinion of the law officers of the Crown was never ascertained.[5]

Before long Selkirk discovered that the influence of the North West Company was strong enough in both Britain and Canada to prevent the arm of the law extending justice as far as Assiniboia. When he heard from Colin Robertson, who was in Montreal, that the Northwesters were planning hostilities against his colony, he applied to Lord

1. Martin, *Selkirk*, p. 91. 2. *Papers Relating to Settlement*, p. 163.
3. William McGillivray to Harvey, June 24, 1815, *Q133*, p. 34.
4. Martin, *Selkirk*, p. 91.
5. *A Letter to the Earl of Liverpool from the Earl of Selkirk, Accompanied by Correspondence with the Colonial Department in the Years 1817–18–19, on the Subject of the Red River Settlement in North America* (London, 1819), pp. 14 ff. Berens to Bathurst, April 19, 1816, February 4, 1818; Hudson's Bay Company memorial to Bathurst, *Q139*, pp. 219 f., *Q150*, Pt. I, pp. 190 ff., *Q134*, Pt. II, pp. 269 ff.

Bathurst, the Colonial Secretary, for protection, for some "measure not of vindictive justice but of precaution and police."[6] Bathurst was not well disposed toward the Earl's business. He had called the Red River scheme "wild and unpromising";[7] and though he had arranged for Selkirk to secure a few guns in 1813,[8] the American war was his real reason. He had then turned the whole question over to the Under-Secretary, Henry Goulburn, a man in close and friendly communication with the North-westers and exceedingly prejudiced against Lord Selkirk and the Hudson's Bay Company. That Goulburn was actually "bought" by the North West Company has been suspected, but never proved. His actions favorable to them provided the basis for the suspicion.[9]

Despite Goulburn's hostility and Bathurst's indifference, Selkirk was able in a personal interview to persuade the Secretary that the colony needed military protection. Instructions were dispatched to Sir Gordon Drummond, Acting-Governor of the Canadas, authorizing him to furnish such protection to the settlers at Red River as could be "afforded without detriment to His Majesty's Service." But it was not assumed that Selkirk's fears were really justified. The step was being taken only that Drummond might "make the necessary inquiries as to the grounds of the fears expressed by them [the Hudson's Bay Company Directors —really Lord Selkirk] on this point." At the same time the Governor was counseled

to take especial care . . . to abstain from doing any act or expressing any opinion which may tend to affect the question in dispute between the Hudson's Bay and North-west companies, the sole object of the present instruction being, to secure the lives and properties of His Majesty's subjects established on the Red River, from the predatory attacks of the Indian nations in the neighbourhood.[10]

It is so difficult to believe that the officials at the Colonial Office could have been entirely ignorant of the state of affairs in the colony that the historian is bound to conclude that they sent these instructions largely in order to get rid of the question for the time being, or to protect themselves from future repercussions. No doubt the remoteness of the

6. Selkirk to Bathurst, March 3, 1815, *PAC SP*, pp. 1476 ff.

7. Halkett to Selkirk, April 17, 1816, *PAC SP*, pp. 2197 ff.

8. Petition of the Governor and Company of Adventurers of England trading into Hudson's Bay for and on behalf of the Right Honourable the Earl of Selkirk, *Q124*, pp. 169 f.

9. J.S. to Halkett, June 29, 1816; Lady Selkirk to Colvile, May 6, 1817; Lady Selkirk to Selkirk, May 7, 1817, *SP SM. PAC SP*, pp. 1815, 1840, 6513. Simon McGillivray to Goulburn, March 14, 1815, *Q134*, Pt. II, p. 329.

10. Bathurst to Drummond, March 18, 1815, *Q136A*, pp. 69 f. Bathurst to Selkirk, March 11, 1815, *PAC SP*, p. 1487.

scene of conflict was constantly in their minds and the potential effort and expense of establishing order there would be powerful deterrents to taking a decisive stand, particularly during the trying period at the close of the Napoleonic wars. With the entire British governing class clamoring for retrenchment and immediate reduction of taxation, the government was anxious to avoid any new and costly adventure in a part of the world which was not only remote but of distinctly secondary importance. At any rate, shortly after receiving these instructions from the Colonial Office the Governor was able to inform the Hudson's Bay Company agents in Montreal, Maitland, Gordon, Auldjo and Company that

if the lives and property of the Earl of Selkirk's settlers are, or may be hereafter endangered, that danger will arise principally from the conduct of Mr. Miles McDonnell, his Lordship's agent, who appears . . . to be actuated by anything but a spirit of moderation and conciliation, in his language and demeanour, towards the Servants of the North West Company. . . . He has, moreover, assumed powers which cannot possibly . . . have been vested in him, or any agent private or public of any individual or of any chartered body.[11]

There was now no doubt about the attitude of the Acting-Governor of the Canadas on the subject of the Red River Colony. Nor is there now any doubt as to where he secured his information and opinions. As soon as he had received Bathurst's instructions his secretary, Colonel Harvey, wrote to the North-wester, William McGillivray, then a legislative councilor for Lower Canada, as follows,[12]

Sir Gordon Drummond has received a communication from high authority, directing him to make enquiry into the foundation for a strong degree of apprehension, which appears to be entertained by the Earl of Selkirk and the Hudson's Bay Company, for the safety of their settlers on the Red River, in consequence of an idea which has been instilled into their minds, by persons resident in Canada, that the Indian tribes in the neighbourhood of that Settlement have been *instigated* to commit the horrid and atrocious act of attempting the destruction of the whole population of that Settlement. I must not conceal from you, that some of the servants of the North-West Company are suspected of being concerned in this diabolical plot. Sir Gordon Drummond, however, feels that he cannot more strongly evince the high respect which he entertains for the heads of that most respectable body, and his perfect confidence in their candour and liberality of sentiment, than by the

11. Harvey to Maitland, Gordon & Auldjo, July 12, 1815, *Q133*, pp. 53 f.
12. Drummond at his dinner table (in the presence of Colin Robertson) discussed the Red River situation very freely with McGillivray; in fact so freely that Robertson wrote to Selkirk that the Governor was so partial to McGillivray that "we can expect little consideration from him." *PAC SP,* p. 1796.

course he has not hesitated to adopt, in applying himself to *them* for the information which they assuredly possess the best means of affording, and which his Excellency is equally assured they are too honourable and conscientious to withhold.[13]

McGillivray vindicated the Governor's respect and assurance by proving too "honourable and conscientious" to remain silent. He replied:

I cannot but express the feelings of indignation to which this calumny gives rise. I deny, in the most solemn manner, the allegations whereon this shameful accusation is founded. . . . Insinuations against the North West company and pretended alarms, brought forward by persons capable of such acts, come indeed from them with an ill grace; but the motives are manifest, and meant to anticipate or counteract the feelings which their own conduct, when known, would naturally produce. . . . Under the guise and cloak of colonization, . . . [the Earl of Selkirk] is aiming at and maturing an exterminating blow against the . . . [North West Company's] trade. Insinuations of alarm and false accusations form part of the system, and his agents and servants are probably instructed to bring them artfully forward, to raise prejudices against us; surely interested representations from such a quarter should be received with caution.[14]

Such was the curious answer of the man who in the preceding year had organized at Fort William the campaign for the total destruction of the Red River Settlement. It is difficult to decide which is more astounding: the fatuousness of the Governor or the barefaced lying of the legislative councilor.

But this striking exhibition of harmony between the North-westers and the government in Canada merely paralleled a similar cordiality which was still being maintained in London. At the same time that Selkirk was begging the government for protection against the machinations of the North West Company, that company's London agents were assuring Goulburn and Bathurst at the Colonial Office that the accusations made against them by Lord Selkirk and the Hudson's Bay Company were "utterly unfounded" and "manifestly malicious," and that the North West Company partners "stationed in the interior of the North American Continent feel too much for the miseries already inflicted upon their unfortunate countrymen, the victims of his lordship's visionary speculations, to add by any action of theirs, to the risks which those deluded emigrants undoubtedly run for the disputes which must arise between them and the Indians."[15] To this assurance that there was

13. June 14, 1815, *PAC SP,* pp. 1537 f.
14. William McGillivray to Harvey, June 24, 1815, *Q133,* pp. 29 ff.
15. McTavish, Fraser & Co., Inglis, Ellice & Co. to Goulburn, March 18, 1815; Simon McGillivray to Bathurst, June 19, 1815, *Q133,* p. 236, *Q134,* Pt. II, pp. 372 ff.

no need of government intervention in Red River, Drummond added the information, in a letter to Bathurst, that it was "decidedly impracticable" to give the requested protection to the Settlement, on account of the enormous expense—"far beyond any idea your Lordship would form of it" and the danger of bringing on a war with the Indians![16]

The climax came, however, when Goulburn actually received the news of the destruction of the colony. Instead of being at last roused to righteous indignation, as one might expect from a civil servant whose main faults were stupidity and ignorance, he was all sympathy for the settlers and all admiration for the generosity of the North-westers. When the Hudson's Bay Company wrote to him, protesting against the outrage in Assiniboia, he had already heard the story from the other side. His reply to the Hudson's Bay Company would have warmed the hearts of the North-westers. "That part of your Letter," he curtly informed Governor Berens, "which relates to the Arms stated to have been seized by the Agents of the North-West Company will be transmitted to the Governor of Canada in order that the arms may be recovered for the public Service."[17]

While it was thus being clearly manifested that it was worse than useless for Selkirk to look to the government for redress for the outrages his colony had suffered, steps were being taken to reply to the North-westers in the only language they really understood and respected—that of force. Even while the lone defenders of the surviving remnant of the Settlement were maintaining a precarious hold, succor was approaching rapidly from two directions, from the Bay and from Montreal. Selkirk had made preparations not only to reinforce his colony with another strong force of settlers, but also to compete with the North West Company in the rich and hitherto undisputed fur country of the Athabasca. For the latter purpose Colin Robertson had for some time been engaged at Montreal in collecting a band of French-Canadian voyageurs.

Robertson was quite familiar with the North West Company's methods from his earlier experiences with them on the Saskatchewan; and, as we have seen, as early as the year 1810 he had urged the English company to adopt the technique of their rivals, push their trade beyond the limits of the charter lands, and seize a part of the rich returns from the fur fields of the Far West. "If," he wrote in 1812, "you could see the returns of the North West Company from the Athabasca, the Lesser Slave Lake and English River region, you should not be idle

16. August 16, 1815, *Q133*, pp. 11 ff.
17. December 14, 1815, *PAC SP*, p. 1815. See also Goulburn to Governor of the Hudson's Bay Company, December 29, 1815, *PAC SP*, pp. 1840 f.

Spectators, especially when your natural Situation might enable you to be the principal *Actors*."[18] The finest furs the Northwest produced came from the Athabasca region; and it was for the Athabasca brigades of the Canadian company that the métis of the Red River prepared their great supplies of pemmican. Under Selkirk's management the Hudson's Bay Company Directors came to see the force of the ex-North-wester's arguments; and thus in 1814 he was sent to Montreal to organize the first Hudson's Bay Company expedition for the Athabasca.[19]

Robertson had a predilection for Canadian canoe men; he maintained that the French Canadians made the best voyageurs in the world. Orkney Islanders, he felt, were "ill calculated for the Country." To quote his advice to the Company Directors,

When an Orkneyman engages in your Service it is more from necessity than inclination; he can find Employment no where else, and when he has accomplished his darling object of gathering a few pounds, he bids farewell to a country that affords him no pleasure. This often obliges you to abandon Posts until a supply of men arrive from those Islands, so that when you reestablish these Posts, you find yourselves Strangers to the Country, and almost forgot by the Natives. An other thing, Orkney men are unacquainted with the manner of voyaging in canoes, by which the Northern business is conducted. It is true they in time would learn but that time is precious; during that period they are doing little or nothing for the interest of the Company, and what is hard, when they are capable of performing their duty, it is then they think of retiring to their native Country.

The Canadians, on the other hand, according to Robertson, were

spirited, enterprising and extremely fond of the Country; . . . easily commanded, . . . they will follow their Master wherever he goes. It is not so with the Orkneymen if the place they are ordered to, has only the name of being hard, or the Voyage difficult to perform, they will throw a hundred obstacles in the way, and when either discontented with the Post or their Master, you can never get them to do their duty but by halves. It is not so with the Canadian, he will sing while surrounded with misery, the toil of the day is entirely forgot in the encampment; they think themselves the happiest people in existence, and I believe they are not far mistaken.[20]

By the spring of 1815 Robertson, assisted by John Clarke, a native of Montreal, had collected about one hundred voyageurs; and all was ready for the blow to be struck in the Athabasca.[21] Clarke, who was to

18. Robertson to Hudson's Bay Company, January 10, 1810, *SP SM. Ibid.*, 1812, *PAC SP.*

19. Pritchard, Narrative, *Q153,* Pt. III, p. 747.

20. Robertson to Hudson's Bay Company, 1812, *PAC SP*, pp. 535 ff.

21. *Narrative of Occurrences,* p. 47.

lead the Athabasca brigade, had had considerable experience in the fur trade. In 1810 he and three others had helped John Jacob Astor found the Pacific Fur Company; and he had also worked for the North West Company.[22]

Early in May Robertson set out from Terrebonne with an advance party of twenty men and followed the usual route to the interior, reaching Jack River about a month after the destruction of Colony Gardens. The news of the breakup of the Settlement was first heard by Robertson and his party when they reached the Lake of the Woods and passed the North-westers who were taking the deserting settlers to Fort William. From the canoe men Robertson learned that the loyal settlers had been driven away by the métis. On hearing this bit of news he hurried toward Jack River, suspecting that the expelled colonists would be waiting there. A short distance from the mouth of the Winnipeg River, on the east side of Lake Winnipeg, he met John Pritchard, who told him the settlers were at Norway House and in a wretched condition. Robertson and his voyageurs reached Jack River in the latter part of July.[23]

In spite of the disastrous events at Red River, Robertson did not now despair but felt confident that all might yet be well. His zeal and hope became infectious; and in a few days he had persuaded all the disheartened settlers to return to Red River with him and begin over again. The return journey was made in August. When the Forks were reached it was discovered that conditions there were not as bad as had been feared. John McLeod, Hugh McLean, Archibald Currie, and James McIntosh, who had been allowed to remain and guard the remnants of the Company's and the colony's property, had cared for the crops that had not been destroyed, made some hay, and repaired some of the fences. With the help of a few free Canadians they had also begun the construction of a new fort at a bend in the Red River about two miles below the Forks.[24] To these encouraging factors was also added the expected arrival of another band of emigrants from Hudson Bay.

22. Clarke to Selkirk, August 10, 1816; Thomas to Hudson's Bay Company, September 15, 1815, *PAC SP*, pp. 1425, 2499 ff. Davidson, *The North West Company*, pp. 133 f., 137.

23. Narrative of Pierre Chrysologue Pambrun of Montreal, formerly lieutenant in the Voltigeur Corps of Lower Canada, March 16, 1819, *Q153*, Pt. III, 712 ff. Hereafter, Pambrun, Narrative, *Q153*. Pritchard, Deposition, *Q143*, p. 340.

24. *Ibid.* Thomas to Hudson's Bay Company, September 15, 1815, *PAC SP*, p. 1425. Peter Fidler, A Narrative of the reëstablishment, progress and total destruction of the Colony in Red River, 1816, with a concise account of the conduct and proceedings of the N.W. Co. in their effecting it, *PAC SP*, pp. 2509 f. Hereafter, Fidler, Narrative, *PAC SP*. Pritchard to Selkirk, August 22, 1816; John McLeod to Selkirk, August 5, 1815; Colin Robertson's Journal kept at Fort Douglas, September 18, 1815, to October 12,

The fifth contingent of settlers sent by Lord Selkirk to Red River had left Scotland early in the summer of 1815 under the command of Robert Semple, newly appointed Governor of the Hudson's Bay Company territories in America.[25] Semple, a native of Boston, Massachusetts, was a cultured man of literary tastes. During the American Revolution his parents had espoused the Loyalist cause. After the war young Semple had gone to London and taken service with an enterprising commercial firm. In a dozen or more years he had served his apprenticeship and become one of the most progressive agents of the concern. His duties had caused him to travel extensively in Germany, Spain, Italy, Asia Minor, the West Indies, Venezuela, Brazil, and South Africa. In 1803 he published his first book, *Walks and Sketches at the Cape of Good Hope*. In the next ten years he wrote five more volumes, many of which were reviewed in the *Edinburgh Review*. His writings show him to have been a man of considerable and varied talent.[26]

What reasons Selkirk had for thinking Semple might cope successfully with the situation at the Settlement, are not known. Later events were to show him somewhat erratic in judgment and prone to underestimate his opponents. But then, the task he had been set was not an easy one—perhaps, even, with the means at his disposal, an impossible one. At first, however, all went well. His followers, mostly from Helmsdale and the parish of Kildonan, were excellent material. Perhaps a better class of men had never landed in America. The journey across the Atlantic was without disturbance, a "good passage, free from Sickness, accidents, and quarrels; the greatest cordiality prevailed among all classes throughout the ship. . . . Perhaps the same number of people under the same circumstances never landed on a foreign shore in higher health and spirits."[27]

When the expedition reached York Factory on August 27, the first news to greet the settlers "was the compleat dispersion of the Colony at Red River." Semple's assurance was somewhat daunted. Such lawless ferocity, he wrote to the Company's officials in London, could be paralleled only in the annals of Indian warfare. But he was firmly convinced that the British Government would do justice.

1815, *PAC SP,* pp. 1595, 1711, 2597. John McLeod to Simpson, n.d., McLeod, Journal, pp. 371 f., *PAC.*

25. Rogers to Selkirk, September 7, 1815; Semple to Hudson's Bay Company, September 20, 1815, *PAC SP,* pp. 1442, 1659 ff.

26. Sketch of Robert Semple, *SP SM. Dictionary of Canadian Biography* (Toronto, 1926), pp. 364 f.

27. Rogers to Selkirk, September 7, 1815; Selkirk to Miles Macdonell, March 23, 1815, *PAC SP,* pp. 1495, 1659 ff.

It is almost a moral certainty that redress will be obtained at home for past aggressions and security against the future. . . . Should our Government refuse immediately to interfere the inevitable consequence will be that Two great Trading Companys of the same nation will be reduced nearly to the State of Two Indian Tribes at War and the scenes of bloodshed and confusion will mark the whole of our tracks from the centre of the Honourable Company's Territories to the extreme limits of the Athapascan.[28]

Such words may have been prophetic of future calamities; but neither Semple's references to the fur-trade war nor to the probable actions of the British Government are easy to explain in the light of the events that have been described above, and of the information which was at his disposal. On the one hand, he seems to have been given to exaggeration, and on the other, to credulity.

Contrary to custom, little time was lost at the Bay, as the officials there gave the expedition every accommodation possible. Thomas Thomas, who had succeeded Auld as Superintendent of the Northern Department, "in particular . . . crowned his long Services by a cooperation so frank & sincere" as to place the Governor "under the greatest obligations."[29] The majority of the colonists left the Factory on September 6 and 7 in four boats. Peter Fidler was in charge of the voyage inland. About September 14 he embarked with the remaining settlers, taking eight head of cattle and six pigs which Selkirk had sent out with the colonists. Semple, accompanied by Thomas and his family, did not set out until September 24. The trip inland proved very difficult and slow, owing to bad weather. It was not until November 2 that the expedition, now assembled in one party numbering about 180, entered the Red River. On November 3 Semple pushed on to Fort Douglas. The others arrived the following day, all in good health and high spirits.[30]

Under the management of Colin Robertson Colony Gardens had in a few weeks' time taken on the appearance of a prosperous settlement. Hay in large quantities had been cut and stacked. The wheat, barley, oats, peas, and potatoes which had been tended carefully by McLeod and his companions, were all harvested and stored. The yield had been good, in spite of the rough tactics of the North-westers and the métis. There were about 400 bushels of wheat, 200 of barley, and 500 of potatoes. The task of constructing a new fort was almost finished. Many

28. Semple to Hudson's Bay Company, September 20, 1815; Rogers to Selkirk, September 7, 1815, *PAC SP,* pp. 1444 ff., 1680.

29. *Ibid.* Auld had been dismissed from the Company's service in 1814.

30. Alexander Macdonell to Selkirk, September 12, 1816; Semple to Selkirk, December 20, 1815, *PAC SP,* pp. 2718 ff., 2735.

of the settlers had built new cabins. Others had made a good start in house building.[31]

Although winter was close at hand, happiness was in the air. A good harvest, an unusual abundance of buffalo, and bountiful supplies of catfish in the river, insured plenty of provisions for the winter. Many of the newcomers were enjoying a reunion with relatives or friends who had come out with previous expeditions. On November 4 the reëstablishment of the colony was formally celebrated. Semple was exultant. "The Colours were hoisted," he wrote, "the guns were fired, at night we laughed and drank and danced, and now the serious Calculations of the Colony Commence."[32]

This optimism was shared by the Hudson's Bay Company traders. The brigade which promised such fair returns from Athabasca set out with pomp and confidence. To Semple the North-westers did not seem at all formidable. Duncan Cameron had returned from Fort William to Fort Gibraltar about the beginning of September. Alexander Macdonell had returned with him, but had gone on to Qu'Appelle. Semple was judging the Canadian company from what he could see at the Forks. "Nothing," he wrote to Selkirk in December, "but the grossest mismanagement on the part of those of the Colony could have enabled such miserable opponents to triumph over them, Half-breeds and Old worn out Canadians! I really did too much honour to this Crew in supposing them to be so formidable."[33] He would have done better to have taken the opinion of Robertson, who really knew the North-westers.[34] At this time, moreover, Auld, the former Hudson's Bay Company official, was in London, intriguing with the enemy. "I really believe, my Lord," wrote Robertson to Selkirk, "that Auld has been one of the greatest enemies your Lordship ever had."[35] The advice was better calculated than timed. Had Auld been removed before the middle of 1811, the Earl's colonizing venture might have avoided many of the disasters which attended it.

Meanwhile the Hudson's Bay Company had been meeting with more discouragements from the British Government. The ordinance for the government of the charter lands, which Selkirk and the Governing Committee had drawn up and submitted to the Colonial Office for the

31. Pambrun, Narrative, *Q153*, Pt. III, pp. 713 f. Semple to Selkirk, December 20, 1815; Fidler, Narrative; Colin Robertson's Journal kept at Fort Douglas, September 18, 1815, to October 12, 1815; Fidler to Keveny, August 11, 1816, *PAC SP*, pp. 1711 ff., 2510, 2560, 2721 f.

32. Fidler, Narrative; Semple to Selkirk, December 20, 1815, *PAC SP*, pp. 2510, 2721 f.

33. *Ibid.*, p. 2723.

34. Robertson to Selkirk, November 12, 1816, *PAC SP*, p. 3033.

35. Robertson to Selkirk, January 1, 1817, *PAC SP*, p. 3037.

opinion of the Crown law officers, had become the subject of a desultory correspondence. As already noted, the policy of the Colonial Office was one of indifference and negligence. Months passed and nothing was done. When almost two years had elapsed and the Directors of the Company had for the third time requested a decision, they were at last told that the question could not be settled until crimes already committed in the territories had been tried in the courts.[36]

When and where such legal action would be taken were matters as yet unknown; so Selkirk, convinced that he could do nothing in Britain to secure justice in Red River, decided at last to go to America himself. He found it difficult to secure a satisfactory representative to leave in Britain, as he had few staunch friends in the Hudson's Bay Company; but he felt that his presence in Assiniboia was essential to the success of his colony;[37] and in September, 1815, he and Lady Selkirk and their two children took passage at Liverpool for New York. On landing in New York Selkirk received his first news of the destruction of the Settlement.[38] But only when he arrived in Montreal did the full seriousness of his position become apparent to him. McGillivray's "arrogance and violence," Drummond's "unaccountable prepossession" in favor of the North West Company, and Goulburn's nefarious influence through the Colonial Office were in evidence everywhere and nearly drove him to despair. Shortly after his arrival in Montreal he wrote to Berens:

I should not entertain a doubt of our obtaining sufficient support from the Government if the matter were fairly investigated, & examined to the bottom. But [such] is the strange ascendency, which the N.W. Co. have obtained over the mind of Lord Bathurst or (perhaps I should rather say) of Mr. Golburne, that I have great doubts, whether the papers will receive so much as a deliberate perusal, unless the Colonial Office be roused to attention by something more than the simple merits of the case. The present Governor of this Province (I am sorry to say) partakes of the same prejudices; & after all that has happened, declines to send a military force to Red River & reposes confidence in the professions of Mr. McGillivray. It will require the utmost exertions to overcome this unaccountable prepossession & I must entreat that you, & all those who feel an interest in our cause, will unite their efforts to obtain a fair hearing. Among all the Gentlemen who are connected with the H.B. Co., there must surely be enough of weight to prevent an under Secretary from throwing aside our representations as waste paper.[39]

36. See this chapter, n. 5.
37. Selkirk to Miles Macdonell, March 23, 1815, *PAC SP,* p. 1501. Andrew Colvile was secured to manage Selkirk's affairs. See Colvile to the Governor, Deputy Governor and Committee of the Hudson's Bay Company, December 5, 1815, *Q134,* Pt. II, p. 274.
38. Selkirk Diary, September 8 to November 1, 1815, *SP SM.*
39. Selkirk to Berens, November 18, 1815, *PAC SP,* pp. 1940 ff.

Not even the firm of Maitland, Gordon and Auldjo was left in peace. It was almost excluded from "society" through the influence of the North-westers.[40]

One of Selkirk's chief purposes in visiting Montreal was to offer to make an amicable settlement with the North West Company, of both the fur-trade rivalry and the Red River Settlement quarrel.[41] At first he found it impossible even to open negotiations. "The natural arrogance & violence of . . . McGillivray's temper (which under any circum-stances would have been a material impediment) . . . [was] consider-ably increased, both by the triumph, . . . which . . . [had] attended his machinations, and by the vindictive spirit, which he . . . [deemed] it necessary to keep up among his followers."[42] Finally, through the offices of John Richardson, Selkirk was enabled to offer his terms.

The Hudson's Bay Company had given the Earl authority either to negotiate a union with the North West Company or to arbitrate their differences. But in the atmosphere of jealousy and suspicion which now enveloped both sides, union was out of the question. Even less were the Canadians disposed to arbitrate. As in the case of an appeal to the courts, they stood to gain nothing by arbitration that they did not al-ready possess; and, on the other hand, they might lose something. They made it clear to Selkirk that they would evacuate the charter lands only when compelled by law; and it was their intention to postpone a legal decision as long as possible. They were, indeed, quite willing to agree to a division of the fur lands; but such a proposal would not even be con-sidered by the English company.

As a result of the really uncompromising attitude of both sides, the attempt at negotiation proved fruitless.[43] Selkirk had hoped that in the event of such a failure his own presence in the Canadas would enable him to secure for his colony that protection which Governor Drummond had hitherto refused. But in this matter he was likewise disappointed.[44] The activities and influence of the North West Company were too much for him; and there was another insidious obstacle. Neither Bathurst

40. Robertson to Selkirk, November 18, 1814, *PAC SP*, pp. 1796 f.

41. Berens, Pelly, Langley, Webb, Colvile, Pitt, Hunter to Selkirk, August 28, 1815, *PAC SP*, pp. 1631 ff.

42. Selkirk to Berens, November 18, 1815, *PAC SP*, p. 1940.

43. The materials relating to the negotiations are voluminous. See especially *PAC SP*, pp. 217 ff., 222 ff., 227 ff., 232 f., 234 ff., 240, 241, 242 f., 244 ff., 252 ff., 1631 ff., 1821 ff., 1842 ff., 1845 ff., 1940 ff., 2184 f., 2227 ff., 2283 f., 2289 f., 2342 ff., 2632 ff., 2635 ff., 2756, 2810.

44. The correspondence relating to the attempts to get military protection for Red River is voluminous. See especially *PAC SP*, pp. 1815, 1840 f., 1974 ff., 2084 ff., 2243 ff., 2248 f., 2342 f. and *Q133*, pp. 116 f., 195 ff., 198 ff., *Q134*, Pt. II, 322 ff., 372 ff., *Q139*, pp. 215 ff., *Q150*, Pt. I, pp. 188 ff.

nor Goulburn nor Drummond would be convinced that Assiniboia was anything better than a howling wilderness or that it was worth saving for the Empire; and they kept this attitude in spite of all representations to the contrary. They had the considered opinions, not only of Selkirk but also of Miles Macdonell, Semple, Robertson, Colonel McDouall, the British commandant at Michilimackinac, and of dozens of the Red River settlers, both that the Northwest was a rich and valuable region in itself and that it was of great value from "a national point of view."[45] None the less, they remained obdurate and contemptuous,[46] while their protégés, the North-westers, jeered at the rival representations.[47] In spite of Goulburn's opposition, however, Selkirk with some trouble did secure the Governor's consent to take with him to Red River a force of fifteen soldiers; but only as a private security against robbery and assault. Even then Drummond found it expedient to account to the North-westers for having made the concession. "With the view of removing any alarm which the measure may excite in the Gentlemen of the North-West Company at Montreal," he wrote, "I shall feel it incumbent on me to explain to them my motives in detaching even this small party." The ironic touch was added when "the Gentlemen" applied for a guard of their own. But it proved unnecessary for the Governor to comply with their request. The De Meuron regiment, which contained Selkirk's "fifteen soldiers," was disbanded, and his Excellency was forced with "regrets" to inform the Earl that he now had "not the means of relieving them by a similar party from any other corps."[48] Disappointed, Selkirk gave up for the moment all attempts to secure government protection.

45. Selkirk to McDouall, March 30, 1816; Selkirk to Sherbrooke, June 17, 1816; Semple to Selkirk, December 20, 1815, *PAC SP*, pp. 2126, 2346 f., 2728.

46. Goulburn to Hudson's Bay Company, December 29, 1815, *PAC SP*, p. 1840.

47. Strachan, *Letter*.

48. Selkirk to Drummond, March 11, 19, April 4, 16, 1816; Drummond to Selkirk, March 15, 23, April 13, 20, 1816; Selkirk to Wilson, May 6, 1816; Harvey to Selkirk, May 14, 1816, *PAC SP*, pp. 2081 ff., 2084 ff., 2105, 2109 f., 2167, 2233 ff., 2237 f., 2239 ff., 2242, 2249.

CHAPTER XVI

THE MASSACRE OF SEVEN OAKS

EVEN after their successes in Red River in 1815 the North-westers were afraid that the Settlement might "rise and be herself again." They had had news of the preparation of the contingents under Robertson and Semple long before these forces had set out for Assiniboia; and they also knew that they themselves were not strong enough to oppose successfully the reoccupation of Colony Gardens.[1] They hoped, however, that in the event of such a contingency, they would again be able to work upon the fears of the bois-brûlés, with the same success as before. The matter was left in the capable hands of the victors of the last campaign, Duncan Cameron and Alexander Macdonell.[2]

The arrival of Robertson and Semple with strong forces at the Forks, however, seemed to shake the allegiance of the bois-brûlés. "Freemen and all" looked upon the Selkirk reinforcements as the real "conquerors." They wished to be on the winning side, and at the moment the future of the North-westers did not look very bright.[3] The slackening confidence of their allies, added to the reoccupation of Colony Gardens, dampened the spirits of the Canadian traders.

Nevertheless, despite these circumstances the two ringleaders of intrigue went vigorously to work. During the fall Alexander Macdonell, with the aid of Cuthbert Grant, who was soon to be appointed captain general or "Generalissimo" of all the métis in the country, succeeded in raising a band of over forty bois-brûlés and freemen.[4] The material had its defects; it was hard to secure and harder to hold. All the freemen, according to Alexander Macdonell, who should have known, were "Damned Rascals" and "few of the Half-breeds little better."[5] It was not until well on in the spring, and after prodigious efforts, that the Canadian traders were well assured of the wholehearted support of the "New Nation" in the coming "sport in Red River." "I am happy to inform you," wrote Generalissimo Grant to Alexander Fraser, a North

1. McGilles to Alexander Macdonell, August 2, 1815; Thain to J. McDonald, June 20, 1815; Alexander Macdonell to Duncan Cameron, October 23, 1815; Simon McGillivray to Archibald McGillivray, July 2, 1815, *PAC SP,* pp. 1868, 1877, 1883, 2383 f.

2. Fidler, Narrative, *PAC SP,* pp. 2510 ff.

3. Alexander Macdonell to Duncan Cameron, October 23, 1815, *PAC SP,* p. 1883.

4. James Sutherland, A Narrative of Outrages Committed against the Hudson's Bay Company Servants by the North West Company at Qu'Appelle during the Winter 1815–1816, *PAC SP,* pp. 1946, 1951. Hereafter, Sutherland, Narrative, *PAC SP.* Fidler to Semple, April 1, 1816, *PAC SP,* p. 2147.

5. Alexander Macdonell to J. D. Cameron, March 3, 1816, *PAC SP,* p. 1864.

West Company clerk, "that they are all united and staunch & ready to obey our Commands."[6]

This great change in the temper of the métis had been facilitated by news from the Athabasca region. The Hudson's Bay Company brigade which had set out in the fall with such confidence had been stricken with disaster. John Clarke, the leader, had seemed sufficiently well qualified for such an undertaking, as he had "an undaunted spirit & much general knowledge of the business of a Trader."[7] He had been accused of being too fond of unnecessary and expensive parade. But why he failed to take provisions for his brigade is a mystery, explicable only in terms of Clarke's strange character. Food was usually plentiful in the farther Northwest, but fur brigades going there for the winter always took plenty of stores to see them through in case of a local shortage. Clarke took none. Eight canoes, fifty men, and six clerks left Lake Athabasca "without a mouthful of provisions . . . except what a Muskegon Indian they brought with them could procure them."[8] For this both Clarke and the Company's officials were to blame. When the brigade had reached Jack River from Canada in the fall of 1815, no supplies awaited it, although Clarke had expected them to be there. The season was too far advanced, Clarke explained later, for the expedition "to remain until the Crafts would arrive from Y F [York Factory] with the necessary supplies required."[9] But by his very use of the words "necessary supplies" Clarke showed that his was the responsibility for the disaster. When a man in charge of an expedition decides for the sake of gain to risk the lives of employees unnecessarily, he is guilty of criminal negligence. Someone had blundered in picking Clarke for the leadership of such a venture.

The North-westers, for their part, did their best to make Clarke's course difficult. Realizing that their richest field was at stake, they hurried off into the Athabasca region ahead of their rivals, cornered provisions, and lured or drove the Indians away. These tactics, under the most favorable circumstances, would have made the task of the Hudson's Bay Company men hard enough; but even the weather fought

6. March 13, 1816, *PAC SP*, p. 1876. See also Grant to J. D. Cameron, March 13, 1816; Alexander Macdonell to Duncan Cameron, March 13, 1816; Alexander Macdonell to J. D. Cameron, March 13, 1816; Sutherland to Semple, March 11, 1816; Fidler to Semple, April 1, 1816; Sutherland, Narrative; Fidler, Narrative; Alexander Macdonell to Selkirk, September 12, 1816, *PAC SP*, pp. 1467 f., 1864, 1881, 1887, 1946 ff., 2080, 2147 ff., 2510 ff., 2736 f. Pritchard, Deposition, *Q143*, pp. 342 ff. Pambrun, Narrative, *Q153*, Pt. III, pp. 714 ff.

7. Thomas to Hudson's Bay Company, September 15, 1815, *PAC SP*, pp. 1425 f.

8. John McGillivray to William McGillivray, January 17, 1816, *PAC SP*, p. 9145.

9. Clarke to Selkirk, August 10, 1816, *PAC SP*, p. 2499. *Robertson's Correspondence*, pp. lxx, xcvii, 60 f.

for the Canadians. The winter of 1815–16 proved so exceptionally severe, and the local supply of provisions so scanty, that even the Northwesters were forced to eat the provisions they had brought with them from Assiniboia. "We would have starved most completely," wrote the bourgeois, John McGillivray, "were it not for the Dried Provisions collected in the Summer."[10] The plight of the Hudson's Bay men was pitiful. At two of their posts, indeed, they managed to secure a bare living; but at Great Slave Lake they were forced to beg their rivals for food, giving up, in return, all the property in their charge for a year; and on the Peace River fourteen men, one woman, and a child starved to death.[11] The first English attempt to invade the Athabasca had been a grim and costly failure.

Meanwhile the winter in Red River was spent with the Selkirk party well in the ascendant. In the late autumn the majority of the settlers were taken to Pembina by Semple and Sheriff Macdonell in order to solve the food problem more easily.[12] At the Forks Colin Robertson ruled triumphant. He had from his first arrival taken a stern attitude toward Duncan Cameron, whose dangerous character he well knew. He was determined to "hold his ground by inches," if necessary; he had early resolved to punish with exemplary severity any "molestation given to our people at Qu'Appelle or any other Post where the N.W. Co. are established."[13] His authority was soon challenged. When the Northwester, Alexander Macdonell, returned to Qu'Appelle in the autumn of 1815 he was greatly displeased at finding the Hudson's Bay traders building storehouses and putting up new stockades around their fort. At once he sent Alexander Fraser, a métis clerk, to John McKay, the officer in charge of the rival post, with an order to leave the place in twenty-four hours, and if the order was not complied with he would "blow him and the Fort to hell." Fraser added, for himself, that as long as he had a heart in his body he would never allow a colony to be established in Red River. McKay's answer was to send an express to Robertson for advice or assistance. Robertson promptly seized Fort Gibraltar and arrested Duncan Cameron. At first he seems to have intended to send Cameron to England by way of York Factory; but upon

10. John McGillivray to William McGillivray, January 17, 1816, *PAC SP,* p. 9146.

11. Clarke to Selkirk, August 10, 1816; Bird to Selkirk, August 12, 1816; Bird to Vincent, August 12, 1816; Fidler to Keveny, August 11, 1816; Forsyth, Richardson & Co. to Inglis, Ellice & Co., August 17, 1816, *PAC SP,* pp. 2499 ff., 2532 ff., 2538, 2546 f., 2560 f. Berens to Bathurst, February 4, 1818; Deposition of George Innes; Pelly to Bathurst, September 13, 1818, *Q150,* Pt. I, pp. 197 ff., Pt. II, pp. 247 ff. *GX,* p. 286.

12. Semple to Selkirk, December 20, 1815; Alexander Macdonell to Selkirk, September 12, 1816; Fidler, Narrative, *PAC SP,* pp. 2512 ff., 2722, 2735.

13. Robertson to Alexander Macdonell, March 19, 1816, *PAC SP,* p. 2493.

the prisoner's "solemnly promising that he would write to his Colleague at River Qu'Appelle to cease further proceedings on the part of the N.W. Co.," and pledging himself "in the most solemn manner that neither he nor any of his associates should in any manner debauch, seduce, or in any other manner disturb the peace & prosperity of the Colony," he released him after twenty-four hours' detention.[14] Cameron gave little trouble for the rest of the winter. Robertson's energetic and rather arbitrary rule seemed to have cowed the opposition.

By spring, however, Robertson had become aware that Cameron and his fellow traders were again plotting the destruction of the Settlement. On the evening of March 19 he went to Fort Gibraltar with fourteen men, seized Cameron, and carried him off to Fort Douglas. This time he had more definite evidence with which to confront the prisoner, for lying on the table in the fort was a letter from Cameron to James Grant, urging that the colony be attacked. "I wish," read the letter, "that some of your *Pilleurs* who are fond of mischief and plunder would come and pay a hostile visit to these sons of Gunpowder and riot. They might make a very good booty if they went cunningly to work." In fairness to Cameron it must be said that he added, "not that I would wish them to Butcher any one *God forbid*."[15]

"Lord Chesterfield," as Robertson was known among the Northwesters, suspecting that a wider and more dangerous plot existed, decided on an unprecedented step—to seize and search the North West Company's "Northern Express." On reading the letters sent with the Express he found that his suspicions had been correct; the North West Company was planning "the most diabolical schemes for the utter extirpation of the Colony."[16]

Governor Semple had spent most of the winter of 1815–16 in and around Pembina.[17] When, after a hurried trip from there, he reached the Forks on March 31 and heard Robertson's story of what was being plotted against the Settlement, he was aghast.[18] He had a firm belief in Selkirk's legitimate title to the land and the authority that went with it, and declared at once that the enemy would be treated as interlopers and vagabonds. But he was readier with words than with deeds. When the vigorous Robertson urged that Fort Gibraltar be torn down and

14. Pritchard, Deposition, *Q143,* pp. 342 f. Fidler, Narrative; Sutherland, Narrative, *PAC SP,* pp. 1946 ff., 2511 f.

15. March, 1816; Semple to Robertson, April 12, 1816; Alexander Macdonell to Selkirk, September 12, 1816; Fidler, Narrative, *PAC SP,* pp. 1466, 2180, 2513 ff., 2736. Pritchard, Deposition, *Q143,* pp. 343 ff.

16. James Hughes to John McTavish, July 27, 1816; Robertson to Alexander Macdonell, March 19, 1816; Fidler, Narrative, *PAC SP,* pp. 2274, 2493, 2517.

17. Fidler to Keveny, August 11, 1816, *PAC SP,* p. 2560.

18. Semple to Robertson, April 12, 1816, *PAC SP,* p. 2180.

Cameron sent to England for trial, by way of the Bay, Semple suggested a more moderate course. This disagreement finally led to an open rupture. The two men had found it difficult to coöperate before; and it had become known in the colony that they were not upon terms of intimacy. Perhaps this hostility was one of personality rather than of principle. "Robertson did certainly oppose Gov. Semple's measures, which probably the latter thought originated more from a spirit of Contradiction than the real benefit which his plans might add to the Concerns of the Colony."[19] But this was just one more example of the chronic absence of unity among Selkirk's various supporters. They lacked the discipline and the singleness of purpose so evident in the rival company. Nevertheless, on this occasion Semple at last came round to Robertson's view.

On June 11 Robertson carried Cameron off to York Factory.[20] On the same day Semple, realizing that he lacked forces sufficient to hold two forts at the Forks, led thirty men to Fort Gibraltar and began to tear it down. In a week he had completed the task. Everything worth moving was floated down to Fort Douglas. Some of this material was used later to complete the construction of the colony fort.[21] Robertson, strangely enough, although he had advised such a course as the razing of Fort Gibraltar, later denied that he had any "participation in suggesting or approving those incautious measures" which, he added, "had a great tendency to produce the second destruction of the Colony."[22] But the Governor's position was now much better than before, as the enemy had no strong place near by, and the Forks was "the Key to all."[23]

Nevertheless, the loss of Fort Gibraltar did not daunt the Northwesters. At various points the métis were getting together armed bands and responding in sentiment to the wishes of their employers. "A storm . . . [was] gathering in the northward ready to burst on the rascals." The Canadian traders were jubilant. "The new nation under their leaders are coming forward," wrote Alexander Macdonell, "to clean their native soil of the intruders and assassins." "Little do they know," declared the same writer, "their situation last year was but a joke."[24]

19. Semple to Duncan Cameron, March 31, 1816; Alexander Macdonell to Selkirk, September 12, 1816, *PAC SP,* pp. 2140 ff., 2737.

20. *Ibid.,* p. 2739.

21. *Ibid.* Fidler, Narrative, *PAC SP,* p. 2524. Pritchard, Narrative, May 4, 1819, *Q153,* Pt. III, p. 770.

22. *PAC SP,* p. 4339.

23. Fidler to Semple, April 1, 1816; Alexander Macdonell to Selkirk, September 12, 1816, *PAC SP,* pp. 2150, 2739.

24. Alexander Macdonell to J. D. Cameron, March 13, 1816; Alexander Macdonell to Duncan Cameron, March 13, 1816. See also R. Henry to Alexander Henry, June 3, 1816, *PAC SP,* pp. 1467, 1864, 1887, 2373.

Cuthbert Grant, in charge of his métis, was equally optimistic. "It is to be hoped," said he, "that we shall come off with flying colours & never see any of them again in a Colonizing way in Red River."[25]

Semple, knowing well what was intended, prepared to defend the colony against a vigorous attack. It soon came. In May Grant started from Qu'Appelle toward the Forks with about fifty bois-brûlés. A short distance below Fort Qu'Appelle they ambushed a Hudson's Bay Company brigade "in a furious manner." The brigade, led by James Sutherland, consisted of six bateaux and twenty men taking provisions and their season's catch of furs to Fort Douglas. The métis seized the food for their own use and carried off a few prisoners. A little later Grant was joined by Alexander Macdonell and his Canadians. From then until Portage la Prairie was reached Macdonell was in supreme command.[26]

Brandon House was the next place to be attacked. Macdonell remained a few miles away while Grant led forty-eight bois-brûlés to the Post, broke open the buildings, and carried away all the stores "in great triumph." The whole expedition then moved on to Portage la Prairie, where they were reinforced by small groups of métis from outlying posts. The Generalissimo was now ready to move against Red River.[27]

Grant's tactics were dictated by the North-westers as part of their grand strategy. The instructions had come from Fort William to Grant and the trader, Morrison. They were signed by A. N. McLeod, Robert Henry, and John McLaughlin, winter partners. The dispatch read:

After various consultations we have come to the resolution of forwarding an express to you to request you will as soon as possible assemble as many of the Indians as you can by any means induce to go to Red River to meet us there. We also mean to take a few of the Lac la Pluie Indians with us: we shall and will be guarded and prudent, we shall commit no extravagancies but we must not suffer ourselves to be imposed upon. Possibly and probably their appearance may suffice, but in any case they shall be well and fully recompensed for their trouble. . . . We shall be in Red River about the 17th of June.[28]

Robert Henry, a member of the party coming from Fort William, however, was not so sure that they would "commit no extravagancies." Writing to his uncle he confessed that he "would not be surprised if some of us left our bones there. If it comes to a Battle many lives must be lost. . . . I am very much afraid it will be a serious business but we

25. Grant to J. D. Cameron, March 13, 1816, *PAC SP*, p. 1881.
26. Sutherland, Narrative; Fidler, Narrative, *PAC SP*, pp. 1953 ff., 2518 ff. Pritchard, Deposition; Pambrun, Narrative, *Q143*, pp. 347 f., *Q153*, Pt. III, pp. 718 ff.
27. *Ibid.* Fidler to Semple, June 2, 1816, *PAC SP*, pp. 2315 ff.
28. *PAC SP*, p. 8612.

must hope for the best.''[29] Later, after the "Battle" was over, he admitted that it was their intention to storm the fort.[30]

It is possible to reconstruct with some exactness the course designed for the métis. Grant had apparently intended to carry out instructions and await at Red River the forces from the east under McLeod. His plan was to leave the banks of the Assiniboine, which he was following, before he came to the Forks, travel across country northeastward until he struck the Red River some distance below Fort Douglas, follow the Red until he met McLeod, and then surrender to that trader the chief command in the attack that was to be made on the Settlement.

On their way down the Assiniboine, Grant and Macdonell met a band of Saulteaux Indians and declared their intentions. Macdonell spoke through an interpreter, Joseph Primeau:

My Friends and Relations, I address you with Bashfulness for not having more Tobacco to present to you. It is the English people who are the cause of it. They have stopped the supplies that were coming for you. You know who I mean—those that make you believe they are cultivating the lands for the good of the Indians, but don't you believe them. They are spoiling the Lands that belong to you, and to your Relations the Metifs [sic] only. They are driving away the Buffaloe, and will render the Indians poor and miserable, but the North West Company will drive them away, since the Indians do not choose to do it. If the Settlers resist, the ground shall be drenched with their blood. None shall be spared. We do not need the assistance of the Indians, but we shall be glad if some of the young men would join us.[31]

This harangue failed to move the taciturn chief, who coldly refused to help the expedition; but it leaves no doubt as to the purposes of the North-wester.

At Portage la Prairie, about sixty miles above the Forks, the bois-brûlé cavalcade was reorganized, and on June 18 Grant started off with his warriors. The band numbered between sixty and seventy men. Alexander Macdonell with more than forty Canadians remained at the Portage to guard the provisions. On June 19 Grant and his men reached Boggy Creek, a stream flowing into the Assiniboine from the north about three or four miles from the Forks. Here a council of war was held.[32] On the same day the Fort William expedition under McLeod was setting out from Bas de la Rivière.[33] Early in the evening the métis

29. Robert Henry to Alexander Henry, June 3, 1816, *PAC SP*, p. 2373.
30. Robert Henry to Alexander Henry, July 22, 1816, *PAC SP*, p. 2373.
31. Pambrun, Narrative, *Q153*, Pt. III, pp. 721 ff.
32. *Ibid.*, pp. 724 ff. Affidavit of Pambrun, August 16, 1816, *Q147*, Pt. I, pp. 171 f. Fidler, Narrative, *PAC SP*, p. 2524.
33. Narrative of Frederick Damien Hueter, late acting Sergeant Major and Clerk

set out from Boggy Creek according to the plan described above, traveling northeastward across country in such a direction that they would avoid the Forks by a distance of about two miles.[34]

All this time Governor Semple was fully aware of the hostile designs of the métis, and his scouts kept him carefully informed of all their movements. He also knew from letters he had intercepted that a force was coming from Fort William to join the band from the west. Hence he was on the lookout for trouble, and apparently was determined to prevent, if possible, the junction of the two enemy bands. When the bois-brûlés, painted and disguised, rode across the plains from the Assiniboine toward the Red River on the evening of June 19 a man in the watchtower at Fort Douglas sighted them and called out that the métis were coming. Immediately there was much excitement and confusion. Settlers and Company men scurried hither and thither. Governor Semple with five or six other men climbed into the loft of a barn and through spyglasses "distinctly saw some armed people on horse back passing along the plains." The man in the watchtower then shouted that they were making for the settlers who were at work along the river bank. The excitement and confusion in the Fort increased. Women and children were crying and men were aimlessly shouting. Governor Semple, either to stop the enemy's advance or to defend the settlers outside the fort from possible attack, ordered a few men to follow him and advanced down the Settlement road toward the moving band of horsemen. At the time there were between sixty and seventy men in the fort. The Governor took with him about twenty-six of these, settlers and Company servants. As this force marched down along the west bank of the Red, they met many panicstricken settlers, who had been working in their fields, scurrying toward the fort and crying out, "The half-breeds! The half-breeds!" Already the enemy had partly carried out their orders to surprise and take prisoners as many of the settlers as they could find in their fields in order to reduce the strength of the defense.[35]

When Semple and his men had gone about three quarters of a mile

in the Regiment de Meuron, March 8, 1819, *Q153,* Pt. III, p. 661. Hereafter, Hueter, Narrative, *Q153.*

34. Affidavit of Pambrun, August 16, 1816, *Q147,* Pt. I, pp. 168 ff.

35. The sources for the Massacre of Seven Oaks are voluminous and in many instances contradictory. The following references are representative: Pritchard, Narrative; Pritchard, Deposition; Affidavit of John Bourke, September 16, 1816; Affidavit of Michael Heden, September 16, 1816; Richardson to Sherbrooke, August 17, 1816; William McGillivray to —, July 17, 1816, *Q153,* Pt. III, pp. 768 ff., *Q143,* pp. 348 ff., *Q147,* Pt. I, pp. 176 ff., 188 ff., *Q137,* pp. 130 ff., *Q140,* Pt. II, pp. 329 ff. Pritchard to Selkirk, August 22, 1816; McPherson to Selkirk, September 4, 1816; Alexander Macdonell to Selkirk, September 12, 1816; Fidler, Narrative; William McGillivray to Simon McGillivray, July 17, 1816; William McGillivray to Johnstone, July 18, 1816, *PAC SP,* pp. 2423 f., 2454 ff., 2525 ff., 2604 ff., 2673 ff., 2738 ff.

they came in sight of a large band of horsemen near a heavy growth of oaks and poplars. When approached more closely the horsemen seemed more numerous, and the Governor made a halt and ordered John Bourke, the colony's storekeeper, to return to the fort for a fieldpiece and as many more men as Sheriff Alexander Macdonell could spare. (Macdonell had been in charge of the Settlement since Colin Robertson's departure for the Bay.) But after waiting only a few minutes, the excited Governor changed his mind and pushed on toward the clump of trees where the horsemen were gathered.

While Governor Semple continued to push forward, Generalissimo Grant divided his force, led one section toward the river across the settlers' line of march, and sent the other around to the right to execute a flanking movement. Before long it had been completed, but all parties continued to move forward. As the settlers, however, got close enough to the enemy to observe the hideous war gear of the métis foe, they lost their nerve and, without orders, began slowly to retreat. Then suddenly a Canadian, François-Fermin Boucher—son of a Montreal tavern keeper, and now a North West Company clerk—galloped out from the ranks of the bois-brûlés and, advancing close up to Semple, called out in broken English, "What do you want?" To which the Governor replied, "What do you want?" Said Boucher, "We want our fort." "Well," answered Semple, "go to your fort." The argument then grew more heated. "Why did you destroy our fort, you damned rascal?" shouted Boucher. Stung to action, the Governor seized the Canadian's bridle, saying, "Scoundrel, do you tell me so?" At this Boucher leaped from his horse, and just then there was a shot. At once the firing became general.[36]

Holte, Semple's lieutenant, was the first man to fall. As the firing continued the colonists were rapidly shot down. The bois-brûlés then rushed upon them and dispatched the majority of the living with "knife, axe, or ball," while "upon the bodies of the dead were practiced all those horrible Barbarities that characterize the inhuman heart of the Savage." Early in the skirmish Semple was shot in the right thigh. Seeing Grant near by, he begged to be conveyed to the fort. The Generalissimo gave his promise, but was called away. An old Canadian, François de Champs, was left with Semple. According to one version, an Indian, the only one in the party, came up after Grant's departure and shot the wounded man in the chest. A more plausible story, and one for which there seems to be good evidence, is that François de Champs himself discharged the fatal ball. Certainly De Champs distinguished himself by his ferocity. It was said that after the "battle" he went over the

36. *Ibid.*

field, slashing open the bodies of the wounded and the dead and uttering "the most horrid imprecations."[37]

The total number of those killed in the "massacre of Seven Oaks," as this fight has been called, was twenty-three. Of these, only one was of Grant's party. The bodies of the Selkirk slain were stripped of their clothing and left lying on the prairie. Only a few of Semple's followers escaped death, some by being made prisoner, others by swimming the river or hiding in the woods. At nightfall the victors encamped at Frog Plain, a short distance north of the battlefield.[38]

Plans were now perfected for the capture of Fort Douglas on the following evening. John Pritchard, who had been taken prisoner, was told by Grant that an attack would that night be made upon the fort, and if the people fired a single shot a general massacre would ensue. "You see," he added, "the little quarter we have shown you, and now if any further resistance is made, neither Man, Woman nor Child shall be spared." Fraser added in French, "Robertson said that we were *Blacks*, and he shall see that our hearts will not belie the colour of our Bodies." Pritchard, "being fully convinced of the inevitable destruction of the Settlers," asked the Generalissimo "if there were any means by which the lives of the Women and Children could be saved." After some time he answered, "Yes," on condition, too, that

the Colonists would give up all the Public property they should be allowed to depart in peace and . . . he would give . . . [them] a safe escort until they had passed the North West Company's track in Lake Winnipeg which he said was necessary to protect . . . [them] from the two other parties of half-breeds that were momentarily expected to come up the river: one of which he said was commanded by William Shaw, son of Angus Shaw, and the other by Simon McGillivray, son of the Honourable William McGillivray.[39]

These terms Pritchard, under guard, was allowed to deliver at Fort Douglas. At first Sheriff Macdonell and the settlers were unwilling to accept Grant's offer; but they soon realized that it was madness to refuse. Giving orders that an inventory of the property of the Settlement be made, Macdonell went to meet him. After making two or three trips to Frog Plain, the sheriff concluded an agreement practically equivalent to the one outlined by Grant to Pritchard. The bois-brûlés then took over the fort. They were keenly disappointed at not finding Colin Robertson there. If they had found him, they told Pritchard, "they

37. *Ibid.*   38. *Ibid.*

39. *Ibid.* See especially the Pritchard documents, Alexander Macdonell's letter, and the affidavits of Bourke and Heden.

would have endeavoured to take him alive and after flaying him, they would have cut his Body into small bits, and boiled it afterwards for the Dogs." Upon the surrender of the property of the Settlement Cuthbert Grant signed each sheet of the inventory as an agent of the North West Company.[40]

By June 22 the colonists were ready to embark. Just then Grant came to them and said that he could not let them go, as Alexander Macdonell had sent an order from Portage la Prairie to hold them until his arrival. This was terrible news, as the settlers were afraid that the bois-brûlés might attack the women. Pritchard

reproached, entreated, and, indeed did all in . . . [his] power to induce Grant to let . . . [them] depart; at last on . . . Sheriff Macdonell's observing that he plainly perceived that . . . Alexander Macdonell wished to defraud Grant of the honour of the day, and take all the praise to himself, Grant's pride was hurt; and he in an intemperate manner said he would keep his word in spite of Macdonell; and desired . . . [them] to depart immediately, without waiting for the escort.

He promised to send it after them in a light canoe. The colonists lost no time, but scrambled into boats and pushed off. This was in the evening of June 22. The bois-brûlés victory being now complete, a messenger was dispatched westward to spread the news far and wide.[41]

When Alexander Macdonell, who had waited at Portage la Prairie since parting from Grant, learned what had taken place at Seven Oaks, he and "all the gentlemen with him . . . shouted with joy." He then went off to announce the news to the rest of his people, shouting in French and with oaths, "Good news! Twenty-two English have been killed!" Immediately afterwards he set out for the Forks; and on his arrival took over from Grant the command of Fort Douglas.[42]

Meanwhile the North West Company expedition which had left Fort William early in June, and Bas de la Rivière on June 19, arrived on June 21 at Rivière aux Morts (Nettly Creek), about forty miles below the Forks. Here they remained until the morning of June 23 waiting for the Assiniboia brigade to join them. They then pushed on up the river hoping to meet their allies at any moment. They had not gone far when they sighted the expelled settlers coming down the stream. Surprised and puzzled, McLeod "ordered his brigade to lower their sails and put

40. *Ibid.* The original "inventory" is in the Selkirk Papers, St. Mary's Isle.

41. *Ibid.* See especially the Pritchard documents, Alexander Macdonell's letter, and the affidavits of Bourke and Heden.

42. Affidavit of Pierre Chrysologue Pambrun, August 16, 1816, *Q147*, Pt. I, pp. 171 ff. Pambrun, Narrative, *Q153*, Pt. III, pp. 726 f.

to shore, and the men at the same time were ordered to load their guns and prepare for action, which they did in great haste." When he had stopped the colonists and heard the news of the massacre, McLeod ordered the whole party to return with him to Rivière aux Morts. Here tents were pitched, some of the leading settlers placed under arrest, and a general search made. The late Governor's trunk was pried open with an axe and its contents rifled; but nothing of great importance was found in it, as Sheriff Macdonell had taken the precaution of giving "the intercepted letters" to a young woman, who carried them around her waist beneath her underclothes.[43]

After about two days of search and inquisition at Rivière aux Morts most of the settlers were allowed to go on their way. John Pritchard, Patt Corcoran, Michael Heden, and another man, John Bourke, were held for later transportation to Canada. A métis, Charles Grant, followed those departing to see that they kept moving. McLeod, who had meanwhile been joined by several wintering partners from the interior, now went on to Fort Douglas, where he was received with discharges of artillery and small arms. Immediately upon his arrival, he took over the chief command from Alexander Macdonell and moved into the late Governor Semple's residence. The bois-brûlés were then assembled in the messroom, where McLeod shook hands with them in turn and thanked them for what they had done and for their attachment to the North West Company. A keg of liquor was opened and all joined in a celebration. The next day the métis were again assembled, this time behind the principal house at Fort Douglas. Again McLeod officiated. In a long speech he thanked the doughty warriors for their heroic deeds, praised them for their noble defense of their lands against the English, and promised them suitable rewards for their great sacrifices. There was clothing for only forty of them now; but the fall canoes would bring sufficient quantities for all. In conclusion they were exhorted to prevent the return of the English to Red River in the future.[44]

After this harangue McLeod and his followers rode in imposing procession to the site of Fort Gibraltar, where a band of Saulteaux Indians was encamped. The commandant addressed them with bitter reproaches for refusing to take up arms against the colony and for permitting the capture of Fort Gibraltar and the arrest of Duncan Cameron. He called them to their faces a band of dirty dogs and threatened

43. Hueter, Narrative, Q153, Pt. III, pp. 657 ff. R. Henry to George Rittson, August 2, 1816; R. Henry to Alexander Henry, July 22, 1816; Alexander Macdonell to Selkirk, September 12, 1816, PAC SP, pp. 2373, 2378, 2743 ff. See also n. 35.
44. Hueter, Narrative, March 8, 1819; Affidavit of Pierre Chrysologue Pambrun, August 16, 1816; Pambrun, Narrative, March 16, 1819, Q153, Pt. III, pp. 666 ff., 726 ff., Q147, Pt. I, pp. 173 f.

them with severe punishment if they ever dared to befriend the English again. But the Indians said nothing. Their chief, Peguis, "who was a master diplomat, looked on with attention and held his peace."[45]

Later in the same day a party of North-westers rode down to Seven Oaks to review the field of slaughter. The bodies of the slain were still lying on the ground, "nearly reduced to Skeletons, there being very little Flesh, then adhering to the bones." Dogs and wolves had been allowed to feed on them. "This spectacle . . . was received with every mark of satisfaction and even exultation" by the reviewing party. The bois-brûlés emulated each other in pointing out their respective feats, especially their deeds of cruelty; while their masters listened and approved. Alexander Macdonell, after hearing old François de Champs tell how he had gone about ripping open the bodies of the dead and dying, remarked, "What a fine vigorous old man he is!"[46]

That night the grand victory was celebrated again. Four kegs of liquor were opened and everyone became merry. The bois-brûlés stripped off their clothes, painted their bodies grotesquely, and to the amusement of the dignitaries present, did an Indian war dance. Festivities over, three days later the Athabasca brigade set out joyfully, honored by a salvo of artillery from Fort Douglas and leaving the New Nation to gloat over its victory and enjoy its rewards.[47] Colony Gardens seemed this time to have been destroyed for good.

45. *Ibid.*   46. *Ibid.*
47. *Ibid.*

CHAPTER XVII

RETALIATIONS

THE steady refusal of the Governor of the Canadas to accede to Selkirk's request for the establishment of a small military unit in the threatened colony, had been somewhat modified in May, 1816, when Drummond's administration ended. Under the new Governor, Sir John Sherbrooke, the influence over the government hitherto enjoyed by the North-westers suffered a decline for a time, while the Earl and Lady Selkirk had suddenly acquired unexpected social power and prestige. When Sherbrooke's appointment became known, Selkirk had remarked:

The success which has so long attended all their [the North-westers'] machinations is in a great measure to be ascribed to their dexterity in deception, & the Bonaparte like effrontery, with which they set forward the grossest misrepresentations in a style of plausibility which has hitherto reached the ears of the Govrs here & thro' them has obtained from the Govt at home a degree of countenance & support to which they have no solid claim whatever. From the account that I heard of Sir Jo. Sh: [Sir John Sherbrooke] I think they will not find that so easy a task with him.[1]

This judgment was sound, though Selkirk had underestimated the power of the Canadian ruling class to bend even the Governor to its views. But for a time the North West Company had been out of favor. "What an unfortunate trade we have got into," wrote William McGillivray to one of his satellites, "hemmed in . . . by a set of unprincipled Agents of a Government on one side and a speculating Nobleman on the other—Equally as it appears bent on the same object—to exclude Canada and Canadian subjects from this too famous trade."[2]

With the wind thus blowing favorably Selkirk had prepared, in June, 1816, to set out for Assiniboia. His wife, on whose judgment and sympathy he had come to rely increasingly, was to remain in Montreal as his principal agent. As a guard for the journey he had thought of the happy plan of enlisting some of the ex-soldiers of the De Meuron regiment—whose disbanding had seemed so unfortunate a few months earlier—and settling them on farms in Red River. There they would form an invincible defense for the colony as a whole. Besides the De Meurons, the regiments of De Watteville and Glengarry Fencibles, stationed at Kingston, had been demobilized and were free for other service. The De

1. Selkirk to William Smith, June 17, 1816, *PAC SP*, p. 2239.
2. William McGillivray to John Johnstone, July 18, 1816, *PAC SP*, pp. 2454.

Meurons were of Swiss, Italian, and other foreign extraction, but had served as mercenaries for Britain in the Napoleonic wars. They had come to Canada in 1812. Most of them and the De Wattevilles were returning to Europe; but a number were remaining in Canada, and to these Selkirk had made his proposals. To each man who would go to Red River he offered a large tract of "open land fit for immediate cultivation" and $8 a month from the time he left Canada until he reached Assiniboia and took possession of his land. On the other hand, if he should decide after visiting Red River not to settle there, he would be brought back to the East and his wages would be continued until he arrived at the place from which he had set out.[3] Of the De Meurons, eighty men and four officers—Captains D'Orsonnens and Matthey, and Lieutenants Fauché and Graffenreid—agreed to go to Red River. They were joined by some twenty De Wattevilles and a few Glengarry Fencibles.[4] All were without arms, but Selkirk arranged to have muskets for them smuggled secretly into Upper Canada from the United States before they set out for the West.[5]

The advance guard of the expedition had been put under the command of Miles Macdonell. Although the North-westers had taken Macdonell to Montreal in 1815 as a prisoner, he was set free soon after his arrival. Rearrested shortly afterwards, he was admitted to bail, but was to appear for trial at the September term of the Court of King's Bench in Montreal.[6] Early in May Selkirk sent him ahead to Red River with four canoes. He still retained the title of Governor, but was to act under Colin Robertson in Assiniboia.[7] He was instructed now to take care to avoid the North-westers on his journey inland. His party was to consist of Lieutenant Simon Clarke, late of the Voltigeurs, a priest, three gentlemen, "Clerks of the concern," a guide named Pelland, and a few Canadians. On May 5 this advance guard set out from the Lake of Two Mountains. The journey to Sault Ste Marie was slow and tedious. The men "continually grumbled and were dissatisfied." One canoe had to be left at Holland Landing, "some of the men not being in a state to proceed"; and another at the Sault, because of desertions. Pelland, the

3. Selkirk to Captain Steiger, May 23, 1816, *PAC SP*, p. 2280. *The Memorial of Thomas Earl of Selkirk to His Grace Charles Duke of Richmond* (Montreal, 1819), p. 18. Hereafter, Selkirk, *Memorial to Richmond*.

4. J.S. (Lady Selkirk) to Kate (Halkett), March 27, 1816; J.S. to Halkett, June 29, 1816, *SP SM. Statement Respecting Settlement*, pp. 59 f., 175, Appendix K.K., pp. lxxxiv ff.

5. Selkirk to Halkett, June 25, 1816, *SP SM*.

6. Selkirk to Berens, May 24, 1816; J. Stewart to Berens, June 22, 1816; Selkirk to Sherbrooke, June 24, August 23, 1816, *PAC SP*, pp. 2287 ff., 2355 ff., 2358 ff., 2620 ff. Selkirk, *Memorial to Richmond*, p. 7.

7. Selkirk to Semple, April 26, 1816, *PAC SP*, p. 2212.

guide, was "a scoundrel" and "a rude brute," who did everything possible to retard the speed of the expedition; and it was discovered later that he was "in the N.W. Co. interest."[8]

A month after Macdonell's departure Captain Matthey with sixty-four De Meurons set out from Lachine. Ascending the St. Lawrence, he stopped at Kingston and picked up the De Wattevilles and Glengarry Fencibles already recruited for Red River. After some provoking delays the party advanced to York, where a number of voyageurs and also some of the ex-soldiers deserted. Like Macdonell's men, Matthey's followers were grumblers. "I found it absolutely necessary, to keep their spirits up after a hard day's work," the captain told Selkirk, "to allow them some Rum every day. Wheening [weaning] them too suddenly of that sweet milk must have produced an unfavourable revolution—moral and spiritual." After more "careless" delays at York the party crossed by way of the Trent River and Lake Simcoe to Georgian Bay.[9]

Selkirk himself left Montreal on June 18, with an order from Governor Sherbrooke to secure seven regular soldiers at Drummond's Island to act as a bodyguard. He had also been made a justice of the peace for the Indian Territories.[10] His fortune seemed to have turned at last. The Hudson's Bay Company was now overshadowing its rivals. At Fort William, among the nabobs already there was uncertainty, fear, and squabbling. A number of them were sick of the fur trade and its exactions. "I really wish," William McGillivray could write in July, 1816, "that I was decently out of it, although I shall never submit to be kicked out of it by any Lord or Commoner in the King's Dominions."[11] Public opinion seemed to be turning against the North-westers. "Every neutral person," J. D. Cameron had admitted, "thinks we are in the wrong."[12] Selkirk, on the other hand, was full of hope and energy. In the spring of 1816 he had received word of the restoration of the colony in the preceding fall and of the subsequent well-being of the settlers. The Earl, on his journey west, planned to avoid the North-westers and follow the southern route by way of Fond du Lac, St. Louis River, Red

8. Miles Macdonell to Donald Macdonell, September 11, 1816, Miles Macdonell, Selkirk Settlement, pp. 191 f., PAC. Miles Macdonell to Selkirk, May 25, 1816, PAC SP, p. 2307. Morice, "Sidelights on the Careers of Miles Macdonell and His Brothers," CHR, X, 317.

9. Matthey to Selkirk, June 8, 29, July 1, 1816, PAC SP, pp. 2330, 2370 f., 2393. Statement Respecting Settlement, p. 60, Appendix K.K., pp. lxxxiv f.

10. J.S. to Halkett, June 29, 1816, SP SM. PAC SP, p. 2313.

11. William McGillivray to John Johnstone, July 18, 1816; Hughes to John McTavish, July 27, 1816, PAC SP, pp. 2274, 2454. Hughes wrote in the same tenor as McGillivray: "I wish sincerely this confounded contest was at an end some way or other."

12. Cameron to —, July 14, 1816, PAC SP, p. 2377.

Lake, and Pembina,[13] territory which for the most part lay within the United States.

Meanwhile Miles Macdonell, hurrying westward, had reached Lac du Bonnet, a short distance above Lake Winnipeg, on June 29, when he heard the news of the massacre at Seven Oaks and the second destruction of the colony. At once he turned and retraced his way with all speed to Sault Ste Marie. Here on July 25 he met the Earl and told him of the disaster. Selkirk was "much shocked at the news . . . but bore it with . . . fortitude becoming the house of Douglas."[14]

The Earl now decided to give up his plan of following the southern route to Red River, because he realized that owing to the massacre there would be no boats or provisions awaiting him at Red Lake, as he had expected, and no supplies at Red River. Also, though he "had not learned all the Circumstances of the Catastrophe, enough had transpired to point out the real character of the transaction, and the influence from which it had arisen," and he had no doubt that by going directly to Fort William "with a force capable of making the Law to be respected very important discoveries would be made." He knew that he might be making a mistake in attacking the enemy by force; but thoughts of what had happened at Red River made him drown his scruples; and he set off with his ex-soldiers straight for the North West Company's headquarters.[15]

Several considerations made this course seem reasonable enough. The government in Britain had refused to pass judgment on the Earl's position in Assiniboia. If he were to seize the chief stronghold of the enemy west of Montreal, the North-westers would be forced either to quit the fur trade or bring the whole question to court. Selkirk felt certain that at Fort William he would find sufficient evidence of his rivals' criminal conduct;[16] and there, too, he knew, were being held as prisoners several of his settlers and a few Hudson's Bay Company men.[17] From the news he had received he was convinced that the North West Company was wholly responsible for the hostility of the métis in Assiniboia.[18] Sel-

13. *Statement Respecting Settlement,* pp. 41 f., 62. Selkirk, *Memorial to Richmond,* pp. 13, 18. Selkirk to Robertson, April 25, 1816, Miles Macdonell, Selkirk Settlement, p. 189, *PAC.* Selkirk to Gore, August 21, 1816; Selkirk to Miller, February 22, 1817, *PAC SP,* pp. 2567 f., 3178.

14. Miles Macdonell to Donald Macdonell, September 11, 1816, Miles Macdonell, Selkirk Settlement, pp. 191 ff., *PAC.*

15. Selkirk to Gore, August 21, 1816, *PAC SP,* pp. 2567 f. Selkirk to Sherbrooke, July 29, 1816, *Q137,* pp. 128 f.

16. *Ibid.* Selkirk to Boulton, August 17, 1816, *PAC SP,* p. 2550.

17. Miles Macdonell to Selkirk, July 7, 1816, *PAC SP,* p. 2405. *Statement Respecting Settlement,* p. 62.

18. Selkirk to Sherbrooke, July 29, 1816, *Q137,* pp. 127 f. Selkirk to Gore, August

kirk denounced, in unmeasured terms, the conduct of the North West Company.[19]

Firmly convinced that his opponents were entirely in the wrong, he was determined to bring to an end the long reign of illegal and dishonest force by which the North-westers had grown rich, and settle in the affirmative, once for all, the question as to whether the rich lands of the Red River Valley were to be safe for British settlers.[20] But when everything has been said in favor of the course he now adopted, it must be admitted that Selkirk, like Macdonell and Semple, underestimated the resources of the enemy. The blood of the slain called too loudly for vengeance for a man of strong sympathies in command of a superior force to exercise cold caution.

Before setting out from Sault Ste Marie, nevertheless, "anticipating the probability of resistance to the process of the Law on the part of men who had so long been accustomed to consider force as the only rule of right, and wishing in these delicate circumstances to have the concurrence of respectable persons who might be above all suspicion of partiality," Selkirk requested two justices of the peace, John Askin of Drummond's Island and Charles Ermatinger of the Sault, to accompany him to Fort William and to afford him their advice and coöperation.[21] Both these gentlemen, however, had "avocations" which prevented them from going. Selkirk was therefore reduced "to the alternative of acting alone, or allowing an audacious crime to pass unpunished";[22] and against the advice of his physician, Dr. John Allen, and Miles Macdonell, he decided to go on.[23] "In these circumstances," he wrote to Sherbrooke, "I cannot doubt that it is my duty to act; tho' I am not without apprehension, that the law may be openly resisted by a set of people, who have been accustomed to consider force as the only true criterion of right."[24]

21, 1816; Minutes of a Council held at Drummond's Island between Katawabetay . . . and Lieut. Col. MacKay, July 22, 1816, *PAC SP*, pp. 2440 ff., 2567 ff.

19. "Its members are perhaps the most unprincipled men who ever had to boast of support and countenance from the British Government . . . with the exception of the Slave traders." Selkirk to Smith, June 17, 1816, *PAC SP*, p. 2340.

"It is the most detestable system of villainy that was ever allowed to prevail in the British Dominions." Selkirk to Boulton, August 17, 1816, *PAC SP*, p. 2550.

20. *Statement Respecting the Earl of Selkirk's Settlement of Kildonan, upon the Red River, in North America; its Destruction in the Years 1815 and 1816* . . . (London, January, 1817), p. 125. *Statement Respecting Settlement*, p. vii.

21. Selkirk to Askin, July 26, 1816; Selkirk to Gore, August 21, 1816, *PAC SP*, pp. 2445 f., 2568 f. Selkirk to Sherbrooke, July 29, 1816, *Q137*, p. 129.

22. Askin to Selkirk, July 27, 1816; Selkirk to Gore, August 21, 1816, *PAC SP*, pp. 2447, 2568 f. Selkirk to Sherbrooke, July 29, 1816, *Q137*, p. 129.

23. Allen to Selkirk, July 31, 1816; Miles Macdonell to Selkirk, July 7, 1816, *PAC SP*, pp. 2404, 2463 ff.

24. July 29, 1816, *Q137*, p. 129.

Captain Matthey had already started for Fond du Lac when Miles Macdonell reached Sault Ste Marie. A messenger was sent after him with instructions directing him to Thunder Bay. On August 12 Selkirk's whole force, having crossed Lake Superior, landed and took up position a short distance above Fort William.[25] On the same day Selkirk demanded from the North-westers the liberation of the colony prisoners; and on the following morning he sent two officers to arrest William McGillivray. There was no resistance. McGillivray "acted as a gentleman," says McNab, one of the men who made the arrest, "read the warrant, and immediately prepared for accompanying us."[26] Along with the prisoner went John McLaughlin and Kenneth McKenzie to offer themselves as bail. Selkirk, suspecting trickery, refused to accept them. Planning to send back to Upper Canada "a Cargo of Criminals of a larger Calibre than usual to come before the Courts of York,"[27] he then proceeded to serve warrants on the other partners. When these resisted, the De Meurons, under Captain D'Orsonnens, seized the fort. The North-westers, after being arrested, were paroled and allowed to return to their regular quarters. Selkirk then issued warrants for the seizure of all available written evidence. Great was the amazement of the Indians and the two hundred Company servants within the fort at seeing the hitherto awe-inspiring nabobs treated like ordinary malefactors.

On August 14 more drastic steps became necessary when early in the morning word came of "clandestine preparations of Hostility" carried on during the night by the paroled partners. At once warrants for a search were issued. A large cache of arms, loaded for use, was discovered in a hayloft; and it looked as if they had been hidden there the

25. The sources for Selkirk's activities at Fort William are voluminous and in many instances contradictory. The following references, many of which have been cited in other connections, are representative: *Statement Respecting the Earl of Selkirk's Settlement upon the Red River; The Memorial of Thomas Earl of Selkirk to . . . Duke of Richmond; A Letter to the Earl of Liverpool from the Earl of Selkirk, Accompanied by Correspondence with the Colonial Department in the Years 1817–18–19, on the . . . Red River Settlement;* Alexander McDonell, *Narrative of Transactions in the Red River Country; from the Commencement of the Operations of the Earl of Selkirk during the Summer of the Year 1816* (London, 1819); *A Narrative of Occurrences in the Indian Countries of North America; Papers Relating to the Red River Settlement: 1815–1819;* Depositions of John Pritchard, Captain D'Orsonnens, Miles Macdonell, Pierre Pambrun, Dr. John Allen, etc., *PAC SP,* pp. 4596 *et seq.;* John McNab, Account of the Arrests of the North West Men at Fort William, August 17, 1816, *PAC SP,* pp. 2541 f. (hereafter, McNab, Account of Arrests, *PAC SP*); The Memorial and Representation of John Richardson of Montreal, one of the Partners of the North West Company, for and on behalf of the said Company, *Q137,* pp. 207 ff. (hereafter, Richardson, Memorial, *Q137*).

26. McNab, Account of Arrests, *PAC SP,* pp. 2541 f.

27. Selkirk to Boulton, August 17, 1816, *PAC SP,* p. 2550.

night before. Not far from the Fort "8 or more Barrels of Gunpowder" were found lying hidden in a swamp. The ground all about them gave clear evidence of very recent disturbance. It was also ascertained that a canoe loaded with powder and guns had been dispatched during the night. As a result of these disclosures Selkirk had most of the North West Company voyageurs pitch their tents on the opposite side of the river, and the De Meurons camp "immediately before the Gates of the Fort." Sentries were placed within the walls and the prisoners "were most strictly guarded, but still left in apartments of their own, notwithstanding that a very good prison was found in the Fort."[28] A more thorough search of the various buildings within the enclosure now revealed further incriminating evidence. Warrants and letters which Selkirk had addressed to Red River in the spring and dispatched by the runner, Lagimonière, were found in the partners' council chamber; and they had been opened. Later it became known that McLeod had issued definite instructions for the runner's capture.[29] Before long, too, the Hudson's Bay Company furs which Cuthbert Grant, on Alexander Macdonell's orders, had seized at Qu'Appelle, were discovered.

All the papers that had been seized were tied up in bundles and sealed by both the contending parties. But the partners proved treacherous. Soon afterwards the Earl learned that some of the bundles had been broken open by one or more of the prisoners, and that letters had been extracted and burned in the kitchen stove. But what gave final and complete proof of the responsibility of the North West Company for the Seven Oaks tragedy was the finding of a list of the names of the métis and free Canadians who had fought, with McLeod's check marks opposite the names of those who had already been paid for their work; and twenty bales of "habilliments" marked with the names not checked off on the list. McLeod had sent eastward, as he had promised, a request for presents for the unrewarded killers; and the partners had responded with the twenty bales of marked goods, to be sent inland with the fall brigade.[30] Selkirk now felt certain that he had evidence against the North-westers sufficient to damn them before any court of law in the British Empire. He made up his mind to spend the winter where he was and make preparations for exacting the full penalty for the crimes committed against his colony.[31]

28. McNab, Account of Arrests, *PAC SP,* pp. 2542 ff.

29. McLeod to Morrison, June 2, 1816, *PAC SP,* p. 8610. Minutes of a Council held at Drummond's Island between Katawabetay . . . and Lieut.-Col. MacKay, July 22, 1816, *PAC SP,* pp. 2440 f., 8610.

30. Deposition of Dr. Allen; Selkirk to Boulton, August 21, 1816, *PAC SP,* pp. 2578 ff., 4596 ff.

31. Selkirk to Ellenborough, October 10, 1816; Selkirk to Gibbs, October 10, 1816;

The decision to winter at Fort William, however, raised the serious problem of supplies. Selkirk had about 130 men to provide for. Supplies for their maintenance on the journey inland had been brought from Montreal, but only enough to support them as far as Red Lake, where the Earl had fully expected to secure provisions. He now knew that all the colony stores in Assiniboia had been either seized or destroyed during the summer hostilities, and that it was too late in the season to procure more, especially as the buffalo hunters had gone from Red River or else were up in arms against the English interests. Food that should have been available at Michilimackinac had all been bought up by the wily North-westers. There was, indeed, still time to return to Montreal; and both Dr. Allen and Miles Macdonell were strongly in favor of doing so.[32] But Selkirk feared that such a course would waste the whole effort that had been made in coming thus far, and would leave little chance for the restoration of the shattered settlement.

In this dilemma the Earl decided to buy from the North-westers the provisions they had secured at Michilimackinac. The situation now obtaining at Fort William made such a course peculiarly feasible. The partners who had been arrested had already on August 18 been sent off to Montreal under military guard.[33] The leading North-wester now at Fort William was the veteran trader, Daniel McKenzie, the very man who had bought the stores. McKenzie proved easy to deal with. Drink and the rigors of the fur trade had broken his health and crumbled any character he had ever possessed. Of late years, too, he had lost the traditional loyalty of the North-wester; he had become jealous of the wealth and power gained by the leading fur traders, and resentful over the fact that he himself got little but hard work and strict orders. As far back as 1809 he had spoken out against the "Froth, Pomp and Ostentation" in his company. Selkirk's arrival, though it meant a short jail term for the old man, was a welcome diversion and an occasion for a long spree. In whatever sober moments he had he did some shrewd thinking and decided to make the most of the situation by selling out his associates. "I owe them no obligations," he wrote, "on the Contrary they have done all in their power to injure me. Henceforth I shall think for myself. . . . Had we thought and acted for ourselves we should now

Selkirk to —, October 10, 1816; Selkirk to Stuart, October 8, 1816; Selkirk to Sherbrooke, August 28, September 3, 1816; Selkirk to Boulton, August 21, 1816; Selkirk to Gore, August 21, 1816, *PAC SP,* pp. 2567 ff., 2577 ff., 2643 ff., 2653 f., 2786 ff., 2805, 2806, 2807.

32. Miles Macdonell to Selkirk, July 7, 1816; Selkirk to Gore, August 21, 1816; Allen to Selkirk, July 31, 1816, *PAC SP,* pp. 2403 f., 2463 ff., 2567 f.

33. Richardson, Memorial, *Q137,* p. 209. *Narrative of Occurrences,* p. 82.

be both Rich and respected" and not known as "McGillivray's Geese."[34] He had already given Selkirk some information and feared that he would be in trouble when the partners recovered their post. But he was worried most about the stores he had bought. He had merely acted as agent for the company, and had not paid for the goods; and if the partners repudiated the purchase, he would be over £1,200 in debt. If he sold the goods to Selkirk, he would be safely out of the transaction. He approached the Earl on the matter and found his offer acceptable.[35]

McKenzie now went much further and agreed on behalf of the North West Company to have all disputes settled according to the plan of arbitration previously proposed by Selkirk in Montreal; the arbitrators were to be selected in England by the Lords Chief Justices of the Courts of King's Bench and Common Pleas. McKenzie was to consign the furs then lying packed for exportation at Fort William, to the arbitrators, to be disposed of by them, the proceeds to be applied, if necessary, to pay any damages that they might award to the Earl. Selkirk, on his part, was to transfer to the arbitrators the conveyance of an estate of £3,000 yearly rental to cover such damages as might be awarded to the North West Company. It was also agreed that all the movable property of the North West Company at Fort William, "except the furs, . . . packed for exportation," should be sold to Selkirk "at a price equal to the cost, added to the charges for transport, and that the price of the property transferred, was to be paid by installments, and that £50 was actually paid the same day by the . . . Earl in gold, to . . . McKenzie, as the first part and earnest of the price thereof."[36]

Only pressing necessity, inflamed feelings, and a persuasion of the injustice of his rivals' conduct could have led Selkirk to adopt a course of such doubtful propriety. Nor was he easy in his mind about it then or later. "I do not know," he wrote to Lord Ellenborough in October, "how far the step I have ventured upon is out of the common path."[37] Yet on the same day he wrote to Lord Gibbs: "I flatter myself that the step which I have taken, tho' perhaps unusual, is not so far out of the common path, as to be in any degree improper. . . . I flatter myself that I have not only accomplished my own object, but cut up by the root one of the most abominable combinations, that ever was suffered to exist in the British dominions."[38] It is true that no pressure had been

34. Daniel McKenzie to Cameron, January 4, 1809; Selkirk to James Stuart, October 8, 1816, *PAC SP,* pp. 2789, 8536.

35. Daniel McKenzie to Selkirk, September 3, 1816; Miles Macdonell to North West Wintering Partners, October, 1816, *PAC SP,* pp. 2685 ff., 2779.

36. Contract, *PAC SP,* p. 2811. *Papers Relating to Settlement,* pp. 229 f.

37. October 10, 1816, *PAC SP,* p. 2805.   38. *PAC SP,* p. 2806.

put on "old Sleepy Head," as Duncan Cameron called McKenzie. He had been freed from custody "long before the transaction was entered into—before even the slightest hint of it was dropped,"[39] and it was he who proposed the sale to which Selkirk agreed "on condition of the arbitration."[40] But was McKenzie legally capable of acting for the company? It was no secret that he was intoxicated most of the time between the seizure of Fort William and the agreement with Selkirk. The Earl's counsel, Stuart and Gale, wrote to inform him that the purchase could never be "maintained in a Court of Justice" and that the agreement to arbitrate was "invalid both under the English and under the Canadian Laws."[41]

That the latter contention was sound is more than probable. Selkirk's promised £3,000 rental was trifling in value compared with the furs upon which the company depended for its very life. Indeed, the Earl admitted that he was deliberately attempting to cripple his rivals. "I do not pretend to deny," he wrote to Sherbrooke, "that I was glad to have it so framed as to keep a part of the Capital of the North-West Company in a state of inaction till the question between us should be decided, so as to limit in some degree their resources for carrying on a system of lawless violence against me."[42] Gale assured him that such would be the result, that "the consequences will be irretrievable to the North West Company." But even when exulting to Sherbrooke over the success of his coup, Selkirk was apprehensive about its ultimate consequences. "Nothing," he went on to admit, "would be more distressing to me than the idea that I could be justly accused of having taken an undue advantage of my situation and if in any point Yr. Ex'y [Your Excellency] should be of opinion that I have gone too far I shall be ready to make any reparation that is in my power."[43] He soon realized himself that he had gone too far. "I have," he admitted to his counsel, "been guilty of great imprudence."[44]

By the time spring came the Earl's imprudence had borne bitter fruit. McKenzie was harshly treated by the North-westers for his betrayal of their interests. At Sault Ste Marie they threw him out of their fort with the promise that he "would rot in Gaol." He was so badgered that he tried to escape by committing suicide,[45] and he was now clay in his partners' hands. At Drummond's Island, on November 11, he signed a "protest" drawn up by the North-westers that while being held a prisoner by Lord Selkirk at Fort William from August 13 to October

39. Selkirk to Sherbrooke, November 12, 1816, *PAC SP*, p. 2920.
40. *PAC SP*, p. 3482.   41. *PAC SP*, pp. 3048 ff.
42. November 12, 1816, *PAC SP*, pp. 2920 f.
43. *Ibid.*, p. 2922.   44. *PAC SP*, p. 3385.
45. Pritchard to Selkirk, January 21, 1817, *PAC SP*, p. 3077.

11, 1816, "during all which time" he was "in a state of inebriety and actual Derangement of Mind," he had been forced to agree to terms "dictated by His Lordship and his Agents."[46] One may wonder what "old Sleepy Head's" condition was when he signed the protest. Perhaps he was still in a state of "inebriety and actual Derangement of Mind."[47] But the partners were exultant over the protest, and soon spread its contents abroad. Selkirk was worried. "The consequences," he confided to his wife, "so naturally and justly arising from my wretchedly ill-judged conduct in September, give room for bitter enough reflections."[48] Lady Selkirk tried to comfort him with good news from Montreal. The Hudson's Bay Company was in a stronger position there than ever before.[49]

Throughout the winter Selkirk remained at Fort William. In November came reports that the North-westers were sending out canoes in small groups from Montreal to assemble finally at Sault Ste Marie and retake their fur emporium "by stratagem or by force, by legal pretexts or open violence."[50] By the middle of October the plan had materialized to the extent of the assemblage of a large fleet of canoes on Lake Superior. But storms made it impossible for the fleet to cross the lake.[51] "The great armada," wrote Lady Selkirk, "with all the warrants and constables, partners, clerks, Iroquois, and guns and Congreve rockets, melts away and disappears, and a little canoe comes dropping in now and then, and one after another the partners return to Montreal, looking very foolish, while all the world is laughing at them."[52]

Nevertheless, as it turned out, a small part of the expedition which succeeded in reaching Fort William played a decisive part in the struggle between the Earl and the Canadians. Even before the seizure of the fort a North West Company canoe had been sent eastward to procure a warrant for Selkirk's arrest. It had not had far to go to find a magistrate, but there was trouble securing a warrant. A pliant tool, however, was found in the person of a Dr. Mitchell of Drummond's Island; "an old man in his dotage, . . . never by any chance sober after mid-day."[53] In the early days of November a constable crossed Lake Superior with a warrant from Mitchell and tried to arrest the Earl. Selkirk, suspecting trickery, refused to submit. The constable had no credentials, the

46. Affidavit of Daniel McKenzie, November 11, 1816; Affidavit of Robert McRobb, December 17, 1816, *Q143*, pp. 8 ff., 24.
47. In 1817 he repudiated the Protest. See J.S. to Halkett, June 12, 1817, *SP SM*.
48. *SP SM*.   49. Lady Selkirk to Selkirk, October 9, 1816, *SP SM*.
50. Selkirk to Gore, November 12, 1816, *PAC SP*, p. 2915.
51. *Narrative of Occurrences*, pp. 108 f.
52. Lady Selkirk to Selkirk (Montreal, 1816), *SP SM*.
53. Selkirk to D'Orsonnens, December 2, 1816, *PAC SP*, p. 2939.

signature on the warrant did not correspond to the rest of the writing, and the journey had been made under difficulties and with a speed unknown in the annals of Upper Canadian justice. It had, moreover, recently become known to Selkirk that Owen Keveny had been murdered in cold blood after being arrested on a warrant signed by a Northwester.[54] "These circumstances," declared Selkirk, "could leave us no doubt of the propriety of treating the Warrant as a trick and the pretended constable as an imposter. I trust it will not be ascribed to any disposition to resist the regular execution of the law."[55] Had he known that the story of his resistance would be noised from the Canadas to London, he might have taken a leaf out of William McGillivray's book and gone quietly along with the "imposter." The North-westers were quick to report the circumstance to the Colonial Office in such a light that almost all officialdom in both Britain and the Canadas had become prejudiced against Selkirk's case before the courts were called upon to decide it.[56]

54. See Bibliography, Simpson, p. 275; Martin, *Selkirk*, pp. 128 ff.
55. Selkirk to D'Orsonnens, December 2, 1816, *PAC SP*, p. 2940.
56. Selkirk to Coltman, July 15, 1817, *Q145*, pp. 42 ff. Selkirk to Gore, November 12, 1816, *PAC SP*, p. 2914. *Statement Respecting Settlement*, pp. 148 ff. *Papers Relating to Settlement*, pp. 232 f. *Narrative of Occurrences*, pp. 109 f.

CHAPTER XVIII

KILDONAN

DURING the fall and winter spent at Fort William, Selkirk extended his "retaliations" to a number of the North West Company posts within close proximity. Shortly after the capture of the great fur emporium a detachment of De Meurons under the command of Pierre Pambrun was sent to Fond du Lac in United States territory, where the Canadian company had a post. James Grant, the trader in charge, was taken prisoner and the goods in the fort confiscated, despite the fact that the merchandise seized at this station had paid duties to the American government and was jointly the property of the North West Company and South West Fur Company. While Fond du Lac was being ransacked, another party of De Meurons was seizing the posts at the Pic and Michipicoten. Donald McIntosh, the partner in charge, and his clerks were arrested and their goods seized. In November McIntosh, Grant, and a few others were sent to Montreal charged with "aiding and abetting the troubles of the previous spring at Red River."[1]

Shortly after the seizure of Fond du Lac and the posts at the Pic and Michipicoten, Selkirk sent another party, under Peter Fidler, to take a company post at Lac la Pluie on the main waterway from Lake Superior to the interior. This post was next in importance to Fort William. J. W. Dease, the clerk in charge, when called upon to surrender, refused; so Fidler, whose force was too small for a successful attack, had to return to Fort William. A party of De Meurons with two field-pieces, under the command of Captain D'Orsonnens, was then sent to Lac la Pluie, and the fort "regularly invested and blockaded." Dease had only seven men with him, and they depended for their subsistence on fishing and gathering wild rice. Being cut off from these supplies by Captain D'Orsonnens, "and that Officer having sent him notice, *that he could not be answerable for the conduct of his soldiers,* if they should be further resisted, Mr. Dease was compelled, by the circumstances in which he was placed, to surrender." The captain and his men thereupon took up their quarters in the company's fort.[2]

As Selkirk was anxious to retake Red River and prepare for the res-

1. John Jacob Astor to James Monroe, December 30, 1816; Affidavit of James Grant, November 23, 1816; William McGillivray to John Jacob Astor, November 23, 1816, Miscellaneous Letters, pp. 210 ff., Department of State, Washington. Astor to Selkirk, May 23, 1817, *PAC SP*, p. 3441. *Papers Relating to Settlement*, p. 224.

2. *Ibid.*, pp. 231 f. McTavish, Fraser & Co. to Goulburn, February 8, 1817, *Q147*, Pt. II, pp. 331 f. *Narrative of Occurrences*, pp. 112 f.

toration of the colony, the next point of attack selected was Fort Douglas. Soon after the capture of Fort Lac la Pluie, as winter was setting in, the expedition got under way. First, Miles Macdonell led a small band of De Meurons from Fort William to Lac la Pluie. Then he and Captain D'Orsonnens concerted a plan of attack. Finally, on December 10, the two leaders set out for Fort Douglas with twenty-eight men and two small fieldpieces on sleds.[3]

It was hoped that the Fort could be taken by a surprise attack. To insure secrecy, the Hudson's Bay traders, who might otherwise have given considerable aid, were not notified of what was being done; and an unusual route was chosen for the expedition. After crossing Rainy Lake Macdonell led his men down Rainy River, across the southern part of the Lake of the Woods, and then through forests and over prairies to Red River. Despite the freezing weather and deep snow the party made very good time; by December 31 it had reached the Red River slightly south of Pembina. From the east bank the guns were trained on the unsuspecting North-westers in their fort on the other side; and Macdonell led his followers, now numbering about sixty, to the attack. There was a little resistance, and Fort Daer was surrendered.[4]

After a few days' rest at Pembina the expedition advanced against Fort Douglas. The cold was terribly severe and a strong wind had to be faced. About ten miles above the Forks Macdonell halted his men and planned a night attack. The Fort was held by fifteen men under Archibald McLellan, and probably could have made little resistance in any case. But when the De Meurons scaled the walls in the moonlight on the morning of January 10, McLellan and his men surrendered without a blow; and at daybreak the Hudson's Bay Company flag was "hoisted on the staff." Macdonell now proceeded to oust the North-westers from Assiniboia; nor was he particularly scrupulous in his methods. McLellan was sent to Canada charged with being an accessory to the murder of Owen Keveny. The Company's servants, however, were soon released.[5]

As soon as he had taken Fort Douglas, Macdonell dispatched a messenger "to obtain intelligence as to the fate of the settlers, and to apprise the survivors that they might return in safety to Red River."[6] They were found at Jack River, where they had been taken by Alexander Macdonell after Seven Oaks. There they had been persuaded by Colin Robertson and James Bird, a Hudson's Bay Company officer, to remain for one year, until Selkirk's "pleasure" should be known. They had vowed, on leaving Fort Douglas, never to return again to Colony

3. Miles Macdonell to Selkirk, March 6, 1817, *PAC SP*, pp. 3233 ff. *Papers Relating to Settlement*, pp. 233 ff. Selkirk to Colvile, August 7, 1817, *SP SM*.
4. *Ibid.*   5. *Ibid.*   6. Selkirk, *Memorial to Richmond*, p. 24.

Gardens; and on their arrival at Jack River they had sent a letter to York Factory requesting passage back to Scotland. As there was no certainty that a ship of sufficient capacity would arrive in the Bay that season, they were advised by Bird that "their best policy would be to remain where they were as their condition would be incomparably worse if reduced to the necessity of wintering on the bleak shores of Hudson's Bay." Upon the further advice of Colin Robertson, but much against their will, they had acquiesced.[7]

The winter spent "on the sterile rocks of Jack River" was perhaps the worst that any of the Selkirk settlers had passed in the New World. They had come to Jack River without provisions, and their prospects of getting what they needed were not good. The staple food of the locality was whitefish, but none of these settlers had been "previously acquainted with the business of fishing." They were, however, able to get equipment from the Hudson's Bay post, and before the winter set in had caught and dried a good store. But the winter was long and cold, and much fishing had to be done through the ice. To supplement this slender and monotonous diet the Bay traders generously supplied quantities of pemmican and wild rice to the unfortunate people. In spite, too, of the rigors of the winter, all the settlers survived and many even gave up their determination to return home.[8]

It was the middle of March when Macdonell's messenger arrived at Jack River. The tidings he brought were received with great joy. At once Sheriff Macdonell with a few of the young men crossed the ice of Lake Winnipeg and returned to the colony to prepare for the return of the others when navigation should open. As soon as the frost was out of the ground the sheriff and his men applied themselves assiduously to the cultivation of the soil. Implements were few and seed scarce, but small patches of wheat, barley, and potatoes were planted. Even some of the De Meurons who had come with Miles Macdonell were equally intent upon that object. The work was done under great handicaps. It was hard to get food, as the buffalo were far from the Fort, hunters were scarce, and fear of the métis kept many men on guard. Had it not been for the zealous attachment of Peguis and his kinsmen, the men at the Forks would have suffered great want. The Indians not only hunted for the colony; they hauled the meat on sleds for great distances, a thing they usually despised doing.

Twice during the spring the settlers' fears of the métis materialized

7. Robertson to Selkirk, August 12, 1816; Alexander Macdonell to Selkirk, September 12, 1816, *PAC SP,* pp. 2508, 2746 ff. Gunn and Tuttle, *Manitoba,* pp. 192 f.

8. Selkirk, *Memorial to Richmond,* p. 24. Petition to His Royal Highness George Prince of Wales Regent of the United Kingdom of Great Britain and Ireland . . ., *Q150,* Pt. II, p. 372.

when Cuthbert Grant led bands of them down the Assiniboine from Qu'Appelle to the Forks with the intention, if circumstances proved favorable, of "surprising the fort, or of cutting off the supply of provisions. By unremitted vigilance these malicious intentions were defeated, and the only mischief which Grant could effect, was to kill two out of the small number of breeding cows that still remained, and to carry off two or three men, who had been sent from the fort to bring in provisions."[9]

Toward the end of the winter Selkirk heard of the success of the Red River expedition, and also of the miserable state of the colonists at Jack River. The news made him more anxious than ever to get to Assiniboia. On May 1 with the opening of navigation the Earl and his ex-soldiers set out from Fort William for Red River. No sooner had they done so than the North-westers reoccupied their fort, and shortly afterwards the posts of Fond du Lac, Lac la Pluie, the Pic, and Michipicoten. After an uneventful journey Selkirk reached the Forks on June 21; and about the same time the settlers who had spent the spring at Jack River returned to the Settlement.[10]

Selkirk's disposition of the affairs of the colony after his arrival at Red River was marked by a wisdom and a generosity which were still spoken of in the country a century later. First he made arrangements for the settling of his soldier-colonists. They had been promised choice lands upon their arrival, if they should desire to remain in the country, or transportation back to Canada at the Earl's expense. A great many of them chose to remain. They were rewarded with small tracts of land on Point Douglas and along Rivière la Seine, a small stream flowing into the Red River from the east, opposite the Point. A road was surveyed between the farms on Point Douglas. It ran from the Point out into the open prairie, and was intended to give all the settlers a common highway by which they could reach the hinterland where they had common rights of pasturage and haymaking. The noncommissioned officers were located on farms among those of the privates; the superior officers were quartered in the Fort and made members of the Colonial Council. Selkirk's purpose in settling the ex-soldiers near the Fort was to afford the colony better protection against attacks. "On a signal being made at headquarters, a few minutes would enable the force to join the commanding officers, rally round their standards and be ready for either attack or defence."[11]

9. Selkirk, *Memorial to Richmond*, p. 24. Selkirk to Colvile, August 7, 1817, *SP SM*.
10. *Ibid.* Selkirk to Coltman, July 7, 1817, *PAC SP*, p. 3674. *Papers Relating to Settlement*, pp. 248 f. Selkirk to Lady Selkirk, July 7, 1817; Selkirk to Colvile, August 7, 1817, *SP SM*.
11. Selkirk to Lady Selkirk, July 7, 21, August 4, 1817; Selkirk to Colvile, August

Having settled the ex-soldiers, Selkirk turned his attention to the other colonists. To each of a number of settlers who had lost everything in the recent destruction of the colony he made a grant of twenty-four "chain lots" of land "in free socage." These lots, commencing a mile below Fort Douglas, had been surveyed only recently by Peter Fidler, the Settlement's first surveyor. The deed of this conveyance was concluded with these words from the Earl:

In consideration of the hardships which the settlers have suffered, in consequence of the lawless conduct of the North West Company, Lord Selkirk intends to grant the aforesaid 24 lots gratuitously, to those of the settlers who had made improvements on their lands, before they were driven away from them last year; provided always, that as soon as they have the means, they shall pay the debts which they owe to the Earl of Selkirk, or to the Hudson's Bay Company, for goods or provisions supplied to them, or for other expenses incurred on their account.[12]

All other colonists who wished land were sold tracts of 100 acres at 5s. per acre payable in produce. Easy terms were offered to those purchasing. Each head of a family was given the privilege of distilling as much whisky as the family would require for its own use, the privilege to go to the descendants "in all time forward."[13]

Two lots, likewise of a 660-foot frontage, were also contributed to the community by Selkirk as sites for a church and a school. "This lot on which we are met today," said the Earl, at the meeting in August at which he gave away the twenty-four farms, "shall be for your church and manse; the next lot on the south side of the creek [Parsonage Creek] shall be for your school and for a help to support your teacher, and in commemoration of your native parish it shall be called Kildonan."[14] The same name he had already given to the colony.[15]

Selkirk also planned public utilities on a generous scale. There was to be a huge experimental farm. "Public roads, by-roads, bridges, mill seats, and other important points were settled"; and a general survey of the colony was ordered.[16] For Selkirk this work must have been highly gratifying; he was carrying out in person the most cherished aims of his life.

While the Earl was in Red River he concluded a treaty with the In-

7, 1817, *SP SM*. Ross, *Red River Settlement*, p. 41. Gunn and Tuttle, *Manitoba*, pp. 199 f.

12. Selkirk to Lady Selkirk, July 21, 1817; Selkirk to Colvile, August 7, 1817, *SP SM*. Ross, *Red River Settlement*, pp. 42 ff. These were 100-acre lots with a frontage of 660 feet and a depth of 1¼ miles. Fidler used the Upper Canada survey system.

13. Gunn and Tuttle, *Manitoba*, pp. 200 f. Memorandum, *SP SM*.

14. *Ibid.*, p. 201.   15. Selkirk to Miles Macdonell, *PAC SP*, p. 1492.

16. Ross, *Red River Settlement*, p. 45.

dians to avoid the possibility of future quarrels over the ownership of the land. For this purpose he assembled as many as possible of the bands of natives in the vicinity. Some of the Crees were opposed to the treaty; but Peguis, the old chief of the Saulteaux, who had much influence among the tribes about Red River, went around and prepared them to accept Selkirk's terms. On the appointed day crowds of Indians were gathered at the Settlement. The Earl, dressed in an imposing costume and attended by a long retinue of followers, greeted them in princely fashion. The savages were then seated on the ground within the Fort; and the speechmaking and pipe smoking began. After lengthy orations and considerable "tact and cunning" on both sides, the high contracting parties concluded the following treaty:[17]

This indenture, made on the 18th day of July, . . . between the undersigned Chiefs and Warriors of the Chippeway or Saulteaux Nation, and of the Killistine or Cree Nation, on the one part, and the Right Honourable Thomas Earl of Selkirk on the other part: Witnesseth, that for and in consideration of the annual present or quit-rent hereinafter mentioned, the said Chiefs have given, granted, and confirmed, and do, by these presents, give, grant, and confirm, unto Our Sovereign Lord the King, all that tract of land adjacent to Red River and Assiniboine River, beginning at the mouth of the Red River and extending along the same as far as the Great Forks at the mouth of Red Lake River, and along Assiniboine River, as far as Muskrat River, otherwise called Rivière des Champignons, and extending to the distance of six miles from Fort Douglas on every side, and likewise from Fort Daer, and also from the Great Forks, and in other parts extending in breadth to the distance of two English statute miles back from the banks of the said rivers; on each side, together with all the appurtenances whatsoever of the said tract of land, to have and to hold forever the said tract of land, and appurtenances, to the use of the said Earl of Selkirk, and of the settlers being established thereon with the consent and permission of our Sovereign Lord the King, or of the said Earl of Selkirk. Provided always, and these presents are under the express condition, that the said Earl, his heirs, and successors, or their agents, shall annually pay to the Chiefs and Warriors of the Chippeway or Saulteaux Nation the present or quit-rent, consisting of one hundred pounds weight of good merchantable tobacco, to be delivered on or before the tenth day of October at the Forks of the Assiniboine River, and to the Chiefs and Warriors of the Killistine or Cree Nation, a like present or quit-rent, of one hundred pounds of tobacco, to be delivered to them on or before the said tenth day of October, at Portage La Prairie, on the banks of the Assiniboine River: Provided always that the traders hitherto established upon any part of the above-mentioned tract of land, shall not be molested in the possession of the lands which they have already cultivated and improved, till his Majesty's pleasure shall be known.

17. *SP SM.*

The treaty was signed by Selkirk and five chiefs, the latter making their totems, rough pictures of animals, by way of signature. In the treaty, as already noted, the Saulteaux are mentioned first. This was not due to the fact that they had a better claim to the country than the others; they really had "no claim at all to the lands of Red River, being aliens or intruders."[18] The Crees and the Assiniboines were the rightful owners. The reason that the Saulteaux played a leading part in the treaty was due to the friendliness of Peguis to the settlers and to his personal influence. Under Peguis the Saulteaux were stronger than they had ever been before in Red River.

This treaty has some significance in British imperial affairs. In thus formally acquiring from the natives the ownership of the soil of Red River, Selkirk was making the first treaty entered into between a British subject and the Indians of Rupert's Land, and was paving the way, both in the matter of precedent and in that of Indian sentiment, for the acquisition by Canada of the whole Northwest half a century later.

Selkirk remained at Kildonan for nearly three months,[19] reëstablishing the Settlement on a stronger footing than it had ever enjoyed before. The results of his efforts, as he viewed them, must have seemed pitifully small when he considered the sacrifices which he and others had made. But he realized better than did any of his contemporaries that the Red River Settlement had failed hitherto largely owing to the halfhearted zeal of some, and the unstinted animosity of others; and that under moderately favorable circumstances it should easily grow into a prosperous community of free agriculturists. When he left Kildonan, the Earl could with reason congratulate himself not only that his judgment of the Red River country as a farming region had been vindicated but also that his efforts to improve the lot of his unfortunate countrymen had not all been wasted.[20]

18. Ross, *Red River Settlement,* p. 12.
19. Selkirk to Lady Selkirk, September 7, 1817; Gale to Lady Selkirk, September, 1817, *SP SM.*
20. Selkirk, *British Fur Trade,* pp. 123 f. Gale to Lady Selkirk, October, 1818, *SP SM.*

CHAPTER XIX

"RETRIBUTIVE JUSTICE"

THE intervention of the government, long requested by Selkirk, between the parties contending for Red River, came at last shortly after the Earl had set out for the West. Reports which had reached Governor Sherbrooke of the activities of both groups had quickly induced him to take action. His first step was to issue a general "Proclamation" on July 16, 1816, under the authority of which all offenders might be brought to trial.[1] Everyone was invited to bring in his prisoners. "And," went the Proclamation, "I . . . strictly charge . . . all Justices of the Peace . . ., and do require all others His Majesty's subjects . . . to make search to discover, apprehend and commit . . . to lawful custody for trial in due course of law . . . all persons . . . guilty of any act . . . of force and violence."[2] There was more point in Sherbrooke's charge to "all others His Majesty's subjects," than to "all Justices of the Peace."

Seven Oaks, bringing about, as it did, Selkirk's determination to send those responsible down to Canada for trial, terminated the long game of hide-and-seek which both sides had been playing with the courts. The justices of the Canadas, it is true, were not thereby persuaded to shake off their lethargy and interfere; but the rival forces themselves could now be trusted to bring into camp the game which the Governor sought.

While the results that the Proclamation would have were still problematical, the Governor decided to appoint commissioners who would go directly to the scenes of conflict, investigate in person, take the depositions of witnesses, and report their findings to the government. In adopting this course Sherbrooke was really carrying out the suggestions of Selkirk and, more particularly, of Lady Selkirk.[3] While at first it appeared that these suggestions would not be accepted, continued solicitations on the part of her ladyship,[4] an urgent appeal from Lord Selkirk for government intervention,[5] and, finally, on September 17, a

1. Sherbrooke to Bathurst, August 24, 1816, *Q137*, p. 125. Selkirk, *Memorial to Richmond*, p. 22.
2. *SP SM.*
3. Selkirk to Sherbrooke, September 3, 1816; Halkett to Bathurst, February 21, 1818, *Q137*, pp. 216 ff., *Q150*, Pt. II, p. 333. Jean Selkirk to Sherbrooke, August 17, 19, 1816; Sherbrooke to Lady Selkirk, August 19, 1816, *PAC SP*, pp. 2252 ff., 2555, 2556 f. Lady Selkirk to Sherbrooke, August 16, 1816, *SP SM.*
4. Lady Selkirk to Colvile, August 24, 1816, *SP SM.* Gale to Selkirk, August 27, 1816, *PAC SP*, pp. 2638 f.
5. Selkirk to Sherbrooke, September 3, 1816, *Q137*, pp. 215 ff.

North West Company memorial beseeching immediate retribution for his lordship's "sack" of Fort William[6] forced Sherbrooke to realize that the government must act at last. Not knowing exactly how to proceed, and feeling that he could not wait for advice from the Colonial Office, the Governor turned to his Executive Council for advice. The Council recommended that since all the magistrates of the Indian Territories belonged to the contending parties, their commissions should be revoked, and they should be superseded by two persons "of influence and impartiality to be sole magistrates of that territory and to proceed thither to exercise their functions; and with further powers as Commissioners of Inquiry to mediate between the two Companies."[7] Upon these recommendations Sherbrooke, late in October, appointed the Commission of Inquiry.[8]

Both commissioners appointed were English-speaking Lower Canadians. On account of "the extensive influence and connections of the North West Company" in Lower Canada, Sherbrooke sought to have the Lieutenant Governor of Upper Canada make the selections; but to no avail.[9] Finally he selected W. B. Coltman, an executive councilor, and John Fletcher, a Quebec police magistrate. In addition to being made justices of the peace and special commissioners, both men were given military rank, Coltman as a lieutenant colonel and Fletcher as a major.[10]

The commissioners set out from Quebec on October 31, and intended to go west in the fall, but owing to delays were forced to spend the winter at York. Here they enjoyed "the society of three or four partners of the North West Company"; and spent considerable time in interrogating North-wester clerks and dependents, and in taking affidavits. Every deposition taken was hostile either to Selkirk's conduct at Fort William or to that of his followers in Red River. No attempt was made to secure evidence of the case from the opposite point of view.[11]

By spring the effects of the news of Selkirk's resistance to arrest, as reported by the North-westers to the Colonial Office, had become manifest. They were disastrous for the Earl's cause. It is not difficult to

6. Richardson, Memorial, *Q137*, pp. 207 ff.

7. Sherbrooke to Bathurst, August 24, 1816; Sherbrooke to Bathurst, October 23, 1816; Sherbrooke to Gore, October 1, 1816, *Q137*, pp. 125 f., 203 ff., 218 ff.

8. Sherbrooke to Selkirk, October 30, 1816, *Q150*, Pt. II, p. 332.

9. Sherbrooke to Bathurst, October 23, 1816; Sherbrooke to Gore, October 1, 1816; Gore to Sherbrooke, October 17, 1816, *Q137*, pp. 205 f., 218 ff., 221.

10. Sherbrooke to Bathurst, November 11, 1816, *Q137*, pp. 229 f.

11. Sherbrooke to Bathurst, November 11, December 21, 1816, *Q137*, pp. 231, 320 f. Sherbrooke to Bathurst, January 1, 2, 1817 (with Robert McRobb's and Daniel McKenzie's depositions), *Papers Relating to Settlement*, pp. 65 ff. Selkirk, *Memorial to Richmond*, pp. 25 f.

anticipate the doom of Selkirk's case in Bathurst's dispatch of February 11:

By resisting the execution of the Warrant issued against him Lord Selkirk has rendered himself doubly amenable to the Laws, and it is necessary, both for the sake of the general principle for the remedy of existing as well as for the prevention of further evils, that the determination of the Government to enforce the law with respect to all and more particularly with respect to Lord Selkirk should be effectually and speedily evinced. You will therefore without delay . . . take care that an indictment be preferred against his Lordship for the rescue of himself detailed in the affidavit of Robert Mc-Robb, and upon a true bill being found against him you will take the necessary and usual measures in such cases for arresting his Lordship and bringing him before the Court from which the process issued. Surrounded as Lord Selkirk appears to be with a Military Force which has once already been employed to defeat the execution of legal process, it is almost impossible to hope that he will quietly submit to the execution of any warrant against himself so long as an opening is left for effectual resistance. It is therefore necessary that the Officer to whom its execution is entrusted should be accompanied by such a Civil, (or if the necessity of the case should require it by such a Military) force as may prevent the possibility of resistance.

If, however, the Earl should succeed in avoiding arrest, a report was to be sent to London at once "in order that I [Bathurst] may in so extraordinary a contingency submit to the consideration of Parliament whether the urgency of the case does not require the adoption of some special measure of severity with respect to his Lordship."[12]

Thus the Earl, unheard and uninformed,[13] was condemned on the word of his rivals and enemies, by the man who really controlled Canadian officialdom. He was similarly condemned by the Commissioners of Inquiry. From York they advised Sherbrooke:

The Earl of Selkirk has resisted the execution of a legal process of arrest . . . and that under colour of an unauthorized transfer, which he had obtained of the property of the North-West company at Fort William, from a retired partner, whom he had kept in a state of coercion and inebriety, he was taking measures for removing the whole of that property to the territories of the Hudson's Bay company.

Sherbrooke forwarded the affidavits on which this charge was based, along with his own dispatch, to the Colonial Office, stating that "the commissioners express an apprehension that the North-West company may be driven to call in the aid of the Indians to prevent" such meas-

12. Bathurst to Sherbrooke, February 11, 1817, *Q151A*, pp. 28 ff.
13. Sherbrooke to Goulburn, March 28, 1818, *Q148*, Pt. I, pp. 169 f.

ures.[14] The chief authorities had thus declared against Selkirk almost as soon as government investigation had begun. The lower orders—the officials of the two Canadas—soon received their cue when Bathurst's dispatch of February 11 and other instructions were surreptitiously circulated among them. The very people who were to sit in judgment on the Earl, though already known to be decidedly favorable to the North West Company, were thus deliberately told what was expected of them by authorities who knew that such a word would be received as law.

The purpose of Bathurst, however, in thus guiding the course of justice was not primarily to injure Selkirk and uphold the North-westers. It was rather to arrange for a drawn battle which would provide a convenient occasion for merging the two fur companies and thus bringing the ancient dispute to an end.[15] That Selkirk would be done an injustice mattered little. The North-westers were already advocating the union openly.[16] Similar suggestions were being made at the Colonial Office in the "hopes of an approach towards an amicable accommodation between the parties."[17] The handwriting on the wall was read clearly by both the judiciary in Canada and the Commissioners of Inquiry. Coltman was well disposed toward Selkirk's case but was "a good-natured Laugh and Grow fat sort of person who had no wish but to conciliate and tranquillize all parties."[18] Coltman, Gale declared,

took it for granted that Government looked upon all parties in almost the same light . . . and like a good subject he has laboured to fulfil what he conceived to be the wishes of Government. . . . He is so anxious to show that both parties have alike been criminal; so eager to equalize matters on both sides. . . . He has declared to me (in private) that he considered the Government as having taken a part and given a decided opinion on the subject . . . the Government was very tenacious in preserving the ground it had taken.[19]

Lady Selkirk was of the opinion that he was "straining every nerve to exculpate and serve the North West Company. Yet such is the man's bonhommie and good nature that none of us can quite attribute bad intentions to him either."[20]

14. Sherbrooke to Bathurst, January 2, 1817 (with McRobb and McKenzie depositions), *Q143,* pp. 6 ff. Sherbrooke to Bathurst, January 1, 1817, *Papers Relating to Settlement,* p. 65.

15. Bathurst to Sherbrooke, January 17, February 7, 1817, *Q151A,* pp. 13 ff., 26 f.

16. Gale to Lady Selkirk, October 23, 1817, *SP SM.*

17. Goulburn to Berens, February 13, 1817, *PAC SP,* p. 4502.

18. Allen to Lady Selkirk, February 18, 1818, *PAC SP,* p. 4564.

19. Gale to Lady Selkirk, October 23, 1817, *SP SM.*

20. J.S. to Halkett, December 30, 1817, *SP SM.*

As for Major Fletcher, little need be said. From the first there was scarcely any doubt that he was prejudiced against Lord Selkirk and the Hudson's Bay Company. Lady Selkirk thought that he was an "honest rogue."[21] His interests seem to have been at all times more military than legal. Fletcher's conduct at Sault Ste Marie early in the summer of 1817 prompted Gale to write that "every person of whatever description, capacity, or profession loses his senses the moment he arrives here. . . . Military fame he is determined to acquire."[22] The major, with an escort from the Seventieth Regiment, on June 6 stopped and detained a party of forty-eight unarmed De Meurons "peaceably travelling in the accustomed route to Red River to establish themselves as Settlers or Colonists," and a party of fifty-five servants of the Hudson's Bay Company, also unarmed and peaceably traveling to the trading posts of the Hudson's Bay Company—both under the direction of Archibald McDonald and J. B. Lemoine. Gale "remonstrated on the illegality of this proceeding, and enquired the reasons for it, but received for answer from the Major in Red, that he had no reason to give, that he had nothing to say as to the law, that he acted 'en militaire' and obeyed orders, adding 'silent leges inter arma.' " After a protracted series of protests on the part of Archibald McDonald and a long-drawn-out correspondence on the part of Gale, the major allowed the party to go on its way as if nothing had happened.[23] "No representations of farce or folly that was ever enacted on any stage," wrote Gale, "could come near to the real life that is exhibited here."[24] Clearly, if Fletcher was not likely to help Coltman much, neither was he likely to hinder him.

Coltman reached Fort Douglas on July 5 in company with several North-westers. Selkirk offered to coöperate with him in every way; but while the commissioner behaved with patience, politeness, and affability, the depositions which he took were hopelessly misleading;[25] and he seemed quite willing to accept the trumped-up claims of the North-westers to lands in Assiniboia. "If the genuine interpretation of the proclamation," Selkirk wrote bitterly to Coltman on August 23, "re-

21. *Ibid.*

22. Gale to Lady Selkirk, June 23, July 6, 1817, *PAC SP,* pp. 3550, 3598, 3681 ff.

23. Gale to Fletcher, June 8, 10, 12, and ?, 1817; Deposition of Archibald McDonald, September 23, 1817; Protest of Archibald McDonald, June 8, 1817; Second Protest of Archibald McDonald, *Q150,* Pt. II, pp. 289 ff., 300 ff., 309 ff., 312 f., 314 ff., 317 ff., 323 ff. Selkirk, *Memorial to Richmond,* pp. 32 ff.

24. Gale to Lady Selkirk, July 6, 1817, *PAC SP,* p. 3683.

25. Selkirk to Lady Selkirk, July 21, 1817; Selkirk to Colvile, August 7, 1817, *SP SM.* Fletcher to Sherbrooke, July 22, 1817; Coltman to Sherbrooke, July 15, 1817; Halkett to Bathurst, February 21, 1818, *Q144,* p. 185, *Q145,* pp. 33 ff., *Q150,* Pt. II, pp. 341 ff. Coltman to Selkirk, July 29, 1817, *PAC SP,* p. 3870.

quires such a concession . . . [that the North West Company be allowed its claims to certain lands in the Settlement] there seems to be no alternative but that the settlers should remove to some situation out of reach of the N.W. Co."[26]

Selkirk was losing faith in the British Government. Possibly it would be better after all if his colonists were to throw in their lot with the Americans. "Under all the circumstances of the case," he wrote to Coltman, "it may perhaps be the most prudent course to allow these people to seek an asylum within the American lines, where at least they will not have to apprehend hostility from the subjects of the same Government and where if they be liable to be attacked it will not be considered as an offence to be prepared for resistance."[27] The lieutenant colonel had no comfort to offer.

Selkirk now began to agree with Gale's shrewd surmise of July 4 "that orders have been received from England for something like a hunt against the Earl of Selkirk thro' the influence of the *under* friends of the North-westers at home."[28] Coltman's conduct certainly gave good grounds for such a suspicion. He had been urged to take depositions which would pave the way for the arrest of Alexander Macdonell and Norman McLeod. After some delay, he did so; but apparently in the meantime he had warned the two gentlemen, as they were seen several weeks afterwards far to the west, and making for the Rockies.[29]

On the other hand, instructions came from the Colonial Office that the Earl and several of his associates were to be bound over for trial at Montreal. Selkirk and his counsel were puzzled. They knew nothing, of course, of the orders coming from the Colonial Office. But such flagrant partiality tended to defeat its own purpose. When Selkirk was bound over for the unheard-of sum of £6,000, Dr. Allen for £2,000, and each of their fellow victims for £1,500,[30] the press in the Canadas and Britain began to expose the false charges of the North-westers. As the Montreal *Courant* put it, the recognizances thus demanded amounted to "a greater sum for an alleged misdemeanour than the total amount . . . taken by the justices of the same court from all the partners and servants of the North-West Company . . ." who were accused of direct responsibility for the murder of twenty-two men.[31]

Selkirk's reply to the manifest hostility and unfairness of the au-

26. Selkirk to Coltman, August 23, 1817, *PAC SP,* p. 3974.
27. *Ibid.*
28. Gale to Lady Selkirk, July 4, 1817, *SP SM.*
29. Selkirk to Colvile, August 7, 1817, *SP SM.* Selkirk, *Memorial to Richmond,* pp. 42 ff. *Papers Relating to Settlement,* p. 197.
30. Coltman to Sherbrooke, August 8, 1817, *Q145,* pp. 71 ff.
31. *SP SM.*

thorities was to submit quietly to everything with the hope of securing justice later. Early in September he left Red River. Coltman tried to persuade him to return by the route he had followed in going to Assiniboia; but Selkirk, knowing that a North-wester by the name of Campbell was waiting at Fort William with a warrant for his arrest, and that "the object of the N.W. was only to have an opportunity of insulting him by causing him to be taken into Campbell's custody, the moment he reached Fort William, which Coltman could not and would not have prevented," decided to travel east by way of the United States.[32] The commissioner was somewhat irritated by this choice, but did not actively interfere.

Selkirk, however, had other reasons for going through the United States. They were in the line of plans which he had made long before, and which had nothing to do with his desire to avoid the North-westers. The Treaty of Ghent, negotiated and ratified in 1814–15 between Britain and the United States, had paved the way for the fixing of the northwestern boundary at the forty-ninth parallel. The decision placed a large section of Assiniboia in American territory. The Earl, accordingly, wished to come to an agreement with the authorities at Washington over the disposal of that part of his grant which lay south of the new boundary; he also wished to arrange for passage through the United States of a band of De Meurons who were returning to Switzerland. And perhaps of greater importance was his intention to buy cattle and sheep in Missouri and Kentucky for Red River.[33]

Many people expected that Selkirk, once in the United States, would never return to Canada to stand his trial. The North-westers at Montreal laid wagers on it, and Bathurst was similarly persuaded. Orders were sent from London to the Attorney-General of Upper Canada "to prosecute . . . criminally for the escape from Dr. Mitchell's Warrant."[34]

Meanwhile Selkirk's journey through the United States had taken him by way of Mendota, now in Minnesota, down the Mississippi to Prairie du Chien and St. Louis, and across Illinois and Indiana to Ohio; from there to Lexington (Kentucky), Washington, Philadelphia, New York, and Albany. He reached York on January 10, 1818,[35] much to

32. Coltman to Gale, September 6, 7, 1817; Selkirk to Coltman, September 7, 1817, *SP SM*.

33. Gale to Lady Selkirk, September, 1817; Lady Selkirk to Colvile, November 19, December 18, 1817, *SP SM*. Berens to Bathurst, November 4, 1818; Mundell to Bathurst, November 5, 1818; William McGillivray to Colonel Ready, October 3, 1818, *Q150*, Pt. II, pp. 386 ff., 394 ff., *Q149*, Pt. I, p. 101.

34. Lady Selkirk to Colvile, December 21, 1817; Selkirk to Lady Selkirk, January 10, 1818, *SP SM*.

35. Selkirk Diary, September 8 to 11, 1817; Selkirk to Lady Selkirk, October 27,

the surprise of his enemies; and set to work, with the help of his associates and Lady Selkirk, to secure from the Canadian courts the justice which had hitherto eluded him.

But the constitution of Canada's ruling class of the time, far more than the Earl could have dreamed, was peculiarly fitted to carry out the compromise policy of the Colonial Office without regard to the wrongs of the Selkirk interests and the crimes of the North West Company. Already the country was well on the way to being completely controlled by the Family Compact, that oligarchy of evil fame so well described a few years later by such men as William Lyon Mackenzie and Lord Durham. The latter wrote of it:

For a time this body of men, receiving at times accessions to its members, possessed almost all the highest public offices, by means of which, and of its influence in the Executive Council, it wielded all the powers of Government; it maintained influence in the Legislature by means of its predominance in the Legislative Council; and it disposed of the large number of petty posts which are in the patronage of the Government all over the Province. Successive Governors, as they came in their turn, are said to have either submitted quietly to its influence, or, after a short and unavailing struggle, to have yielded to this well-organized party the conduct of affairs. The bench, the magistracy, the high offices of the Episcopal Church, and a great part of the legal profession, are filled by the adherents of this party: by grant or purchase they have acquired nearly the whole of the waste lands of the Province; they are all-powerful in the chartered banks, and, till lately, shared among themselves almost exclusively all offices of trust and profit.[36]

But the pecuniary interests which had helped weld together and strengthen in union this powerful combination were not the only, or the strongest ties which bound. The secret of their greatest strength is contained in their name. Widespread intermarriage had knit them together with a host of overlapping and crisscross bands. They were, literally, a compact family.

It is true that when Selkirk was about to begin his struggle in the Canadian courts this Family Compact was not as strong and bold as when Durham wrote. But to the extent that it had not become so, it was all the more subservient to the original source of its place and power—

November 3, 24, December 16, 31, 1817, January 10, 1818; Selkirk to Colvile, December 28, 1817; Lady Selkirk to Colvile, January 6, 1818, *SP SM*. Benj. O'Fallon to Ninian Edwards, February 19, 1818, *Niles' Weekly Register,* XIV, 388 f.

36. Sir C. P. Lucas, ed., *Lord Durham's Report on the Affairs of British North America* (Oxford, 1912), II, 147 f. The Family Compact took its name, of course, from the famous "Family Compacts" of the Bourbon rulers of France and Spain in the eighteenth century.

the British Government; and at this time that government was pressing for Selkirk's defeat.

Moreover, even aside from the wishes of the Imperial authorities, the Earl's prospects in the Canadas were hopelessly dark. The North West Company's leaders were hand in glove with the Family Compact, whose "family tutor and political schoolmaster," the Rev. Dr. Strachan, had already struck the keynote of the attitude of his whole clique toward the Earl of Selkirk's Red River venture, by declaring it "one of the most gross impositions that ever was attempted on the British public."[37] As far as that interested group was concerned, Selkirk was already indicted, tried, and condemned before he returned from Assiniboia to Upper Canada. As early as 1815 Dr. Strachan, writing of the Earl's colonizing activities, had declared that "retributive justice is due; and I flatter myself that, among the many great examples of disinterested benevolence so common in Great Britain, one may be found sufficiently powerful to compel Lord Selkirk and his brother Proprietors, to make ample compensation to the Survivors of the Colony for . . . the miseries they have endured."[38]

He could not have asked for a better instrument of "retributive justice" than the judiciary which was about to handle Selkirk's case. The judges at the time held office at the will of the Executive, and at least in some instances were shamelessly servile and corrupt. Among those outside the ruling cliques in both the Canadas there was a good deal of distrust of the judiciary, from the judges of the Supreme Court down to the rural magistrates.[39]

Since the judges held their remunerative offices at the pleasure of the provincial Executive, they were only too apt to see eye to eye with authority, so much so that the local reformers and other critics of the ruling powers were loud in their complaints of judicial subservience and corruption.[40] Thus all those who were interested in effecting the down-

37. Strachan, *Letter,* p. 10.   38. *Ibid.,* Preface.

39. John Charles Dent, *The Story of the Upper Canadian Rebellion* (Toronto, 1885), I, 84.

40. John Mills Jackson, *View of the Political Situation of the Province of Upper Canada* (n.p., 1809), has left the following vivid description of the lower courts:

"The shopkeepers are Justices of the Peace. They have the means of extortion, and the power of enforcing payments. They are first the criminals, then the judges; and the court of appeal seems to be so constructed as to prevent an honest verdict from passing into effect. The practice of the court is unjust, oppressive, and influenced. Favourite attorneys were made deputy clerks of the peace, so that process might be entered and writs obtained most partially. The crown lawyer is allowed nearly seven pounds sterling for every criminal prosecution! an inducement to listen to trifling complaints, and prefer frivolous indictments, when, if power was gratified and independence harassed, it was a sufficient excuse for an inflated contingent account."

fall of Selkirk could be reasonably certain of sympathetic consideration from the Canadian courts. Some of the trials which now followed were conducted in Upper Canada; and what has been said above of Canada's ruling class applied directly to that province. It is sufficient to say of Lower Canada, where most of the trials were to take place, that conditions were very similar to those of the sister province, but worse, because "the Scotch Party," as the ruling clique there was called, was an even more powerful and corrupt oligarchy than the Family Compact; and its resources were even more completely at the disposal of the partners of the North West Company, with its headquarters in Montreal.

That when Selkirk arrived at York in January, 1818, he was still largely unaware of both the power of the North-westers in the Canadas and the effect there of Bathurst's dispatch of February 11, 1817, is surprising and yet true. This is apparent from a report which he sent to the Hudson's Bay Company in February, 1818. "The time is at hand," he wrote, "when the true character of that association [the North West Company] must be completely exposed to the public view, and it is impossible so far to doubt the justice of the British Government as to suppose that such a system can be much longer tolerated."[41] It is not known just how soon he realized that in hoping to secure justice in the Canadas he had been living in a fool's paradise, but certainly it was not until after he had committed himself irrevocably to involved litigation.

The first and most important phase of this litigation was concerned with the attacks on the Selkirk party which had been instigated by the Colonial Office. The Earl had been bound over by Coltman to appear in Montreal for trial in March, 1818.[42] On a bill of indictment preferred against him in Upper Canada he was also required to appear in the following month at the quarter sessions in Sandwich.[43] Neither Selkirk nor his counsel could understand the importance which was being attached to the crime with which he was charged—resistance to arrest. The chief justice at York, William Dummer Powell, explained that "the charge of resistance to legal process was of a peculiar nature; that the Law with respect to it was particularly severe; and that the offence was not bailable."[44] The Acting Solicitor-General of Upper Canada, Henry Boulton, admitted that "instructions from the Secretary of State had been communicated to him containing directions to institute criminal

41. *PAC SP*, p. 4536.
42. Coltman to Sherbrooke, August 8, 1817, *Q145*, p. 71.
43. *PAC SP*, p. 4347.
44. Halkett to Bathurst, January 30, 1819, *Q153*, Pt. II, p. 505.

proceedings against Lord Selkirk."[45] Then the Court of King's Bench confirmed the enormous bail, £6,000, demanded by Coltman.[46]

But Selkirk's suspicions, though already aroused by Sherbrooke's warning in the preceding year of his "determination to carry his orders strictly and fully into effect, however painful that duty might be,"[47] did not become full belief until it was too late; and such belief was not confirmed until a copy of Bathurst's dispatch of February 11, 1817, accidentally came into Selkirk's hands.[48] It was only in the light of this latter document that the Earl saw his past difficulties and mistakes in their true colors.

The first court action took place in Sandwich. Selkirk was charged with having "feloniously stolen" the arms of the North-westers at Fort William. The very man, Jasper Vandersluys, who had been behind the issuing of the warrant had previously declared on oath that Fort William had been captured before the arms were seized. Dr. Mitchell, who had issued the warrant, knew that a regular search warrant had been provided for the seizure of the arms. "The Magistrate by whom that warrant [against Selkirk] had been granted, and also the two others, who had acted with him in taking the information upon which it was grounded, were among those present on the Bench" before which the Earl was now to be tried. It was not difficult for Selkirk to show conclusively that Vandersluys' information was inconsistent and false, and that therefore no reliance could be placed on any of his testimony. The court, accordingly, "set aside the warrant, and discharged the parties from their arrest."[49] This summary dismissal of the case was a fitting introduction to the continued mockery of justice which was to follow.

The other main charges against Selkirk, resistance to arrest, and assault and false imprisonment, had a similar, if more protracted fate. The first of these two cases was moved from Sandwich to Montreal, with bail lowered from £6,000 to £50; and then back to Sandwich, with bail raised from £50 to £6,000. All this time the Earl had to support his witnesses and move them about as required. When the case finally came up in Sandwich "the Bill was thrown out by the Grand Jury,"[50] after a short deliberation. The second case also forced the Earl to make a

45. *Ibid.*, pp. 507 ff.

46. Gale to Lady Selkirk, March 24, 1818, *SP SM*.

47. Sherbrooke to Selkirk, May 3, 1817, *SP SM*.

48. This dispatch was shown to Coltman, who made a copy of it. When some documents were being sent to Selkirk, this copy, "by one of those accidents that will often happen among a multitude of papers, slipped among the others and fell into his hands." Sherbrooke to Goulburn, March 28, 1818, *Q148*, Pt. I, pp. 169 f.

49. Halkett to Bathurst, February 21, 1818, January 30, 1819, *Q150*, Pt. II, pp. 339 ff., *Q153*, Pt. II, pp. 507 ff.

50. *Ibid.*, pp. 524 ff.

second trip to Sandwich with his witnesses. This was in September, 1818. A few days before the quarter sessions opened, the Attorney-General, John Beverley Robinson, after some judicial maneuvering, directed that the indictment be quashed. Thereupon Elliott, the counsel for the North West Company, moved that it should be quashed. The magistrates, however, refused to quash it and the case was postponed. Selkirk returned to Lower Canada. The case was put off repeatedly and nothing was done to terminate it until all the Earl's witnesses had long since scattered and he himself had gone to Britain.[51]

All the remaining charges against Selkirk were now gathered together under the heading of "Conspiracy to injure or destroy the Trade of the North West Company." After the grand jury had spent three days in examining forty witnesses, and two in deliberation, the Attorney-General seems to have come to the conclusion that another of his bills was going to be thrown out. Without assembling the grand jury to explain his reasons, the chief justice adjourned the court *sine die.*[52]

The course of the Crown's prosecution of Selkirk was complicated enough, but the litigation between the Earl and the North West Company was almost hopelessly involved and bewildering. The charges and countercharges were legion. The North West Company was confronted with the following charges: murder or complicity in murder, 42; arson, 18; burglary, 9; robbery, 16; stealing in boats on navigable rivers, 9; grand larceny, 9; and malicious shooting, 9. The Hudson's Bay Company and the Red River Settlement faced these charges: robbery, 5; grand larceny, 6; stealing in dwelling houses, 9; riot and pulling down houses, 5; false imprisonment, 3; and assault and battery, 1.[53]

From the first Selkirk found his efforts baffled by his enemies' influence. His counsel were refused their proper share in the proceedings against the North-westers. Selkirk protested to Sherbrooke that until "within twenty-four hours of the time when the trial was to be opened" neither the Attorney-General nor the Solicitor-General had seen "some of the most material witnesses," and that "neither of them was very ready in the use of the French language"; but the Crown refused to permit private counsel to help conduct the prosecution or even to examine witnesses. A committee of the Executive Council, after considering the question, were "humbly of opinion" that they could not interfere. Thus

51. *Ibid.,* pp. 514 ff.   52. *Ibid.,* pp. 526 ff.

53. *Ibid.,* pp. 535 ff. *Papers Relating to Settlement,* pp. 251 *et seq.* A. Amos, *Report of the Trials in the Courts of Canada relative to the Destruction of the Earl of Selkirk's Settlement on the Red River* (London, 1820). Hereafter, Amos, *Report of Trials.* Selkirk, *Memorial to Richmond,* pp. 38 ff.

the Crown officials were left free to spare the guilty whenever they saw fit.[54]

Selkirk had many other causes for complaint against Canadian justice. Late in 1818, after twenty-two true bills of indictment had been found against the North West Company, the whole Lower Canadian part of the litigation was removed to Upper Canada. The expense to the Earl of maintaining and moving witnesses was enormous. Then, on one pretense and another, the chief offenders were allowed to escape. George Campbell, of ill fame for his part in the destruction of the colony in 1815, was able to leave jail *via* the hospital and get away to the United States through what was really a conspiracy on the part of two judges and a private physician.[55] For the other leading prisoners, however, more regular processes of delivery were employed. Cuthbert Grant was being held at Montreal with no less than thirteen true bills against him, two of which were for murder. Admitted to bail on a small recognizance, he fled to the Indian Territories and never returned. A similar method of escape was provided for a number of other prisoners who had been involved in the violences at Red River.[56]

In the one case in which Selkirk was able to secure a conviction success was nullified by a failure to execute. Charles de Reinhard, the murderer of Owen Keveny, was tried, found guilty, and sentenced to be hanged. He even admitted his guilt. But a dispute arose over the boundaries involved in the case, the sentence was referred to the Prince Regent in Council; and, after further and unnecessary delays, the case was shelved. True bills for murder were also found in both Quebec and Montreal against Archibald McLellan, the North-wester who had been in charge of Keveny. Bail was refused in Montreal and then granted in Quebec. After many farces and mistakes the prisoner was acquitted,[57]

54. Selkirk to Sherbrooke, March 4, 30, April 13, 1818; Sherbrooke to Selkirk, March 30, 1818; Sherbrooke to Bathurst, April 7, 1818; Bathurst to Sherbrooke, June 13, 1817, *Q153*, Pt. III, pp. 624 f., 626 ff., 636 ff., 646 ff., *Q148*, Pt. I, pp. 194 ff., *Q151A*, pp. 95 ff.

55. Halkett to Bathurst, January 30, 1819, *Q153*, Pt. II, pp. 535 ff. Selkirk to Liverpool, March 25, 1819, *PAC SP*, p. 6012. Selkirk, *Memorial to Richmond*, pp. 54 ff.

56. Halkett to Bathurst, January 30, 1819, *Q153*, Pt. II, pp. 545 ff. Allen to Gale, June 16, 1818; Robertson to Selkirk, June 11, 1818, *PAC SP*, pp. 5011, 5035.

57. William S. Simpson, *Report of the Trial of Charles de Reinhard for Murder . . . May 1818 . . .* (Montreal, 1819). *Report of the Trials of Charles de Reinhard and Archibald McLellan for Murder . . ., May 1818* (Montreal, 1818). Halkett to Bathurst, January 30, 1819, *Q153*, Pt. II, pp. 551 ff. Selkirk to Robinson, June 4, 1818, *PAC SP*, p. 4972. The story of the murder of Keveny is long-drawn-out. In 1816 Keveny was arrested on a warrant issued by Norman McLeod, put in charge of De Reinhard—an ex-De Meuron sergeant—and dispatched to Fort William. At the Falls of Winnipeg De Reinhard killed his prisoner.

although, as Dr. Allen wrote, "every one admits McLellan's guilt, even his own friends."[58]

Under the strain of the struggle and the disappointment of defeat the Earl's health began to give way.[59] The rest of the cases against the North-westers only served to aggravate his condition. Vigorous opposition was still offered to the removal of the cases to Upper Canada; but to no avail. Witnesses had to be removed to Upper Canada and retained there at great expense. Some left the scene of litigation altogether. The Earl was too ill to appear; the lawyers of Upper Canada refused to let those from Lower Canada practice in their courts; and the North West Company had "retained every lawyer of influence or talent in Upper Canada." When the cases were sent back to Lower Canada, many of them were dropped as being too indefinitely described; and the Lower Canadian officials "stood on their dignity and would no longer try cases that had once been assigned for trial in Upper Canada."[60]

Furthermore, after the transfer of these cases had been decided upon, the Deputy Attorney-General was instructed by a committee of the Executive Council to admit to bail all the North-westers except those involved in the Keveny case.[61] "The persons so liberated, with hardly an exception, made their escape into the Indian countries."[62] Of those charged with the murder of Governor Semple, only Paul Brown and François Boucher were tried. The evidence at their trial was confused and contradictory. Several important witnesses were absent. In keeping with these chaotic proceedings was the fact that six North-westers, charged with being accessories to the murder of Semple, were tried and acquitted before judgment was passed upon the principals. Of all the charges against the North West Company, over 150 in number, only one, that against Reinhard, resulted in a just verdict; and that verdict was never carried out. The North-westers boasted that their conduct had been completely vindicated.[63]

Little different from these futile proceedings were those brought against the Red River officials. From term to term and from year to year the trials of such men as John Spencer, Miles Macdonell, and Colin Robertson were postponed. During all this time these men were

58. *PAC SP,* p. 5037.

59. Selkirk to Stewart, August 14, 1818; J.S. to Kate, October 26, 1818; J.S. to Halkett, October 26, 1818, *SP SM.*

60. Halkett to Bathurst, January 30, 1819, *Q153,* Pt. II, pp. 557 ff. *PAC SP,* pp. 4205, 5490, 5720, 5772. Martin, *Selkirk,* pp. 153 f. Amos, *Report of Trials,* p. xiii.

61. Minutes of the Executive Council, Lower Canada, State I, 288, *PAC.*

62. Amos, *Report of Trials,* p. xviii.

63. *Ibid.,* pp. ix, 189 ff. Halkett to Bathurst, January 30, 1819, *Q153,* Pt. II, pp. 535 ff.

supported by Selkirk. Finally prosecution was dropped in all cases but those of Robertson and four others. In May, 1818, all five were tried for riot and for tearing down Fort Gibraltar. The jury "after a few minutes consideration," acquitted them all.[64]

The results of these four weary years of litigation inspired Andrew Amos, a Fellow of Trinity College, Cambridge, the London lawyer who prepared the elaborate reports of the trials for publication, to describe the Canadian situation as "a state of Society of which no British colony has hitherto afforded a parallel:—Private vengeance arrogating the functions of public law:—Murder justified in a British Court of Judicature, on the plea of exasperation commencing years before the sanguinary act;—the spirit of monopoly raging in all the terrors of power, in all the force of organization, in all the insolence of impunity." The "disposition, the abilities, and the leisure of the Crown officers" determined the action that would be taken in the case of criminal offenses.[65] A terrible indictment, indeed, but, if anything, an understatement. The only excuse that can be made for the Canadian judicature was its subordination to the Colonial Office. Bathurst and Goulburn had chosen the instrument and given the orders. In the last analysis theirs was the chief guilt.

That guilt was not small. They and their protégés had not only succeeded in well-nigh bringing to nought the Earl's Red River Colony and his private fortune. They had also given him his death wound. The exertions and the hardships of the months in America had undermined his health, until he contracted tuberculosis of the lungs. In the autumn of 1818 he returned to England.[66] His wife followed in the spring after witnessing further and costly defeats of his cause in the Canadian courts.

64. *Ibid.*, pp. 566 ff. Amos, *Report of Trials*, pp. 1 ff.
65. *Ibid.*, pp. xxiii f.
66. Selkirk to Stewart, August 14, 1818; J.S. to Kate, October 26, 1818; J.S. to Halkett, October 26, 1818; J.S. to Kate, March 23, 1819; Selkirk to Lady Selkirk, November 7, 1818, *SP SM*.

CHAPTER XX

THE UNION OF THE COMPANIES

DESPITE his failing health and his disappointments in America, Selkirk was not willing, on his return to Britain, to give up the fight against the North West Company. A "swollen tide of corruption" had overwhelmed him in the Canadas; but he hoped that the British Government, partial as he believed it to be, would inquire into what had taken place, and reverse the judgment of his enemies. "Justice," he wrote, "is all I desire."[1] He had not been long in England when his friends rallied to his cause. Soon they were demanding the attention of the government. Some members of the House of Commons felt that there should be "an attack on Lord Bathurst."[2] Such action was not practicable; nor would Selkirk have sanctioned it. He was unwilling to have "the object of his whole life" degenerate into a sordid party quarrel. Then, too, the nature of the case was personal rather than political.[3]

When the Cabinet was approached on the subject of the instructions sent by the government to Canada, it was discovered that several members of the Cabinet were totally ignorant of the contents of Bathurst's fateful letter of February 11 as well as those of many others. Selkirk was equally surprised. To Lord Hopetown he wrote:

I must own that I thought it could bear but one interpretation and that I was to find a decided enemy, not in Lord Bathurst only, but in every member of the Cabinet. It was with very great surprise, that on meeting Lord Melville and Lord Sidmouth[4] [Selkirk's two friends in the Cabinet] within these two days, both of them assured me that they had never till now been informed of the orders sent out by Lord Bathurst on the 11th of February 1817.[5]

Nor was the Colonial Secretary himself as deliberately responsible for the part he had played as events in the Canadas might have seemed to indicate. In the first place he had been long in office and had come to leave too much of his work to subordinates. The voluminous documents from Drummond and Sherbrooke on the Red River disturbances he had read only perfunctorily, or had turned over to Goulburn to be dealt with. Then, too, he was a rather dull, slow-thinking, narrow-minded, and perverse man.[6] Such men have little desire or capacity to do justice

1. Selkirk to Colvile, December 11, 1819, January 8, 1820, *SP SM.*
2. *PAC SP,* p. 6156.   3. Martin, *Selkirk,* p. 160.
4. J.S. to K., March 26, 1812, *SP SM.*   5. February 2, 1819, *PAC SP,* p. 5861.
6. Selkirk to Colvile, January 8, 1820, *SP SM.* Halkett to Selkirk, April 17, 1816, *PAC SP,* pp. 2197 ff.

to the side opposed to the one they happen to have espoused. Had Bathurst been an abler man, or even a harder worker, he might easily have prevented much of the corruption and futility which marked the Selkirk litigation.

More culpable than Bathurst was the Under-Secretary, Henry Goulburn. Bathurst's worst faults were negligence, prejudice, and perversity. Goulburn really betrayed his office.[7] It was his duty to keep clear of outside influence, yet he allowed himself to become the cat's-paw of the master mind in the plot, Edward (Bear) Ellice, the shrewdest and most influential among the partners of the North West Company. William McGillivray controlled the company's affairs in Canada, while Ellice manipulated the political strings in England; and Henry Goulburn danced at the end of one of them. Ellice and Goulburn together were almost entirely responsible for the hostility of the British Government to Selkirk.[8] This was no secret to the Earl. "I should not entertain a doubt," he told Berens, "of our obtaining sufficient support from the Government if the matter were fairly investigated, & examined to the bottom. But [such] is the strange ascendency, which the N.W. Co. have obtained over the mind of Lord Bathurst or (perhaps I should rather say) of Mr. Goulburne [sic], that I have great doubts."[9]

Since the year 1815 it had been the policy of both Ellice and Goulburn to delay any definite pronouncement of the Crown law officers on the rights of the Hudson's Bay Company in the charter lands even though crime should rage there unchecked and unpunished. Successive requests from the Hudson's Bay Company for an official decision in respect to the maintenance of law and order in Assiniboia were either refused or put off with one excuse or another. "Nothing short of a fatal encouragement," wrote Berens to Bathurst in 1818, "has been thereby held out to the North-West Company."[10] Every request made by Lord Selkirk and the Hudson's Bay Company for the protection of the Red River settlers was ignored or refused by the government, while the North West Company was permitted to infringe upon charter rights, murder innocent people engaged in peaceful pursuits, wantonly destroy property upon which the living of poor pioneers depended, and inflict upon the English trading company a loss of from £40,000 to £50,000.[11]

After a copy of the dispatch of February 11 had fallen into Sel-

7. *Ibid.* J.S. to Halkett, June 29, 1816, December 30, 1817; Lady Selkirk to Colvile, April 27, May 6, 1817; Lady Selkirk to Selkirk, May 7, 1817; Colvile to Lady Selkirk, April 3, 1818, *SP SM.*

8. Simon McGillivray to Goulburn, January 11, 1817, *Q147,* Pt. II, p. 300. *PAC SP,* pp. 6513 ff.

9. Selkirk to Berens, November 18, 1815, *PAC SP,* p. 1942.

10. February 4, 1818, *Q150,* Pt. I, p. 195.   11. *Ibid.,* pp. 188 ff.

kirk's hands, John Halkett wrote to Bathurst,[12] describing "faithfully and without exaggeration" the wrongs suffered by the Earl through the actions of the Colonial Office. "It is evident," he declared, "that he [Lord Selkirk] has been treated with marked and signal injustice, and it cannot be expected that a man who has been so injured is to sit tamely down and have his rights of Property trampled upon, and what is of more importance, his character wantonly traduced."[13] The response from Goulburn, however, was anything but encouraging. In answer to the charge that the dispatch of February 11 had been based on insufficient evidence, he referred to the irregular manner in which Selkirk had secured a copy; and to Halkett's detailed complaints, he countered that the quotations from the dispatch were "very inaccurate."[14] Goulburn's idea of what made the quotations very inaccurate is decidedly revealing: twelve letters capitalized in the copy but not in the original, two proper names misspelled, and half a dozen commas either misplaced or deleted.[15]

Having failed to move the Colonial Office, Selkirk tried to bring his case directly before the Prime Minister, Lord Liverpool, and the Privy Council;[16] and for a time his prospects seemed hopeful. The Prime Minister was cordial and promised him "a careful consideration of the Documents," and the response from the other members of the Cabinet was sympathetic rather than hostile.[17] On June 24, 1819, Sir James Montgomery, a lifelong friend of Selkirk, moved in the House of Commons for

Copies or Extracts of the Official Communications . . . between the Secretary of State and the Provincial Government of *Upper* or *Lower Canada,* relative to the destruction of the Settlement on the Red River, to any legal Proceedings thereon in the Courts of *Upper* or *Lower Canada,* or to any Complaints made of those Proceedings by Lord *Selkirk,* or the Agents of *The Hudson's Bay* or the *North-West* Companies;—also, for copies or Extracts of the Reports made by the Commissioners of Special Inquiry, appointed to inquire into the Offences committed in the *Indian* Territory. . . .

Three weeks later the report was made and it was ordered that it be printed.[18]

12. January 30, 1819. See also Halkett to Bathurst, February 21, March 10, 1818, *Q153,* Pt. II, pp. 495 ff., *Q150,* Pt. II, pp. 330 ff., 358 ff.
13. Halkett to Bathurst, January 30, 1819, *Q153,* Pt. II, pp. 609 f.
14. February 9, 1819, *SP SM.*
15. Halkett to Bathurst, February 11, 1819, *SP SM.*
16. March 19, 1819, *SP SM.* This letter was published in London, 1819, under the title, *A Letter to the Earl of Liverpool from the Earl of Selkirk.* . . .
17. Martin, *Selkirk,* p. 164.   18. *Papers Relating to Settlement.*

Public opinion also seemed to be shifting toward Selkirk. The influential Zachary Macaulay promised his aid and the humane William Wilberforce spoke of desiring "some opportunity of doing justice to him," with the certainty that the Red River Settlement "had been undertaken with a view to the improvement and benefit of your fellow creatures." By the middle of the year the future looked so bright that Selkirk became quite optimistic. "I have of late had the satisfaction," he wrote in August, "of finding the public beginning to be sensible of the infamy of the proceedings in Canada . . . and I believe truth and justice will at last prevail."[19]

There were two forces at work, however, which made the Earl's optimism ill-founded. One of these was the disease which was killing him; the other was the desire of many powerful interests to unite the two fur companies. After his return to England from the Canadas, Selkirk suffered intermittently from hemorrhages and complete exhaustion. A hacking cough disturbed him constantly. He had to keep to his room for days at a time. Occasionally better prospects of success would seem to restore his strength and even promise ultimate recovery. But the strain under which he was living more than made up for these gains. In the fall hemorrhages became more frequent. From then on "he had nothing but anxiety, sorrow, labour of body, and heart break."[20] As a last resort it was decided that he should spend the winter at Pau, in southern France. He hoped that the warmer climate would help him and that he would return to the attack in the spring.[21] But he was beginning now to realize that final union between the fur companies was inevitable, and this he could never agree to.[22] "There was no place for him in the exigencies of a practical settlement."[23] Death solved his problem. He never returned from his trip abroad but died at Pau on April 8, 1820.[24]

Just twenty-seven days before Selkirk's death Sir Alexander Mackenzie also had passed away. His death at this time was symbolic. The North West Company, in spite of successful violence in Assiniboia and dishonest victory in the Canadian courts, had been beaten to its knees. The Hudson's Bay Company, inspired by the Selkirks with new vigor since 1811, had encroached steadily on the trade of its rivals. As the strain of the struggle grew more severe, some of the Canadian partners wished that they were "decently out of" the fur trade.[25] They feared for the future. Victory in the courts was expensive and brought no posi-

19. Martin, *Selkirk,* p. 164.
20. J.S. to K., March 23, 1819; Note by Lady Katherine Halkett, *SP SM.*
21. J.S. to Halkett, February 1, 1820; J.S. to K., April 1, 1820, *SP SM.*
22. Selkirk to Colvile, December 11, 1819, January 20, 1820, *SP SM.*
23. Martin, *Selkirk,* p. 165.   24. J.S. to K., April 17, 1820, *SP SM.*
25. William McGillivray to Johnstone, July 18, 1816, *PAC SP,* p. 2454.

tive gains. Profits had fallen dangerously.[26] Alexander Ross states that the cost of the struggle to the North West Company was £55,000 sterling.[27] If this is true, it had lost £15,000 more than its competitor. In 1822 the agreement between the Montreal partners and the winterers would expire.[28] There was little prospect of its being renewed. The winter partners thought that their profits were too small and their hardships too great. As old Daniel McKenzie had complained, "party work was the madness of many for the gain of a few."[29] The few did not include the winterers. But knowledge of their attitude made the partners in London and Montreal anxious to have the trade war ended speedily.

Before Selkirk's death Edward Ellice had made the first move toward a settlement. Some time in the latter part of 1819 Lord Bathurst sent for him and asked him if it was possible to do anything toward a union between the companies. "I undertook that matter," stated Ellice some forty years later, "not only at his request, but from obvious considerations of interest."[30] In December, 1819, and during the early months of 1820, many letters passed between him and Andrew Colvile. These letters indicate that Ellice was acting on behalf of the North West Company; but more probably he was really speaking only for himself, especially at first. On December 2, 1818, he had sent a list of proposals to Colvile, in which it was suggested that the legal strife between the two companies be stopped at once, that the North West Company buy a controlling interest in the Hudson's Bay Company, and that the North West Company "agree to such conditions as A. Colvile may think necessary or expedient, to assure to such Settlers as have been sent into Red River by Lord Selkirk, if they should be disposed to remain in that Country, the same support which Lord Selkirk . . . has promised to them." Any settlers to whom the plan should prove unacceptable would be transported free of charge to either the United States or Canada.[31]

Lord Selkirk, when he saw these proposals, became enraged. His reply to Colvile was bitter and reproachful. By no manner of means would he trust his property or his colonists to an association which had already proved itself so steeped in treachery. He wrote:

You are aware of the repugnance which I feel to any transaction, which would make me the instrument of putting power into the hands of a set of unprincipled miscreants. To hand over to them the sovereignty as it may be

26. *Report on H.B.C.*, pp. 323 f.
27. Alexander Ross, *The Fur Hunters of the Far West* (London, 1855), I, 278.
28. Davidson, *North West Company*, p. 175.
29. McKenzie to Cameron, January 14, 1809, *PAC SP*, p. 6493.
30. *Report on H.B.C.*, p. 324.
31. Colvile to Lady Selkirk, November 24, 1819; Ellice to Colvile, December 2, 1819, *SP SM*.

called, of an extensive country, where we had the prospect of doing so much good, is a transaction to which I cannot easily reconcile myself, and I would reckon it immoral as well as disgraceful, if it were done from any views of pecuniary advantage. . . . With respect to giving up the settlement or selling it to the North West, that is entirely out of the question. . . . I consider my character at stake upon the success of the undertaking, and upon proving by the result that it was neither a wild and visionary scheme nor a trick and a cloak to cover sordid plans of aggression. . . .[32]

Ellice, nevertheless, continued his overtures. The North West Company was on the brink of ruin. In his difficulty Ellice turned to Goulburn, and as usual got a sympathetic hearing. The Under-Secretary "urged the expediency of a compromise without obliging the Council to decide, because the decision might be unfavourable to both," and he added that "Government might be disposed to go into and confirm any arrangement the Parties might make between themselves."[33]

In addition to the Colonial Office and the North West Company, many of Selkirk's friends and relatives were desirous of a settlement. They had suffered enormous financial losses through their association with the Earl; and his financial condition being now even worse than theirs, there seemed no prospect of recovery unless peace was made.[34] Still Selkirk defied necessity, while virtually admitting that something had to be done. "It is," he wrote, "only the impossibility of holding out against the Colonial Office and the North-West Company together, that can justify it, as I agree fully with what you say of the chances that are against us in carrying on the contest, and the ruinous expenses that it necessarily involves. But we are surely not yet reduced to the point of giving up all in despair."[35]

Such a defiant hope was magnificent, especially in view of the fact that it was soon to be answered. At the very moment when the Earl was writing, a letter was on the way from Samuel Gale, Selkirk's counsel in Montreal, with the thrilling news that the forces of the enemy were breaking up. Robertson's brilliant analysis of the North West Company's vital weakness had at last been vindicated. The wintering partners of the Canadian concern, acting as a body, had indicated privately their willingness to come to terms with the Hudson's Bay Company. Robertson's Athabasca plan had at last borne splendid fruit. Continued English incursions into the North-westers' choicest fur preserves, and recurring violence, had brought things to such a pass that the Canadian winterers faced the prospect of losing everything. Rather than incur

32. Selkirk to Colvile, December 11, 1819, *SP SM.*   33. *SP SM.*
34. Colvile to Lady Selkirk, November 24, 1819, *SP SM.*
35. Selkirk to Colvile, December 11, 1819, *SP SM.*

such a loss, they would make a separate peace. The Hudson's Bay Company was now really master of the situation. Selkirk was jubilant. He had lived long enough to know that he and his friends were the real victors in his life's greatest struggle. Yet at first, after receiving the news, so concerned was he for the welfare of his colony that he wished to continue conversations with Ellice with a view to securing the future of that all-important venture. His opinion, however, was overridden or perhaps reversed by Lady Selkirk, who at this time may well have had a clearer vision than the dying Earl.

In conformity with Lady Selkirk's views and with the support of Halkett and Pelly, Colvile decided to reject the Ellice proposals and enter into negotiations with the winterers. Time passed and many as yet unknown proposals passed back and forth between the Company on the one hand and the two disunited groups on the other. Colvile seems to have been afraid to press his advantage home, partly because he felt that his concern was still too insecure financially to win a drastic victory, partly, perhaps, with an eye on the dangers of future discord. As a result, when terms were finally agreed upon among all parties, the Canadians, especially the Montreal partners, were given the fullest concessions that they could possibly have hoped for, and vastly more than they might easily have been forced to accept.[36]

Selkirk had been dead just a year when the agreement between the rival interests was brought to completion. On March 26, 1821, the two great companies united under the name of the Hudson's Bay Company. Had the Earl been living, doubtless the agreement would have been less favorable to the North West Company. According to the final settlement the new arrangement was to last for twenty-one years, "commencing with the outfit of 1821 and ending with the returns of the outfit of 1841." The details are rather complicated but, roughly, the Hudson's Bay Company was to receive 45 per cent of the profits and the North-westers 55—30 per cent for the Montreal partners and 25 for the winterers. The Hudson's Bay Company officials were dissatisfied with the arrangement, as were the winterers.[37] The McGillivrays were highly elated. But their joy was comparatively short-lived. Within a few years the older company, which had kept control of the trade by way of the Bay, was able to monopolize the fur business as never before, and to bring ruin upon the Montreal houses. The McGillivrays,

36. *Robertson's Correspondence,* pp. civ ff. Colvile to Gale, December 4, 1819, *SP SM.* Martin, *Selkirk,* p. 166.

37. Deed of Covenant executed by the Hudson's Bay Company and the McGillivray's and Ellice, 1821, Davidson, *North West Company,* pp. 305 ff. Colvile to Lady Selkirk, Saturday, n.d.; Colvile to Lady Selkirk, Thursday, n.d.; Colvile to Lady Selkirk, March 30, 1821, *SP SM.*

broken in fortune, declined in power. William went to Britain to die. Simon, "the old Fox," was in 1836 "leading the life of a vagabond and adventurer." Inglis, Ellice & Company of London went bankrupt.[38] But the Hudson's Bay Company went on prospering. With its great Canadian competitor eliminated and as yet no important rivals to disturb its equanimity, it settled down again into its former quiet, secretive, money-making traffic with the natives. Selkirk's wrongs had been avenged.

38. Selkirk (sixth Earl of) to Lady Selkirk, September 17, 1836, *SP SM*.

CHAPTER XXI

PERMANENT SETTLEMENT

WHEN Selkirk set out from Red River in the summer of 1817, he left behind him a colony which at last was to prove permanent. Not that the establishment was in itself immeasurably stronger than before, but the enemies who had destroyed it in the past were now either dispersed or discouraged, and there seemed to be no other foe who would be likely to attack it in force. The métis, when not inspired by the North-westers, were fairly easy to placate; the local Indians were still consistently friendly to the colonists; and Assiniboia was well beyond the range and ambitions of the main body of the Sioux.

The men who had accompanied Selkirk to Red River, moreover, possessed a sort of discipline which had its value for an infant colony in a wilderness; and the decision of some of them to remain permanently seemed a further promise of future stability. While the chief protagonists in the fur-trade war were feverishly busy in Canada and England with the last phases of their ruinous rivalry, these new settlers were engaged in adapting themselves to their new home.[1] During the summer months of the next year more settlers arrived at Red River—"Orkney men with their wives, white and brown and their children." They took up lots on the Assiniboine, a few miles up the river from Fort Douglas, and laid the foundations of Orkney-town.[2] With the settlement of the ex-soldiers and Orkneymen in Assiniboia had come practical peace, if not harmony.

Unfortunately, however, the De Meurons made better soldiers than settlers. The officers among them had brought a certain amount of culture with them; and some of the men had the admirable steadiness of character often possessed by veteran soldiers. But a mercenary career had given many of them bad habits and a selfish, dishonest outlook on life. "They were," states a contemporary, "a medley of almost all nations—Germans, French, Italians, Swiss and others; and, with few exceptions, were a rough and lawless set of blackguards. . . . They were bad farmers, as all old soldiers generally are, and withal very bad subjects; quarrelsome, slothful, famous bottle companions, and ready for any enterprise, however lawless and tyrannical."[3] Another contempo-

1. Miles Macdonell to Captain Roderick MacDonald, June 25, 1818, *SP SM*.
2. Matthey to Selkirk, August 30, 1818, *SP SM*. It may be explained that some of the Orkneymen had been in the country for several years.
3. Ross, *Red River Settlement*, p. 41.

rary, writing in 1821, brands them as "lawless banditti and, almost to
a man drunkards."[4] A visitor at Red River in 1822 found "most of the
Meurons . . . extremely mutinous."[5] Two years later a company official, George Simpson,[6] declared: "I should be rejoiced to see every
Meuron in the Colony away, they will never pay a farthing of their
debts, are continually in distress, would not consider themselves half
paid for the services they have rendered his Lordship, if his estate was
divided among them, and are ripe for outrage and violence whenever an
opportunity offers."[7] A more specific charge against the De Meurons
was that they soon became adepts at "rustling" cattle, and thus increased the size of their own herds at the expense of their Scottish neighbors. They rather despised mere farming as it had to be carried on in
Red River.[8]

Prominent among the many real or fancied grievances of the ex-
soldiers was the dearth of marriageable women. None of the De Meurons
had brought a wife with him, and scarcely any brides were available in
Red River. But steps were soon taken by Selkirk to meet the difficulty.
In January, 1820, he sent Captain de May, a British ex-mercenary, to
Switzerland to recruit settlers for Red River. In some respects the captain was well fitted for the task. He was a native of Berne and spoke
French, German, Italian, and English with "decided fluency." He was
gifted with a winning personality. He also had a keen appreciation of
the value of advertising. Having drawn up a highly colored emigration
tract, he went to work in the cantons of Neuchâtel, Vaud, Geneva, and
Berne, and at the end of a few months had secured 170 emigrants. Three
quarters of these were French-speaking; the rest spoke German.[9]

Opinions were to differ as to the quality of these recruits. According
to one authority, "all were Protestants, and generally intelligent and
well-to-do persons, some of them possessed of considerable means."[10]

4. Nicholas Garry, "Diary," *Transactions of the Royal Society of Canada,* VI,
sec. II, p. 163. Hereafter, Garry, Diary, *RSC.*

5. Halkett to Lady Selkirk, October 19, 1822, *SP SM.*

6. Simpson was appointed Governor of the Northern Department of the Hudson's
Bay Company Territories shortly after the union of the companies. In 1826 he was
made Governor-in-Chief of the Company's territories in North America, a position
he continued to hold until his death in 1860. See E. E. Rich, ed., *Journal of Occurrences in the Athabasca Department by George Simpson, 1820 and 1821, and Report.
With an Introduction by Chester Martin* (London, 1938), p. lvi.

7. Simpson to Colvile, May 31, 1824, *SP SM.*

8. Ross, *Red River Settlement,* p. 106.

9. Simpson to Colvile, September 5, 1821; Halkett to Lady Selkirk, October 19,
1822, *SP SM. Prospectus D'Un plan d'envoyer des colons à la colonie de la Rivière-
Rouge dans l'Amérique Septentrionale,* Berne le 24. Mai 1820. Garry, Diary, *RSC,*
VI, sec. II, pp. 162 ff., 192.

10. "Early Days at Red River Settlement . . . .: Reminiscences of Mrs. Ann
Adams, 1821–1829," *Minnesota Historical Collections,* VI, 77. Hereafter, *MHC.*

On the other hand, most of the reports were unfavorable. George Simpson described them as "most injudiciously selected, men of no character, some taken out of jails, others out of work and mad houses."[11] John Halkett refers to their coming to Red River as the "invasion of that horrible importation sent from Switzerland."[12] According to Nicholas Garry, Deputy Governor of the Hudson's Bay Company, who visited Kildonan in 1821, "many of the Swiss, both male and female," were "bad characters"; but also, "many of them are excellent, particularly one Family, where there are six Daughters who merit a better Fate than will probably await them."[13]

The one shortcoming of the Swiss upon which all critics agreed was that as a group they were not farmers. "Many of them were watch and clock makers, pastry cooks and musicians."[14] Simpson complains that "instead of useful hardy agriculturists, they are of all ages, and unaccustomed to laborious work, being chiefly watchmakers, jewellers, pedlars etc." But the chief blame for this blunder must be charged to De May—"that swindler," as Halkett calls him. De May certainly seems to have valued quantity higher than quality in his recruiting. Simpson concluded, "from the rabble" De May had sent out, that he must have been paid "by head money."[15] This was indeed the case; and it is not unfair to say that the captain was "more intent upon gaining Louis d'ors [sic] than upon honourably fulfilling the trust reposed in him."

The Swiss were at least as much sinned against as sinning. "From the printed prospectus . . . circulated through the Swiss Cantons by Mr. de May," admits Governor Bulger of Assiniboia, "it is but too apparent that these wretched people have not been fairly dealt with. This is not the country, which Mr. de May has, in that prospectus, represented it to be." The historian must concur in Bulger's judgment that it was "most unfortunate that . . . de May should have been intrusted with so important a mission."[16]

The Swiss came to Red River in 1821 by way of Hudson Bay. They finished the ocean voyage in good health and spirits; but when they reached Assiniboia they discovered, like so many others who had preceded them in former years, that no preparations had been made to receive them. At first they were lodged in tents near Fort Douglas; afterwards they were moved across the Red River and settled along the

11. Simpson to Colvile, September 5, 1821, *SP SM*.
12. Halkett to Lady Selkirk, October 19, 1822, *SP SM*.
13. Garry, Diary, *RSC*, VI, sec. II, pp. 162 ff.
14. Ross, *Red River Settlement*, p. 57.
15. Simpson to Colvile, September 5, 1821; Halkett to Lady Selkirk, October 19, 1822, *SP SM*.
16. Bulger to Colvile, August 4, 1822, *SP SM*.

banks of the Rivière la Seine with the De Meurons. In this task of settlement most of the ex-soldiers gave their help with enthusiasm, though it was remarked that they confined most of their attentions to the families in which there were marriageable daughters. The English clergyman, the Reverend John West, who had come out to Assiniboia in the preceding year, was soon busy marrying the Swiss girls to the De Meurons.[17]

Yet the arrival of even these attractive newcomers was not an unmixed blessing. From the first, food was scarce in Kildonan, but in later years the chronic scarcity had been greatly aggravated by the depredations of locusts. This pest had appeared in the Red River Valley some thirteen years before the first establishment of the colony. Then it had disappeared, to return in 1818, on a day late in July. In the morning the gardens and the fields of grain promised an excellent harvest. In the afternoon the sky was darkened by locusts in vast swarms, sweeping in from the great dry regions lying to the south and west; and, next morning, when the people awoke, all their hopes were blighted! "Crops, gardens, and every green herb in the settlement had perished, with the exception of a few ears of barley, half ripe, gleaned in the women's aprons." This was an almost crushing disaster. Yet it was not as dreadful as it would have seemed a few years earlier. The colony was becoming acclimatized. The settlers had now become good hunters; "they could kill buffalo; walk on snow-shoes; had trains of dogs trimmed with ribbons, bells and feathers, in the true Indian style; and in other respects, were making rapid steps in the arts of savage life." Food being too scarce at Kildonan after the locust plague to support them for the winter, they turned confidently toward Pembina.[18]

After spending a comparatively good winter at Fort Daer, the Red River people returned to Kildonan in the spring of 1819 and industriously set about planting what little seed grain still remained in the colony storehouses. Barely had the crops sprung up, however, when young locusts came out of the ground in swarms, hatched from eggs laid in the preceding year.

As early as the latter end of June, the fields were overrun by this sickening and destructive plague; nay, they were produced in masses, two, three, and in some places, near water, four inches deep. The water was poisoned with them. Along the river they were to be found in heaps, like sea-weed, and

17. Simpson to Colvile, September 5, 1821, *SP SM*. Simpson to Colvile, May 20, 1822, *PAC SP,* pp. 7589, 7590, 7595. Garry, Diary, *RSC,* VI, sec. II, pp. 162 ff.

18. Matthey to Selkirk, August 30, 1818, *SP SM*. Ross, *Red River Settlement,* pp. 47 ff. Simpson to Colvile, May 20, 1822, *PAC SP,* pp. 7589 ff. The "grasshoppers" were what we now call "Rocky Mountain locusts."

might be shovelled with a spade. . . . Every vegetable substance was either eaten up or stripped to the bare stalk . . . and the grain vanished as fast as it appeared above the ground. . . . Even fires, if kindled out of doors, were immediately extinguished by them, and the decomposition of their bodies when dead, was still more offensive than their presence when alive.[19]

Once again the poor settlers were forced to seek a winter refuge at Pembina.

Perhaps the worst feature of the locust plague of 1819 was that it left Kildonan without seed grain. To secure this necessity in time for the next seedtime, a score of settlers journeyed in the dead of winter all the way to Prairie du Chien on the Mississippi. This was, at the time, the nearest American settlement, although in 1819 a military establishment, later know as Fort Snelling, had been set up at the forks of the Minnesota and Mississippi rivers. As early as 1817, while journeying from Kildonan through the American West, Lord Selkirk had "had occasion to observe the great facilities which nature offers, for a commercial intercourse between [Kildonan] . . . & the American settlements in the Missouri & Ilinois Territories," and had realized that "our people might draw their supplies of many articles, by way of the Missisipi, & River St. Peters [Minnesota], with greater facility than from Canada or from Europe." He was confident that "this traffic, tho' it might be of small account at first, would increase with the progress of our Settlements . . ."; and on reaching Baltimore he wrote to the American Secretary of State, John Quincy Adams,[20] expressing these hopes, and suggesting that the American Government facilitate matters by permitting the granting of the requisite passports for trade across the intervening territory, which was then part of the Indian country. In making this suggestion Selkirk was thinking specifically of an arrangement which would "afford an opportunity to my settlers to obtain a supply of cattle & sheep, to replace those which had been destroyed by the lawless partisans of the North West Company."

Whether or not Selkirk was responsible for the decision of the colonists to go to Prairie du Chien in 1819 is not known; but the journey was quite in conformity with his ideas. At this time they purchased 250 bushels of wheat, 100 bushels of oats, 30 bushels of peas, and some chickens. These supplies were loaded on three Mackinac boats and transported up the Mississippi and Minnesota rivers and then down the

19. Ross, *Red River Settlement*, pp. 49 f.

20. December 22, 1817, Miscellaneous Letters, pp. 178 f., State Department, Washington. John Perry Pritchett, "A Letter by Lord Selkirk on Trade between Red River and the United States," *CHR*, XVII, 418 ff. The westward advance of American settlement will be discussed in chap. xxii.

Bois de Sioux and Red to the devastated colony. The whole expedition cost the Selkirk estate the sum of £1,040 sterling. Although the seed did not reach Kildonan until well on in June, it was planted at once and grew well, enough ripening to provide sufficient seed for the following year.[21]

Red River was not yet freed of the destructive locust, but its worst ravages were past. In 1820 only part of the crops was destroyed. "The grasshoppers have again visited us upon the 8th of July," wrote the Governor, Alexander Macdonell, "and continued till they had eaten a good deal of our barley, but they did not appear to be so destructive as upon the former occasion, [and] they do not injure the wheat. . . . The Indian corn they do not touch but they injured some young potatoes."[22] Once again in the following year, the pest returned. "The grasshopper, I am extremely sorry to say," reported Simpson, "continues its destructive influence, the crops have been seriously injured, and in many parts wholly destroyed."[23] He was referring to the earlier part of the season. At the end of August John Pritchard was able to tell a different story. "Since the arrival of the grasshoppers the country has never been so free from them as at present, and so propitious has the season been, that the crops considered as totally destroyed have, since the grasshoppers left shot up again, and now hold out a very fair promise."[24] Fortunately the locusts had themselves been attacked by a blight and had suddenly disappeared.[25] They were not to reappear in the Red River Valley for many decades.

But the effect of this succession of locust plagues had been extremely disturbing to the spirits of the settlers. Even as early as 1818, partly on account of the depredations of the insects, the De Meurons became "rather disheartened" and developed "a determination to abandon their homes."[26] At this juncture a few new settlers arrived and the ex-soldiers were persuaded to remain.[27] But after the departure of the locusts a number of settlers decided to migrate. Several families of Swiss and De Meurons proceeded to the States *via* Prairie du Chien, "with a hope of mending their fortunes." The journey had its hazards, as was seen in the fate of a Scotchman, a blacksmith, Tully by name, and his family, who for several years had been attached to the establishment at Fort

21. *The Nor'-Wester,* March 1, 1861. Henry H. Sibley, "Reminiscences; Historical and Personal," *MHC,* I, 470. George A. Belcourt, "Department of Hudson's Bay," *MHC,* I, 220. Ross, *Red River Settlement,* pp. 50 f.

22. Alexander Macdonell to Colvile, August 8, 1920, *SP SM.*

23. Simpson to Colvile, September 5, 1821, *SP SM.*

24. Pritchard to Colvile, August 31, 1821, *SP SM.*

25. Simpson to Colvile, May 20, 1822, *PAC SP,* pp. 7591, 7595.

26. Matthey to Selkirk, August 30, 1818, *SP SM.*

27. *Ibid.*

Douglas. The poor man and his wife were murdered by the Sioux about sixty or seventy miles beyond Pembina, and his two children had been taken by the Indians.[28] Such a prospect may have helped to deter other settlers who were still hesitating to emigrate. But for most of these the question was settled definitely a few years later, in 1826, when the Red River Valley was devastated by a new enemy—a flood. For twenty-two days the river had risen higher and higher, and it was slower in going down again. When it had gone down "the industrious among the people returned to the possession of their houseless lands. They soon repaired many of the inroads caused by the flood, and such was the increased fertility of the soil that crops in general sprouted above the surface in three days." But the Swiss and De Meurons who were still in Assiniboia "bent their course to the States," while a number of Canadians returned to Canada, those who left, it was estimated, "making a total of 180 big and small."[29] A later estimate was much higher. "By our latest accounts," says Donald Mackenzie in January, 1827, "the families which emigrated to the States took boats at the American Trading Posts of Lake Travers, and descended the River St. Peter's. From the date of setting out they were considerably augmenting [sic] along the way. We have not been able . . . to ascertain exactly . . . but believe the number which left the settlement to be little short of 300 of every denomination."[30] Earlier he had declared that this exodus "was a consummation much to be desired," the emigrants consisting "mostly of idle and turbulent characters who had infested the colony for several years."[31] He was still able, in 1827, to assure Andrew Colvile that "among the industrious portion of the population but few or none have taken their departure."[32]

These outgoing settlers and the ruined crops and equipment of the locust and flood years were not the only losses suffered by the colonists and proprietors of Assiniboia in the years immediately following Selkirk's departure. There was the added loss of the ownership as well as the jurisdiction of those Assiniboia lands which lay south of the forty-ninth parallel. Selkirk himself had become aware of this possibility as soon as news reached him of the terms of the boundary agreement; but the quarrel with the North West Company, added to the other cares of colonization, had prevented him from taking any steps to secure his rights south of the new boundary before his visit to Red River in 1817.

28. Simpson to Colvile, May 31, 1824, *SP SM*.
29. Donald Mackenzie to Colvile, August, 1826; Simpson to Colvile, October 22, 1826, *SP SM*.
30. Mackenzie to Colvile, January 30, 1827, *SP SM*.
31. Mackenzie to Colvile, August, 1826, *SP SM*.
32. Mackenzie to Colvile, January 30, 1827, *SP SM*.

It was partly with a view to enlisting the help of the authorities at Washington in obtaining a good American title to the lands which had been cut off that he had decided to return from Assiniboia to Canada through the United States.[33]

At one time he had had some prospect that "a Company might be formed to purchase & settle that part on speculation." As his American confidant and assistant in these matters he had selected one John Greig, an old legal acquaintance from Canandaigua, New York, and had ended by "giving him carte blanche as to what should be done as to the disposal of the American R R lands." Due to his failing health Selkirk was unable to remain in the United States to look after his own interests, or to return there later as he had fully intended to do.[34] When nothing came of Greig's part in the land scheme, and when Selkirk had given up all hope of returning to the New World, he conveyed his title to "the lands south of the 49th degree" to Halkett, and advised the latter to go to America and do what he could to obtain a sound title to the property and attempt to dispose of it.[35] Halkett made the journey in 1821, but he "soon saw enough and heard enough" to convince him that Lord Selkirk's views respecting the disposal of American Assiniboia could not be carried through in the present state of agricultural depression in North America.[36] On this account Halkett concluded that to go to any expense to secure a definite American title to the lands in question would be idle, and that the only thing they had to do was to have their claims preferred, and maintain their title to them until it was advisable to take possession of the land.[37] This was a mistaken view, as later events were to show. Fifteen years afterwards when Dunbar James Douglas, the sixth Earl of Selkirk, was in Washington, he discussed the whole matter with Daniel Webster, the legal representative of the Selkirks in America. Webster said that "everything remained as it was" when Halkett was in Washington. He seemed sanguine as to the chances of the claims being admitted. He hinted, however, that an Act of Congress might be of use to affirm the right, adding that "if the good understanding between the countries still continued as at present, he did not think there would be any difficulty in getting it passed." But nothing was done, due largely to the fact that Webster was a candidate for the presidency. "There is another wheel in the concern," the young Earl

33. See chap. xix.
34. Selkirk to Lady Selkirk, November 9, 1818, January 9, 23, February 26, 1819; Selkirk to Greig, December 2, 1818, *SP SM*.
35. Selkirk to Halkett, September 19, 1819; Memorandum by Halkett, April 27, 1823, *SP SM*.
36. Halkett to Colvile, November 22, 1821, *SP SM*.
37. Halkett to Colvile, February 9, 1822, *SP SM*.

wrote to his mother, "which is this: Webster is candidate for the Presidency, and even if he has no chance now, he will I think try to oust Van Buren at the end of four years. . . . Now I believe if he thought there was to be any stir up about this land he would throw us over, rather than risk his popularity."[38] In the end the Selkirk estate was forced to relinquish its claim to Assiniboia south of the boundary.

The fixing of the boundary in the Red River Valley at the forty-ninth parallel in 1818, however, was less important as disturbing property rights than as shifting the incidence of political sovereignty. Whoever might own the soil south of that line, the government of that region and the allegiance of its inhabitants were henceforth to be American instead of British. The importance of this change was to become more evident with the passage of time. But even as early as 1822 the first fruits were beginning to show: the Red River authorities dismantled Fort Daer and the Hudson's Bay Company post at Pembina. This was partly the work of Halkett, who visited Red River after his trip through the United States. "I have done everything," he wrote in October, 1822, "to break up the whole of that unfortunate establishment, and I daresay by this time both Fort Daer and the Company's trading post, are floating down the river in the shape of rafts to repair their buildings at the Forks."[39]

This did not mean that the Hudson's Bay Company officials had no intention of continuing to trade south of the boundary. But they realized that such trade would in future be very precarious. In 1821 Simpson admitted, speaking of any Company claim to trade south of the border, "it is probable the Americans, who are very tenacious of their rights, may complain and if they do it will be necessary to withdraw it."[40] It was to be many years before the Company was to discontinue all incursions south of the line, but after the retirement from Pembina the Selkirk Settlement may be said to have been confined in fact as well as in theory to the region lying north of the treaty boundary. Yet though this is largely true as regards Old World settlement, it scarcely applies to the disposition of the more native population and to the movements of local trade. These had been determined from the first by regional rather than by political forces; and it was long in their case before the new order became practically effective.

The loss in territory thus occasioned to Assiniboia and the loss in population due to this and other causes were compensated for, however, about this time by an influx of new settlers. In fact, during the years

38. Selkirk (sixth Earl of) to Halkett, n.d.; Selkirk to Countess of Selkirk, January 1, 1836, *SP SM*.
39. Halkett to Lady Selkirk, October 19, 1822, *SP SM*.
40. Simpson to Colvile, September 5, 1821, *SP SM*.

1820–22 the population of Red River was doubled. The change was largely a by-product of the reorganization of the fur companies following their union in 1821. On that occasion hundreds of employees— English, Scotch, French-Canadian, and métis—were discharged as superfluous labor; many others resigned rather than work under a name they despised. Most of these men had been traders, trappers, or voyageurs. Few of them returned to Canada. Some crossed over into the United States and became a valuable asset to the American Fur Company; in 1822 others, together with a few Americans, organized the Columbia Fur Company, whose chief establishment was strategically located on Lake Traverse. But the majority were content to take up their permanent abode in or about Red River. Many of them intermarried with the Indians or with métis women, as their forerunners had been doing for decades; and the mixed-breed element of the population attained a larger proportion than before.[41]

By the early 'twenties, then, the Red River Colony presented a most heterogeneous picture, most of the chief nationalities of Western Europe, as well as the natives and varying degrees of mixtures of the two, being well represented. The character of this people was as diverse in quality as its blood. Governor Simpson, in a lengthy report to Andrew Colvile on May 31, 1824,[42] neatly classifies and describes the chief groups.

"The Meurons and Swiss generally speaking," he wrote, "are wretched settlers; being neither industrious nor provident, they are continually begging and talking of leaving the settlement if their wants are not supplied. We conceive it would be highly advantageous if they did withdraw, therefore no steps are taken to prevent them; on the contrary we are inclined to render them every facility to that end." Clearly no one was disappointed at their decision to leave. They were never fitted for Red River life.

Just the contrary seems to have been true of the immigrants from Scotland, although Simpson as a Company man found many of them unprofitable debtors. As he told Colvile, the Scotch

are steady and well disposed, and consider Red River as much their home as the land of their nativity formerly was; they never will think of leaving the colony, unless some evil which is not to be anticipated should arise; they live

41. Matthey to Selkirk, August 30, 1818; Colvile to Gale, February 23, 1820; Simpson to Colvile, September 5, 1821, September 8, 1823, May 31, 1824; Bulger to Colvile, August 4, 1822; Halkett to Lady Selkirk, October 19, 1822, *SP SM*. Simpson to Colvile, May 20, 1822, *PAC SP*, pp. 7589 f., 7625 ff. William H. Keating, *Narrative of an Expedition to the Source of St. Peter's River* (London, 1825), I, 445. Hereafter, Keating, *Narrative*.
42. *SP SM*.

in great comfort, but grumbling is the characteristic of Highlanders, and neither a change of country nor circumstances will alter their nature; they talk nothing but Gaelic, and do not mix with the other settlers; they are honest in their dealings with all, except the Company and executors, and debts contracted with them they have no idea of paying; they complain bitterly that we do not give superfine cloth, and Hyson tea, on credit, although they did not know such articles even by name in their own country.

Not a discreditable picture, in view of the almost endless series of misfortunes which had been the lot of the Old World emigrants.

For the former servants of the Company now settled at Red River, Simpson had an even better word than for the Scotch. Not that they really made better colonists. But they were less troublesome to the neat-minded official. "The Company's old Canadian servants," he contends, "are the least troublesome and most attached to us; either in starvation or in plenty we can do anything with them; if they have but a hatchet and hoe, a little ammunition and a few hooks and lines, they can shift for themselves and are of that happy thoughtless disposition that they are never discontented or out of humour." This resembles strongly Colin Robertson's eulogy of the same class of people, and draws credibility not only from the circumstance that it was one of the few points upon which the two men were in harmony but also from its close agreement with the accounts left by others.

Simpson's approval, however, bestowed so freely upon the Scotch and the ex-Company settlers, was certainly not extended to the freemen and the métis. These he classed rather with the Swiss and the De Meurons—with this reservation, that he saw in their greater numbers a growing danger to law and order. To them he devotes a more considerable space.

The freemen and half-breed population is now growing very formidable in point of numbers and lives entirely by the chase; the produce of their hunts, Buffalo meat, has hitherto met a ready sale in the colony, but in the course of another year or two that market will be shut up, or the stock of domestic cattle will render the inhabitants perfectly independent of the plain; these people will then I apprehend be the greatest danger the colony has to fear; they are fond of dress show and liquor, which they cannot then procure, they are accustomed to an erratic life, and cannot immediately be brought to agricultural pursuits, they possess all the savage ferocity of the Indians with all the cunning and knowledge of the whites, so that unless early means are taken to bring them round to industrious habits and withdraw them from the plains, I do most seriously apprehend that they will in due time be the destruction of the colony. They never inter-marry with the whites, but on the contrary all the best looking women among them are picked up by the whites, and this produces everlasting jealousies, and when their present means of living terminates, there is every prospect that they will become a most alarming banditti who will have recourse to acts of violence and barbarity in order to gratify their love of plunder and revenge.

Simpson then goes on to explain how he has sought to control the bois-brûlés by influencing their leader—a policy to be followed by the Company with success for some years:

I have made it my business to secure [Cuthbert] Grant's attachment, and good offices; he is to us a useless expense further than keeping him out of harm's way, and by management I have got him to retire from the service, and turn settler; I have got an order . . . to transfer his money into the hands of the Company . . . he is regularly married . . . and related to, or connected with the principal freemen or half-breeds who look up to him as their chief and great man. . . . He this spring became a settler and has got a grant of land on the White Horse Plains, about 12 miles above this place, on the Assiniboine, where he is joined by . . . about 80 or 100 families of half-breeds. These people will turn their attention to agriculture and to the rearing of cattle immediately, and may form comparatively speaking a well regulated village; if the season is prosperous and the plan succeeds, it will induce others to follow, and in the course of a year or two I hope it will draw all those people from the plains. . . . Grant is turned very serious (religious) and by management will become a useful man to the colony and Company, but he requires good management being an Indian in nature.

This was an early instance of the use of the policy of "smoothing" by which the Company for many years managed to remain on tolerably good terms with the freemen and métis.

Another instrument which lent itself with promise to this scheme was the Catholic Church. Priests had come into the Red River Valley from Lower Canada as early as 1818 and had soon acquired a strong influence over the numerous adherents of their faith. At first they made Pembina their chief center of activity. "The R.C. Church at the Forks," noted Halkett on his visit to Assiniboia, "has never been finished, nor the residence for the Priests built, while their whole establishment at Pembina has been finished and kept up in high style." He regarded as "impudence" his being asked "for £100" to help "finish the church at the Forks."[43] Simpson was more politic, realizing that the clerical influence could be valuable to the Company in helping to settle and tame the plainsmen. "The Catholic Bishop," he notes, "enters into the scheme, and proposes erecting a chapel." The extraordinary influence which the priests had "acquired over the minds of their followers" proved very useful a few years later when the failure of the buffalo reduced the

43. Halkett to Lady Selkirk, October 19, 1822, *SP SM*.

hunters to desperate want.[44] "Indeed," admitted Simpson, "it is to the Catholic Mission we are alone indebted for the safety of the Company's establishments and the peace of the Colony . . . as their followers . . . had made up their minds to seize the grain we had provided for the consumption of our Brigades, and had they once commenced the work of plunder, it would not have been confined to provisions, and the consequences would have been dreadful."[45] It was fortunate for the Red River Settlement that such a strong restraining influence had thus come to be exerted over the nomadic hunters at this time, and without expense to the settlers.

The salutary influence of religion was also exercised over many of the Red River Protestants in these years. In this case there was less danger of disorder. But the Old World settlers were naturally afflicted with homesickness, and every amenity associated with their former life helped to bridge the painful gap. The Reverend John West had not proved a signal success in his missionary labors. "I am in great hopes," writes Simpson after that minister's departure, "that Mr. West will not return; he would not have a single hearer." But a successor, the Reverend David Jones, was well fitted for his task. "Mr. Jones fully comes up to the opinion I had formed of him," is Simpson's verdict; "his church is well attended and he is most zealous in the discharge of his duties . . . he is a great favourite with the people, and the Scotch do not now trouble their heads about the ritual of the Church of England, which was formerly so obnoxious; indeed they say they never knew a Presbyterian clergyman who pleased them so much, although one half of them do not understand English."[46] This optimistic judgment of the feelings of the Scotch Presbyterians may be taken with a grain of salt, without discounting the positive results of the labors of the Reverend David Jones.

In other matters the influence of the authorities was not noticeably successful. "Governor Pelly and I," admits Simpson, "have turned our attention very much to the formation of schools, but as yet to little or no purpose. . . . Pritchard's Buffalo wool concern I fear is not likely to turn out well." An experimental farm did not represent a very useful expenditure.[47] Several of the members of the local Council were men of a "mean despicable character," and the others were not of great ability.[48] But in spite of these more superficial weaknesses the Red River

44. Simpson to Colvile, May 31, 1824, *SP SM.*
45. Simpson to Colvile, June 14, 1826, *SP SM.*
46. Simpson to Colvile, May 31, 1824, *SP SM.*
47. *Ibid.* Simpson to Colvile, September 5, 1821, *SP SM.* Simpson to Colvile, May 20, 1822, *PAC SP,* pp. 7597, 7609, 7614.
48. Simpson to Colvile, May 31, 1824, *SP SM.*

Settlement was now a permanent, well-established colony. It "extended from Nettley Creek up to Pembina, a distance of about one hundred miles," and the population was numerous, "exceeding two thousand souls."[49] The disastrous floods of 1826 were yet to come, but they were to demonstrate the essential stability of the community. "This settlement is now so firmly established, and the bulk of its inhabitants so much attached to the soil," says Simpson, "that if the Company and executors were even inclined to abandon it and disperse its population, they could not accomplish it, and nothing but superior force of arms could remove them." The secret was in the people and in the country. It was a good country and there were good people in it.[50] "The state of things in this quarter," writes Donald Mackenzie in February, 1826,[51] "has gone forward in a way that was prosperous and tranquil. . . . The settlers live in perfect harmony with us as well as with each other, the natives likewise keep admirably quiet, crops have been most productive, in quality better than usual. The new mill goes at length in operation, the flour fine, and fully answerable to all demands." The essence of Selkirk's dream was at last being practically fulfilled. The Red River Settlement had become a permanent reality.

49. *Ibid.*   50. *Ibid.*
51. Mackenzie to Colvile, February 5, 1826, *SP SM*.

CHAPTER XXII

THE UPPER MISSISSIPPI

THE struggles which attended the efforts of Selkirk and his followers to establish an agricultural settlement in the Red River Valley had been occasioned entirely by the exigencies of the British and the Canadian fur trades; they had, almost wholly, been phases of the natural rivalry between the St. Lawrence and the Nelson River systems. Until the time of the union of the hostile fur companies and the termination of their violent strife the Mississippi Valley and the people of the United States had not entered very actively into the history of Red River. Reference has been made to the journey which the colonists made to Prairie du Chien in 1819 to secure seed grain and other supplies, to Selkirk's hopes of American trade for his settlers, and to the loss of southern Assiniboia. Mentioned, too, was the presence of American fur traders in the regions south of the border. But in all these instances there was little or no pressure on the Red River Valley from the south. What pressure there was came from the north, from the Settlement itself. Yet the existence of these American forces so near the Selkirk colony was a sign of what was to come. Gradually—yet swiftly, considering the spaces and the distances involved—the American frontier was sweeping westward and northward toward the Mississippi and the British-American boundary; and the time would not be long before Red River would feel the dynamic impulses of the great and growing nation to the south, thrusting its advance guard forward along the valley of the upper Mississippi.

Owing to the dreams of a Selkirk and the requirements of two fur companies European settlers had been taken from the Old World and dropped down in the middle of the North American Continent, far from their fellows and quite removed from other agricultural groups. This was not the method followed as a rule in the United States. There the spread of the white man's frontier, though rapid and not unplanned, was the outcome of more natural and less exceptional circumstances. During the seventeenth and eighteenth centuries the regions which were to form the Eastern States were populated from Europe by people seeking relief from the pressures of an old and complex civilization. One of these pressures was active persecution; another was the need of rising generations for new space in which to expand; a third was a craving for land and the dignity and freedom which it connotes. When the eastern portions of the United States had become saturated with this overflow of population and with their own natural increase, there was a movement to the west where land was still plentiful. The Louisiana Purchase of 1803 was both a cause and a symbol of the expansion that was to come. Within the next two decades the forerunners of settlement, the fur traders, advanced rapidly to the northwest, penetrated the Red River Valley, and reached the Selkirk Settlement.

This wave of traders, naturally enough, had had its forerunners. In both the French period before 1763 and the British period which followed, men seeking furs had gone southward and westward from Lake Superior.[1] Besides these men intent on profits the region had also received a few scattered explorers. In 1798 David Thompson, a surveyor and astronomer in the service of the North West Company, returning from a surveying expedition which had taken him as far as the Missouri, entered the American Northwest. Having come down the Assiniboine to its mouth, "he proceeded up the Red River to the Red Lake River, whence he made his way to Red Lake and Turtle Lake, which he assumed to be the northern sources of the Mississippi. From here he descended the latter river to Sandy Lake and at length reached Lake Superior by way of the Savannah portage and the St. Louis River."[2] A few years later, following the Louisiana Purchase, President Jefferson took steps to have the upper Mississippi explored. As a result, on July 30, 1805, Lieutenant Zebulon M. Pike, stationed at St. Louis, was ordered "to proceed up the Mississippi with all possible diligence." Pike's instructions indicate both the state of official knowledge and the trend of official purpose in respect to the upper Mississippi at that time. He was ordered "to record his topographical observations in a diary"; to note the "population and residence" of the Indians, and to spare no pains to conciliate them; to look for positions suitable for military posts; and to ascend the main branch of the Mississippi to its source. More significantly, he was instructed "to obtain permission from the Indians who claim the ground, for the erection of military posts and trading houses, at the mouth of the river St. Pierre, the Falls of St. Anthony, and every other critical point which may fall under your observation."[3] In the course of his journey to carry out these instructions Pike visited Prairie du Chien, "then a village of about 370 people," and at this time the extreme frontier post in this region. Continuing on up the river, he decided to winter in the country. At Sandy Lake and

1. Wilson Porter Shortridge, *The Transition of a Typical Frontier* . . . (Menasha, Wisconsin, 1922), p. 12.

2. William Watts Fowell, *A History of Minnesota* (St. Paul, 1921), I, 111. Hereafter, Fowell, *Minnesota*.

3. *American State Papers: Miscellaneous*, I, 942.

again at Leech Lake he was hospitably received by the agents of the North West Company in their trading posts. With equal courtesy and formality Pike declared "that British goods must not be introduced till after payment of duties at Mackinac; that the English flag must on no pretense whatever be hoisted over . . . trading posts; that no political dealings shall be had with the Indians; and that the commerce of the company shall be regulated by American law." After visiting Upper Red Cedar Lake (Cass Lake) which, with Leech Lake, Pike took to be the source of the Mississippi, the expedition returned early in 1806 to St. Louis.[4]

It had expanded, in some measure, the bounds of geographical knowledge, and secured the release by the Indians of two pieces of land—one at the mouth of the St. Croix River and the other at the Falls of St. Anthony. But it had had no practical influence on the activities of the North West Company. As a part, however, of the process by which the United States gradually assumed military control of the upper Mississippi Valley and thereby gave protection to the American fur trader, lumberman, and settler, it had considerable significance. By the treaty of 1783 the United States had secured nominal ownership of the region south and west of the Great Lakes. But the British continued to influence the Indians, dominate the fur trade, and hold strategic posts by force. The Americans attempted to take over the trade of the region by economic means. But in this they were, on the whole, unsuccessful until the State stepped in and forced the interlopers to withdraw—first from the Lower Lake region, by the Jay Treaty of 1794; and then from the Upper Lake and upper Mississippi regions in the years following the War of 1812. Thus American expansion in the northern Mississippi country was first really effected by political action, of which Pike's expedition was a part and a symbol.

Yet even in these early years the American fur trader was advancing with some success beyond the limits of actual political force and was preparing the ground for much greater activity in the near future. In the years following the Revolutionary War there were hundreds who left the Eastern States and invaded the fur fields of the interior. It was out of a combination of many similar ventures that the great North West Company of Canada was formed. But for a variety of reasons the Americans were slower in combining; and for over a quarter of a century their efforts were individual rather than collective. Perhaps it was on this account that there arose within their ranks the man who

4. See Elliott Coues, ed., *Expeditions of Zebulon Montgomery Pike to the Headwaters of the Mississippi River, through Louisiana Territory, and in New Spain during the Years 1805–6–7* (New York, 1895), I, *passim*.

became in several respects the greatest and most portentous figure to be met with throughout the annals of the North American fur trade.

John Jacob Astor[5] was a German who had spent some time in London and who came to America in the winter of 1783–84. It is an interesting though probably unimportant coincidence that the year 1783 also witnessed the acquisition by the United States of the region south and west of the Great Lakes, and also of the political sovereignty by which the title would be enforced. Astor was to profit equally from both events. But that was to be many years hence. Meanwhile he began to learn the fur business as an obscure and humble clerk working· for a New York fur merchant, Robert Bowne. This was in the year 1784.

John Jacob seems to have been an apt pupil as well as an able businessman. Within a year he was sent, with goods to trade for furs, into the country of the Six Nations. Here for the first time he came into contact with that force which for over thirty years was to challenge his patience and ingenuity, but which was also to teach him many a valuable lesson. This was the British trading influence. Astor's response was the one he was to adopt toward his Northern rivals as long as they were able to oppose him—compromise and, as far as possible, association and coöperation. Another opportunity soon presented itself. By this time, 1787, Congress was refusing to allow Canadian furs to be brought into the country. Robert Bowne decided to buy his furs in Montreal and ship them direct to London. As his agent he selected Astor,[6] who thus began to play a direct part in that great inland traffic which was to be such a dominant factor both in his own life and in the opening up of the American Northwest.

Before long the agent became his own master and widened his activities. Having made friends with a group of Montreal traders, including Alexander Henry, he not only, by some means or other, soon succeeded in building up a yearly trading business between Montreal and London, as well as between New York and Europe, but in the end he was also able to go West as a fur trader with the North West Company's brigades and visit the fur emporium at the Grand Portage. How he, no Montreal trader but a man from New York and a natural rival of the Canadian fur dealers, could so impose himself and his business on the jealous and masterful North West Company is at first glance puzzling, to say the least.[7] "Possibly," it has been said, "it was his continental personality, his foreign manner and broken speech, which differentiated

5. Kenneth Wiggins Porter, *John Jacob Astor, Business Man* (Cambridge, Mass., 1931). Hereafter, Porter, *Astor.*

6. Arthur D. Howden Smith, *John Jacob Astor* (Philadelphia, 1929), pp. 34 f. Hereafter, Smith, *Astor.*

7. Porter, *Astor,* I, 31 ff.

him from the hated Yankees. Possibly Henry and other Canadian friends contributed to the result. Certainly, he was a winning fellow when he wished to be, of a pleasantly virile personality, rugged in physique, hardy, a good talker, and popular for his gift of music, always welcome at any campfire."[8] But besides all these personal reasons there was probably the telling fact that Astor always had money and was accepted as another but temporary partner in a concern which was as yet an agglomeration of individual traders and had not hardened into a self-sufficient machine. Yet unknown to itself the company was taking to its bosom and enriching with its secrets the man who was to become its most successful individual opponent and was to be more responsible than any other for the winning by American interests of the vast fur fields of the northwestern United States.

Throughout this process the American fur traders and the United States Government were to work hand in hand, and Astor was to be the chief fur trader. In 1783 the United States secured the Northwest; subsequent legislation excluded Canadian furs; in 1796, by the Jay Treaty,[9] the British garrisons were forced to leave their United States posts such as Oswego, Niagara, Detroit, and Mackinac; and by this time Astor had built up his fur business to such a point as would enable him, given a good opportunity, to take over most of the fur trade of the United States. The Louisiana Purchase whetted his appetite and vastly enlarged his prospects.

In the meanwhile he had entered the China trade; and he now began to visualize a fur business of transcontinental proportions controlled by himself and continuing in its ramifications across the Pacific Ocean. By the year 1808 he felt the need of a more impersonal organization to serve his interests and on April 6 secured from the State of New York a charter for "The American Fur Company."[10] It is worth while noting that by this time he was on intimate terms with the government. Jefferson, then President, was keenly interested in the success of the American fur traders and wrote to Astor that "in order to get the whole of this business passed into the hands of our own citizens, and to oust foreign traders . . . every reasonable patronage and facility in the power of the Executive will be afforded."[11] This was no idle promise, as time was to show; but meanwhile Astor proved that he was getting at

8. Smith, *Astor*, p. 50.
9. *Treaties, Conventions, International Acts, Protocols, and Agreements between the United States of America and Other Powers, 1776–1909*, I, 590 ff. (61st Cong., 2d Sess., Sen. Docs., No. 357, ser. 5646.)
10. *Private Laws of the State of New York* (31st Sess., Jan. 26, 1808), pp. 160 ff.
11. April 13, 1808, *Thomas Jefferson, The Writings of* (Monticello ed., Washington, 1903–5), XII, 28.

least a good share of the fur-trade profits when he provided all the capital, $500,000, required by the new company.[12]

That the creation of this concern was not due entirely to Astor, however, but was partly the result of more impersonal forces such as the spreading power of the United States Government, is indicated by the fact that within a year a rival fur company was organized in St. Louis by Manuel Lisa, one of the ablest of the Missouri traders.[13] St. Louis was the logical center for an opponent of the American Fur Company. The latter at the time was based on Mackinac, while St. Louis, in the decade from 1805 to 1815, was a center for much of the more western fur trade. Lisa's concern was the first of a series of such companies, which were formed to fight the larger and more "trust"-like Astor organization. These smaller, more individualistic bodies were well served by the most enterprising and experienced traders. But owing to their comparative lack of capital they were forced in time either to sell out to their larger rival or move farther into the wilderness.[14] This running fight between the American Fur Company and its opponents was a potent factor for a generation or more in the push westward and northward of the American advance guard of settlement. Thus, "as was true in most other sections, it was the fur trade that brought the upper Mississippi country into commercial relations with the civilized world." In view of this fact it becomes manifest why "the presence of Indians on the frontier hastened rather than retarded the settlement of new areas by white men" and how "among the influences making for settlement the fur trade had a very important relative position."[15]

Indeed, a perfect deluge of westward migration coincided with the first few years following the formation of Astor's company. It is known in American history as "the great migration." A wave of westward settlement following the Revolutionary War had terminated some time before the year 1803, which brought the admission of the State of Ohio into the Union. For the next few years the prosperity which arose in America as a result of the European war kept people in the East. But the commercial struggle into which the United States was soon drawn again created hard times, and the movement westward was resumed. There were other reasons, of course, for this trek. The West was well advertised and by the most diverse agencies. There was the purchase of Louisiana, the accounts of western explorers such as Pike, the Indian wars, and the War of 1812 as well as the fur trade. But the chief stimu-

12. Washington Irving, *Astoria* (New York, 1861), chap. ii.
13. Smith, *Astor*, p. 136.
14. Hiram Martin Chittenden, *The American Fur Trade of the Far West* (New York, 1902), I, 138, 146, 262. Smith, *Astor*, p. 136.
15. Shortridge, *Typical Frontier*, p. 11.

lus seems to have been economic. "The hard times that persisted in much of the East after 1807 were not fully relieved until after 1819. . . . The accelerated flow of population is clearly visible after 1811 and assumes huge proportions after 1815. It shows itself in the noise of the migration, in the heavy sales of western lands, and in the creation within six years of six new border States: Indiana (1816), Mississippi (1817), Illinois (1818), Alabama (1819), Maine (1820), and Missouri (1821)."[16]

While the frontier of American settlement was thus rapidly approaching and crossing the Mississippi River, the fur-trade frontier and the fortunes of John Jacob Astor were making equally spectacular advances. Two years after the incorporation of the American Fur Company, Astor, when he had vainly tried to interest the North West Company in a Pacific fur company, formed one with his own capital, at the same time "luring to his service" five of his rivals' ablest factors.[17] In the following year "Astor and several partners of the North West Company who were operating at Mackinac under the name of the Montreal-Michilimackinac Company formed a merger known as the Southwest Company." It argues much for the strength of the new concern that "an arrangement was made with the Northwest Company whereby the latter was to confine its trading operations to the Indians north of the boundary line, and the former to those within the limits of the United States."[18] This mention of the boundary is also significant, associating as it does the fortunes of John Jacob Astor and the American fur trade with the political power of the United States. But while significant, it was a little premature, as the War of 1812 disorganized the fur trade and finally forced the South West Fur Company to dissolve.

With the return of peace Astor proceeded to revive the American Fur Company. But no longer was he disposed to share the trade with rivals. During the war his Columbia River post, Astoria, had been seized by the British; and it is said that as a result "he swore an unending vendetta against the Northwest Company,"[19] whose partners had been the chief promoters of the deed. At any rate he now began to seek active support from the Federal Government; and "there was more than a hint of malice in the energy with which he went about the task of convincing the Administration that alien traders should be barred from the territory of the United States."[20] As by this time Astor was one of the directors of the Bank of the United States and was eclipsed in fortune

16. Frederic L. Paxson, *History of the American Frontier, 1763–1893* (Boston, 1924), pp. 186 ff.
17. Porter, *Astor*, I, 181 ff.
18. Fowell, *Minnesota*, I, 132. Porter, *Astor*, I, 194, 252 ff.
19. Smith, *Astor*, p. 186.   20. *Ibid.*, p. 193.

by only two or three other men in the country, he was easily able, "by adroitly arousing the pride and patriotism of leading men at Washington,"[21] to secure the passage through Congress of an act providing that "licenses to trade with the Indians within the territorial limits of the United States shall not be granted to any but citizens of the United States, unless by the express direction of the President."[22] There is some basis for a contention that has been made that Astor was not perfectly satisfied with this act, that he was almost as anxious to exclude private American traders from the fur field as to shut out foreign companies; and such a contention is scarcely out of harmony with the other known facts of his career.[23] Nevertheless, his success as a result of the act, passed on April 29, 1816, was very great.

Immediately, "on his own terms,"[24] Astor "secured not only the interests of the Southwest Company but also all the posts and outfits of the Northwest Company south of the Canadian boundary, and established its headquarters at Mackinac." In addition, he "adopted the policy of retaining the old *engagés* and *voyageurs* of the Northwest Company, but replaced its clerks and agents by enterprising young Americans, who easily adapted themselves to the situation and soon became efficient." By thus taking over existing machinery the revived American Fur Company "in the course of two years . . . was doing business throughout the upper valley of the Mississippi." Of course Astor did not have things entirely his own way in this region. There was still the opposition of his lesser American competitors to reckon with. More important, there was an influx of new independent opponents as "the former traders of the Northwest Company speedily obtained naturalization papers and, as American citizens, continued in the business."[25] Such was the origin of leading American fur men like Joseph Rolette, Sr., Joseph Renville, Jean-Baptiste Faribault, Alexis Bailly, Louis Provençalle, and Joseph Laframboise. Knowing the country and possessing the confidence of the Indians, and driven by the competition of their great rival, these men and others like them found it advisable to push westward and northward into the more virgin fur fields of the upper Mississippi and the Red River south of the British border. Here in a very real sense they played the part not only of fur traders, but also of American pioneers.

This function and its importance the United States Government now continued to recognize by extending its military protection farther into

21. Fowell, *Minnesota,* I, 132.
22. *United States Statutes at Large,* III, 332 f.
23. Chittenden, *American Fur Trade,* I, 310 f. Marcus L. Hansen, *Old Fort Snelling, 1819–1858* (Iowa City, 1918), p. 44 n. Porter, *Astor,* II, 1143 ff.
24. Smith, *Astor,* p. 193.   25. Fowell, *Minnesota,* I, 133.

the wilderness. During the War of 1812 the process had been suspended. But the close of the war had been followed by the termination of the formal British control of the fur trade in the American Northwest, the British garrison withdrawing from Prairie du Chien in 1815;[26] and the advance was again resumed. In this "the first step was the negotiation of a treaty with the Sioux at the Portage des Sioux, near St. Louis, on July 19, 1815, by which these Indians agreed to resume friendly relations with the United States and to acknowledge the president as their only Great Father."[27]

The following year a detachment of American soldiers advanced to Prairie du Chien and there built a fort, Fort Crawford.[28] Further advances were forecast a year later when the Secretary of War announced that officers had been appointed "to examine the whole line of our frontier, and to determine on the position and extent of works that may be necessary to the defence of the country."[29] In the summer of the same year Major Stephen H. Long was sent up the Mississippi from St. Louis to the Falls of St. Anthony to report on sites for military establishments. Late in 1818 the Secretary of War reported to Congress that "our posts are now, or will be shortly, extended, for the protection of our trade and the preservation of the peace of the frontiers, to Green Bay, the mouths of the St. Peter's and the Yellow Stone river, Bellepoint, and Natchitoches."[30] On February 10, 1819, Lieutenant Colonel Henry Leavenworth was ordered to proceed with troops from Detroit by way of Green Bay and Prairie du Chien to establish a military post at the mouth of the St. Peter's.[31] The order was duly carried out and in the course of the next few years a fort was erected which later became known as Fort Snelling.[32]

Under the protection of the American political authority which was thus extended into the region which included the upper parts of the Mississippi and Red River valleys, the fur traders and the missionaries were now free to come and go at will. Of the latter it has been said that their annals might fill a volume but that they themselves had so little effect "on either the red man or the white," that their story is not

26. Wayne E. Stevens, "Organization of the British Fur Trade," *Mississippi Valley Historical Review,* III, 172 ff.

27. Fowell, *Minnesota,* I, 133 f.

28. Bruce E. Mahan, *Old Fort Crawford and the Frontier* (Iowa City, 1926), pp. 71 ff.

29. *American State Papers: Military Affairs,* I, 669.

30. *Ibid.,* p. 779.

31. Calhoun to Brown, October 17, 1818, J. Franklin Jameson, ed., "Correspondence of John Caldwell Calhoun," *Annual Report of the American Historical Association for the Year 1899,* II, 147.

32. Hansen, *Old Fort Snelling,* chap. ii.

worthy of treatment except for the thrilling interest of its fascinating details.[33] More important in this case as a prelude to settlement were the fur posts which were now set up.

Between 1819 and 1834 several trading posts were established within the limits of what later became Minnesota Territory. The principal post was at New Hope (also called St. Peter and later Mendota), just across the St. Peter's river from Fort Snelling. In 1826 Major Taliaferro, the Indian Agent at that point, listed seventeen posts in the upper Mississippi country.[34]

Of these ten belonged to the American Fur Company, six to the Columbia Fur Company, and one to the Cheyenne American Fur Company. Several were located in or on the borders of the Red River Valley.[35] The posts of the American Fur Company were controlled by Joseph Rolette, Sr., from Prairie du Chien. This concern "made it a practice to form partnerships with men of proved ability as fur traders by which the company furnished the goods to the trader on credit, the trader gave his time, and the profits were divided between them." Rolette was such an agent.

In 1834 Henry Hastings Sibley "came to the Mississippi country . . . as a partner in the American Fur Company, jointly with Rolette and Dousman." It thus became necessary to divide the territory, and "Sibley took charge of all the country from Lake Pepin to the Little Falls of the Mississippi, north and west to Pembina in the Red River valley; also all the valley of the St. Peter's river and westward to the sources of the streams which flowed into the Missouri River."[36] In 1835 Sibley inspected the posts under his control and found the following traders in charge: Joseph R. Brown at Lac Traverse; Joseph Renville at Lac Qui Parle; Louis Provençalle at Traverse des Sioux; Jean-B. Faribault at Little Rapids; Joseph Laframboise at Coteau de Prairie; and Alexander Faribault at Cannon River. Besides these there were in the locality other prominent traders such as Alexis Bailly, Norman W. Kittson, James Wells, Hazen Mooers, Philander Prescott, and François Labathe.[37] It was these men and their associates who brought the American fur frontier to the Red River country and held it there until it was overtaken by the lumberman and the settler.

Meanwhile, in 1834, the fur career of John Jacob Astor had come to an end. Throughout the decade and a half after the founding of Fort

33. Fowell, *Minnesota*, I, 170.   34. Shortridge, *Typical Frontier*, pp. 12 f.
35. Taliaferro to Alexis Bailly, April 2, 1826, Sibley Papers, Minnesota Historical Society, St. Paul. Hereafter, *SbP MHS.*
36. Shortridge, *Typical Frontier*, pp. 13, 15.
37. Sibley, "Reminiscences of the Early Days of Minnesota," *MHC,* III, 245 ff.

Snelling he had watched his business grow and his competitors fall one by one into his hands. In 1822 he had established an additional center for his company in St. Louis, buying out the local concern of Stone, Bostwick and Company.[38] Four years later he was able to absorb another powerful rival, the Columbia Fur Company, which had been established by Joseph Renville.[39] The process went on rapidly until by the year 1829 "the American Fur Company had made its monopoly absolute." The next decade was the heyday of the fur trade in the upper Mississippi Valley. After that it declined. It was quite in keeping with Astor's business foresight or good luck that he should retire at the right moment. "All he touched turned to gold, and it seemed as if fortune delighted in erecting him a monument of her unerring potency."[40] The year he selected for withdrawing was 1834. The occasion was marked by a reorganization of the American Fur Company and the accession of a new president, Ramsay Crooks.

In the first few years following the retirement of Astor the fur business increased in volume and value. But it reached its peak in 1837. "The fur trade in Minnesota was in its most flourishing condition in the years immediately preceding. . . . New trading posts were established during this period, particularly in the region of the Red River of the North. Prices of furs were higher in 1836 than they had been for years and higher, in fact, than they were to be after 1837."[41] This change in the fur trade coincided in time with a change in the ownership of land. In the year 1837 "a delegation of Sioux Chiefs was taken to Washington and a treaty was negotiated for the cession of lands east of the Mississippi," in the future Minnesota Territory.

The reason for making this treaty was "primarily to open up the pine forests of the St. Croix valley to the lumberman, the advance guard of the next wave of civilization."[42] The passing of the fur trade was now definitely in sight, and this was indicated by a change in the business of the fur traders. On the one hand, the Indian tended to give up agriculture and trapping and become an annuity-drawing indigent, dealing with the traders no longer in furs, but in cash.[43] On the other, white men coming into the country for purposes other than the fur trade promoted the retail business of the traders. "When white settlement increased still more, the fur company undertook banking opera-

38. Porter, *Astor*, II, 718, 734.   39. *Ibid.*, II, 744 ff.

40. Smith, *Astor*, pp. 100 f.

41. Taliaferro to Sibley, September 14, 1836; Crooks to Sibley, September 14, 1836, *SbP MHS*. Shortridge, *Typical Frontier*, pp. 20 f.

42. *Ibid.*, p. 22.

43. H. H. Sibley, "Reminiscences; Historical and Personal," *MHC*, I, 461.

tions, making loans, cashing drafts brought into the region by prospective settlers, and selling exchange on the New York office to those who wished to send money out of the region."[44]

At the same time, in the years after 1837 the routes by which freight was shipped in and out of the country were changed. Before 1838 goods were sent from New York to Mackinac, and from there by way of Prairie du Chien to Mendota. In that year Sibley began to buy goods for the fur trade from Pierre Chouteau, Jr. and Company in St. Louis. By 1840 this company ceased to import by way of Albany and Buffalo and was bringing goods *via* Philadelphia and Pittsburgh, by river to St. Louis and thence up the Mississippi to Mendota. The change in route was further emphasized in 1841 when the Pierre Chouteau company "began to secure furs from Minnesota, thus challenging the monopoly of the American Fur Company."[45] Two years later regular communications by cart line were established between Pembina on the Red River and St. Paul near Fort Snelling. As goods from the East were now, in some cases, being brought to St. Louis and Mendota by way of New Orleans, transportation independence had practically been established in the Mississippi Valley as connected with that of the Red River.

The cart line from Pembina to St. Paul marked the convergence of two frontiers and was the connecting link between them. Since its construction in 1819 Fort Snelling had remained the nearest official American outpost to Red River. One of the primary reasons for the establishment of this post had been to protect the interests of the American Fur Company from the encroachments of traders from Canada and the Hudson's Bay Company's territories. For more than a decade after the close of the great migration, which ended about the time Fort Snelling was being built, American westward expansion was more or less at a standstill, and there was no movement of settlers from the East to disturb the "peace" of the Indians and the military. Nevertheless it was in these years that the first permanent agricultural settlers in the Minnesota-to-be arrived at the Fort. These were the Swiss and De Meuron emigrants from Kildonan. Between 1820 and 1835 more than five hundred persons left Red River for the United States.[46] Some of these people were allowed to "squat" upon the lands belonging to the Fort Snelling military reservation, and this constituted the first real settlement in Minnesota.[47]

Before many years were to pass others were to be added to it as a

44. Shortridge, *Typical Frontier*, p. 23.   45. *Ibid.*, p. 24.
46. Taliaferro Journals, No. II, pp. 77, 83, No. IV, p. 78, No. IX, pp. 30 f., 147, 152 f., 228; J. Stevens to Henry Hill and Rev. D. Greene, Mss. 74, No. 8, p. 2, *MHS.*
47. Fowell, *Minnesota*, I, 216 f.

continuous line of settlements from the East came into the upper Mississippi region on the crest of a new tide of immigration. "The opening of the Ohio Canal marks the beginning of another period comparable to the great migration. . . . From 1832 until 1837 this wave of population flowed, swelled, and broadened over the regions of the older settlements and out upon the public domain."[48]

By the close of the 'thirties the advance guard of this "Jacksonian" wave of American pioneers had pushed into the rich and beautiful lands on the eastern side of the upper Mississippi. In 1836 the Wisconsin Territory was organized, with its western limits reaching to the Mississippi. The growth of Wisconsin was so rapid that by 1847 its population numbered more than 200,000 whites; and in 1848 it was admitted into the Union with the St. Croix River and the Mississippi as its western boundary.

At this time (1848) there were about 5,000 settlers in that part of what had been Wisconsin Territory, lying between the St. Croix and the Mississippi. They now had no institutions of government; but they sent a delegate, Henry Hastings Sibley, to Congress; and he was allowed to sit and to draw his salary. Sibley soon introduced a bill to create a Territory of Minnesota; and in March, 1849, this bill became a law.[49] Of course the mere passing of a law does not create a community; and, indeed, it cannot be said that by this time Minnesota was primarily an agricultural settlement. But it was on the verge of becoming one. "As the decade of the thirties was the heyday of the fur trade in Minnesota, so the decade of the forties found lumbering the predominant industry and the decade of the fifties marked the transition to agriculture."[50] Thus by the end of the 'forties the frontier of American colonization had advanced to within a comparatively short distance of the Selkirk Settlement in Assiniboia; the Mississippi Valley was joining hands vigorously with the Valley of the Red River.

48. Paxson, *American Frontier*, p. 274.
50. Shortridge, *Typical Frontier*, p. 30.

49. *Ibid.*, pp. 286, 292 f., 398 f., 424.

CHAPTER XXIII

TRADERS AND SMUGGLERS

THE key to the history of the relations between the Hudson's Bay Company and the Red River Settlement after 1821 lies in the character of the additions made to the population as a result of the union of the fur companies. The majority of these newcomers were traders and trappers, rather than farmers; and they naturally found the temptation to engage in the fur trade too strong to be resisted. The Hudson's Bay Company in its grant of Assiniboia to Lord Selkirk had expressly reserved to itself two prerogatives, "all rights of jurisdiction whatsoever granted to said Company by their Charter," and the complete monopoly of "trade and traffick." It was stipulated specifically that neither Selkirk nor his heirs nor his colonists should "carry on or establish or attempt to carry on or establish . . . any trade or traffick, in or relating to any kind of furs or peltry."[1]

These reservations were the Company's first attempt to safeguard itself against possible encroachments on the part of the Red River settlers. During the first eight or ten years of settlement there was scarcely any attempt to infringe upon the Company's rights, as the problems of colonization were paramount. But the Directors had not changed. They had accepted Selkirk's scheme of settlement only with great reluctance. They remained thoroughly convinced that the purposes of colonization and the interests of the fur trade were incompatible. It was only on account of Lord Selkirk's predominant influence, and the current opposition of the North West Company, that fur-trade activities had been subordinated in any way to colonization, or that the latter had been permitted at all. After Selkirk's death and the fusion of the companies, the fur-trade interests once more prevailed. But the settlement of Red River was now a reality, there was no North West Company to frighten the settlers, and the new ex-trader elements knew all the tricks of the fur trade.

As early as 1821 several of the new settlers had become independent merchants and traders in Red River. Supplied with food, clothing, ammunition, and other goods, they had slipped out into the prairies and begun to barter with the Indians for furs. Nor was it long before they had also built up a *sub rosa* trade across the border with the American fur traders, with whom they had first come into contact on buffalo

1. Grant of Assiniboia to Lord Selkirk, by the Hudson's Bay Company, June 12, 1811, *SP SM*.

hunts that took them into United States territory. When the local officers of the Hudson's Bay Company became aware of this traffic, which they termed "illicit," they at once adopted methods for its suppression.[2] Forty-nine of the leading inhabitants of the colony, all Europeans, were persuaded to sign an agreement binding the Settlement not to "engage in the sale of spirituous liquors or the fur trade."[3] The agreement never became effective; and the bois-brûlés even refused to admit that they did not have a natural right to trade when and where they saw fit.

Even before 1821, the Company had been forced to concern itself with the approach of the Americans. In 1816 the American Fur Company had established a trading post at Red Lake; it already had fur houses at Sandy Lake and on the Minnesota; and in 1822 it occupied three other important posts between Rainy Lake and Lake of the Woods.[4]

The illicit Red River fur traffickers found their way into Minnesota by trails well marked. The North West Company had extended its enterprises to the Minnesota and Mississippi rivers; and in 1816 and 1817 the British trader, Colonel Robert Dickson, was located with his men on Lake Traverse at the head of the Minnesota River. Dickson was accustomed to getting his goods and supplies from the Selkirk Colony, and bringing them up the Red River "in carts made for the purpose." The Hudson's Bay Company also had carried its operations up the Red River into Minnesota. In the spring of 1818 the Company sent Louis Bellain and two other agents to the American Fur Company's establishment at Red Lake. Here they bartered goods and liquor with the Indians and made preparations for a winter outfit near by.[5] Such activities as those of Bellain and Dickson offered a very bad example to the Red River colonists, since, on account of the Act of Congress of 1816 excluding foreign fur traders from the territories of the United States, such business was illegal and could only be described as "poach-

2. Simpson to Colvile, September 5, 1821, September 8, 1823, *SP SM*. Simpson to Colvile, May 20, 1822, *PAC SP,* pp. 7598 ff. Governor, Deputy Governor and Committee of the Hudson's Bay Company to Simpson, May 21, 1823, Bulger Papers, M 151, p. 215, *PAC. The Globe* (Toronto), July 20, 1857. Keating, *Narrative,* I, 445.

3. Pritchett, "Some Red River Fur-Trade Activities," *Minnesota History Bulletin,* V, 407.

4. Ramsay Crooks and Robert Stuart to John Jacob Astor, July 21, 1817; Crooks to Astor, June 21, 1819, November 30, 1821; Stuart to David Stone, May 19, 1823, Mackinac Register, Astor House, Mackinac. Astor to James Monroe, December 30, 1816 (with enclosures), Miscellaneous Letters, pp. 210 ff., Department of State, Washington.

5. Eustache Roussain to George Boyd, July 17, 1819; Crooks and Stuart to Boyd, July 14, 1819, Mackinac Register, Astor House, Mackinac. Selkirk to Lady Selkirk, August 4, October 27, 1817; Selkirk to Colvile, August 7, 1817; Alexander Macdonell to Colvile, August 8, 1820; Simpson to Colvile, September 5, 1821, *SP SM*. Simpson to Colvile, May 20, 1822, *PAC SP,* pp. 7615 ff. *Niles' Weekly Register,* XIV, 388.

ing." The Hudson's Bay Company was thus indulging in the same sort of "illicit" traffic which it forbade the Selkirk settlers to practice.

An account has already been given of Selkirk's expectations and approval of trade between his colony and the American frontier settlements, and of the official expedition from Red River to Prairie du Chien in 1819 to secure seed grain and other commodities. This was the beginning of a sporadic but spontaneous commercial intercourse across the border in the Red River Valley. It continued and grew in the following years. As has been said, the cattle and sheep whether brought from Europe or purchased by the Selkirk colonists had been either killed or lost during the troubles with the North West Company. About the year 1819 British traders had driven a few head of cattle from Sault Ste Marie through the United States Indian country to the Settlement;[6] but these did not meet all demands. In 1820 Hercules L. Dousman, merchant and fur trader at Michilimackinac and Prairie du Chien, contracted to furnish Kildonan with cattle. A drove was got together at Prairie du Chien, but they starved there in the winter, and none ever reached the settlement.[7] Joseph Rolette, onetime North-wester, managed, despite considerable difficulty, to drive a few cows to the colony in 1821. All were bought up "with great avidity." Dousman made a second attempt in 1821; he got his cattle as far north as the Hudson's Bay Company post at Lake Traverse, but many of them were lost during the winter.[8]

In subsequent years, however, a number of American stockmen bought up droves of cattle and flocks of sheep in Louisiana, Kentucky, Wisconsin, and Missouri, and sold them in Kildonan at a good profit. Frequent mention of cattle and sheep passing through Minnesota to Red River during the 'twenties is made in the journals kept by Lawrence Taliaferro, Indian agent at Fort Snelling from 1819 to 1840.[9] During the winter of 1821–22, Dousman made a trip to Kildonan with the idea of establishing a regular commercial intercourse with the settlers and the Hudson's Bay Company. The principal commodities which he offered to supply were pork, flour, spirits, and tobacco. He extended to the Company "a tender to deliver any quantity [of tobacco] from 50 to 100,000 lbs deliverable at Sault St. Marys at 18^d plb Twist & 15^d

6. Roussain to Boyd, July 17, 1819, Mackinac Register, Astor House, Mackinac.

7. Simpson to Colvile, May 20, 1822, *PAC SP*, pp. 7616 f.

8. *Ibid*. Halkett to Colvile, November 22, 1821; Bulger to Colvile, August 4, 1822, *SP SM*. Crooks to Rolette, March 28, 1822, Mackinac Register, Astor House, Mackinac.

9. See also Donald Mackenzie to Colvile, February 5, 1826, *SP SM*. John Pritchard to Miles Macdonell, June 16, 1825, Miles Macdonell, Selkirk Settlement, p. 211, *PAC*. *The Nor'-Wester*, May 14, 1860. L. C. Sutherland, ed., "Driving Sheep from Kentucky to the Hudson's Bay Country," *Annals of Iowa. A Historical Quarterly*, XV, 243 ff.

plb for Carrot."[10] Alexander Macdonell, Governor of the Colony, John Pritchard, manager of the Buffalo Wool Company, and James Bird, now retired Company Factor, ordered "sundry articles," the produce of the country, to the approximate amount of £4,500.[11] By such transactions as these American trade influence began to filter across the British frontier, and the hunters and trappers of Red River acquired a market for their goods.

Throughout the 'twenties this activity was not seriously opposed. Not that the Company officials regarded it with a tolerant eye. They would have enforced their monopoly over the colonists "even to the extent of forbidding them to buy horses, leather, or provisions from the Indians." But the Governor of Assiniboia in 1822 and 1823, Captain Andrew Bulger, protested to the Selkirk trustees against the policy of the local officials; and as a result, the Directors of the Company were persuaded to order the removal of restrictions on trade in Red River and to advise the Governor of Rupert's Land, George Simpson, that the late proceedings in "the interest of the Fur Trade . . . were most unwarrantable as well as extremely imprudent and indiscreet." In the next year Simpson was further informed that the Governor and Committee of the Company in London "would not suffer the fur trade to oppose or oppress the Settlement, and if it be attempted, the expence of redressing the evil must and will fall on the fur trade as in Justice it ought."[12] From this time on until the middle 'thirties, when Assiniboia was returned by the sixth Earl of Selkirk to the Hudson's Bay Company, freedom of trade in Red River was more or less undisturbed.[13]

With the transfer, when the Company attempted to establish civil government in the colony, and also at the same time enforce its charter monopoly of trade, the public freedom was sacrificed to private gain. Almost the very first act of the new governing body, the Council of Assiniboia, was the placing on February 12, 1835, of a tariff of 7.5 per cent on Red River imports and exports. The revenue thus raised was to be used to meet the expenses incurred in the "maintenance of tranquillity" and the enforcement of the "laws, rules and regulations."[14] The inhabitants of Red River were to have the privilege of financing a sys-

10. Bulger to Colvile, August 4, 1822, *SP SM*. Simpson to Colvile, *PAC SP*, p. 7616.
11. Crooks to Maitland, Gordon and Auldjo, March 28, 1822, Mackinac Register, Astor House, Mackinac.
12. Governor, Deputy Governor and Committee of the Hudson's Bay Company to Simpson, May 21, 1823, Bulger Papers, M 151, pp. 215 ff., *PAC*. Simpson to Colvile, September 8, 1823; Colvile to Simpson, March 11, 1824, *SP SM*.
13. The date of the "reconveyance" was May 4, 1836, *SP SM*.
14. E. H. Oliver, ed., *The Canadian North-West; Its Early Development and Legislative Records* (Canadian Archives, Publications, No. 9, Ottawa, 1914), I, 267 f. Hereafter, Oliver, *Canadian North-West*.

tem of monopoly directed against themselves! The new regulations struck directly at the independent traders and merchants who were now carrying on a flourishing smuggling traffic with St. Louis, Prairie du Chien, Mendota, and other American outposts. There was an outburst of anger throughout Red River, particularly from the French métis element. Protest meetings were held before the gates of Fort Garry, the Company's headquarters, and the obnoxious laws were openly and systematically violated. Finally, the leaders of the opposition petitioned Alexander Christie, the district governor, for its repeal. The answer was that they should pay the duties and "their request for exemption would meet with favorable consideration." On this assurance many paid the tax, but the Company said nothing more about "exemption." In 1836, at the request of the London officers, the Colonial Council reduced the tariff to 5 per cent, and again in the next year, to 4 per cent. It remained at this level until 1870, when Canada took over the territory.[15]

Notwithstanding the submission of some to the 1835 tariff and the vigilance of the local Hudson's Bay Company officials, a number of free traders, or smugglers, continued to carry on their lucrative enterprises across the border; and they defied every effort of the authorities to enforce the laws. Quantities of furs—beaver, fisher, mink, marten, raccoon, and buffalo robes—as well as other local products, were secretly carried south and exchanged for American produce. Usually those engaged in the business departed in the dark of night and avoided the commoner routes so as to keep clear of the Fort Garry constabulary. Pembina, on the American side of the boundary line, was the smugglers' rendezvous. Merchandise brought from the American trade centers was left at Pembina until an opportunity came for smuggling it into the Settlement. Of course the trade involved many risks. The trails between Pembina and the Mississippi crossed a wild stretch of country inhabited by hostile Indian tribes. To the Red River smugglers the American markets were, nevertheless, very attractive. In them peltries and hides brought far higher prices than in the posts of the Hudson's Bay Company. The Red River trade was also highly remunerative to the American settlements; and American merchants and traders naturally encouraged and contributed greatly to the success of such illicit business.[16]

Previous to 1829 the American Fur Company had established fur-trading posts at Grand Forks and Pembina.[17] In 1840 Joseph Rolette,

15. Gunn and Tuttle, *Manitoba*, pp. 286, 298. H. G. Gunn, "The Fight for Free Trade in Rupert's Land," *Mississippi Valley Historical Association, Proceedings*, IV, 81.

16. *The Globe* (Toronto), July 20, 1857. *Report on H.B.C.*, p. 283.

17. A manuscript trader's ledger kept at Lake Traverse from 1829 to 1831 con-

a son of the famous upper Mississippi British trader of the early years of the century, was put in charge of the Company's affairs in the Pembina region. So successful was he in competing with the Hudson's Bay Company and in sustaining the illegal fur traffic across the boundary that in 1843 he started a line of carts from Pembina to St. Paul. In the same year Norman W. Kittson, the "Yankee trader," was made general manager of the American Fur Company's operations in northern Minnesota, and Rolette became his chief representative.[18] Until the introduction of steam navigation, Mendota was the southern terminus of the American Fur Company's cart line from Pembina. The carts used were the famous Red River carts,[19] constructed entirely of wood and leather, and pulled by oxen or shaggy ponies. Those used in the fur trade traveled in trains. A train would set out from Pembina late in the spring because travel was easiest then, and would arrive at its destination in July. The journey took from thirty to forty days. When the cart line was first established, about half-a-dozen carts were enough to carry all the goods being shipped by the fur company.[20] But so rapidly did the business develop that by the close of the decade the number of carts engaged in the trade had grown to nearly two hundred, and the value of the furs carried to about $20,000.[21] In 1849 the American Fur Company transferred its headquarters to St. Paul. Soon afterwards several other companies were organized to handle furs and supplies, and the trade to Pembina and Kildonan increased very rapidly. Contemporary Canadian and American newspapers are replete with comments upon the importance of the Red River trade.

During the decade a hotly contested trade war was waged along the boundary. Private hunters and trappers in Red River increased rapidly in number and became more determined in their illegal enterprises. Kittson and his employees added much to the ferment; and in other ways American influence was very powerful. On March 2, 1846, Kittson wrote to Henry H. Sibley, the Chouteau partner and chief factor at Mendota: "We have created quite a sensation in our favour in their [the Hud-

tains an "Inventory of Goods sent to the Big Fork of Red River—Sept. 18th 1829," *SbP MHS*.

18. Pritchett, "Some Red River Fur-Trade Activities," *Minnesota History Bulletin*, V, 413. Clarence W. Rife, "Norman W. Kittson, A Fur-Trader at Pembina," *Minnesota History*, VI, 227 ff.

19. There are many excellent contemporary descriptions of the Red River cart. See especially "The Red River Trail," *Harper's Magazine*, XVIII, 615 f., and *Minnesota Pioneer* (St. Paul), March 4, 1852.

20. *Weekly Pioneer and Democrat* (St. Paul), December 16, 1858.

21. *The Argus* (Kingston, Ontario), August 11, 1846. *Minnesota Register* (St. Paul), July 26, 1849. *Weekly Pioneer and Democrat* (St. Paul), December 16, 1858. *The Nor'-Wester*, January 15, 1866. W. B. Hennessy, *Past and Present of St. Paul, Minnesota* (Chicago, 1906), pp. 77 f.

son's Bay Company's] colony, which is working strongly against
them."[22] During the period from 1844 to 1849 numerous petitions
signed by Red River métis were sent to American governing officials requesting leave to establish themselves within the United States as citizens. But in spite of the popularity of the Americans among the people
of Red River it is extremely doubtful whether the American Fur Company was making money in the Settlement. At the beginning of each
season Kittson wrote optimistic letters to headquarters, but the fur
and peltry returns were almost always discouraging.[23] The Hudson's
Bay Company was also losing heavily in Assiniboia. Those who really
reaped most of the benefit from this clandestine trade were the Red River
settlers, especially the free traders, and the Americans at Mendota, St.
Paul, and other centers, who profited indirectly from the traffic. Thus
through the course of historical change on the American side of the
boundary, in the upper Mississippi Valley and the upper Red River
Valley, the Hudson's Bay Company's monopoly of trade in Assiniboia
was being challenged with increasing success as the middle of the century drew near.

The Company, however, kept up the unequal struggle and did all in
its power to meet the challenge successfully. A new step was its adoption of a more rigorous system of espionage, which fell as heavily upon
the innocent as it did upon the guilty. On the slightest suspicion or
provocation a search would be made for contraband goods. The settlers complained that traders who were suspected of having furs or
peltries were stopped on their way to Minnesota by armed police, their
trunks broken open, and their goods confiscated. Within the colony
constables with musket and bayonet ransacked the houses of the settlers. If there was resistance, entrance was obtained by force. "Every
cranny and crevice that could conceal anything was turned inside out.
Even the tall chimney that formed an indispensable feature of these
humble homes was made to yield up its secrets; a stout pole, which invariably formed part of the armament of a deputation of this sort,
being used for the purpose." Out on the prairies Cuthbert Grant, the
warden of the plains, and his emissaries, conducted similar arbitrary
expeditions. All peltries and skins found were confiscated, and the offending parties were either arrested and thrown in jail to await trial

22. *SbP MHS. Report on H.B.C.*, p. 135. In September, 1842, the American Fur
Company broke up. The next year Pierre Chouteau, Jr., and Company took over its
business. The name American Fur Company was applied to this concern more commonly than its real name.

23. John McLaughlin to James Buchanan, October 22, November 14, 1845, Miscellaneous Letters, State Department, Washington. Kittson to Sibley, December 4, 1848;
Belcourt to Sibley, January 15, 1848, *SbP MHS.*

or "made to suffer the pains and penalties on the spot." It was not at all uncommon for the violators of the fur law to have their shanties burned to the ground.[24]

Despite such vigorous repression the independent traders steadily increased in number and daring. The Fort Garry authorities, realizing that their methods were inadequate, decided in 1844 to tighten up their control. By this time Kittson had become well established at Pembina, had made fur-trading arrangements with Andrew McDermott and James Sinclair, the leaders of the free-trade movement in the Settlement, and had begun, as he wrote later, to spare "no trouble in giving them [the Hudson's Bay Company] the 'Devil.' "[25]

On December 7, 1844, Governor Christie issued a proclamation which denied to all persons who interfered with the Company's fur trade the privilege of importing goods from England on board the Company's ships. The proclamation[26] reads in part:

Whereas certain persons are known to be trafficking in furs, I hereby give notice that . . . the Hudson's Bay Company's ship will henceforward not receive at any port goods addressed to any person whatever, unless he shall, at least a week before the day appointed for the departure of the winter express, lodge at the office of Upper Fort Garry a declaration to the following effect: "I hereby declare that . . . I have neither directly or indirectly trafficked in furs . . . moreover, if before the middle of August next I shall appear to have acted contrary to . . . this declaration, I hereby agree that the Hudson's Bay Company shall be entitled either to detain my imports of next season at York Factory for a whole year, or to purchase them at original cost of the goods alone."

Again, on December 20, 1844, the Governor ordered that all letters must be sent to Fort Garry for perusal. "Every letter must have the writer's name written by himself in the left hand corner below," so that if he was suspected of trading in furs, it could be opened and examined. Letters not addressed in conformity with this regulation would not be carried. In less than three years, however, this measure became ineffective, as the free traders began to send their mail by the Kittson express to Fort Snelling.[27]

24. *The Globe* (Toronto), Oct. 1, 1856, July 20, 1857. Donald Gunn in *The Nor'-Wester,* June 28, 1860. Gunn, "Fight for Free Trade in Rupert's Land," *Mississippi Valley Historical Association, Proceedings,* IV, 84. Gunn and Tuttle, *Manitoba,* p. 296.

25. August 24, 1848; see also McDermott to Sibley, June 3, 1844; Kittson to Sibley, May 7, July 16, 1844, *SbP MHS.*

26. *Report on H.B.C.,* p. 272.

27. *Ibid.,* p. 265. Sinclair to Sibley, January 30, 1848; Kittson to Sibley, January 3, 1849, January 27, February 7, 1850, *SbP MHS.*

In the furtherance of this coercive policy, Adam Thom, the Recorder of Rupert's Land, proposed at a Council meeting on June 16, 1845, a new set of resolutions for the control and regulation of imports to the Settlement; and at a Council meeting held three days later they were carried unanimously. Every British subject in Assiniboia who was not an actual resident and not an illicit fur trader was allowed to import once a year from Great Britain or St. Paul, goods exempt from duty to the amount of £10 local value. But he had to declare that such imports were intended altogether for his own use. It was further enacted that in case anyone in the Settlement "personally accompanied both his exports and imports," and declared that such goods were "to be consumed by himself or to be sold . . . to actual consumers, within the settlement," he could import free of duty merchandise to the amount of £50 local value. In the previous month the Governor and Council levied a 20 per cent *ad valorem* impost on all goods and supplies from Great Britain and the United States coming to persons suspected of trading in furs or of aiding others to do so. All other importers, in order to be exempt from the tariff, had to take out a license.[28]

In addition to these various enactments, the Company devised another scheme for protecting its monopoly. A new type of land deed was drawn up, which compelled anyone before he secured land from the Company to agree to certain conditions. First, he must promise that he would not

without the licence or consent of the said Governor and Company . . . carry on or establish, or attempt to carry on or establish in any parts of North America, any trade or traffic in or relating to any kind of skins, furs, peltry, or dressed leather, nor in any manner directly or indirectly aid or abet any person or persons in carrying on such trade or traffic.

He must also agree not to "infringe or violate the exclusive rights, powers, privileges, and immunities of commerce, trade and traffic, . . . of or belonging . . . to . . . the said Governor and Company." Finally, he must give assurance that he would not "at any time during the said term [*one thousand years*] underlet, or assign, or otherwise alienate, or dispose, or part with, the actual possession of the said land hereby devised or any part thereof, for all or any part of the said term, or any interest derived under the same, without the consent in writing of the said Governor and Company."[29] If any of these provisions were violated, the deed would thereby be rendered invalid and the land for-

28. Oliver, *Canadian North-West*, I, 317 ff., II, 1303 ff. *The Globe* (Toronto), October 10, 1856.
29. *Report on H.B.C.*, pp. 361 f.

feited. But the Company got little chance to use this elaborate instrument of tyranny. People who wanted land in Assiniboia defied the law by simply squatting on the land without bothering to obtain a deed.[30]

While the people of Red River were thus evading the Company's various monopolistic restrictions, they were also moving slowly in the direction of a more positive and legal protest. Of course, this was largely a reaction from the repressive policy of the authorities rather than a spontaneous demand for self-government. One of the strongest forces working on the settlers to this end was the administration of justice in Assiniboia. The only court in the country was controlled by recorder Adam Thom. As an employee of the Company, Thom found it advisable to take the side of authority whenever he could, and in general, to support the trading monopoly against the people. The most important after-effect of the recorder's bias was to bring together the French and English bois-brûlés, who had hitherto held apart, in a common determination and effort to bring to an end the trade restrictions which oppressed them both.[31]

During the course of the strife occasional appeals were made to the Canadian and British governments as well as to the local authorities. In 1845 a group of métis petitioned Governor Christie to give a definite answer to a number of questions pertaining to their status and rights. Their contention was that as métis they were entitled to the same privileges as those enjoyed by the Indians. The Governor, in reply, stated that as métis they did not "possess certain privileges over their fellow citizens, who have not been born in the country," and that they could hope to exercise only the rights of British subjects. In answer to another query, he admitted that any purchaser of lands would have the right to trade in furs if he had not "willed" it away by assenting to any "restrictive condition"—this with reference to the new form of land indenture described above. But he went on to qualify his admission with the peculiar statement that "such an assumption, of course, although admissible of itself, is inconsistent with your general views; the conditions of land tenure have always been well understood to prohibit any infraction of the company's privileges."[32]

It is not surprising that the discontent of the métis was augmented rather than appeased by the Governor's answers. Soon afterwards two petitions complaining of the onerous nature of the Company's rule were framed by the French and English inhabitants, respectively, and sent

30. *Ibid.*, p. 96. *The Globe* (Toronto), October 10, 1856.

31. *The Globe* (Toronto), May 15, 1852. George Bryce, "The First Recorder of Rupert's Land," *Historical and Scientific Society of Manitoba* (Winnipeg, 1890), *Transaction*, No. 40.

32. Alexander Begg, *History of the North-west* (Toronto, 1894), I, 261 ff.

to London. Here on February 17, 1847,[33] they were presented to the Imperial authorities by Alexander K. Isbister, a London lawyer and educator. Isbister was himself a "quarter-breed," born at Cumberland House on the Saskatchewan and educated in England. Naturally he sympathized with the Red River settlers rather than with the Company, and was ready to give them active aid in attempting to win their freedom.[34]

In response to the memorials presented at this time, the Colonial Office proposed to get a more definite and more accurate statement of the charges which had been made. Isbister interpreted the answer to mean that the Imperial Government intended sending an investigating committee to Red River. He complained that such a commission would be unsatisfactory; that it would likely be influenced and prejudiced by the Fort Garry officials because it would be dependent upon the Company "for conveyance and support." On February 17, 1848, Earl Grey, the Colonial Secretary, informed Isbister that the Colonial Office did not "contemplate the appointment of a 'Commission of Inquiry' into the allegations against the Hudson's Bay Company."[35] But in the meantime letters of inquiry had been dispatched by Grey to Lord Elgin, Governor General of Canada, W. B. Caldwell, Governor of Assiniboia, and Sir John H. Pelly, London Governor of the Hudson's Bay Company.[36] Pelly denied the various accusations. The reports sent by Lord Elgin and Governor Caldwell were also favorable to the Company. After these returns, spirited arguments ensued for some time. Both parties secured statements from various interested friends. Isbister questioned the validity of the Company's charter. Earl Grey replied that the charter, which had been recognized by acts of Parliament, was unquestionably valid. He also considered that there were "no grounds for making any application to Parliament on the subject of oppression alleged . . . to have been suffered by the inhabitants of the territory over which the powers of the Hudson's Bay Company extend"; and concluded by saying that he felt sure that the Company would willingly "consider any representations which might be made of substantial grievances."[37]

Isbister was not at all satisfied with this answer and continued to

33. *Copy of Memorial and Petition from Inhabitants of the Red River Settlement, complaining of the Government of the Hudson's Bay Company, and Reports and Correspondence on the subject of the Memorial,* pp. 1 ff. (*PP GB, HC,* 1849, XXXV, No. 227).

34. George Bryce, "Late A. K. Isbister," *Manitoba Historical and Scientific Society* (Winnipeg, 1883), *Transaction,* No. 2. *Chronicle and News* (Kingston), March 3, 1849. *The Nor'-Wester,* January 28, 1860. *The Globe* (Toronto), March 9, 1857.

35. *Copy of Memorial . . . from Inhabitants of the Red River . . ., and Reports and Correspondence, op. cit.,* pp. 97 ff.

36. *Ibid.,* pp. 6 ff.   37. *Ibid.,* pp. 8 f., 18, 20 ff., 101 f., 113.

plead the cause of the Red River people. At last on July 5, 1849, the House of Commons addressed the Crown asking for an inquiry "to ascertain the legality of the powers in respect to territory, trade, taxation, and government . . . claimed or exercised by the Hudson's Bay Company on the continent of North America." The Crown assented; and Earl Grey accordingly asked the Hudson's Bay Company for an ex parte statement of those claims. Its report was laid before the Imperial juris-consults, Sir John Jervis and Sir John Romilly, on October 30, 1849. Having examined the document, they gave it as their opinion "that the rights claimed by the Company do properly belong to them"; but they went on to suggest that if it were thought desirable, the question might be referred to the judicial committee of the Privy Council by means of a petition to the Crown embodying the charges against the Company. Earl Grey then asked Isbister if he would appear as a party to the prosecution. Isbister declined to do so. His chief reason for refusing was probably the fact that the party who prosecuted would have to defray all the expenses of the investigation. Isbister and his friends were not in a position to do this; and so the inquiry ended abruptly in 1850.[38]

During the interval between the preparation of the petitions and their presentation to Earl Grey the British Government had sent out to Red River a regiment of soldiers under the command of Colonel J. F. Crofton. In the autumn of 1846 military government was proclaimed and the complainants were cowed for the time being.[39] But two years later, when the troops were withdrawn, popular feeling began to be manifest again. The regulars were then replaced by some fifty-six pensioners under Lieutenant Colonel William Caldwell, but they "were neither respected nor feared" and did little or nothing to prevent illegal trading.[40]

The local situation was, soon afterwards, brought decisively to a head. In the spring of 1849 there was much agitation in the Settlement. Guillaume Sayer and three other métis were arraigned before the court of Assiniboia charged with illegal trafficking in furs. The métis and other free traders now made up their minds that, in case of a conviction, no punishment should be inflicted, and that if they could not prevent it by peaceful means, they would resort to violence. On the day set for the trial the excitement was intense. Under the leadership of Louis Riel, father of the famous "rebel" of 1869, some 500 or 600 armed

38. Hudson's Bay Company, pp. 3 ff. (*PP GB, HC*, 1850, XXXVIII, No. 542).

39. Kittson to Sibley, February 11, 1847, *SbP MHS. The Argus* (Kingston), June 19, December 4, 29, 1846. *Report on H.B.C.*, pp. 169 f.

40. *Ibid.*, pp. 298, 307. John McLaughlin to Sibley, June 10, 1848, *SbP MHS. The Globe* (Toronto), July 20, 24, 1857, July 19, 1864.

métis "assembled in a mob around the court-house, and fired several volleys of musketry." The court was intimidated. To quote a contemporary, one of the judges, Hugh Poleson,

was seized with a panic in his body and limbs, besides feeling rather uneasy *himself*. His Honor felt like taking an airing—fatigued probably with the confinement of the court house, concluded to get away from the "noise and confusion"; or perhaps felt disgusted with the drudgery of business—or— well, no matter why; his Honor was taken with a sudden leaving. With most uncharacteristic liberality, he paid a by-stander $5 to take his seat on the bench (a bass wood man might have answered the same purpose) and sneaked out through the crowd; mounted his horse and fled at full speed.

The jury found Sayer guilty, but he was let go unpunished. At this the métis concluded that they had gained their objective, free trade, although the court had made no mention of free trade for the future. Like wildfire the cry, *Le commerce est libre—vive la liberté*, spread throughout the land; and the outcome was, indeed, freedom of trade. The Hudson's Bay Company's fur monopoly in Assiniboia was now a thing of the past even in name; and the creaking Red River carts continued to make their way, unmolested, over the level plains and down to St. Paul.[41]

Just what was the chief cause of this outcome of the fur-trade struggle is not easy to discover. It is an interesting coincidence that it was in the decade of the 'forties, when questions of free trade were being hotly debated in England, that they were being similarly contested in Assiniboia; and that the year 1849, which saw the Sayer trial at Fort Garry, also witnessed the repeal of the British Navigation Acts. Was there a definite connection between the recall of the troops from Red River and the end of protection throughout the British Empire? It is difficult to believe that they were entirely unconnected. More important, however, for the winning of free trade in Red River were the advance of the American frontier and the activities of the American Fur Company. These two factors, taken in conjunction with two others—the large métis population at Red River, with its hunting and fur-trading traditions, and the natural facilities for communication between the Red River Settlement and such frontier communities as Mendota and St. Paul—are sufficient in themselves to explain the breakdown of the chartered fur-trade monopoly.

41. *Report on H.B.C.*, pp. 306 f., 310. *Minnesota Pioneer* (St. Paul), July 26, August 2, 1849. *The Globe* (Toronto), July 20, 24, 1857, January 13, 1858. Donald Gunn in *The Nor'-Wester*, June 28, 1860.

CHAPTER XXIV

THE VALLEY OF THE RED RIVER

THE Sayer trial and its outcome mark the close of one phase of the history of the Red River Valley and the opening of another. The period of domination by the Hudson's Bay Company, beginning actually in the year 1821, and legally about fifteen years later, had now come to an end as far as the fur monopoly was concerned, and was to be succeeded by two decades of practical freedom. In a sense the political condition of the people of Assiniboia in this period between 1849 and 1870 was to be more akin to that which had obtained in the years before the Selkirk Grant than to anything which had been seen in the meantime, or has been seen from 1870 to the present. Outside control, in one form or another, had characterized the period from 1812 to 1849; and it was likewise to characterize that which was to be ushered in after 1870, when the Dominion of Canada would assume control. In contrast with these eras of foreign domination, the period which came before 1812 and that between 1849 and 1871 are both distinguished by conditions of comparative local autonomy. It seems fitting, then, that this history, which began with the intrusion of the Selkirk settlers, controlled from Europe, into a region hitherto largely self-determining, should end with the recovery, by its people, of practical self-government. It also seems appropriate that a historical narrative which has confined itself largely to details of fact and to particulars of exposition should be reintegrated at its close by a discussion of its larger aspects and its subsequent direction.

The main lines of cleavage which give shape and pattern to the subject of this study are geographical, economic, and political. In its first chapter reference was made to the chief geographical features which have affected the history of the Red River Valley; and there and in subsequent pages the leading economic and political aspects were described or referred to. It remains to be shown how these larger factors, which tend to be lost sight of, at times, in the masses and mazes of historical change, retain at all stages of the story of Assiniboia their dominating force, and not only for the most part mark the limits within which the conduct of the actors is bound but also determine in large measure the direction and the effect of individual actions themselves. This is not to claim that the course of history is predetermined or inevitable. It is merely to assume what cannot reasonably be denied, that the subject of history consists of more than historical events—that it contains what seem to be larger and more impersonal elements which, though they do not make history, condition it immeasurably, and are therefore decidedly worthy of the historian's investigation.

The Red River Valley, as was observed at the beginning, lies at the center of the continent of North America and is most accessible, from the ocean, through three drainage basins—the St. Lawrence, the Nelson, and the Mississippi. It is also a link binding these three regions together at one point, and a convenient stepping-off place for a further penetration of the territories lying farther to the west. Before and during the first half of the nineteenth century the chief value of the region consisted in furs and food. The fur trader came looking for furs, and for provisions to support him in his business; the settler came looking for land from which to gain a living by farming. Both came by each of the three great river systems. The Nelson was followed by the Hudson's Bay Company and the Selkirk settlers; the St. Lawrence, by the North West Company and by its servants who became independent traders or farmers; the Mississippi, by the American Fur Company and its subsidiaries, and by the flood of agriculturists who, in the year 1850, were pouring into the future State of Minnesota.

Each of these three river systems, moreover, including the group of men who followed it, was associated with a particular political sovereignty which tended to accompany its adherents into the Red River Valley and to establish itself there to the exclusion of other sovereignties. By the Nelson River system came the political authority of the Hudson's Bay Company, absolute, within certain limits, under a charter granted by the British Crown and recognized by the British Parliament. From the St. Lawrence, after the British conquest of Canada, there spread westward with the fur traders a certain amount of *de facto* authority which in time came to be identified with that of the Canadian Government and to be specifically subordinated to that of the Canadian judiciary, both of which, in theory at least, were under the control of the United Kingdom. Finally, up the Mississippi River system the power of the government of the United States was being extended both by the process of immigration and by the express action of law. Three sovereignties, supported by three groups of men and following three drainage basins, were thus advancing simultaneously toward the heart of the North American continent and the valley of the Red River. The story of the consequent actions and reactions, within certain time limits, has been the subject of this study.

The first in the field, in a sense, were the men from the St. Lawrence. It has been noted above that the Great West was penetrated about the middle of the seventeenth century by Radisson and Groseilliers, and its fur resources discovered. These Frenchmen soon went over to the English and helped bring the Hudson's Bay Company to the Nelson River. But the system thus inaugurated long confined itself to the shores of Hudson Bay; and years before this policy was changed the La Vérendryes from the St. Lawrence had advanced all the way to the Red River and beyond, and won for French Canada the wealth, and some control, of the West. The Seven Years' War and its outcome interrupted but did not change this process; and it was not until almost another quarter of a century had passed that the Hudson's Bay Company began to awake from its lethargy and to exploit the trading possibilities of its peculiar location.

The truth of the matter was, and still is, that the Red River Valley and the regions to the west of it are by nature far more accessible from the sea through the valley of the Nelson River system than through the valley of the St. Lawrence. What had given the latter its long start in the race for the Western furs was its agricultural possibilities and its priority in settlement. As long as the English company confined its operations to the shores of Hudson Bay, men from the St. Lawrence had every encouragement to go west for furs because they had a favorable system of waterways to carry them and abundant supplies of cheap food at their base. When at last they reached a point in their expansion where their trade came into conflict with the English system, then, and not till then, did it pay the Hudson's Bay Company to depart from its traditional policy and pursue its rivals to their posts. Other things being equal, this struggle could have only one outcome, victory for the English concern. But for the time being, other things were not equal. In the first place, the St. Lawrence traders had built up an organization magnificent in its flexibility, resourcefulness, and striking power; and in the second place, most of the provisions used by the men from the Bay had, at first, to be brought all the way from Europe. Thus when the two river systems, represented by the two fur-trading groups, came into conflict over the wealth of the West, it was apparent that a long time would be required for men who followed the shorter inland route to make their advantage decisive over the men who followed the longer inland route.

When, in 1811, Lord Selkirk came actively into the scene, thirty-seven years had elapsed since the Hudson's Bay Company had first invaded the interior, and still the St. Lawrence group was strongly in the ascendant. Their peculiar advantages had served them well; and in the meantime had grown greater, if anything. This growth was due partly to accident, partly to deliberate planning. The accident was the appearance in the Red River Valley, in those years, of the métis nation, a by-product of the fur trade, which quickly took to the plains on horse-back, hunted the buffalo for its food value, and prepared great quanti-ties of pemmican for the use of the fur traders, who were thereby en-abled to extend their operations with still greater speed and facility. The planning consisted largely in heroic and finally successful negotia-tions among the various St. Lawrence fur interests to unite their forces into one organization in order successfully to defy the inroads of the men from Hudson Bay. It is true that the English traders had taken great strides forward in their opposition; but they still lacked their rivals' power of organization and they were still, almost as much as ever, hampered for food. The slowness of the older company to develop a system fit to rival that of the Canadians was due partly to the force of long-established habit and partly to the character of its personnel. The men who managed it were European businessmen, with conservative views and methods. The men who served as laborers were mostly inhabit-ants of the Orkneys, who were engaged for short terms, and who de-manded food they were used to. They would not, like the Canadian la-borers, give their lives to the fur trade and relish pemmican.

The entrance of Lord Selkirk into the affairs of the Hudson's Bay Company promised speedily to remedy its defects, because he was will-ing to make great personal sacrifices in order to establish on the fertile soil of Assiniboia a colony of agriculturists who would supply the Bay traders with "civilized" food, and because he also brought with him into the Company a group of wealthy men who were bound to demand returns on their investment and whose business force and acumen, united to Selkirk's own, might well serve sufficiently to revivify the personnel of the trade in America. The course of Selkirk's subsequent career, with its successes and disasters, has been traced. But perhaps too much stress has been laid on the disasters, and too little on the successes.

When Selkirk secured Assiniboia in 1811 his rivals were strong, rich, and aggressive; and the Hudson's Bay Company was weak, poor, and discouraged. Within half a decade the nobleman had succeeded not only in planting his colony, and reviving his own company, but he had also threatened the North-westers with ruin, and had driven them to resort to suicidal violence in order to combat his moves. It is in these years that the question of sovereignty assumes its great importance. Selkirk was able to secure a title to Assiniboia through the charter rights of the Hudson's Bay Company; he was able to threaten the great St. Law-rence company with ruin through a title deed conferred in the seven-teenth century.

On the other hand, his enemies were able to strike back through their strong *de facto* authority in the Red River Valley and through their great political and judicial power in the Canadas. It was left to the Canadian Government to employ force in the Northwest, and to the Canadian judiciary to bring culprits from there to be tried in Canada. Selkirk was thus, on the smaller issue of certain specific actions, defeated and ruined, and even driven to death, by the power in Red River of the political sovereignty of the colonies along the St. Lawrence. But he was soon revenged by nature and by the food base he had established. With the union of the rival companies the Bay traders prospered, but the Canadian organization died away; the charter powers of the English company were extended over Red River as never before, while the Canadas even lost memory of the West; the Nelson drainage basin replaced, in the affairs of the united Company, even as far east as Sault Ste Marie, the drainage basin of the St. Lawrence.[1]

Meanwhile, the Mississippi Valley had been slow to take a part in the struggle. The Spaniard had never had the desire, or the power, to utilize his early opportunity there; and the French and the Spanish who controlled the region successively in the seventeenth and eighteenth centuries failed for various reasons to colonize and exploit it in any large measure, especially in its upper areas. It was not until the United States had come into being with its free institutions and its enormous undeveloped wealth—both so attractive to potential European immigrants—that the region drained by the Mississippi was ready to begin competing actively for the wealth of Red River and the American Northwest.

Outstanding in the early beginnings of this competition were such events as the coming of John Jacob Astor and the Louisiana Purchase of 1803. Then, almost immediately after its foundation in 1808, the American Fur Company was able to force the North West Company to recognize its right to the fur trade south of the boundary. The War of 1812, it is true, checked this expansion. But the assistance given to American traders by their government after the war more than compensated for the check, and the revived American Fur Company replaced the North West Company even as far as the upper Mississippi Valley.[2] It has been claimed that this narrowing of the fur fields open to the Canadian and the English companies intensified the struggle between the two.[3] This is questionable. But there can be little doubt that the activities of the American company weakened the Canadian concern

1. *Report on H.B.C.*, Appendix No. 8, pp. 387 ff. *Hansard* (3d Series, 1857), CXLIV, 223 f., 229. Morton, *Canadian West,* pp. 690 *et seq.* Innis, *The Fur Trade in Canada,* pp. 288 ff.
2. See chap. xxii. 3. Paxson, *American Frontier,* p. 214.

by depriving it of valuable fur sources and enticing away many of its servants; and thereby it helped pave the way for its elimination.[4]

The advance of the American Fur Company's agents into the Red River Valley and their competition there with the Hudson's Bay Company have been sketched above. Noted, too, was the coming of American settlement. The combination of fur trader and settler south of the boundary proved too strong for the Company in its attempt to enforce its fur monopoly, and enabled the inhabitants of Assiniboia to secure what was practically free trade for themselves. Even the Company itself found it profitable in time to bow to the attractions of the Mississippi Valley facilities and to import goods from and through the United States.[5] If nature could have had her way the fertile soil and the easy routes offered by the southern drainage basin would have combined to eliminate from the competition for the control of Red River, even the Nelson system with its short inland route.

But at this point political forces stepped in with a view to restoring to the St. Lawrence region once more the possession and control of the Red River country. About the middle of the nineteenth century a group of Canadians, mostly Upper Canadians, began to revive in their country a realization of the great value of the British Northwest; and at the same time they started an agitation for the transfer of the control of the region to the Government of the Canadas. In the two decades following the Sayer trial other Canadians with similar ambitions migrated to Red River, and used their influence there for the same purpose. These men were never great in number, nor were they popular in Assiniboia; but they were part of the movement to make Red River Canadian, and as such their influence in the end was of importance in the taking over of the West by Canada.[6]

While the St. Lawrence region was thus threatening to reassert its control over Red River, the Nelson region, through the Hudson's Bay Company, was striving to keep its recently enfeebled grip on the country; and the Mississippi, through trade and also by means of some slight political activity, was constantly increasing its influence north of the boundary. But neither of the two latter forces was to be the chief

4. Solon J. Buck, *Illinois in 1818* (Chicago, 1917), pp. 23 ff., 27 ff.

5. *The Nor'-Wester,* January 14, 28, July 28, September 14, 1860. *St. Paul Pioneer,* October 23, 1862. *St. Paul Press,* May 7, July 26, September 17, 1863, January 1, August 27, December 31, 1864, June 27, 1865. *St. Paul Daily Press,* August 9, 1867. Russell Blakeley, "Opening of the Red River of the North to Commerce and Civilization," *MHC,* VIII, 45 ff.

6. See particularly: Morton, *Canadian West,* pp. 825 ff.; George F. G. Stanley, *The Birth of Western Canada. A History of the Riel Rebellions* (New York, 1936), pp. 44 ff.; Reginald George Trotter, *Canadian Federation* (Toronto, 1924), chaps. xvii, xviii.

antagonist of the Canadians in the struggle for Red River which was now beginning. It has been observed above that the métis or mixed-breed element was the strongest potential force in the country, especially after the fusion of the fur rivals in 1821. It was largely the power of these métis, too, which had defied and finally broken the local fur monopoly. The same power was now to be the leading force opposed to political control from the East. There are several main factors which account for this.

First, the great majority of the métis were of French extraction. This did not prevent them from associating in a friendly manner with the other inhabitants of Red River, or with the Americans, or even with the Hudson's Bay Company men. But it did separate them by a wide gulf from the people of Upper Canada, and especially from those English-speaking Canadians who were now coming into the West to spy out and exploit its possibilities. There was no doubt in the minds of the Red River French métis that the distinction of race had long been used in Lower Canada to enable the crowd of fortune hunters who flocked in after the Conquest to batten upon the labor of a subject people, and they were equally convinced that theirs would be a similar fate if the Upper Canadians, with their domineering spirit of racial bigotry, were allowed to control the Hudson's Bay Company's territories. Principally they feared for their lands.

Religious and cultural considerations served only to emphasize the point of view. In the early pages of this study it was noted that not long after the first appearance of native métis in the West many of the young were sent down to French Canada to receive academic and religious instruction. As a result, they became permanently French in speech and Roman Catholic in religion. The process was intensified and made constant, beginning with the year 1818, by the establishment in Assiniboia of a Roman Catholic Mission from Lower Canada. When in the 'fifties the Upper Canadians began to agitate for control of the West, the métis in Red River began to fear for their language and for the freedom which their religion enjoyed. Their fears were not unfounded. The Canadas had long been the scene of bitter cultural and religious contentions. Peculiarly enough, bitterness was injected into the quarrel not so much in Lower as in Upper Canada.

This was explainable as a natural accompaniment of the clash and contest between English-speaking Upper Canada and French-speaking Lower Canada which increased in intensity as the former approached equality in population and wealth and more and more resented Lower Canada's control of the Atlantic ports.

Now knowledge of such views was not slow in penetrating to Red

River in the years under discussion; because if it had not been carried by the French clergy, it would certainly have been brought by the new settlers from Upper Canada. The coming of these men and their activities in Red River during the 'fifties and 'sixties are not a definite part of this study. But it may be observed here that if their intention was to alienate the French métis community from the prospect of union with Canada, they certainly were not disappointed.

No doubt there were faults on both sides of what was in essence a contest between the whole pattern of living which was cherished by the métis and the threats to it which were represented by aggressive Easterners. When religious differences came into play, leaders as well as followers fell into strange courses. Be that as it may, when the time came for Canada to assume control of the West, while the Hudson's Bay Company was selling out its ancient charter rights and the Canadian Government was paying the price and sending out an official representative to Assiniboia, the métis decided to resist the change by force. It is significant of the artificial nature of the new union that the Lieutenant Governor of Rupert's Land, William McDougall, appointed by Canada in 1869, found it most convenient to approach his new dominions through the United States; and that both the Hudson's Bay Company officials and certain American citizens and sympathizers in Red River have been accused of helping to foment a métis rising.

The leader of the insurrection which now shook Red River was Louis Riel, whose father had led his countrymen at the Sayer trial in 1849. Riel was a man of some education and much native ability; and his followers, long disciplined in the buffalo hunt, had the striking power of a brigade of cavalry and an unrivaled knowledge of the country. But when a military expedition, following the old North West Company's canoe route, came west from Canada to establish Canadian authority in Assiniboia, Riel lacked a force sufficiently large to resist with any good prospect of success. Nor could his friends from the north and the south help him. The local Hudson's Bay Company officials, even granting that they wished to aid Riel, had practically no power; and the Americans, both in and out of Red River, who might have given armed assistance, were either too few in number to risk interference or had alienated Riel, or Riel's associates, by their annexationist ambitions.

The métis leader did not wish to jump out of the Canadian frying pan into the American fire. He probably shared the French-Canadian Catholic clergy's loyalty to the British Crown, and gratitude for the freedom it seemed to guarantee. Or perhaps he, or his more influential associates, were satisfied with the prospect of securing justice from the Canadian Government. Riel had been willing to live quietly under the mild rule of the Company. Failing that, he had dreams of an independent state, preponderantly French métis and Roman Catholic, flourishing along the banks of the Red and Assiniboine rivers.[7]

This, however, was not to be. As in the earliest times of European penetration to the West, the natives were too few and too poor to resist aggression from without. Had Canada not taken over the West, probably the United States would have purchased it in the course of time, as they had already purchased Louisiana and other regions. As it was, Riel slipped away quietly in the face of overwhelming force; and the valley of the Red River north of the forty-ninth parallel became Canadian territory. There the St. Lawrence had triumphed over both the Nelson and the Mississippi; both north and south of it politics had beaten geography, if not economics.

Was this settlement of the question permanent? For decades it seemed as permanent as such settlements can be. But in more recent times the situation has changed somewhat. Naturally enough, the changes have come through what may be called the pressure of geography and economics. On the one hand, as the Canadian West was peopled, its exporting interests began to demand a cheaper route to the sea than the one provided by the St. Lawrence Valley. That agitation secured, at last, the Hudson Bay Railway.

On the other hand, the primary producers of the West saw their need for manufactured goods being, as they thought, exploited by a profiteering Eastern Canada; and their thoughts often turned to at least economic union with the great regions to the south which were geographically one with theirs.

What the next or the most permanent outcome of this triple tug will be, no one knows. Will the West become independent, as Riel seemed to wish, and trade by way of the Nelson drainage basin? Will it form with the Mississippi drainage basin an economic union?—a political union? Or will it resist the pressure from both the Nelson and the Mississippi systems and remain indefinitely, both politically and economically, a vassal of the St. Lawrence? The answers to these questions will be given by the future.

7. See especially: Stanley, *The Birth of Western Canada;* Morton, *Canadian West;* A. G. Morice, *A Critical History of the Red River Insurrection* (Winnipeg, 1935); Ruth Ellen Sanborn, "The United States and the British Northwest, 1865–1870," *North Dakota Historical Quarterly,* VI, 5 ff.; Theodore C. Blegen, "James Wickes Taylor: A Biographical Sketch," *Minnesota History Bulletin,* I, 153 ff.; Lester Burrell Shippee, *Canadian-American Relations, 1849–1874* (New Haven, 1939), pp. 180 ff.

BIBLIOGRAPHY

No attempt is made here to furnish a complete bibliography. Only those authorities are included to which reference has actually been made.

I. MANUSCRIPT SOURCES

BOARD OF TRADE PAPERS, Series I, Vol. 42, No. 36, and Series V, Vol. 18, No. 438, Public Record Office, London.

BOOK OF DEEDS, Land Office, Albany, N.Y.

BULGER PAPERS, Public Archives of Canada.

COLONIAL OFFICE RECORDS, Series G, Vols. 10; 54, Pt. I; 55, Pt. I, Public Archives of Canada.

COLONIAL OFFICE RECORDS, Series Q, Vols. 123; 124; 130, Pt. I; 130, Pt. II; 133; 134, Pt. II; 135, Pt. I; 136A; 137; 139; 140, Pt. II; 143; 144; 145; 147, Pt. I; 147, Pt. II; 148, Pt. I; 148, Pt. II; 149, Pt. I; 150, Pt. I; 150, Pt. II; 151A; 153, Pt. II; 153, Pt. III; 293, Public Archives of Canada.

LAND BOOK E, Upper Canada, Public Archives of Canada.

LAND BOOK G, Upper Canada, February 28, 1806, to March 29, 1808, Public Archives of Canada.

JOHN MACDONELL JOURNAL, Masson Collection, McGill University Library, Montreal.

MILES MACDONELL, Selkirk Settlement, 1811–1812, and Various, 1763–1812, Public Archives of Canada.

MACKINAC REGISTER, Astor House, Mackinac.

JOURNAL OF JOHN McLEOD, Sr., Chief Trader, Hudson's Bay Company, 1811–42, Public Archives of Canada.

MINUTES OF THE EXECUTIVE COUNCIL, Lower Canada, State I, Public Archives of Canada.

MISCELLANEOUS LETTERS, Department of State, Washington.

ONEIDA RECORDS, Oswego County Clerk's Office, Oswego, N.Y.

SELKIRK PAPERS, Public Archives of Canada.

SELKIRK PAPERS, St. Mary's Isle.

SIBLEY PAPERS, Minnesota Historical Society, St. Paul.

STATE BOOK, Lower Canada, G, Public Archives of Canada.

TALIAFERRO JOURNALS AND PAPERS, Minnesota Historical Society, St. Paul.

II. PRINTED SOURCES

A LETTER TO THE EARL OF LIVERPOOL FROM THE EARL OF SELKIRK. Accompanied by correspondence with the colonial department in the years 1817–18–19, on the subject of the Red River Settlement in North America. London, 1819.

AMERICAN STATE PAPERS: Military Affairs, I. Washington, 1832.

AMERICAN STATE PAPERS: Miscellaneous, I. Washington, 1834.

AMOS, A. REPORT OF THE TRIALS in the courts of Canada relative to the destruction of the Earl of Selkirk's settlement on the Red River. London, 1820.

A NARRATIVE OF OCCURRENCES in the Indian countries of North America, since the connexion of the Right Hon. the Earl of Selkirk with the Hudson's Bay Company, and his attempt to establish a colony on the Red River. . . . London, 1817.

BURPEE, LAWRENCE J., ed. Journals and letters of Pierre Gaultier de Varennes de la Vérendrye and his sons, with correspondence between the governors of Canada and the French court, touching the search for the western sea. Toronto, 1927.

COPY OF MEMORIAL AND PETITION from inhabitants of the Red River Settlement, complaining of the government of the Hudson's Bay Company, and reports and correspondence on the subject of the memorial. Great Britain, Parliamentary Papers, House of Commons, 1849, XXXV, No. 227.

COUES, ELLIOTT, ed. New light on the early history of the greater Northwest. New York, 1897. 3 vols.

—— Expedition of Zebulon Montgomery Pike to the headwaters of the Mississippi River. . . . New York, 1895. 3 vols.

FLEMING, R. HARVEY, ed. McTavish, Frobisher & Company of Montreal. *Canadian Historical Review,* X.

—— The Origin of "Sir Alexander Mackenzie and Company." *Canadian Historical Review,* IX.

GARRY, NICHOLAS. Diary. In: Transactions of the Royal Society of Canada, VI, Sec. II.

GUNN, DONALD, AND TUTTLE, CHARLES R. History of Manitoba from the earliest settlement to 1835 and from 1835 to the admission of the province into the Dominion. Ottawa, 1880.

HANSARD'S PARLIAMENTARY DEBATES, 3d Series, 1857, CXLIV.

HARMON, DANIEL WILLIAMS. A Journal of voyages and travels in the interior of North America. Andover, 1820.

HENRY, ALEXANDER. Travels and adventures in Canada and the Indian territories between the years 1760 and 1776. New York, 1809.

HUDSON'S BAY COMPANY. Copy of the existing charter or grant by the crown to the Hudson's Bay Company. . . . Great Britain, Parliamentary Papers, House of Commons, 1st session, 1842, XXVIII, No. 547.

HUDSON'S BAY COMPANY. Great Britain, Parliamentary Papers, House of Commons, 1850, XXXVIII, No. 542.

INNIS, HAROLD A., ed. The North West Company. *Canadian Historical Review,* VIII.

IRVING, WASHINGTON. Astoria. Author's revised ed. New York, 1861.

JACKSON, JOHN MILLS. View of the political situation of the province of Upper Canada. n.p., 1809.

JAMESON, J. FRANKLIN, ed. Correspondence of John Caldwell Calhoun. In: Annual Report of the American Historical Association for the Year 1899.

JEFFERSON, THOMAS. The Writings of. Monticello ed. Washington, 1903–5. 20 vols.

KEATING, WILLIAM H. Narrative of an expedition to the source of St. Peter's River. . . . London, 1825. 2 vols.

KING, CHARLES R., ed. The Life and correspondence of Rufus King. . . . New York, 1894–1900. 6 vols.

LA ROCHEFOUCAULT-LIANCOURT. Travels in Canada 1795 with annotations and strictures by Sir David William Smith, edited with notes by William Renwick Riddell. Thirteenth Report of the Bureau of Archives for the Province of Ontario, Toronto, 1917.

LIANCOURT, DUC DE. Voyages dans l'Amérique. Paris, An 7.

LUCAS, SIR C. P., ed. Lord Durham's report on the affairs of British North America. Oxford, 1912. 3 vols.

McDONELL, ALEXANDER. Narrative of transactions in the Red River country; from the commencement of the operations of the Earl of Selkirk during the summer of the year 1816. London, 1819.

MACKENZIE, ALEXANDER. Voyages from Montreal, on the river St. Lawrence, through the continent of North America to the frozen and Pacific oceans; in the years 1789 and 1793. With a preliminary account of the rise, progress, and present state of the fur trade of that country. London, 1801.

MACKENZIE, WILLIAM LYON. Sketches of Canada and the United States. London, 1833.

M'KEEVOR, THOMAS. A Voyage to Hudson's Bay, during the summer of 1812. London, 1819.

MASSON, LOUIS. Les Bourgeois de la compagnie du Nord-Ouest; Reminiscences of Roderic McKenzie. . . . Quebec, 1889.

MILTON, VISCOUNT, AND CHEADLE, W. B. The Northwest passage by land. . . . 6th ed. London, 1865.

MORTON, ARTHUR S., ed. The Journal of Duncan M'Gillivray of the North West Company at Fort George on the Saskatchewan, 1794–5. With Introduction, Notes, and Appendix. Toronto, 1929.

O'CALLAGHAN, E. B., ed. Documents relative to the colonial history of the state of New York . . ., VII, IX. Albany, 1853–87. 15 vols.

OLDMIXON, JOHN. The British Empire in America. London, 1741.

OLIVER, E. H., ed. The Canadian North-West; its early development and legislative records. Canadian Archives, Publications, No. 9. Ottawa, 1914–15. 2 vols.

PAPERS RELATING TO THE RED RIVER SETTLEMENT: 1815–1819. Great Britain, Parliamentary Papers, House of Commons, No. 584.

PRITCHETT, JOHN PERRY, ed. A Letter by Lord Selkirk on trade between Red River and the United States. Canadian Historical Review, XVII.

PRIVATE LAWS OF THE STATE OF NEW YORK, passed at the thirty-first session of the legislature; begun and held at the city of Albany, the twenty-sixth day of January, 1808.

PROSPECTUS D'UN PLAN D'ENVOYER DES COLONS à la colonie de la rivière-Rouge dans l'Amérique septentrionale. Berne le 24. Mai 1820.

REPORT FROM THE SELECT COMMITTEE on the Hudson's Bay Company; together with the proceedings of the committee, minutes of evidence, Appendix and Index. Great Britain, Parliamentary Papers, House of Commons, 2 Session, XV, No. 240.260.

REPORT OF THE CANADIAN ARCHIVES, 1891. Ottawa, 1892.

REPORT OF THE TRIALS of Charles de Reinhard and Archibald McLellan for murder . . ., May, 1818. Montreal, 1818.

RICH, E. E., AND FLEMING, R. HARVEY, eds. Colin Robertson's correspondence book, September, 1817 to September, 1822. London, 1939.

RICH, E. E., ed. Journal of occurrences in the Athabasca department by George Simpson, 1820 and 1821, and report. With an introduction by Chester Martin. London, 1938.

ROBSON, JOSEPH. An Account of six years' residence in Hudson's bay, from 1733 to 1736, and 1744 to 1747. London, 1752.

ROSS, ALEXANDER. The fur hunters of the far west. London, 1855. 2 vols.

—— The Red River Settlement: its rise, progress, and present state. London, 1856.

SCULL, G. D., ed. Voyages of Peter Esprit Radisson, being an account of his travels and experiences among the North American Indians, from 1652 to 1684. Boston, 1885.

SELKIRK, THOMAS DOUGLAS, 5th Earl of. A Sketch of the British fur trade in North America, with observations relative to the North-West Company of Montreal. London, 1816.

—— Letter on the subject of parliamentary reform. n.p., 1809.

—— On civilization of the Indian in British America. n.p., n.d.

—— Observations on a proposal for forming a society for the civilization and improvement of the North American Indians within the British boundary. London, 1807.

—— Observations on the present state of the highlands of Scotland, with a view to the causes and probable consequences of emigration. London, 1805.

—— Speech on the defence of the country, 1807.

SHORTT, ADAM, AND DOUGHTY, ARTHUR G., eds. Documents relating to the constitutional history of Canada, 1759–1791, Pt. I. Sessional Paper No. 18, Canadian Archives. Second and revised edition, Ottawa, 1918.

SIBLEY, HENRY H. Reminiscences; historical and personal. In: Minnesota Historical Collections, I.

—— Reminiscences of the early days of Minnesota. In: Minnesota Historical Collections, III.

SIMPSON, WILLIAM S. Report of the trial of Charles de Reinhard for murder. . . . May, 1818. Montreal, 1819.

SOME ACCOUNT OF THE TRADE carried on by the North West Company. Dominion of Canada Report of the Public Archives for the Year 1928. Ottawa, 1929.

SOUTHESK, EARL OF. Saskatchewan and the Rocky mountains, a diary and narrative of travel, sport, and adventure, during a journey through the Hudson's Bay Company's territories, in 1859 and 1860. Edinburgh, 1875.

STATEMENT RESPECTING THE EARL OF SELKIRK'S SETTLEMENT of Kildonan, upon the Red river, in North America; its destruction in the years 1815 and 1816. . . . London, January, 1817.

STATEMENT RESPECTING THE EARL OF SELKIRK'S SETTLEMENT upon the Red river, in North America; its destruction in 1815 and 1816; and the massacre of governor Semple and his party. . . . London, 1817.

STATUTES, DOCUMENTS AND PAPERS bearing on the discussion respecting the northern and western boundaries of the province of Ontario. . . . Compiled by Direction of the Government of Ontario. Toronto, 1878.

STRACHAN, JOHN. A Letter to the right honourable the Earl of Selkirk, on his settlement at the Red River, near Hudson's Bay. London, 1816.

SUTHERLAND, L. C., ed. Driving sheep from Kentucky to the Hudson's Bay country. Annals of Iowa. A Historical Quarterly, XV.

THE MEMORIAL OF THOMAS EARL OF SELKIRK to his grace Charles Duke of Richmond. Montreal, 1819.

TREATIES, CONVENTIONS, INTERNATIONAL ACTS, PROTOCOLS, AND AGREEMENTS between the United States of America and other Powers, 1776–1909, I (61 Congress, 2d session, Senate Documents, No. 357—serial 5646).

UMFREVILLE, EDWARD. The Present state of the Hudson's bay, containing a full description of that settlement, and the adjacent country; and likewise of the fur trade. London, 1790.

UNITED STATES STATUTES AT LARGE, III.

WALLACE, W. S., ed. John McLean's notes of a twenty-five years' service in the Hudson's Bay Company. Toronto, 1932.

III. SECONDARY MATERIALS

ADAMS, Mrs. ANN. Early days at Red River settlement and Fort Snelling, or reminiscences of Mrs. Ann Adams (1821–1829). In: Minnesota Historical Collections, VI.

BEGG, ALEXANDER. History of the North-west. Toronto, 1894. 3 vols.

BELCOURT, GEORGE A. Department of Hudson's Bay. In: Minnesota Historical Collections, I.

BLAKELEY, RUSSELL. Opening of the Red River of the north to commerce and civilization. In: Minnesota Historical Collections, VIII.

BLEGEN, THEODORE C. James Wickes Taylor: A biographical sketch. Minnesota History Bulletin, I.

BRYCE, GEORGE. Late A. K. Isbister. In: Manitoba Historical and Scientific Society, Transaction, No. 2. Winnipeg, 1883.

—— Mackenzie, Selkirk, Simpson. Makers of Canada, VII. Toronto, 1905.

—— The First recorder of Rupert's Land. In: Historical and Scientific Society of Manitoba, Transaction, No. 40. Winnipeg, 1890.

—— The Life of Lord Selkirk. Coloniser of western Canada. Toronto, n.d.

—— The Romantic settlement of Lord Selkirk's colonists. Toronto, 1909.

Buck, Solon J. Illinois in 1818. Chicago, 1917.

Chittenden, Hiram Martin. The American fur trade of the far west. . . . New York, 1902. 3 vols.

Cowan, Helen I. Selkirk's work in Canada. *Canadian Historical Review,* IX.

Davidson, Gordon Charles. The North West Company. In: University of California, Publications in History, VII. Berkeley, 1918.

De Koven, Mrs. Reginald. The Life and letters of John Paul Jones. New York, 1913. 2 vols.

De Land, Charles E. The Vérendrye explorations and discoveries. In: South Dakota Historical Collections, VII.

Dent, John Charles. The story of the Upper Canadian rebellion. Toronto, 1885. 2 vols.

Fowell, William Watts. A History of Minnesota. St. Paul, 1921. 4 vols.

Goodrich, Albert M., and Nute, Grace Lee. The Radisson problem. *Minnesota History. A Quarterly Magazine,* XIII.

Gunn, H. G. The Fight for free trade in Rupert's Land. In: Mississippi Valley Historical Association, Proceedings, IV.

Hansen, Marcus L. Old Fort Snelling, 1819–1858. Iowa City, 1918.

Hennessy, W. B. Past and present of St. Paul, Minnesota. Chicago, 1906.

Hitchcock, Ripley. The Louisiana purchase and the early history and building of the west. Boston, 1903.

Hodge, Frederick Webb, ed. Handbook of American Indians north of Mexico, Pts. I, II. Washington, 1907.

Holand, Hjalmar R. Radisson's two western journeys. *Minnesota History. A Quarterly Magazine,* XV.

Hough, Franklin B. A History of Jefferson county in the state of New York, from the earliest period to the present time. Albany, 1854.

Innis, Harold A. The Fur trade in Canada. New Haven, 1930.

Johnson, Grisfield. History of Oswego county, New York, with illustrations and biographical sketches of some of its prominent men and pioneers. Philadelphia, 1877.

Libby, O. G. Some Vérendrye enigmas. *Mississippi Valley Historical Review,* III.

Lockhart, J. Q. Memoirs of the life of Sir Walter Scott. Philadelphia, 1839.

Mackintosh, W. A. Prairie settlement. The geographical setting. Canadian Frontiers of Settlement, I. Toronto, 1934.

Mahan, Bruce E. Old Fort Crawford and the frontier. Iowa City, 1926.

Martin, Chester. Lord Selkirk's work in Canada. Oxford, 1916.

Morice, A. G. A Canadian pioneer: Spanish John. *Canadian Historical Review,* X.

—— A Critical history of the Red River insurrection. Winnipeg, 1935.

—— Sidelights on the careers of Miles Macdonell and his brothers. *Canadian Historical Review,* X.

Morton, Arthur S. A History of the Canadian west to 1870–1871. Toronto, n.d.

—— La Vérendrye: commandant, fur-trader, and explorer. *Canadian Historical Review,* IX.

MURCHIE, R. W., AND GRANT, H. C. Unused lands of Manitoba (Dept. of Agriculture and Immigration, Winnipeg, 1926).

NUTE, GRACE LEE. Radisson and Groseilliers' contribution to geography. *Minnesota History. A Quarterly Magazine,* XVI.

—— The Voyageur. New York, 1931.

PAXSON, FREDERIC L. History of the American frontier, 1763–1893. Boston, 1924.

PORTER, KENNETH WIGGINS. John Jacob Astor. Business man. Cambridge, Mass., 1931. 2 vols.

PRITCHETT, JOHN PERRY. Some Red River fur-trade activities. *Minnesota History Bulletin,* V.

RIFE, CLARENCE W. Norman W. Kittson, A Fur-trader at Pembina. *Minnesota History Bulletin,* VI.

RIPPY, J. FRED. Rivalry of the United States and Great Britain over Latin America 1808–1830. Baltimore, 1929.

ROBERTSON, WILLIAM SPENCE. The Life of Mirando. Chapel Hill, 1929.

ROBINSON, DOAN; DE LAND, CHARLES E.; LIBBY, O. G. Additional Vérendrye material. *Mississippi Valley Historical Review,* III.

RYDJORK, JOHN. Foreign interest in the independence of new Spain. An introduction to the war of independence. Durham, N.C., 1935.

SANDBORN, RUTH ELLEN. The United States and the British Northwest, 1865–1870. *North Dakota Historical Quarterly,* VI.

SHIPPEE, LESTER BURRELL. Canadian-American relations 1849–1874. New Haven, 1939.

SHORTRIDGE, WILSON PORTER. The Transition of a typical frontier. . . . Menasha, Wis., 1922.

SMITH, ARTHUR D. HOWDEN. John Jacob Astor. Philadelphia, 1929.

STANLEY, GEORGE F. G. The Birth of western Canada. A history of the Riel rebellions. New York, 1936.

STEVENS, WAYNE E. Organization of the British fur trade. *Mississippi Valley Historical Review,* III.

TROTTER, REGINALD GEORGE. Canadian federation. Its origins and achievement. Toronto, 1924.

WHITAKER, ARTHUR PRESTON. The Mississippi question 1795–1803. A study in trade, politics, and diplomacy. New York, 1934.

WILLSON, BECKLES. The Great Company (1667–1871), being a history of the honourable company of merchants-adventurers trading into Hudson's Bay. London, 1900. 2 vols.

IV. NEWSPAPERS AND PERIODICALS

CHRONICLE AND NEWS (Kingston, Ontario), March 3, 1849.

MINNESOTA PIONEER (St. Paul), July 26, August 2, 1849; March 4, 1852.

MINNESOTA REGISTER (St. Paul), July 26, 1849.

Niles' Weekly Register, XIV.

St. Paul Daily Press, August 9, 1867.

St. Paul Pioneer, October 23, 1862.

St. Paul Press, May 7, July 26, September 17, 1863; January 1, August 27, December 31, 1864; June 27, 1865.

The Argus (Kingston, Ontario), June 19, August 11, December 29, 1846.

The Globe (Toronto), May 15, 1852; October 1, 10, 1856; March 9, July 20, 24, 1857; January 13, 1858; July 19, 1864.

The Nor'-Wester, January 14, 28, May 14, June 28, July 28, September 14, 1860; March 1, 1861; January 15, 1866.

The Red River Trail. *Harper's New Monthly Magazine,* XVIII.

Turner, F. J. The Diplomatic contest for the Mississippi valley. *Atlantic Monthly,* XCIII.

Weekly Pioneer and Democrat (St. Paul), December 16, 1858.

INDEX